RETHINKING PEACE MEDIATION

Challenges of Contemporary Peacemaking Practice

Edited by
Catherine Turner and Martin Wählisch

BRISTOL
UNIVERSITY
PRESS

First published in Great Britain in 2021 by

Bristol University Press
University of Bristol
1-9 Old Park Hill
Bristol
BS2 8BB
UK
t: +44 (0)117 954 5940
e: bup-info@bristol.ac.uk

Details of international sales and distribution partners are available at bristoluniversitypress.co.uk

British Library Cataloguing in Publication Data
A catalogue record for this book is available from the British Library

ISBN 978-1-5292-0819-1 hardcover
ISBN 978-1-5292-0821-4 ePub
ISBN 978-1-5292-0820-7 ePdf

Cover design: Liam Roberts
Front cover image: istock-695789274

Bristol University Press uses environmentally responsible print partners

Printed and bound in Great Britain by CPI Group (UK) Ltd, Croydon, CR0 4YY

FSC
www.fsc.org
MIX
Paper from responsible sources
FSC® C013604

Contents

List of Abbreviations

AI	Artificial Intelligence
AIDC	Association Internationale de Droit Constitutionnel
AMISOM	African Union Mission to Somalia
APSA	African Peace and Security Architecture
AQAP	al-Qaeda in the Arabian Peninsula
AQIM	al-Qaeda in the Islamic Maghreb
ASEAN	Association of Southeast Asian Nations
AU	African Union
AUCISS	African Union Commission of Inquiry on South Sudan
B4P	Business for Peace
CEWARN	Conflict Early Warning and Response Mechanism
CMFPR	Co-ordination of the Movement of Patriotic and Resistance Fronts
COMESA	Common Market for East and Southern Africa
CMI	Crisis Management Initiative
CPA	Comprehensive Peace Agreement
DCM	Democracy-building & Conflict Management
DRC	Democratic Republic of Congo
EAC	East African Community
ECOWAS	Economic Community of West African States
EEAS	European External Action Service
EIP	European Institute of Peace
EITI	Extractive Industries Transparency Initiative
EU	European Union
FARC	Revolutionary Armed Forces of Colombia
FSA	Free Syrian Army
GAM	Free Aceh Movement
GATIA	Imghad Tuareg Self-Defence Group and Allies
GCC	Gulf Cooperation Council
GCCA	Gulf Cooperation Council Agreement
GPC	General People's Congress
HCUA	High Council for the Unity of Azawad
HD	Humanitarian Dialogue

HD Centre	Centre for Humanitarian Dialogue
HQ	Headquarters
HRW	Human Rights Watch
IAI	Istituto Affari Internazionali
IACtHR	Inter-American Court of Human Rights
ICC	International Criminal Court
ICG	International Contact Group
ICJ	International Court of Justice
IDEA	Institute for Democracy and Electoral Assistance
IFC	International Finance Cooperation
IFI	International financial institution
IGAD	Intergovernmental Authority on Development
IMF	International Monetary Fund
INGO	International Non-Governmental Organization
IO	International Organizations
IOM	International Organization for Migration
IPS	Inclusive Political Settlements
IPKF	Indian Peacekeeping Force in Sri-Lanka
ISGS	Islamic State for the Greater Sahara
JEP	Special Jurisdiction for Peace
JMP	Joint Meeting Parties
LFP	Legal Framework for Peace
LGBTI	Lesbian, Gay, Bisexual, Transgender and Intersex
LNA	Libyan National Army
LRA	Lord's Resistance Army
LTTE	Liberation Tigers of Tamil Elam
MAA	Movement of Arab Azawad
MECO	Military Economic Cooperation
MILF	Moro-Islamic Liberation Front
MNLA	National Movement for the Liberation of the Azawad
MSA	Mouvement pour le Salut de l'Azawad
MSN	Mediation Support Network
MSU	Mediation Support Unit
MUJAO	Movement for Oneness and Jihad in West Africa
MWMN	Mediterranean Women Mediators Network
NAP	National Action Plan
NDC	National Dialogue Conference
NGO	Non-Governmental Organization
NWM	Nordic Women Mediators
OECD	Organisation for Economic Co-operation and Development

OHCHR	Office of the United Nations High Commissioner for Human Rights
OSCE	Organization for Security and Co-operation in Europe
OSE	Office of the Special Envoy
OSESGY	Office of the Special Envoy of the Secretary-General to Yemen
OTP	Office of the Prosecutor
PYD	Kurdish Democratic Union Party
R2P	Responsibility to Protect
REC	Regional Economic Community
SCICN	Stanford Center on International Conflict and Negotiation
SDG	Sustainable Development Goals
SIDA	Swedish International Development Agency
SPLM	Sudan People's Liberation Movement
SPLM-IO	Sudan People's Liberation Movement in Opposition
SRSG	Special Representative of the Secretary-General
STC	Southern Transitional Council
UAE	United Arab Emirates
UK	United Kingdom
UN	United Nations
UN DPPA	United Nations Department for Political and Peacebuilding Affairs
UNDAF	United Nations Development Assistance Framework
UNDP	United Nations Development Programme
UNGA	United Nations General Assembly
UNIP	United Nations Institute of Peace
UNITAR	United Nations Institute for Training and Research
UNMIS	United Nations Mission in the Sudan
UNMISS	United Nations Mission in South Sudan
UNSC	United Nations Security Council
UNSCOL	United Nations Special Coordinator for Lebanon
UNSG	United Nations Secretary-General
UPDF	Uganda People Defence Forces
US	United States
VTC	video-tele-conferencing
WIIS	Women in International Security
WMC	Women Mediators Across the Commonwealth
WOSCAP	Whole of Society Conflict Prevention and Peacebuilding
WPS	Women, Peace and Security
YECO	Yemeni Economic Corporation

Notes on Editors and Contributors

Editors

Catherine Turner is Associate Professor of International Law at Durham University. She is the deputy director of the Durham Global Security Institute, where her areas of research and teaching expertise include international law, peace mediation, transitional justice, and women in mediation. She has published widely in the fields of peace mediation and transitional justice, in addition to several policy papers on the subject of advancing women in mediation. In addition to her academic work Catherine has extensive experience as a practitioner and trainer in mediation and good relations in Northern Ireland. She now specializes in training and facilitation in mediation and transitional justice. She is currently a Board Member of Mediation Northern Ireland and MediatEUr.

Martin Wählisch leads the Innovation Cell in the Policy and Mediation Division in the Department of Political and Peacebuilding Affairs of the United Nations (UN DPPA). He supports peace initiatives and good office initiatives around the world, including conflict prevention efforts, national dialogues and formal high-level political peace negotiations. His scholarly work focuses on peace agreements, international law, and system theory aspects of international conflict resolution. He holds a PhD (Dr. jur.) in Public International Law from the Humboldt University of Berlin and a postgraduate MA in Mediation from the European University Viadrina. He has been a fellow at Columbia University, the University of Cambridge, Durham University and the American University of Beirut and has published widely on the nexus of law and politics in peace processes.

Contributors

Emmanuel De Groof works in diplomacy for the Belgian Ministry of Foreign Affairs. He is an associate to the Political Settlements Research Programme (University of Edinburgh); a visiting lecturer at the University of Maastricht; a visiting professor at the University of Kigali; and a scholar in the fields of international law, diplomacy and development cooperation. An alumnus of the European University Institute (EUI) and formerly a Fulbright-Schuman scholar at NYU School of Law, Emmanuel has won various awards including at the Charles Rousseau and Manfred Lachs competitions. He has worked at the European Centre for Development Policy Management ('Pelican House'), the EUI, the Brussels Bar and as a Law Clerk for Justice Albie Sachs at the South African Constitutional Court.

Irene Fellin is senior researcher on gender and security issues at the Istituto Affari Internazionali (IAI), where her focus is the implementation of United Nations Security Council Resolution 1325 (2000) on 'Women, Peace and Security' in the Mediterranean area within the frameworks of NATO, OSCE and the UN. She was the project coordinator for the establishment of a Mediterranean Women Mediators Network. She holds a Masters in 'Women's Rights and Gender Issues' from the Middle East Technical University (METU) in Ankara and prior to joining IAI she worked as Gender Advisor of the Special Representative of NATO Secretary-General for 'Women, Peace and Security'. She is founder and President of the Italian antenna of WIIS – Women in International Security.

Andreas Hirblinger is a postdoctoral researcher at the Centre on Conflict, Development and Peacebuilding, at the Graduate Institute of International and Development Studies in Geneva, where he conducts research on peacebuilding, with a special interest in the role of knowledge production. His past research has focused on questions of inclusion in peace processes and the governance of difference. More recently, Andreas's research has investigated the role of technology in peacebuilding, for instance in facilitating digital inclusion, enabling new forms of conflict analysis, or navigating uncertainty in peace processes. Andreas holds a PhD from the University of Cambridge, Department of Politics and International Studies, and an MA from the Department of War Studies at King's College London. His research has been published in *Security Dialogue*, the *Journal of Intervention and Statebuilding*, and the *Journal of Eastern African Studies*.

Anne Holper is Co-Director of the Center for Peace Mediation at European University Viadrina. Heading the 'Tough Choices Cluster' of Viadrina, ETH Zurich, swisspeace and Kiev Mohyla Academy, her research focuses on dilemma management in peace processes and breaking deadlocks between politically polarized groups. Within the Center's Mediation Hub she provides scientific support to the German Federal Foreign Office. After specializing on EU–China relations in her PhD in Political Philosophy and Applied Ethics, her regional focus is now on Ukraine, where she has worked with local dialogue actors. As a supervisor and coach, she works with various actors from the peacebuilding sector. She is a faculty member of the Master in Mediation and the Master of International Human Rights and Humanitarian Law Programs at Viadrina and teaches at the Training Academy for International Diplomats at the German Federal Foreign Office.

Philipp Kastner is a Senior Lecturer at the Law School of the University of Western Australia. He holds degrees from McGill University, Canada (DCL and LLM) and the University of Innsbruck, Austria (Dr. iur. and Mag. iur.). He researches and teaches in the areas of the resolution of armed conflicts and transitional justice, international criminal law, public international law and legal pluralism. Publications include *Legal Normativity in the Resolution of Internal Armed Conflict* (Cambridge University Press, 2015) and *International Criminal Justice* in bello*?* (Martinus Nijhoff, 2012). He is also the editor of *International Criminal Law in Context* (Routledge, 2018).

Josie Lianna Kaye is a peace and conflict researcher-practitioner with a particular expertise on business engagements in complex environments. Since 2013, Josie has been the Director of TrustWorks Global, which engages public and private actors to resolve intractable conflicts and sustain peace; in this capacity she has advised and supported international organizations, governments and business actors on conflict prevention, conflict-sensitivity, multi-stakeholder dialogues, and process and programme design. In 2020, Josie successfully defended her PhD on the role of business actors and peace mediation at the University of Oxford.

Lars Kirchhoff is Co-Director of the Center for Peace Mediation and Director of the Institute for Conflict Management and the Master's Program in Mediation at the European University Viadrina. After pursuing graduate studies in Passau, Dublin and Berlin, and holding research positions at the Organization for Security and Cooperation in Europe (OSCE), he specialized in alternative dispute resolution (ADR), international law and international commercial arbitration during his postgraduate studies at Yale Law School and at the US District Court of Northern California. In addition to his practical work as a mediator, he teaches mediation and ADR skills at the German Academy of Judges, Bucerius Law School, the United Nations and the Training Academy for International Diplomats at the German Federal Foreign Office. He is a faculty member of the Master of International Human Rights & Humanitarian Law.

Julian Klauke is Junior Project Manager in the Department of Global Learning for Conflict Transformation at the Berghof Foundation. His principal interests lie in the interfaces of peace mediation with other fields and the psychological mechanisms involved in conflict transformation. Currently, he is involved in a joint project with the UN-MSU that is exploring the role of constitutional issues in peace processes. He has previously worked on cultural external relations with the German Federal Foreign Office. He obtained his Master's degree in Peace and Conflict Studies from the University of Marburg and his bachelor's degree in Psychology from the University of Jena.

Dana M. Landau is Senior Researcher at swisspeace, where her research focuses on inclusive peace mediation processes and approaches to diversity in peacemaking and peacebuilding. She holds a DPhil in Politics from the University of Oxford, where her research focused on post-conflict peace- and state-building in Kosovo. She previously worked at the Graduate Institute of International and Development Studies in Geneva with the Inclusive Peace and Transition Initiative (IPTI), as well as in Kosovo for UNDP, the Swiss Agency for Development and Cooperation, and the European Centre for Minority Issues in the fields of women's security, transitional justice and minority rights. She has published in the *Journal of Intervention and Statebuilding, Nationalities Papers* and *Security Dialogue*.

Mir Mubashir is Advisor for dialogue and mediation support at the Berghof Foundation. He is particularly interested in approaches of insider mediation and whole-of-society peacebuilding, and in dynamics of Resistance and Liberation Movements. In his conceptual and practical work he engages with the systemic, indigenous, cultural, religious, generational and aesthetic aspects of conflict and conflict transformation. A practitioner of interactive theatre for social transformation, he is zealous about incorporating the language, approaches and methods of theatre into the Berghof training and workshops he designs and facilitates. Currently, he is involved in a joint project with the UN-MSU that is exploring the role of constitutional issues in peace processes.

Asli Ozcelik is Postdoctoral Research Associate in International Law at the University of Glasgow and the Academic Coordinator of the Glasgow Centre for International Law and Security. Her principal research interests concern the role of international law in peacemaking. More broadly, she works in the fields of public international law, international human rights law, international criminal law and comparative constitutional law, with a particular interest in the issues of non-state actors, self-determination, transitional justice and post-conflict constitution making. She has published on peacemaking issues in *International Journal of Constitutional Law* and *Melbourne Journal of International Law*.

Julia Palmiano Federer completed her PhD at the University of Basel and an MA in International Affairs at the Graduate Institute of International and Development Studies in Geneva. Before joining swisspeace in 2013, she started her career with the United Nations Office for the Coordination of Humanitarian Affairs, Human Rights Watch and the Centre for Humanitarian Dialogue. She has also worked as a research assistant for the Political Science Department of the University of British Columbia and as a project assistant for the Department of Foreign Affairs, Trade and Development Canada. She also currently works as an Associated Researcher in the Mediation programme at swisspeace with a geographic focus on Myanmar and a thematic focus on inclusivity, process design and gender in mediation.

Jamie Pring is a visiting postdoctoral researcher at the Center for Transnational Relations, Foreign and Security Policy at the Freie Universität Berlin. Supported by the Swiss National Science Foundation, she conducts a comparative study of regional conflict prevention institutions in the Global South. Her PhD at the University of Basel examines the promotion of inclusivity in the mediation of the Intergovernmental Authority on Development (IGAD) in South Sudan from 2013 to 2015. She worked for swisspeace, the Geneva International Centre for Humanitarian Demining, the Geneva Centre for Security Policy, the Graduate Institute Geneva, and the Philippine Department of National Defense.

Jeff Seul serves as Co-chair of the Peace Appeal Foundation, an international conflict resolution NGO founded with a mandate from five Nobel Peace Laurates, including Nelson Mandela and Desmond Tutu;

Lecturer on Peace Studies at Harvard Divinity School; and a partner in the international law firm Holland & Knight. He has served as a mediator or mediation advisor in numerous armed conflicts and other contexts. His research and practice interests include the design and conduct of peace and national dialogue processes; the relationships among religion, conflict, and peacebuilding; and the transformation of conflicts involving deeply held moral values.

Elisa Tarnaala is Senior Adviser at CMI (Crisis Management Initiative), and holds the title of docent at the University of Helsinki. She is currently working on North and West Africa, and Colombia in South America, with a focus on peace, conflict and transitional processes. Dividing her time between actual mediation and dialogue projects and academic research, she has engaged in field work and participative projects with activists, memory collectives in conflict-affected communities, victims' organizations, and youth groups. She has been grant researcher of academic foundations in Finland and abroad, senior analyst in a think-tank, and consulted for international organizations on themes of democracy, conflicts, human rights and gender. In addition to teaching at graduate and undergraduate levels, she has conducted international training in conflict resolution and analysis.

Emma Van Santen is a researcher at the Centre for Development Studies at the University of Cambridge researching the adaptation of peace process design to new political economies of conflict. Before Cambridge, she worked for nine years on climate change, humanitarian and peace-building policy, programme design and evaluation for the Australian Agency for International Development (AusAID)/Department of Foreign Affairs, advising missions in Jakarta, UN New York and Suva. She carries out design and evaluation consultancies for international non-government organizations and governments, and lectures on peace-making at the University of Cambridge. She is also a CEDR-accredited mediator, specializing in land and environment disputes.

Miguel Varela is a lecturer in sociology, mediation and international development at the University of Valladolid. He provides process design, facilitation and communications advice to NGOs and international organizations, having worked most intensively in the Ukrainian process of peace. He is a sociologist with an MSc in Peace and Development Work from Linnaeus University and an MA in documentary photography from the University of the Arts London. His research interests include the role of social media and images in social identity and conflict, and the use of online platforms to enhance mediation processes.

Luxshi Vimalarajah is Senior Advisor for mediation and negotiation support at the Berghof Foundation. She is both conceptually and practically involved in designing and facilitating dialogue and mediation processes and providing training and on-demand support for negotiators, advisors, special envoys and mediators involved in peace negotiations. In the past, she was engaged in dialogue and negotiation processes in Sri Lanka, Nepal, Macedonia, Myanmar, the Basque Country and Yemen. She led the conceptual work on National Dialogues and Insider Mediation at the Berghof Foundation. Currently, she is engaged in some discrete processes in Europe and Latin America. She is also involved in a joint project with the UN-MSU that is exploring the role of constitutional issues in peace processes.

Siniša Vuković is Senior Lecturer of Conflict Management and Global Policy, and Associate Director of the Conflict Management Program at Johns Hopkins University's School of Advanced International Studies (SAIS). He is also a visiting professor at the Institute of Security and Global Affairs, Leiden University, and at the Amsterdam University College, University of Amsterdam. His research focuses on various forms of international conflict resolution, negotiation and mediation. He has published in a range of scholarly journals such as *Washington Quarterly*, *Cooperation and Conflict*, *Studies in Conflict and Terrorism*, *Millennium Journal of International Studies*, *International Journal of Conflict Management*, *International Negotiation*, *Asia and the Pacific Policy Studies* and *Acta Politica*, policy-relevant outlets such as Foreign Affairs, Foreign Policy, World Economic Forum, Sustainable Security and Policy Forum, and has contributed to several edited volumes.

Francis Ward works in Middle East and North Africa regional department of the Centre for Humanitarian Dialogue (HD), focusing on political mediation processes at the local, regional and international level. Before assuming his current position in 2013, he worked with HD to assist with the national transitional process in Libya and to facilitate multiple local tribal and ethnic conflict mediation processes across the country. During the conflict in 2011–12, Francis was stationed in Libya working on negotiating humanitarian access and the provision of humanitarian assistance in frontline areas. Previously, he was based in Afghanistan, where he worked on humanitarian and development projects across the central and northern provinces. He has a Bachelor's degree in History from the University of Nottingham and a Master's degree in War Studies from Kings College London.

Acknowledgements

This book presents and builds on a series of conversations at a workshop on the theme of "Re-thinking Peace Mediation", held in New York City in November 2018. We are grateful to the German Federal Ministry of Foreign Affairs and the United Kingdom Foreign and Commonwealth Office for their kind support, including through the Permanent Mission of the United Kingdom and the Permanent Mission of Germany to the United Nations.

Permission has been received from SAGE publications to reproduce Chapter 7, which is an early version of an article published as follows:

Hirblinger, A.T. and Landau, D.M. (2020). 'Daring to differ? Strategies of inclusion in peacemaking', *Security Dialogue*, 51(4): 305–22, copyright © 2020 by the Authors
Reprinted by Permission of SAGE Publications, Ltd.

We would also like to acknowledge the contributions of those who took part in the workshop in addition to the contributing authors: Karin Aggestam, Elodie Convergne, Sophia Dawkins, Vesna Markovic Dasovic, Harriet Fildes, Anna Hess, Elshaddai Mesfin, Fabio Oliva, Olufemi Oloba, Juan Diaz Prince, Mareike Schomerus and Christina Steenkamp. Their insights have strengthened the analysis offered on the themes presented in this collection.

Work on this collection was facilitated by the award of a Christopherson/Knott fellowship to Catherine Turner from the Institute of Advanced Study (IAS) at Durham University. We also gratefully acknowledge the support of the IAS for the work of Irene Fellin, who was an IAS Fellow during Michaelmas term 2019.

We are thankful to Sarah Clowry and Juline Beaujouan-Marliere of Durham University School of Government and International Affairs for their outstanding research assistance and support with the preparation of this collection. We warmly thank Teresa Whitfield and anonymous reviewers for reviewing the manuscript – all remaining errors are ours.

We also thank Robert Pfeiffer from the European Viadrina University for his kind assistance with the organization of the authors' workshop.

Opinions expressed in this book are those of the authors and do not necessarily reflect views of their represented organizations, including the United Nations.

1

Rethinking Peace Mediation: Trends and Challenges

Catherine Turner and Martin Wählisch

Introduction

This volume comes at a time when the United Nations, regional organizations and their Member States are actively seeking new ways of better using mediation to sustain peace. It is also a moment where multilateralism and the principles of the rules-based international order for conflict resolution are under strain. Operational and practical challenges for mediators have multiplied in a world where the global–local nexus has become tighter and is overshadowed by growing transnational threats such as terrorism, cybercrime and climate change. Conflicts have fundamentally changed since the end of the 20th century, moving away from interstate conflicts, or conflicts between states and secessionist movements that can easily be characterized as conflicts about sovereignty, to conflicts that engage whole societies and involve multiple conflict actors with multiple competing priorities (Griffiths and Whitfield, 2010).

In this context there is renewed international attention being paid to mediation as a form of conflict resolution. The term 'peace mediation' is increasingly used as a catchall term to include a wide range of activities ranging from high-level diplomacy to grass roots peacebuilding, reflecting a much greater interest in the idea of multi-track diplomacy and the contribution that mediation can make at all levels of a conflicted society. In 2016 the UN General Assembly (UNGA) acknowledged that 'effective mediation and mediation support require systematic efforts at all levels'.[1] In a landmark resolution adopted by consensus of all Member States, UNGA underlined that 'timely conflict analysis, development of case-specific strategic road maps for mediation drawing on best practices and lessons learned, and identification of appropriate expertise' are vital.[2] This turn reflects a significant evolution in dominant understandings of mediation and peace support in policy and practice that started with the shift from an exclusively state-centric approach towards a model rooted in the 'liberal consensus' on the value of rule of law and rights-based approaches to peacemaking (Richmond, 2018). It is a new direction from the UN within the context of its 75-year mandate for mediation and good offices.

The evolving discourse on peace mediation shows that the bar for providing assistance and support to conflicted parties is being set progressively higher, reflecting, for some, the aspirations of the international community to handle conflict more effectively and more sustainably. The system-wide debate in the UN about the 'sustaining peace' agenda stands as a symbol for this trend – driven by the hope that closer coordination of the prevention, resolution and peacebuilding continuum could diminish the risk of recurring violence.[3]

However, as the field expands there is perhaps inevitably an increasing lack of common understanding about the means and the ends of peace mediation. Recent scholarship in the field reveals new contestation of mainstream and settled postulations of how best to mediate and end conflict (Hinton et al, 2019). This collection contributes to this body of scholarship by bringing together scholarly and practitioner perspectives on the altering landscape of international peace mediation. Through each of the chapters the collection explores new trends and invites readers to think critically about the future of peace mediation within the broader global political context. Through their analysis of key trends in peace mediation the chapters reveal key conceptual and practical challenges that face mediation scholars, policy makers and practitioners, as well as revealing disciplinary blind spots and contradictory approaches that risk hampering effectiveness. By bringing these insights and analyses together within the overarching thematic frameworks of norms, inclusion and engagement, the collection aims to deepen understanding among scholars and practitioners alike of the challenges facing the field of peace mediation and stimulate informed debate on how to address them.

1 General Assembly resolution 70/304, 26 September 2016.

2 General Assembly resolution 70/304, 26 September 2016.

3 Security Council resolution 2282 (2016), 27 April 2016.

Trends and Developments in Peace Mediation: An Altering Landscape

The move away from state-centric models of mediation towards a broader understanding of mediation within the context of liberal peacebuilding has been accompanied by a move towards norm-based interventions, and the professionalization of actors in the field (Von Burg, 2015; Convergne, 2016). Within this contemporary framework, peace mediation policy is now connected to broader goals of social reconstruction and liberal peacebuilding with new thematic areas of priority, such as constitution making, gender aspects and attention to local, bottom-up peacebuilding initiatives (Lehti, 2017). As a result there has been a gradual move away from the model of a single high-level mediator towards the institutionalization of multi-track mediation in which mediation occurs simultaneously across different levels of society and includes a broad range of actors. High-level mediation processes are now routinely supported by a range of external actors, including quasi-governmental and non-governmental organizations that are specialized in process design or thematic areas related to peace mediation (Lehti, 2017). There are two points to note in respect of this recent evolution of the field. The first is the existence of a normative turn in which mediation came to be analysed in light of legal norms and the values of the mediation actor. The second is the increased reliance on technical expertise which underpins mediation support activities to deliver the normative goals. Both these trends are reflected in the policy guidance that has been issued by the United Nations within the past decade.

In 2012 the United Nations consolidated a growing trend towards the professionalization of peace mediation in its Guidance for Effective Mediation (United Nations, 2012), stressing that peace processes need to be 'well supported' to achieve durable solutions. The UN underlined that external state and non-state actors can help to galvanize peace efforts by strengthening negotiation capacities, providing capacity-building support, consulting stakeholders on thematic issues or facilitating the engineering of peace mediation efforts. As a normative direction, the UN recommended that mediators should 'not accept conditions for support from external actors that would affect the impartiality of the process',[4] underscoring that 'coherent support' and consistent messaging to the conflict parties are critical aspects in creating an environment conducive to mediation. In the context of an increasingly crowded peace mediation field (Lanz and Gasser, 2013) it is perhaps unsurprising that some form of

[4] Security Council resolution 2282 (2016), 27 April 2016.

regulation would be required to ensure coherence of approach. The move towards thematic guidance and professionalized approaches to mediation should be seen in this context.

The normative turn in mediation is increasingly reflected in the number of Guidance notes and toolkits for implementation that guide not only UN practice, but also that of other organizations though a trickle-down effect. To take an example, the UN Guidance on Effective Mediation includes, as core principles, inclusivity and regard for international law and normative frameworks. A separate guidance note has also been produced to assist with the operationalization of norms related to gender and mediation arising from the Women Peace and Security Agenda (United Nations, 2017). These principles are balanced in the 2012 Guidance against the traditionally more political aspects of mediation, including consent and national ownership. The focus of Guidance notes and toolkits for implementation rests on the translation of international norms into practice through the development of the skills of the mediator. In this way political problems are reframed as technical problems to be resolved. However, whether these developments have led to an improvement in terms of smoother peace processes, strengthened confidence of stakeholders and eventually more sustainable peace agreements remains open to question. As case studies in this volume show, mediation support actors often promise to honour conflict sensitivity but risk imposing predefined models and solutions that suit the interests of donors and agendas of influential conflict bystanders. In an ideal instance, peace mediation support entities would reflect about how and why a desired change is expected to happen in a particular context, applying a critical approach of methodology for planning, participation and evaluation of their work. However, in practice, peace mediation support is often less grounded in concrete strategies and can be, at worst, disorganized (Lehmann-Larsen, 2014). In this regard, the proliferation of practitioner guidance and normative directions for mediators poses additional challenges to the field as the expectations for due diligence and 'properly' performed mediation have risen.

While professionalization and multi-track efforts have been part of a response to trends and developments in peace mediation practice, new challenges have emerged. First, a question remains over how best to manage the diversity of voices now present in the mediation space. Just as the scope of conflicts has been fundamentally transformed since the end of the 20th century, so too has the range of actors who must be engaged in mediation processes (Griffiths and Whitfield, 2010). As mediation was traditionally understood as a form of peace diplomacy, research has focused on themes such as the choice and motivation of the mediator, the limits of statecraft and soft power, as well as the techniques of peacemaking in this context (Croker, 2001; Bercovitch and Gartner, 2010; Svensson, 2014). Analysis has centred on the relationship between the different actors within the process, and the successes, failures and limitations of particular approaches (Darby and MacGinty, 2003; Sisk, 2009; Vukovic, 2015). Less attention has been paid to the substance of those interactions, the role of support actors, or indeed to the nature of the relationship between mediation and peace (Convergne, 2016; Clowry, 2019). Mediation support entities bring their own values, priorities and understanding to the mediation field. As a result, the practices of mediation support actors inevitably shape the norms they purport to implement. This has led to a creeping lack of conceptual clarity about the core functions, motivations and responsibilities. These contemporary dynamics bring not only practical challenges in terms of co-ordinating the efforts of the different actors, but also normative challenges when different players promote different values and objectives to the process. As a result, in some cases mediation efforts are complementary to each other, while in other instances they are lacking strategic links and mutually counterproductive (Lehmann-Larsen, 2014).

There is still a lack of clarity, or indeed consensus, on what the lived 'core' principles underpinning mediation actually are. For example, it is now widely accepted that as a matter of best practice mediation should be inclusive and that it should observe the rules of international law. And yet there is very little clear consensus on what these terms mean or how they are ought to be operationalized. For example, there are clear tensions in trying to create space for civil society actors to engage in a state-centric model of mediation. Not only does the dominance of the foreign policy paradigm risk preventing meaningful engagement with local processes and local actors, but the epistemic biases of the mediator will also have a significant bearing on who is invited to engage in the process and who remains excluded. This is particularly true in respect of the rules on 'terrorism', which profoundly shape how mediators engage with armed actors. Addressing these challenges requires looking beyond a limited understanding of inclusion as adding new actors and towards new paradigms for engagement that fundamentally rethink why new groups are included and how they contribute to the substance, and as a result, the effectiveness of mediation.

Finally, despite vast efforts to make peace mediation more effective, ordered and utilized, conflict remains a reality of international affairs and maintains intrastate fragility in many regions of the world. Humanity's fascination with war, high military expenditures and constant developments to weapons systems make the 'peace industry' look comparatively minor.

Added to this, rapid advances in technology, changing demographic trends and economic connectivity all challenge mediators to adapt to new realities. Despite the rapid increase in the number of mediation support actors in recent years, peace mediation as a field remains rooted in traditional models of diplomacy and interstate bargaining. Indeed the techniques of what might be called 'old school' mediation, such as shuttle diplomacy and the convening of face-to-face talks, are still very much standard components of mediation practice. Yet while some diplomats claim that they are the genuine peacemakers with the necessary finesse to bring others together and talk them out of military escalation, very few foreign office officials have been properly trained and mentored to cope with the role of being an impartial third party equipped with skills that go beyond formal diplomacy techniques and rituals. As the chapters in this collection discuss, traditional interstate rivalries continue to influence the ways in which mediation is offered. Governmental actors continue to hold power and influence when it comes to the design of mediation processes and the actors who will be included. With the resurgence of geopolitical polarization there is a risk that the liberal consensus that has allowed for the professionalization and expansion of the peacemaking field now gives way to a more instrumental use of peace mediation in service of larger strategic aims. In particular, it is possible that mediation becomes exclusively a cover for the promotion of specific foreign policy agendas which would have long-term negative consequences for its acceptance as a form of dispute resolution at any level. A breakdown in consensus on the value of mediation, or the hijacking of its ostensibly impartial process to mask foreign policy interventions is a real concern, and one which peace mediators must be willing to address.

As various chapters in this collection discuss, it is noticeable that in recent years mediation has become an overt tool for the projection of the values of the international community, such as inclusivity and the respect for the rules of international law. Yet as other chapters reveal, the re-emergence of global political rivalries and polarization with the loss of entrusted multilateralism presents new challenges to the overarching consensus on mediation as a key instrument to sustain peace.

Outline of the Book

Critical thinking has been a common theme in conflict resolution studies, not least as part of self-awareness, its contribution to process empowerment and its scholarly philosophy that is intrinsic for both teaching and learning about peace and conflict (Rothman, 2014). This collection aims to contribute to this overall objective to continuously gain deeper perspectives, explore new skills and challenge contemporary assumptions concerning peacemaking. The evolution of peace and conflict theory has progressed precisely because perceived dogmas of correlation–causation equations, conclusions from regional studies, process design parameters and other issues have been constructively questioned, tested and modified over time. The combination of orthodox and heterodox approaches to peace and conflict in international relations has eventually resulted in the rich variety of mediation, conflict resolution, conflict transformation and peacebuilding understandings that currently exist to make sense of order, norms, structures, power, the role of international organizations and intergroup dynamics (Richmond, 2010). The eclectic and interdisciplinary field of peace studies, considering its multiple teleologies, canons, influences and biases, has evolved whenever new, experimental and unconventional views contested the mainstream and settled postulations of how to best mediate and end conflict (Hinton et al, 2019). This volume stands in this spirit of constructively 'rethinking' peace mediation based on practitioner–scholarly collaborations for the betterment of peacemaking.

This volume is structured along three main themes which have emerged from recent scholarship on peace mediation and reflect the challenges mentioned earlier, namely normativity, inclusivity and engagement. Each of the themes is interrogated in a series of chapters that take both theoretical and empirical approaches to the theme.

The first theme of normativity considers the normative framework within which peace mediation actors now operate. As noted earlier, there has been a significant normative turn in mediation in recent years. The full consequences of this have not been fully explored. Each of the chapters offers insight into both the explicit and the implicit effects of the normative turn in mediation. Rather than focusing specifically on the norms themselves, each chapter considers the complex relationship between actors and norms and the ways in which norms shape or are shaped by the practices of mediation actors. Philipp Kastner in his contribution considers the role of norms in the professionalization of the field. Scrutinizing documents promulgated by the United Nations, the European Union, the African Union and the Centre for Humanitarian Dialogue, he highlights that the growing trend to depict peace mediation as a professionalized activity is promoted mainly by experts in this field. He notes how the multiplication of actors in the field and the articulation of a normative framework as an ostensive route to 'professionalization' can, in itself, contribute to the legitimization of peace mediators, thereby rendering mediation processes more effective. However,

Kastner also sounds a note of caution. Confronted with the shrinking number of peace agreements, he calls for more flexibility in mediation practices and experts' scope for action. Continuing the interrogation of the relationship between actors and norms, Emmanuel de Groof in his chapter highlights the methodologies and practices that shape the normative framework of peacemaking, offering a multidimensional analysis of the way in which peacemaking practices are narrated by key actors. Navigating three normative layers of peace processes, he investigates the connexion between, first, the professional deontology of peacemakers, mediation practices and values; second, domestic laws and constitutions; and third, the progressive development of international law in relation to transitional governance. De Groof contemplates the potential consequences of this 'jurisgenerative train' arising from the connection between actors and norms on peace practices, the credibility of practitioners, and eventually, on peace processes. In their contributions Siniša Vuković and Julia Palmiano Federer examine the processes of norm diffusion through NGO actors in peace processes. Vuković interrogates the way in which norms are diffused by international actors as a means of controlling the practice and assumptions of mediation itself. Following her analysis Federer concludes that non-governmental organizations can function as both norm makers and norm takers during peace processes despite, and perhaps due to, their frequent lack of an official mandate. Moreover, she underlines that they lack awareness concerning their power to encourage particular norms, and to support their broader diffusion within international society. In the final contribution to this part Asli Ozcelik presents an empirically grounded analysis of the role of norms in the Colombian peace process. Focusing on the ways in which norms pertaining to justice shaped the Colombian process, she neatly illustrates the practical challenges of 'legalized peacemaking'. Through her analysis she highlights how the norm-driven approach to peace mediation, particularly as it pertains to international law, must be assessed with care. Based on the applied case study, Ozcelik warns that international law has a limited prescriptive reach in providing clear and specified normative parameters, and that such regulation risks being strategically instrumentalized during mediation. She emphasizes that international law is political and stresses that claims that compliance with international law renders mediation legitimate or durable should therefore be viewed with a degree of caution.

The second part focuses on the concept of inclusion, exploring both conceptual and practical challenges to inclusive process design. From the contributions to this part it becomes clear that inclusion is not simply a matter of adding new groups to the existing structures of mediation, but rather that a genuine commitment to inclusion might require a radical rethinking of some of the assumptions that currently underpin mediation theory and practice. The section begins with a meta-level exploration of the concept of inclusion from Andreas Hirblinger and Dana Landau. Their chapter presents a detailed typology for understanding inclusion in peacemaking theory, which the authors use to assess instructions for inclusive peace processes put forward in key UN documents. Their analysis reveals a tension between the international normative framework – which promotes the protection of included groups – and mediation guidance documents – which emphasize the merit of relational framing. They suggest that a relational inclusion strategy may foster a peace that is both more contextually grounded and more focused on long-term conflict transformation. The theme of tension between the strategy of inclusion and its implementation in practice is continued by Elisa Tarnaala in her contribution on women's peace advocacy and inclusive processes. Tarnaala invites her readers to rethink mediation from the perspective of political transition and social mobilization, arguing that post-conflict political transition and inclusive peace processes must be negotiated in the light of two key factors: the regime type and the historical space for civil society. She calls for mediation practices that would demonstrate greater sensitivity to national processes and local trajectories. Tarnaala contends that mediation should be considered beyond political transitions that are not contingent on specific time frames, but rather as episodes where claims and actors involved durably shape the future relations between powerholders and challengers. This theme is continued by Emma Van Santen in her chapter, in which she highlights how current mediation practice is rooted in the liberal peacebuilding paradigm which itself inherently excludes certain groups of social actors from mediation processes. Analysing inclusion through a case study on the politics of inclusion of violent non-state actors in the Mali peace process, Van Santen analyses the manner in which the drive to render mediation 'inclusive' is adapting to contemporary intrastate conflicts. She suggests that 'new' mediators are less constrained by the liberal peacebuilding agenda and are thus uniquely placed to encompass traditionally excluded 'criminal' elements within negotiations. She urges peace practitioners to redevelop their understanding of the notion of inclusion, ensuring the norm encourages engagement by mediators at the local level. This theme is also explored by Jeffrey R. Seul in his contribution on mediating across worldviews. Seul suggests that mediation is currently ill-equipped to mediate where the fundamental drivers of conflict can be attributed to worldviews. In addition to greater local engagement, meaningful inclusion in this context would require grappling with two profound questions: how are worldviews entwined with power structures within the international system, and how might the system need to change if we were to take more seriously other worldviews that have had relatively less influence in international affairs up until now? Finally, Josie Lianna Kaye explores another group traditionally excluded from the 'political' business of peacemaking – the business community. Working through the case study of the conflict in Yemen from 2011 to 2016, Kaye critically evaluates the inclusion and exclusion of business leaders from the UN-supported peace process. The marginalization of local businesses, she warns, underscores the imperative of extending the discourse and political practice of inclusion that would give a greater role to local actors. Kaye describes the potential power of influence of local business leaders as an 'untapped resource' and makes a case for considering mediation practices through a 'business lens'. She considers the latter to be particularly appropriate to overcome the gap between peacemaking and post-conflict reconstruction processes.

The final part brings together aspects that impact, sustain and accelerate engagement in peace processes. Beyond the idea of inclusion, the chapters presented in this part explore the questions of 'who' engages, 'how' they engage, and 'when' in terms of the strategies that they use. In this regard it presents a diverse range of strategies for engagement, and reflections on their strengths and weaknesses. Each of the chapters provides important insights into new trends and challenges for mediation actors. In his contribution Francis Ward analyses options for non-state mediators in the age of multilateral proxy conflicts, outlining a typology of proxy conflicts and highlighting the challenges that this new trend poses for peace mediation. Building on the analysis of the engagement of multiple actors in peace processes, Jamie Pring highlights the ways in which states compete for influence in the peace mediation sphere, revealing the risks this poses for the coherence of mediation support efforts. Using the relationship between the UN, the African Union and the Intergovernmental Authority on Development (IGAD) as a case study, Pring highlights the divergent interests and practices of different organizations and suggests that this divergence in values could hinder collaboration during peace processes. In this context, she urges that capacity building for mediators should be accompanied by frank discussions concerning deviating normative priorities. This chapter adds an extra layer of depth to the analysis of Kastner in that it highlights the realities of competing values on mediator behaviour. Turning to one of the most recent innovations in mediation, Irene Fellin and Catherine Turner present a comprehensive overview of the establishment of the new networks of women mediators. Their chapter outlines the emergence of these networks from the field of women peace and security and provides not only a detailed overview of the development of networks as a strategy to increase the representation of women in mediation, but also a careful critique of some of the potential barriers and limitations faced by the networks in fulfilling their role. Central to their analysis is the question of 'how' networks engage in the peace mediation field. Continuing the inquiry as to 'how' new actors engage in mediation, Miguel Varela assesses the implications of online communications for peace mediators. Highlighting and addressing the growing importance of social media in the modern world and peace practices, he concludes that the survival of the profession may depend on mediators' capacity to embrace the prospect of working with digital technologies and to move towards a 'technology of peace or mediation'. Varela also argues that technologies should be contemplated and used as an opportunity to strengthen the link between local and international practitioners, as well as to create more inclusive and better-coordinated mediation processes that have a measurable impact on decision making. In their contribution, Mir Mubashir, Julian Klauke and Luxshi Vimalarajah consider the relationship between peace mediation and constitution making. In particular they ask the question of 'when' constitution making should be addressed, suggesting that a closer collaboration between the two processes – which draw on similar techniques – would benefit the field of mediation. They make a case for rethinking and (re)assessing the conceptual and practical relation between mediation and constitution making. They also assess how an interdependent relationship may be forged to better contribute to the transformation of conflict for sustaining peace, calling for the creation of a complex and adaptable design of peace (sub)processes to allow multiple and diverse actors to engage collaboratively with the dynamic nature of the nexus.

Finally, the contribution of Anne Holper and Lars Kirchhoff reflects on the professionalization of peace mediation with reference to the previous chapters, exploring whether and how professionalization and regulation affect the outcomes of mediated negotiations. Noting that we do not yet know whether the attempts over the last decade to better regulate mediation have had an impact on the effectiveness of peacemaking, they propose an analytical framework for carrying out precisely this assessment, incorporating the insights of the preceding considerations in this volume. Holper and Kirchhoff described the professionalization process as being 'advanced yet highly volatile' and conclude by calling for further, more detailed research into the causal mechanisms at work during peace mediation.

Conclusion

There is no doubt that the landscape of international peace mediation has shifted enormously in the past decades. A range of new actors and methods have been introduced, along with increasingly institutionalized approaches to designing and delivering mediation processes. There are undoubtedly challenges arising from the changing nature of mediation. These challenges are now amplified by the current state of flux in global affairs whereby a multilateral system that had been taken for granted as the foundation of peaceful interstate relations is coming under strain. The role of peace mediation is likely to become more, not less, important in this context.

Rethinking Peace Mediation describes a compact between scholars and practitioners to jointly pursue innovation and critical approaches to peacemaking. It is a call to engage in the challenges of our time. In this spirit, we hope that this volume will motivate further interdisciplinary efforts, challenge thoughts on perfect and imperfect solutions, and nurture constructive curiosity to improve collective efforts to sustain peace.

References

Bercovitch, J. and Gartner, S. (2010) *International Conflict Mediation: New Approaches and Findings* (Routledge).

Clowry, S. (2019) 'Review: International Negotiation and Mediation in Violent Conflicts: The Changing Context of Peacemaking', *Peacebuilding*, DOI 10.1080/21647259.2019.1633120.

Convergne, E. (2016) 'Learning to Mediate: The Mediation Support Unit and the Production of Expertise by the UN', *Journal of Intervention and Statebuilding*, 10(2): 181–99.

Croker, C.A. (2001) *Turbulent Peace: The Challenges of Managing International Conflict* (USIP).

Darby, J. and MacGinty, R. (2003) *Contemporary Peace Making: Conflict, Violence and Peace Processes* (Palgrave Macmillan).

Griffiths, M. and Whitfield, T. (2010) *Mediation Ten Years On: Opportunities and Challenges for Peacemaking* (Centre for Humanitarian Dialogue).

Hinton, A., Shani, G. and Alberg, J. (2019) *Rethinking Peace: Discourse, Memory, Translation, and Dialogue* (Rowman & Littlefield).

Lanz, D. and Gasser, R. (2013) 'A Crowded Field: Competition and Co-Ordination in International Peace Mediation', Centre for Mediation in Africa: University of Pretoria.

Lehmann-Larsen, S. (2014) 'Effectively Supporting Peace Processes: Developments, Challenges and Requirements', HD Centre Oslo Forum Papers, No. 3.

Lehti, M. (2017) *The Era of Private Peacemakers: A New Dialogic Approach to Mediation* (Palgrave).

Richmond, Oliver P. (2010) 'A Genealogy of Peace and Conflict Theory', in O. Richmond, ed., *Palgrave Advances in Peacebuilding: Critical Developments and Approaches* (Palgrave) 14–38.

Richmond, Oliver P. (2018) 'A Genealogy of Mediation in International Relations: From "Analogue" to "Digital" Forms of Global Justice or Managed War', *Cooperation and Conflict*, 53(3): 301–19.

Rothman, J. (2014) 'Reflexive Pedagogy: Teaching and Learning in Peace and Conflict Studies', *Conflict Resolution Quarterly*, 32(2): 109–28.

Sisk, T. (2009) *International Mediation in Civil Wars: Bargaining with Bullets* (Routledge).

Svensson, I. (2014) *International Mediation Bias and Peacemaking: Taking Sides in Civil Wars* (Routledge).

United Nations (2012) 'Guidance for Effective Mediation'.

United Nations (2017) 'Guidance on Gender and Inclusive Mediation Strategies'.

Von Burg, C. (2015) *On Inclusivity: The Role of Norms in International Peace Mediation* (swisspeace).

Vuković, S. (2015) *International Multiparty Mediation and Conflict Management: Challenges of Cooperation and Coordination* (Routledge).

PART I
Normative Influences on Mediation

2

Promoting Professionalism: A Normative Framework for Peace Mediation

Philipp Kastner

Introduction

Different actors involved in peace mediation, above all the United Nations (UN), have started to articulate a normative framework for their activities in recent years, seeking to promote professionalism and to provide normative guidance to mediators. The most prominent example consists in the publication of a document entitled *Guidance for Effective Mediation*, annexed to the Secretary-General's 2012 report on the mediation activities of the UN. Within this framework, international legal norms, such as the prohibition to include in peace agreements amnesties for alleged perpetrators of genocide, crimes against humanity and war crimes, play a particularly prominent role. Other organizations, including regional organizations and specialized non-governmental organizations (NGOs), have also adopted and publicized guiding principles and codes of conduct that govern their activities.

This trend of rendering explicit certain norms pertaining to peace mediation is not only intriguing from a scholarly perspective; the articulation of a normative framework can also affect the practice of peace mediation and, ultimately, the success of negotiations. Therefore, it seems useful to try to understand the reasons for rendering explicit what used to be largely implicit. Indeed, given the apparent imperative to make these norms explicit, something seems to have changed, at least in the perception of mediation organizations. As will be argued, however, norms have never been absent from an intermediary's attempt to resolve armed conflicts through peaceful means, and peace mediation has always been governed by certain principles. Moreover, presumably universal rules, such as the (non-)neutrality and impartiality of a mediator, have never existed as absolutes and have always been qualified in some way.

Scrutinizing the main documents promulgated by organizations that have developed a particular expertise in the field of peace mediation, namely the UN, the European Union, the African Union and the NGOs Centre for Humanitarian Dialogue and Crisis Management Initiative, the chapter demonstrates that peace mediation is increasingly presented as a professionalized activity to be carried out by experts. Certain more specific principles, such as those pertaining to the impartiality and (non-) neutrality of mediators, have been engaged with and further defined, and the relevance of existing norms, in particular those stemming from international human rights law and pertaining to rendering peace negotiations more inclusive, is increasingly highlighted.

While it is difficult to assess already the impact of this recent articulation of a normative framework on the actual practice and effectiveness of peace mediation activities, the chapter also tries to grasp some of the likely effects. Despite some inherent drawbacks of an explicitly stated normative framework, being clear about the values and norms governing peace mediation can potentially fulfil considerable expressive and symbolic functions and contribute to the legitimation of the peace mediator in question, thus possibly rendering mediation processes more effective. The chapter concludes with some thoughts on the allegedly problematic over-regulation of peace mediation and the potential of the currently dominant approach, which is affected by the articulation of a normative framework, to resolve certain types of conflict but not others.

A Field in Need of Professionalization

The field of peace mediation has undergone significant changes and has arguably become much more complex over the past few decades. This is related to the types of armed conflict that intermediaries seek to help resolve. Whereas inter-state conflicts used to be the main challenge, most armed conflicts now take place within states, even if they are often internationalized in some way. Internal armed conflicts, which rarely oppose two, or several, relative equals, are typically much more difficult to resolve than conflicts between states, where the conflict parties can, in a way, agree to disagree but do not necessarily have to (re)build a thorny relationship (Kastner, 2015: 5).

Seeking to peacefully resolve internal armed conflicts, in other words, is a complex endeavour. More conventional, high-level diplomatic interventions that attempt to resolve a well-defined dispute still occur, and diplomats or politicians may still be able to rely on a conventional approach to conflict resolution when acting as intermediaries to reach, for instance, a ceasefire agreement between two warring states. However, such an approach is unlikely to bear fruit in the context of internal armed conflicts, where multiple issues need to be taken into account and worked out. Usually, a more comprehensive approach needs to be adopted, and a greater number of actors – and experts – involved. States and their representatives, who were traditionally the main players, with diplomats or politicians acting as mediators to contribute to the resolution of armed conflicts between or within other states, are, of course, still involved in peace mediation today, but international and non-governmental organizations (NGOs) play an increasingly important role. International organizations, above all the UN, but also regional organizations like the European Union and the African Union, have developed a particular expertise in peace mediation. Moreover, a number of specialized NGOs, such as the Centre for Humanitarian Dialogue and the Crisis Management Initiative, which were established in 1999 and 2000 respectively,[1] have been created to act as peace mediators or to support peace mediation initiatives.

The fact that numerous actors are now involved in peace mediation may also explain the desire for further regulation. Indeed, peace mediation has, according to some, become a 'crowded field', which is increasingly characterized by competition between the different actors involved in peace mediation (Lanz and Gasser, 2013). While unhelpful competition, which risks undermining peace negotiations, can be addressed by enhancing cooperation between the actors involved (Lanz and Gasser, 2013), more established organizations also try to distinguish themselves by underlining their expertise, competence and also normative ambition. To avoid every kind of involvement of a third party in the context of a peace process being called 'peace mediation', which would, in the long run, risk watering down the very meaning of peace mediation, standards and principles have been established, and norms promulgated.

[1] The Centre for Humanitarian Dialogue's website is accessible online, available from: https://www.hdcentre.org/who-we-are/about/ (accessed 25 July 2019); the Crisis Management Initiative's website is accessible online, available from: http://cmi.fi/about-us/ (accessed 25 July 2019).

Related to this shift in the type of actors involved in peace mediation, it can be observed that the task of peace mediation has become a more and more specialized and professionalized activity. Whereas peace mediation used to be largely ad hoc, and approaches to mediation varied greatly, the activity has become increasingly institutionalized and standardized (Splinter and Lüttmann, 2014). The best example probably consists in the publication of the UN's *Guidance for Effective Mediation* in 2012 (UNSG, 2012) and in the institutionalization of mediation activities within the UN, in particular through the establishment of the Mediation Support Unit (MSU) in 2006.[2] In the *Guidance*, the UN highlights that mediation is not only 'one of the most effective methods of preventing, managing and resolving conflicts' but also 'a speciali[z]ed activity' (UNSG, 2012: 1, 4), thus underlining its conviction that peace mediation must be approached in a professional manner and take place within a normative framework.[3]

The policies of the European Union and the African Union can be considered in a similar light. These regional organizations, which have been involved in peace mediation in a number of conflicts, also seek to underline and enhance their competence in the area of peace mediation. As noted in a key document entitled *Concept on Strengthening EU Mediation and Dialogue Capacities*, which was adopted by the Council of the European Union in 2009, '[w]hile mediation is not a new area to the EU, a more coordinated and focused approach will enhance the EU's ability to play a more active international role in this area' (Council of the European Union, 2009: 2). The *Concept* even notes that mediation has been used, so far, 'in a rather ad hoc fashion' (Council of the European Union, 2009: 4). Similarly, the African Union's *Mediation Support Handbook*, first published in 2012 and updated in 2014, recalls that mediation processes necessitate 'a planned and professional approach, rather than being conducted through ad hoc diplomatic initiatives' (ACCORD and AU, 2014: 7).

The normative framework of peace negotiations, especially those seeking to end internal armed conflicts and given the absence of a single, hierarchical legal order, could be seen as still being primarily generated by the negotiating parties, but the fairly recent 'mushrooming' of norms (Hellmüller et al, 2015: 7), which build on and even spell out otherwise implicit, underlying values and seek to ensure a quality process, represent a considerable change. In fact, compared to other contexts, such as family

[2] The Mediation Support Unit's website is accessible online, available from: https://peacemaker.un.org/mediation-support (accessed 25 July 2019).

[3] In addition to the general *Guidance*, more specific guides have been published by the United Nations, such as on gender issues and on natural resources.

and employment disputes, peace negotiations and peace mediation are, relatively speaking, still only thinly regulated. In the literature on domestic mediation, this approach has been called 'norm generation' (Waldman, 1997). In this traditional approach to mediation, the mediator guides the parties through the process and also encourages them to generate the norms that will help resolve the dispute. Norms external to the process are largely irrelevant in this approach, which usually works well in the context of a private dispute between relative equals. However, peace negotiations can hardly be considered a private dispute as the underlying conflict affects entire populations and may threaten regional or even international peace and security. Moreover, as already mentioned, such negotiations are rarely conducted between relative equals but are highly asymmetrical, especially in the context of an internal armed conflict. Protective norms, established by and of concern to the international community, such as human rights, are also routinely affected (Kastner, 2015: 73). As a 'Background Note' on *Global Challenges and Trends in International Peace Mediation and Diplomacy*, prepared and published by the Mediation Support Team of the European Union usefully notes,

> those mediating in conflicts today are faced with clearer, more comprehensive, but also more complex, international legal and normative frameworks that attempt to define what is (and what is not) acceptable in negotiations to end armed violence. This applies for example to the protection of human rights in the context of international peace mediation, impunity and expectations with regard to transitional justice in dealing with perpetrators of violence and abuse, as well as victims' needs. In many instances, EU policy has become or is in the process of becoming more defined ([eg] transitional justice); efforts to address impunity at international level ([eg] sexual violence in conflict) is also clearer. Such codifications inevitably affect mediators' work to broker lasting peace agreements. (EEAS Mediation Support Team, 2016: 2)

It is useful to recall that the broader field of mediation in the domestic context has witnessed increasing attempts at regulation, either by the state or through the profession of mediators (Spencer and Brogan, 2006).[4] The

[4] However, as Spencer and Brogan conclude with respect to the regulation of alternative dispute resolution in Australia, there is still 'little control over the level of training and experience by the various training providers, or assessment of the ability of individual after such training has been completed' (Spencer and Brogan, 2006: 379).

idea is to put the legitimacy of intermediaries – similar to those of judges – on a more solid foundation, prior to and largely independent from the specific approval of the negotiating parties, to ground the involvement of mediators on general principles, and to render mediation ultimately more effective (Kastner, 2015: 90). Indeed, when compared to judges, who can be considered to be pre-legitimated by the state when part of a judicial system built on the rule of law, mediators used to obtain their legitimacy solely through the consent of the parties. While such consent is still essential, various training programmes, certificates and codes of conduct increasingly seek to ensure certain quality standards and to protect potential clients from unskilled and dishonest individuals. However, official regulation and clear entry standards are lacking in many areas, and the question as to whether and how mediation should be regulated in the domestic sphere remains heavily debated (Hinshaw, 2016). Among other things, given the usually broad definitions of mediation and the strong commitment to diversity and flexibility in the field, there is no clear consensus as to what competent mediation actually looks like (Waldman, 1996).

Moreover, regulating and professionalizing the activity of mediation bears certain dangers. These include the promotion of a dominant model that silences alternative approaches and hence does not take into account the fact that a diversity of approaches may be valuable when dealing with diverse conflicts – a danger that also exists in the field of peace mediation. As it has been argued with respect to mediation more generally, 'there is a steady development of ethical standards which promote North American dominant culture values of individual autonomy and objectivity, without acknowledgement of the diversity of cultures and practices in the field of dispute resolution' (Morris, 1997: 344).

As illustrated by the 'guidance', 'concepts', 'handbooks' and similar documents that have been published, attempts at guiding and regulating the activity of mediators in the domestic sphere have also reached the more specific field of peace mediation, even if with some delay, and many of the desired benefits and feared shortcomings of such regulation resurface here as well. In light of this recent tendency to professionalize the field, notably by articulating a normative framework for peace mediation and by defining more formally and explicitly certain procedural and substantive norms governing peace negotiations, peace mediation can increasingly be understood as norm based, with mediators assuming the role of norm educators and even norm advocates.[5] The *Guidance*, for instance, not only mirrors the UN's commitment to render efforts by mediators mandated by

[5] This language draws on Waldman (1997).

the organization itself more professional and legitimate (Wählisch, 2016), but is also meant to be relevant and useful for other peace mediators. In this sense, the UN clearly voices a normative ambition and aims to assume a leadership role in the field of peace mediation and to regulate this activity of 'experts' (Kastner, 2017). The standards and principles promoted by the UN are, without doubt, very influential and have even been explicitly endorsed by other actors. For instance, the Crisis Management Initiative, one of the most prominent non-governmental peace mediation organizations, declares on its website that it is 'committed to international mediation standards' and that 'our work programme is aligned with the United Nations Guidance for Effective Mediation' (Crisis Management Initiative, nd).

It can be argued that the normative guidance spearheaded by the UN, along with the institutionalization of mediation – the UN's MSU being the prime example – also signals a commitment to depoliticizing the practice of peace mediation. The UN, in particular, seems to privilege generic, technical and international expertise over insider or local knowledge of political actors (Convergne, 2016). In this sense, seeking to professionalize the field and to articulate a normative framework for peace mediation also implies an attempt to recast political problems as technical problems.

Impartiality and (Non-)neutrality: Refining Key Principles

One of the key normative principles of mediation that several peace mediation organizations have affirmed relates to the impartiality and (non-)neutrality of mediators. This principle has arguably always been – and continues to be – essential for any engagement of a mediator, but certain mediation organizations, above all the UN, have clearly felt the need to affirm and further define it.

The UN's *Guidance* contains general advice to peace mediators on how to render their involvement more legitimate and a mediation process more effective, for instance by being well prepared; by making clear that mediation is a voluntary process and by cultivating consent; by being committed to an inclusive process, such us through the engagement and inclusion of 'the different perspectives within civil and other stakeholders, throughout the various phases of the peace process'; and – most notably for our discussion here – by remaining impartial, with impartiality being described as a 'cornerstone' of mediation (UNSG, 2012). With respect to the normative baggage and potential bias of a mediator, the *Guidance* clarifies that impartiality is, in the view of the UN, not the same as neutrality: for instance, a mediator, as in the case of mediators mandated by the UN, may be required to 'uphold certain universal principles and values' (UNSG, 2012: 10).[6]

The African Union's *Handbook* also recalls important principles and contains specific guidelines for mediators. Among other things, it stipulates that 'mediators must be impartial', that 'civil society must be involved in the mediation and negotiations' and that 'the process must address the regional dimensions of national conflicts' (ACCORD and AU, 2014: 15–16). Interestingly, and somewhat contrary to the increasing trend towards norm-based mediation, the *Handbook* also states that 'mediators must be flexible, creative, responsive and adaptive' (ACCORD and AU, 2014: 16). The European Union's *Concept* is less explicit in this regard but, as will be discussed later, it does address the relevance of existing normative frameworks and the European Union's general commitment to human rights and international law. And while specialized NGOs are not necessarily neutral and unaffected by normative frameworks like international law, they often continue to highlight their independence. Probably the most prominent NGO active in the field, the Centre for Humanitarian Dialogue, highlights in its *Charter* the principles of impartiality and independence, whereas neutrality is not mentioned (Centre for Humanitarian Dialogue, nd).

The recognition by certain players that peace mediators do not necessarily have to be neutral, or should, in some instances, not be neutral, appears to have crystallized only quite recently. In fact, mediation is never a perfectly neutral or disinterested endeavour, even if mediators often claim and try to assert their neutrality (and related concepts, such as impartiality, unbiasedness and independence). First of all, the negotiating parties are inevitably influenced by the presence of a mediator and change their behaviour, communication and negotiation strategy accordingly (Bowling and Hoffman, 2003), even if the mediator does not clearly articulate a particular normative agenda. Moreover, the very idea that a mediator can be perfectly neutral should never be taken for granted. This does not

[6] It should be noted that the concepts of mediator neutrality and impartiality are interconnected, with one often being used to define the other. However, there are, indeed, important differences: 'Neutrality, on the one hand, can be associated with the more general condition and stance of the mediator vis-à-vis the conflict. Enquiring into a mediator's neutrality means asking what he or she brings to the table, such as particular interests, prior relationships with the parties or potential benefits to be gained from the outcome of the mediation. Impartiality, on the other hand, relates more to the process and the way a mediator behaves towards the parties in the course of that process than to the background of the mediator' (Kastner, 2015: 94).

only concern mediators who are mandated by organizations like the UN and whose activities are hence restrained – or guided, in a more positive sense – by certain norms; in fact, mediators cannot leave their normative baggage at the door when entering a particular negotiating room. They have been educated and trained in certain ways, they come from a certain place in this world and, as a result, have a particular background that can never be completely effaced, and certainly not in the perception of the negotiating parties and of other actors involved in a peace process.

In other words, mediation is never an entirely neutral activity. Although mediators may claim to be neutral concerning the interests and positions of the parties, being engaged in mediation implies affirming certain values (Webb, 1988: 16). Such values can relate to the process and procedural norms, such as the inclusion of civil society actors (Hellmüller, 2019) as well as the outcome of negotiations and associated substantive norms, such as upholding, or rather not violating, fundamental human rights. As a matter of fact, mediators usually have some interest – if not an openly declared stake – in the result of the negotiations, which has been described as a form of '*bias of outcome* that points out a range of possible solutions that a mediator is willing to endorse' (Vuković, 2015: 419; emphasis in original). The involvement of a mediator, from a private citizen to an envoy of the UN Secretary-General, is hence always affected by an interrelated set of assumptions, values, norms and interests, some of which are likely to differ from those of the negotiating parties. As I have argued elsewhere, 'whether implicitly or explicitly, consciously or unconsciously, a mediator will always have to manage some tensions between the parties' objectives and his or her own normative beliefs and principles' (Kastner, 2017: 81).

One of the problems is that dominant norms are often accepted as so 'normal' that they are not even recognized anymore as culture-specific, potentially biased and contestable norms. As has been affirmed in the more general context of mediation,

> people who are enculturated within a given social system often consider the prevailing norms, however unfair, to be 'objective'. … The ideal of autonomous objectivity does not recognise the fact that mediators are influenced far more than they may realise by the culture and social setting in which they live, and the political, social and power structures within which they operate. (Morris, 1997: 330)

Some mediators may believe, often in good faith, that they can hide their normative baggage under a Rawlsian 'veil of ignorance'; yet even those actors who do not represent states and who may therefore be considered to be uninfluenced by geopolitical considerations have certain interests and objectives. These interests and objectives may, once again, be voiced clearly, or they may remain tacit, but they always play a role. For instance, certain non-governmental actors, including faith-based organizations, may claim to be strictly neutral and not to have any interests – political, economic or other – in a particular peace process. As a member of the Roman Catholic Community of Sant'Egidio, which was, among others, instrumental in bringing about the 1992 peace agreement in Mozambique, asserted, '[t]he real factor behind the success … is the fact that St. Egidio is interested solely in putting an end to the conflict; it has no other interests to defend and considers any contribution that can work to this end useful and welcome' (Giro, 1998: 87). However, when considering 'interests' more broadly, it becomes apparent that a Roman Catholic community evidently represents and promotes certain values. Similarly, while generally perceived as a neutral actor, the Inter-Religious Council of Sierra-Leone, which was established by the country's religious leaders in 1997 and facilitated negotiations between the parties to the ongoing armed conflict in the country, clearly promoted such values as forgiveness and reconciliation through their involvement (Jessop et al, 2008; Kastner, 2015).

In sum, mediators carry with them assumptions, values and normative expectations that often remain implicit and may hence not be seen as impacting the neutrality of mediators and the negotiating process; yet these assumptions, values and normative expectations do matter. As discussed, some peace mediation organizations have started to be more explicit about some of the values and norms that govern their activities. It should, however, not be forgotten that these explicitly discussed values and norms only represent a fraction of the normative assumptions and expectations that actually guide and affect a mediator.

Engaging With Existing and Emerging Norms

In addition to reflecting more explicitly on and further defining the notion of mediator impartiality and (non-)neutrality, peace mediation organizations have also started to be more outspoken about the relevance of existing normative frameworks that are, in principle, external to the negotiations. These norms can also affect, among others, a mediator's (non-)neutrality. It is peace mediators themselves that will typically introduce such norms into the negotiations. Mediators might not see themselves as advocates for such norms, but they might feel a moral or legal obligation to at least bring these norms to the attention of the negotiating parties. As the Centre for Humanitarian Dialogue notes in its *Charter*, one of its 'standards' consists in 'ensur[ing] that parties to a conflict are aware of obligations to punish the most serious international crimes, and provide access to international expertise, when needed, on issues pertaining to transitional justice' (Centre for Humanitarian Dialogue, nd). Moreover, from a more pragmatic conflict resolution perspective, certain external norms, such as those stemming from international law, can be a used as a starting point or presented as an outer limit for the negotiations, and they can also be seen as bestowing greater legitimacy on the process (Hellmüller et al, 2015: 14). It should be noted that norms that are already well accepted will, of course, always be easier to introduce into the process than those that are more controversial or unsettled. Unsurprisingly, mediators are, at least implicitly, hence likely to prioritize 'settled' over 'unsettled' norms (Hellmüller et al, 2015: 14), although the question as to whether a norm is settled or unsettled remains a highly subjective one (Hellmüller et al, 2015: 7).

In fact, mediation never takes place in a normative vacuum and is always norm based to some extent. Since mediator flexibility and adaptability and, especially, the negotiating parties' ownership over the process continue to be highlighted and valued as key principles of peace mediation in various documents, the frank recognition in the UN's *Guidance* that peace mediation takes place 'within normative and legal frameworks' (UNSG, 2012: 16) is quite remarkable. International law naturally plays a particularly prominent role in the UN's approach to mediation. As the *Guidance* notes, '[c]onsistency with international law and norms contributes to reinforcing the legitimacy of a process and the durability of a peace agreement', and international humanitarian law and human rights, refugee law and international criminal law are explicitly mentioned (UNSG, 2012: 16).

In addition to such increasingly accepted binding international legal obligations, certain 'normative expectations', or what could be considered 'emerging legal obligations' (Kastner, 2015: 182), such as with respect to the inclusion of civil society and to transitional justice, are also relevant. For instance, a red line is established regarding amnesties for serious crimes: mediators, it is noted in the *Guidance*, should 'be clear that they cannot endorse peace agreements that provide for amnesties for genocide, crimes against humanity, war crimes or gross violations of human rights, including sexual and gender-based violence' (UNSG, 2012: 17). As for process-related obligations in this context, the *Guidance* contains a more elusive statement, advising mediators that they should 'limit contacts with actors that have been indicted by the International Criminal Court to what is necessary for the mediation process' (UNSG, 2012: 13). A few additional process-related norms resurface throughout the *Guidance*, with the one on the inclusion of women and gender-balancing being particularly noticeable. For instance, mediators are reminded that they should 'include a balance of men and women on mediation teams' and that they should 'encourage conflict parties to include women in their delegations' (UNSG, 2012: 7, 13). Moreover, the 'gender dimension of all issues should be clearly articulated, as agreements that are gender neutral have often proven detrimental' (UNSG, 2012: 21).[7]

The European Union's *Concept* is not as explicit as the UN's *Guidance* with respect to the (non-)neutrality of EU-mandated mediators and the relevance of existing normative frameworks, such as the sometimes alleged prohibition on amnesties – a word that is not even mentioned in the *Concept*. However, the fact that conflicting normative commitments may limit the scope of engagement of the organization is addressed, even if rather elusively: 'potential tensions between the EU's normative commitments in the area of human rights and international law and short-term conflict management objectives may pose additional challenges and prevent the EU from becoming involved in a mediation process' (Council of the European Union, 2009: 7). Moreover, mediation initiatives, it is noted, 'need to be guided by the principle of policy coherence and undertaken in the broader context of EU policy objectives in external relations' (Council of the European Union, 2009: 6). The inclusion of women also features prominently in the *Concept*:

> [T]he EU should contribute to promoting women's equal and full participation in the prevention and resolution of conflicts, peace negotiations, peace-building, peacekeeping, humanitarian response and in post-conflict reconstruction. … The EU needs to promote the representation of women and the availability of adequate resources for dedicated mediation gender expertise from an early stage of mediation processes onwards. (Council of the European Union, 2009: 8–9)

[7] In this context, the use of the word gender *dimension* in the singular is quite telling: it is as if gender could have only one dimension or was one-dimensional. In reality, the gender *dimensions* of peace negotiations can take numerous forms, and mediators will, explicitly or implicitly, adopt a certain approach or have to navigate between different approaches, with formal and substantive equality being the most obvious alternatives. For an attempt to capture the complex gendered dimensions of peace negotiations, which draws on insights from a substantive equality approach and masculinities theory, see Kastner and Roy-Trudel (2019).

With respect to existing norms that may guide African Union mediators in their activity, the *Handbook* also adopts a noticeably lighter tone than the UN's *Guidance*. For instance, although the core principles of the Constitutive Act of the African Union are recalled, such as the 'condemnation and rejection of unconstitutional changes of governments' (ACCORD and AU, 2014: 15), these principles are not noted as guiding the activities of African Union mediators. Similarly, international law is barely mentioned, and the *Handbook* does not elaborate on the substance of any rules. Somewhat elusively, the *Handbook* stipulates that international law 'highlights norms that can provide a useful starting point for, and place outer limits on, a peace negotiation and the resulting agreement' (ACCORD and AU, 2014: 155). The *Handbook* hence seems to recognize that international law not only 'highlight[s]' certain norms, but that a mediator may actually be restricted by them. Recalling that mediators 'need to work in an even-handed, non-judgemental manner', the *Handbook* also states that 'the non-condemning approach does not mean that perpetrators of human rights violations or even war crimes should not be addressed, tried and judged' (ACCORD and AU, 2014: 83). However, such considerations are relegated to the realm of ethics not to be effected by a mediator:

> [Y]et, it is not the mediator's role to implement ethical considerations. His/her job is to focus solely on the mediation mandate and to bring the violent conflict to an end. Hence – although restricted by the mandate and international law – the mediator has a wide range of options and approaches to choose from to engage with the belligerent parties. (ACCORD and AU, 2014: 83)

In other words, certain international legal norms are seen as 'restricting' African Union mediators, but the *Handbook* does not offer any guidance in this regard. Most notably, the *Handbook* does not say anything about the increasingly accepted prohibition of amnesties for certain serious crimes, which is probably the most obvious example of an at least emerging international legal norm. The *Handbook* merely defines amnesty in the glossary as 'the granting of a pardon for past offences, especially political ones – for example human rights violations and war crimes' (ACCORD and AU, 2014: 175), without any normative discussion as to when offering amnesties may not be advisable or may even be contrary to international law. In fact, the only time the word 'amnesty' is mentioned in the *Handbook* itself is in the context of a brief case study, namely the amnesty offered to the Lord's Resistance Army by the government of

Uganda before the signing of a ceasefire agreement in 2006 (ACCORD and AU, 2014: 147). No further analysis or commentary of this amnesty is offered.

While specialized NGOs clearly try to uphold their independence and flexibility with respect to certain substantive norms, such as individual accountability for serious crimes, they tend to be outspoken about their commitment to an inclusive process. For instance, representatives of the Centre for Humanitarian Dialogue, as it is noted in its *Charter*, shall 'support or engage in processes where all parties – including civil society and women – who could contribute to preventing, reducing and resolving violent conflict can be involved' (Centre for Humanitarian Dialogue, nd). Similarly, the Crisis Management Initiative emphasizes its independence but also affirms on its website that

> [t]he inclusion of women and their interests in peacemaking is essential from the standpoint of equal rights, and for the quality of any peace process. Women play a key role in introducing a wider variety of viewpoints and narratives of the conflict to expand the scope of sustainable solutions. Without women, a substantial part of society may reject an agreement and refuse to participate in its implementation. Women's inclusion can pave the way for democratization and more just societies. (Crisis Management Initiative, nd)

In sum, the organizations discussed here, which are all actively involved in peace mediation and have acquired a particular expertise in this regard, seek to promote professionalism and to provide normative guidance to mediators, partly drawing on existing norms. The organizations clearly do so to varying degrees, although certain shared commitments have emerged. Explicitly engaging with – and sometimes further developing – relevant norms is meant to enhance the legitimacy and ultimately the effectiveness of peace mediation endeavours. While the articulation of a normative framework can play an at least symbolic role regarding the legitimation of mediators, as will be discussed in the concluding section, a danger of over-regulation certainly exists. It is because of these tensions that a single normative framework governing peace mediation activities as a whole has not crystallized, although important normative trends, such as with respect to rendering peace negotiations more inclusive, can be identified.

Concluding Thoughts: the Future of 'Regulating' Peace Mediation

Given the multitude of actors now sharing the field of peace mediation, articulating a normative framework can arguably contribute to clarifying what values a particular organization stands for and which norms it considers relevant, and what the negotiating parties can hence expect from a mediator mandated by this organization. This, in turn, can fulfil considerable expressive functions and increase the mediator's legitimacy, at least symbolically, which can be explained by the typical focus and practice of international organizations. As Michael Barnett and Martha Finnemore have argued, 'because IO [international organizations'] practices reflect a search for symbolic legitimacy rather than efficiency, IO [behaviour] might be only remotely connected to the efficient implementation of its goals and more closely coupled to legitimacy criteria that come from the cultural environment' (Barnett and Finnemore, 2004: 37). The professionalization of the field of peace mediation and the related articulation of a normative framework for the involvement of mediators by international organizations and NGOs can be seen in this light: whereas the effectiveness and efficiency of peace mediation interventions certainly matter, with successful outcomes being the main concern, the first step consists in establishing the symbolic legitimacy of the mediator to be involved.

Nevertheless, some mediator flexibility may be required in certain situations, which is why peace mediation – and mediation more generally – can still not be considered to be regulated to a significant extent. In fact, flexibility still seems to be highly valued in the field. As a senior mediator with an extensive record mediating for the UN has put it,

> the international community should tread much more carefully than it is doing nowadays with the mushrooming normative framework to which it claims to subject peacemaking. However attractive it may be to fuse peacemaking requirements with all the other values the international community currently stands for, this temptation must be resisted, not embraced. (Arnault, 2014: 25)

Indeed, recent qualitative research in the form of interviews with senior mediators and UN officials has confirmed that some mediators perceive the normative principles contained in the *Guidance*, such as the one pertaining to amnesties, as restricting their scope for action, and sometimes the *Guidance* is even disregarded completely (Convergne, 2016: 189).

From a practical conflict resolution perspective, the *marge de manoeuvre* of mediators can definitely be increased through the cooperation between different peace mediation organizations, some of which do not pursue their activities according to an explicitly stated normative framework or agenda. Certain NGOs, states or individuals, for instance, may not have any trouble dialoguing with groups that have been proscribed as 'terrorist organizations' by the UN or certain powerful states or with individuals against whom an arrest warrant has been issued by an international criminal tribunal. In other words, keeping some communication channel open, even if indirectly and via another organization, can be highly valuable for the official mediator. Some actors may also be able to engage in mediation activities more discretely, without the public scrutiny and media attention typically given to Special Envoys of the UN Secretary-General. For instance, the Crisis Management Initiative, highlighting its independence and the complexity of contemporary violent conflicts, states that '[o]ur independence gives us space to act where official actors cannot … We can flexibly move between the various formal and informal processes and actors, bridging gaps where they exist and adding to the overall effectiveness of peace efforts' (Crisis Management Initiative, nd).

It should be noted that the currently dominant approach to norm-based mediation is characterized by an often unhelpful binary logic that only allows either-or choices. This greatly diminishes the scope of action and normative agency of mediators and, in fact, is opposite to the very idea of mediation, which is about transcending the logic of binary positions. Negotiations with so-called terrorist organizations are again a good example. As Palmiano Federer has highlighted, the 'dichotomy between liberal and illiberal norms … constrains mediators to a single normative standard, rendering only liberal and illiberal views possible' (Palmiano Federer, 2018: 20). This binary logic means that mediators are supposed to take sides and choose between adhering to the norm that proscribes a particular group and the norm pertaining to inclusive processes. As a matter of fact, the inclusivity norm itself has been created by and further entrenches an unhelpful binary logic, as if the main question were about exclusion or inclusion, whereas a much more nuanced thinking about different ways of inclusion is needed (Pfaffenholz, 2014).

Finally, it must be said that the increase in the quantity and diversity of actors involved in peace mediation, as well as their greater expertise and preparedness, do, unfortunately, not mean that more conflicts are actually being resolved through mediation nowadays. In fact, there have been fewer 'success stories' in recent years (Lehti and Lepomäki, 2017: 103). The number of peace agreements that can be considered to have been successful has declined, and although organizations that have been at the forefront of peace mediation, such as the UN, are still solicited on a regular basis, their efforts have not necessarily led to positive outcomes (Harland, 2018).

Since the more and more explicit articulation of a normative framework and the apparently diminished effectiveness of peace mediation activities have occurred in roughly the same period, one does wonder if the former is responsible for the latter. While there is no clear evidence supporting this, a correlation cannot entirely be ruled out and would merit further investigation. What is clear is that some of the challenges for contemporary peace mediation initiatives are directly related to increasingly accepted norms, such as those pertaining to an inclusive process. The fact that mediation is now more frequently conducted in the open and under the close scrutiny of the media, and that some peace mediation missions have grown into unwieldy bureaucracies, with numerous advisers pursuing their own agendas, has arguably 'eroded' some of the features of successful mediation (Harland, 2018: 7). As David Harland, the Executive Director of the Centre for Humanitarian Dialogue has argued, less discretion and agility, among other things, has drastically reduced the scope for 'real mediation' (Harland, 2018: 8).

A few studies have tried to identify more methodically the reasons for the relative decline of successful peace negotiations. One of the more persuasive ones – in addition to the suspicion that at least some high-level mediators have remained unaffected by attempts at professionalizing the field and are actually not conducting mediation in a competent manner – is that the nature of conflicts that could, and arguably should, be the subject of mediation has, again, changed. Whereas the field of peace mediation was able to adapt to, and even matured because of, the imperative to resolve internal armed conflicts in the post-Cold War period, it has had great difficulties making a useful contribution to the resolution of conflicts involving radical groups that are sometimes labelled or even proscribed as terrorist organizations. Conflicts in the Middle East and in Northern Africa seem particularly resistant to a mediated resolution. As Magnus Lundgren and Isak Svensson have demonstrated, conflicts over religion – and in particular those with an Islamist dimension, which have increased significantly over the past two decades – are less frequently the subject of mediation attempts than other conflicts (Lundgren and Svensson, 2017). Moreover, conflicts in some regions, like Europe and Africa, are over-mediated, whereas those in other regions, like East and Southeast Asia, are under-mediated (Lundgren and Svensson, 2017).

This means that there is a lot of room for further engagement of peace mediators, although in different contexts from those that are usually in the spotlight. In other words, while it would be imprudent to jump to the conclusion that the currently dominant approach to peace mediation, which conceptualizes peace mediation as a professional activity to be conducted by experts according to certain rules, is flawed, it does have important shortcomings and appears better suited to resolving certain types of conflicts but not others.

References

ACCORD and AU (African Union) (2014) *Mediation Support Handbook*, [online] Available from: https://www.accord.org.za/publication/african-union-mediation-support-handbook/ (accessed 25 July 2019).

Arnault, J. (2014) 'Legitimacy and Peace Processes: International Norms and Local Realities', *Accord*, Issue 25.

Barnett, M. and Finnemore, M. (2004) *Rules for the World: International Organizations in World Politics*, Ithaca, NY: Cornell University Press.

Bowling, D. and Hoffman, D.A. (2003) 'Bringing Peace into the Room: The Personal Qualities of the Mediator and Their Impact on the Mediation' in D. Bowling and D.A. Hoffman (eds) *Bringing Peace into the Room: How the Personal Qualities of the Mediator Impact the Process of Conflict Resolution*, San Francisco, CA: Jossey-Bass, pp 13–48.

Centre for Humanitarian Dialogue (nd) *The HD Charter – Mediation for Peace*, [online] available from: https://www.hdcentre.org/wp-content/uploads/2016/06/The-HD-Charter.pdf (accessed 25 July 2019).

Convergne, E. (2016) 'Learning to Mediate? The Mediation Support Unit and the Production of Expertise by the UN', *Journal of Intervention and Statebuilding*, 10(2): 181–99.

Council of the European Union (2009) *Decision 15779/09 on Concept on Strengthening EU Mediation and Dialogue Capacities*, 10 November, [online] available from: http://eeas.europa.eu/archives/docs/cfsp/conflict_prevention/docs/concept_strengthening_eu_med_en.pdf (accessed 25 July 2019).

Crisis Management Initiative (nd) *Programme*, [online] available from: http://cmi.fi/our-work/programme/#mediation-and-dialogue (accessed 25 July 2019.

European External Action Service (EEAS) Mediation Support Team (2016) *Global Challenges and Trends in International Peace Mediation and Diplomacy: A Background Note*, [online] available from: http://eeas.europa.eu/cfsp/conflict_prevention/docs/20160519-global-challenges-and-trends_final_en.pdf (accessed 25 July 2019).

Giro, M. (1998) 'The community of Saint Egidio and its peace-making activities', *The International Spectator*, 33(3): 85–100.

Harland, D. (2018) 'The Lost Art of Peacemaking', *Centre for Humanitarian Dialogue*, [online] available from: https://www.hdcentre.org/wp-content/uploads/2018/07/The-Lost-Art-of-Peacemaking.pdf.

Hellmüller, S., Palmiano-Federer, J. and Zeller, M. (2015) *The Role of Norms in International Peace Mediation*, swisspeace.

Hellmüller, S. (2019) 'Beyond Buzzwords: Civil Society Inclusion in Mediation' in H-W. Jeong (ed) *Conflict Intervention and Transformation*, London and Lanham, MD: Rowman & Littlefield, pp 47–63.

Hinshaw, A. (2016) 'Regulating Mediators', *Harvard Negotiation Law Review*, 21: 163.

Jessop, M., Aljets D. and Chacko, B. (2008) 'The Ripe Moment for Civil Society', *International Negotiation* 13(1): 93–109.

Kastner, P. (2015) *Legal Normativity in the Resolution of Internal Armed Conflict*, Cambridge: Cambridge University Press.

Kastner, P. (2017) 'International Peace Mediators: The Normative Involvement of an Epistemic Community' in H. Cullen, J. Harrington and C. Renshaw (eds) *Experts, Networks, and International Law*, Cambridge: Cambridge University Press, pp 70–92.

Kastner, P. and Roy-Trudel, E. (2019) 'Addressing Masculinities in Peace Negotiations: An Opportunity for Gender Justice' in R. Shackel and L. Fiske (eds) *Rethinking Gender Justice: Transformative Approaches in Post-conflict Settings*, New Work, NY: Palgrave, pp 145–63.

Lanz, D. and Gasser, R. (2013) 'A Crowded Field: Competition and Coordination in International Peace Mediation', *Centre for Mediation in Africa*, Mediation Arguments No. 2, Pretoria: University of Pretoria.

Lehti, M. and Lepomäki, M. (2017) *The Era of Private Peacemakers: A New Dialogic Approach to Mediation*, New York, NY: Palgrave Macmillan.

Lundgren, M. and Svensson, I. (2017) 'A Not So Crowded Stage: The Shortfall of International Mediation in Armed Conflicts', *Paper presented at the Annual Meeting of the International Studies Association*, 22–25 February, Baltimore, MD.

Morris, C. (1997) 'The Trusted Mediator: Ethics and Interaction in Mediation' in J. Macfarlane (ed) *Rethinking Disputes: The Mediation Alternative*, Toronto: Edmond Montgomery Publications, pp 301–47.

Palmiano Federer, J. (2018) 'We Do Negotiate With Terrorists: Navigating Liberal and Illiberal Norms in Peace Mediation', *Critical Studies on Terrorism*, 12(1): 19–39.

Pfaffenholz, T. (2014) 'Civil Society and Peace Negotiations: Beyond the Inclusion-Exclusion Dichotomy', *Negotiation Journal*, 30(1): 69–91.

Spencer, D. and Brogan, M. (2006) *Mediation Law and Practice*, Cambridge: Cambridge University Press.

Splinter, D. and Lüttmann, C. (2014) 'Friedensmediation organisiert sich', *Konfliktdynamik*, 3(4): 340–6.

United Nations Secretary-General (UNSG) (2012) 'Guidance for Effective Mediation' in United Nations General Assembly, *Resolution A/66/811 on Strengthening the role of mediation in the peaceful settlement of disputes, conflict prevention and resolution*, [online] 25 June, available from: https://undocs.org/A/66/811 (accessed 24 July 2019).

Vuković, S. (2015) 'Soft Power, Bias and Manipulation of International Organizations in International Mediation', *International Negotiation*, 20(3): 414–43.

Wählisch, M. (2016) 'Normative Limits of Peace Negotiations: Questions, Guidance and Prospects', *Global Policy*, 7(2): 261–6.

Waldman, E.A. (1996) 'The Challenge of Certification: How to Ensure Mediator Competence While Preserving Diversity', *University of San Francisco Law Review*, 30: 723–56.

Waldman, E.A. (1997) 'Identifying the Role of Social Norms in Mediation: A Multiple Model Approach', *Hastings Law Journal*, 48(4): 703–69.

Webb, K. (1988) 'The Morality of Mediation' in C.R. Mitchell and K. Webb (eds) *New Approaches to International Mediation*, Westport, CT: Greenwood Press, pp 16–28.

3

Norm Diffusion in International Peace Mediation

Siniša Vuković

Introduction

Contemporary scholarship on international mediation has extensively examined a wide range of material-based factors that motivate and condition mediators' involvement. Yet in shaping specific outcomes mediators also inevitably promote, invoke and/or safeguard specific ideational aspects, such as principles, norms and values, which may be threatened by an escalating conflict (Vuković and Hopmann, 2019). Promotion of new norms in circumstances where a related norm has already been contested by participating actors represents a form of norm diffusion. Norm diffusion has been studied on case-to-case basis as a distinct dynamic that shapes and guides conflict management processes. These studies have ranged from reflections on the role civil society can play in such processes (Boesenecker and Vinjamuri, 2011) to how specific countries may use norm diffusion to advance their own normative agenda (Björkdahl, 2007; Kurusu, 2018), as well as how norms can be diffused through specific global practices such as peacekeeping (Björkdahl, 2006), responsibility to protect (Jacob, 2018) and post-conflict peacebuilding (Tholens and Groß, 2015). While all these studies are unequivocally insightful and rich in detail, they highlight an important limitation:

namely that there is no commonly agreed-upon taxonomy on how norm diffusion unfolds, and which methods/mechanism norm diffusion encompasses. So far, the gold standard used to explain norm diffusion comes from the seminal work by Finnemore and Sikkink, who looked at the norm dynamics through three stages: emergence, cascade and internalization. In the first phase, the norm emerges once the norm entrepreneur frames the issue saliency, offers a specific language for it, and as a consequence formulates an alternative norm that creates new perceptions of appropriateness and related interests (Finnemore and Sikkink, 1998: 897). Once the parties accept the new norm, they gradually become an integral part of a socialization process that punishes confrontational and deviant behaviour, and rewards cooperation and coordination between actors. In the last phase, once the norm has been adequately integrated into the existing normative framework, it may be fully internalized by the parties, consequently making it both commonsense and the only form of appropriate behaviour. As will be highlighted in this chapter, mediators go through the same three phases when they want to get their normative ideas diffused. Although there is an evident link between the dynamics of international peace mediation and norm diffusion there has been surprisingly little conceptual attention to this nexus. Building on existing peacemaking literature, this chapter addresses this gap and examines which factors enable or deter norm diffusion through mediation, and their impact on mediators' choices in peacemaking.

In order to fully unpack the parallels between peace mediation and norm diffusion, this chapter will first explore a broader connection between two conceptually distinct yet practically highly interrelated dynamics: norms and conflict. Norms represent a fundamental lynchpin for the establishment, maintenance and evolution of social order. They assist social actors to foster a sense of shared purpose and synchronize their activities accordingly. A willingness to cooperate and the ability to coordinate reduce the likelihood of social conflict (Axelrod, 1984, 1986; Nye and Welch, 2016). Yet norms are neither universally accepted nor permanent in time; they are rather subject to frequent contestation and prone to continued evolution. As this chapter will show, norm contestation does not automatically degenerate into violent conflict. Contestation can be done through established channels and in an agreed-upon manner. On occasion, however, it can degenerate into violence and destruction of social bonds. This constructive–destructive dichotomy is also present in conflicts. The purpose of peace mediation is to assist conflicting parties to refrain from harmful and destructive means in achieving their goals, and explore the viability of a mutually acceptable solution to their perceived differences. As parties express their disagreement about the norm that should regulate their relations, they may seek or be offered assistance by a mediator who can provide new perspectives on how their differences should be regulated. In such a way mediators affect the existing and/or promote a whole new norm that becomes central in organizing the relations of the conflicting parties. As mediators are not motivated by altruism, but by specific self-interests, they will protect and/or promote a norm that is in line with their own normative agenda, thus becoming norm entrepreneurs intended to diffuse particular norms. In order to understand how norms are diffused through peace mediation, this chapter will present a novel conceptual framework that contrasts known models of norm diffusion with different types of strategies and tactics mediators employ in peace processes.

Conflicts as a Process of Norm Contestation

Conflicts have been most commonly understood as a social dynamic where two or more parties perceive their goals and interests as mutually incompatible, and consequently challenge each other in order to maximize their own utility (Pruitt and Kim, 2003; Kriesberg, 2007). Along with this interest-based approach, conflict can also be viewed as a dynamic process of norm formation through contestation. Norms have been broadly defined as 'standards of appropriate behavior for actors with a given identity' (Finnemore and Sikkink, 1998: 891). In other words, they have the capacity to assign meaning by classifying different actors within a given system and categorizing their specific actions, identities and interests (Wendt, 1999; Wiener, 2014). At the same time, the aforementioned behaviour is contingent on the actors' ability to define acceptable justifications for a given behaviour (Hurrell and MacDonald, 2013: 61). As Risse noted, this justification is rarely articulated as a projection of self-interest, rather the grounds for justification are found in a widely accepted value (Risse, 2000: 17). Consequently, norms represent 'intersubjective constructs' that 'provide reference points for which actions others consider acceptable' (Stimmer, 2019: 271). As for any social construct, norms may provoke diverging understandings, interpretations and applications across a broad range of actors that use a given norm as a reference point for appropriate behaviour. Such divergence may incite discussions, queries and challenges to a given norm, and call into question its social status. Wiener refers to this aspect as a 'dual quality of norms as structuring and constructed' (Wiener, 2004: 191). Continued scrutiny may generate new meanings for norms which can consequently encourage or hamper further iterations of their contestation. Many scholars recognize this as constructive feature. Competing views participate in the debate over a specific norm, permeate further its social legitimacy and facilitate improved understanding of what is considered as appropriate behaviour (Acharya, 2004, 2011; Wiener, 2004, 2014). On the other hand, contestability may also generate adverse effects as it may further propagate and legitimize established prejudices, ideational frames, and power structures (Epstein, 2008; Evers, 2017).

In exploring norm contestation, Deitelhoff and Zimmermann note that there is an inherent difference between contestation over an application of the norm and over its validity. In the former case, contestation may lead to further specification of how and where a norm should be applied. In the latter case, contestation may lead to the weakening of a norm (Deitelhoff and Zimmermann, 2013). Offering further clarification on this matter, Stimmer (2019) distinguishes between disagreements over norm frames (that is, justification) and claims (that is, action). According to her typology, when actors agree only on the frames, this dynamic reduces the range of available actions that can be perceived as legitimate, generating 'norm recognition' among actors. In cases where actors agree solely on the actions that can be taken, but have no convergence on which norm should apply, the system is characterized by 'norm neglect'. Both norm recognition and norm neglect can result in further debates that shape the normative framework but as she notes, 'norm neglect is an unstable outcome: it produces a temporary and partial consensus that will eventually result in either a norm impasse or norm clarification' (Stimmer, 2019: 276). Since there is no normative agreement, actors may at first concur on the necessary course of action as an exceptional compromise. On the one hand, this may lead to a socialization process where they gradually develop an agreement over both frames and actions to be taken, and as such offer 'norm clarification'. On the other, the transitory nature of their agreed-upon action may revert to circumstances where actors agree neither on frames nor on the claims, and as a consequence produce a 'norm impasse' (Stimmer, 2019: 277).

Stimmer's typology offers a useful clarification on the degrees to which actors actually share an idea over norm suitability to prescribe behaviour. In fact, as Niemann and Schillinger argue, norm contestation is a perpetual process as there is no scenario that can assume an unequivocal consensus among all actors over any existing norm (Niemann and Schillinger, 2017). Disagreement over norms may lead to non-compliance. In cases when specific actors perceive an inherent discrepancy between their preferences – which may comprise both tangible priorities and intangible beliefs – and the existing norm, they may start challenging its prescriptive character. While non-compliance by a single actor may not be sufficient to degenerate a norm, it may incite other actors to gradually join the process of contestation. The more the norm is contested the more it loses its legitimate ability to prescribe behaviour. As Panke and Petersohn note, 'norm precision combined with the stability of the environment, as well as the presence of rival norms, are crucial for the dynamics and outcomes of norm degeneration processes' (Panke and Petersohn, 2012: 735). According to their study, even when norms are very specific, thus leaving no doubt about instances of norm violation, the lack of a sanctioning mechanism for norm violation accelerates norm degeneration. At the same time, when norms are imprecise, thus allowing for deviation to be camouflaged with an appearance of norm-compliance, and the system is relatively stable so that major norm violation can easily be detected while smaller ones are ignored, norm degeneration will be more gradual. Both paths of norm degradation may lead to norm substitution, if and when a competing norm is articulated. In the absence of a contender, a degenerated norm may simply disappear (Panke and Petersohn, 2012: 735). Building on this line of reasoning, in a subsequent study they found that norm contestation takes the form of norm violation mainly in cases where there is no institutional framework with set rules for negotiating normative change. Consequently 'negotiations always played a role in cases of institutionally embedded norms' (Panke and Petersohn, 2016: 15).

Current scholarship on norm contestation seems to suggest that norm contestation may assume a form of destructive conflict, when parties aspire to unilaterally impose a new or revised norm by challenging the existing one or those intended to preserve the status quo. However, in some cases where there are pre-established procedural rules as to how contestation should be articulated, then parties may develop a more constructive conflict, where they negotiate their way out of the impasse and find a mutually acceptable normative framework. There is a clear nexus between norm contestation and conflict dynamics, which has been surprisingly overlooked by contemporary scholarship. Yet the debates over norm contestation may clearly benefit from a more nuanced application of theories related to conflict analysis. In all social conflicts, conflicting parties face a strategic choice, whether to pursue unilateral solutions (that is, imposition) or opt for a compromised multilateral engagement (that is, negotiation) (Iklé, 1967; Pruitt, 1983; Hopmann, 1996; Zartman and Alfredson, 2010). The key appeal of a negotiation process stems from the expectation that it provides structure and predictability between conflicting parties. Moreover, negotiations promote the spirit of the possibility of compromise and cooperation by accentuating the utility of mutuality in formulating viable solutions to the underlining disagreement.

In a similar fashion, norms also promote order by providing a means for international actors to coordinate their behaviour through tacit agreements that create common expectations and a shared frame of reference (Cortell and Davis, 2000: 65).

International Mediators as Norm Entrepreneurs

In his seminal work on the evolution of norms, Axelrod noted (1986: 1096) an intrinsic link between conflict management and the existence of norms, arguing:

> Large numbers of individuals and even nations often display a great degree of coordinated behavior that serves to regulate conflict. When this coordinated behavior takes place without the intervention of a central authority to police the behavior, we tend to attribute the coordinated behavior and the resulting regulation of conflict to the existence of norms.

Coordinated behaviour is possible even in the most adversarial circumstances, through a process of 'mutual adjustment' which does not require a formal agreement. According to George, the process of creating the mutual adjustment produces norms that offer a sense of certainty, predictability and order (George, 1988: 650). The international system is innately characterized by the absence of a stable and consolidated overarching structure that can enforce existing norms in an uncontested manner. Within this systemic void, disagreements over the interpretation and/or application of a specific norm may trigger conflict escalation that is difficult to regulate. When parties are unable or unwilling to settle on a commonly agreed solution, their conflict may attract the attention of one or more external actors that can mediate a compromise solution (Bercovitch, 2009; Vuković, 2014, 2019).

Mediation is neither aimless nor altruistic in scope. In order to effectively shape parties' relationships and incite a regime of cooperation between them, mediators are expected to commit considerable tangible and intangible resources. Consequently, they may be driven more by their self-interests, norms and beliefs than by altruistic and humanitarian impulses (Touval and Zartman, 1985). As Bercovitch and Jackson point out, 'mediators bring with them consciously or otherwise, ideas, knowledge, resources and interests, of their own or of the group they represent' (Bercovitch and Jackson, 2009: 35). Since conflicts do not occur in a vacuum, mediators will inevitably develop specific ideas and expectations about the conflict they are expected to manage. These assumptions are based on their previous experience with similar situations, prior interactions with conflicting parties, and, most importantly, their interests and principles regarding the contested issue or norm. Therefore, mediators may be entrusted to establish the rules of procedure, decide which actors will be included in the process, define which issues will be placed on the agenda, and establish a timeline within which a solution has to be adopted (Vuković, 2019; Vuković and Hopmann, 2019). In essence mediators delineate the normative framework within which they are willing to operate, and as such project a normative bias as to what kind of future behaviour are they willing to sanction.

Mediators can be considered as very active norm entrepreneurs, engaged in diffusing norms that they deem most appropriate for managing a specific conflict (Hellmüller et al, 2017; Palmiano Federer, 2019). As norm entrepreneurs, mediators aspire to persuade and incite conflicting parties to embrace new norms, or redefine existing ones, in order to find a normative framework acceptable to all parties in conflict (Finnemore and Sikkink, 1998: 895). These efforts take place within a context that is already characterized by prevailing norms. The existing normative framework sets the standards of appropriate behaviour, or 'appropriateness'. When a new norm is introduced within this framework, if it is in line with the existing norms then that norm may gain persuasiveness, while those non-aligned with the existing framework will find resistance and fail to find immediate support (Björkdahl, 2006). As such, mediators are faced with the task of persuading the conflicting parties about the appropriateness of the new and/or reconstructed norm, through the actions of norm localization, which prescribes 'active construction (through discourse, framing, grafting, and cultural selection) of foreign ideas by local actors, which results in the former developing significant congruence with local beliefs and practices' (Acharya, 2004: 245). At the same time, it is crucial to note that when mediators get involved in formulating a new or redefined norm, they are faced with an existing normative framework that already includes both 'settled norms' which are not the source of conflict, as well as those that are contested by one or more conflicting parties. Therefore, when norms associated with the mediation process manage to fit within the existing normative system on all these levels, this will increase the chances for these new and redefined norms to become future settled norms.

Henry Kissinger's peacemaking efforts in the Middle East are a good example in this context. Mandell and Tomlin point out that mediation may produce new norms if it manages to support a process of *new learning*, through the alteration of conflicting parties' preference structures (Mandell and Tomlin, 1991: 53). Through a process of incremental change, Kissinger also fostered a spirit of *repetition* which can be associated with gradual internalization of the new norms by conflicting parties. In order to strengthen the new behaviour, Kissinger consistently *used incentives* that can alter parties' preference, perceptions and priorities. Lastly, as Mandell and Tomlin note, 'Kissinger facilitated congruence with other transnational norms dealing with conflict management by compelling the parties to make public their new intentions to the international community at large' (Mandell and Tomlin, 1991: 54). In other words, Kissinger managed to persuade the parties to make their new behaviour unequivocally *visible* in order to deter defection and highlight the utility of conforming to the new normative framework.

As norm entrepreneurs, mediators can trigger new patterns of behaviour through facilitated dialogue, repetition and tailor-made incentive structures, all of which promote the emergence of new norms aimed at restraining conflict. At first, these are most likely to be informal, actor-specific norms, which focus on the substantive content of appropriate behaviour. Yet over time, three essential patterns emerge which are fundamental for the parties' ability to restrain their own confrontational behaviour and develop a cooperative regime through which they can coordinate their activities in order to manage their differences. First of all, as exchanges and tradeoffs that are facilitated and formulated by a mediator begin occurring with sufficient frequency, this may encourage a sense of reciprocity between the parties. As a consequence, parties may begin to view exchange as expected, and coordinated behaviour as a useful mechanism that guarantees expected utility. Secondly, at least initially, the emergence of a norm may be limited to a specific dynamic, for instance functional cooperation, allowing parties to cooperate on a particular issue but remain adversarial on others. As such, norm creation should be seen as an incremental process rather than a binary one. Third, the more the parties rely on mediators and the mediation process, the more a new or redefined norm will consolidate and have parties willingly surrender authority to a mediator to prescribe behaviour and shape the potential outcome.

International Mediation and Norm Diffusion

Within an unstructured international system, mediators take on the task of providing predictability and a sense of direction for the conflicting parties. They offer a frame of reference for the parties about what kind of solution they may expect and what kind of future behaviour will find international support. In order to persuade parties about the validity of these goals, mediators may facilitate impaired communication, which may provide much-needed clarification about normative compatibility between conflicting parties. Mediators may suggest new interpretations of a contested norm, help parties redefine what they may deem as appropriate behaviour, and offer specific incentives that can routinize these new normative expectations (Beardsley, 2011). Mediators may also provide essential political cover that can be used to justify a new norm for the parties' relative constituencies. Mediators may also offer implementation assistance to the parties that can expedite the process through which a specific behaviour becomes routinized and consequently internalized by the parties themselves. Lastly, as mediators are expected to find an appropriate normative formula that takes into account existing international norms, their own promoted norms, settled norms between the parties, and those norms that are contested, mediators may present this new formula as form of behaviour that will enjoy international legitimacy.

Mediators' power to confer legitimacy (legitimate power or normative power) represents their ability to prescribe behaviour for the conflicting parties, whose consent to this prescription is based in a specific norm. Although parties may be apprehensive about losing autonomy of their decision making, and as such prefer to view mediators' involvement as provision of constructive assistance rather than nudging, legitimate power placates these concerns by grounding suggestions and recommendations in norms that have been widely recognized by parties as appropriate. Carnevale argues that legitimate power 'derives from a norm that has been accepted by the disputants … and influence rests on a judgment of how one should act, and the authority determines the standard' (Carnevale, 2002: 28). In line with this argument, Raven (2004) distinguished four specific social norms that can produce legitimate power: position, reciprocity, equity and responsibility. Accordingly, actors may be compelled to conform to the instruction given by those that hold specific positions within formal or informal social structures. Moreover, if an actor has benefited from others' actions it may perceive an obligation to reciprocate with further constructive and beneficial behaviour. Similarly, those that created benefits may expect an equitable response from the other. Lastly, actors may have a moral responsibility to assist those that depend on their action and are unable to assist themselves. Legitimacy on the international level entails a moral dimension as well. When discussing the legitimacy of international organizations, Buchanan and Keohane point out that legitimacy 'is the right to rule, understood to mean both that institutional agents are morally justified in making rules and attempting to secure compliance with them, and that people subject to those rules have moral, content-independent reasons to follow them and/or to not interfere with other's compliance with them' (Buchanan and Keohane, 2006: 411). Using their analytical framework for international organizations, it can be argued that mediators may be deemed morally acceptable and their instructions morally justifiable if they conform with norms that do not generate grave injustices, there is no evident alternative actor that could undertake the mediating role in a better way, and are able and willing to structure a predictable and fair process for the parties (Buchanan and Keohane, 2006: 419).

While mediators may use tangible resources in order to incentivize certain behaviour, the localization of those norms and internalization by the parties may be jeopardized by the coercive nature of those activities. *Diffusing norms through coercion* implies a form of pressure that mediators exercise towards conflicting parties in order to induce them to adopt certain policies, accept distinct rules and comply with specific standards. Pressure may take the form of tangible threats (that is, sanctions) in response to parties non-compliance with mediators' instructions, as well as various forms of rewards for cooperative behaviour (that is, financial assistance, developmental aid, access to specific funds and so on). So far the literature on norm diffusion has linked coercion to two specific settings: the activities of international financial institutions (IFIs) in linking their help to recipient governments with specific types of domestic reforms, and policies of conditionality used by the EU towards countries that aspire to become member states (Gilardi, 2012). As evidenced by a series of studies, IFIs' pressure policies have not managed to produce meaningful domestic reform due to the recalcitrant nature of recipient governments and their normative frameworks, which are not sufficiently developed to internalize requested change (Weyland, 2006; Brooks, 2007; Mukherjee and Singer, 2010). Similarly, policies of conditionally have not managed to induce complete reform within aspiring member states as these actors frequently use norms-based 'rhetorical action' to manipulate accession criteria and achieve their short-term self-interests, without internalizing any normative change (Schimmelfennig, 2001, 2008). In line with these trends, the most assertive form of mediation – which presupposes the development of tailor-made tangible incentive structures that mediators use in order to put pressure on the parties to conform to certain behaviour – has also been associated with very limited success in realizing desired change. Beardsley argues that this has to do with the artificial nature of the incentive structure that tangible resources imply (Beardsley, 2008). The parties will comply with assigned behaviour as long as they can exploit the tangible incentives which do not require any type of internalization of this change. Once these structures are no longer present, parties may revert to confrontation and escalation. As Zartman and Touval argue, 'left alone to their own devices, parties may fall out of an agreement just as it is being made or implemented' (Zartman and Touval, 1985: 44).

As noted by Mandell and Tomlin, the success of Kissinger's initiatives in the Middle East was not based solely in incentive structures he provided to the parties, but in the learning process he fostered, which in turn was only supported by those incentives (Mandell and Tomlin, 1991). In other words, while coercion may not suffice to diffuse norms on its own, it may provide the necessary support mechanism for *norm diffusion through learning*. Gilardi defines learning as 'the process whereby policy makers use the experience of other countries to estimate the likely consequences of policy change' (Gilardi, 2012: 463). Using Bayesian updating, he also points out that 'within this perspective, policy makers have prior beliefs regarding the consequences of a policy, which they update on the basis of information coming from other countries' (Gilardi, 2012: 464). In conflict dynamics this information may be either incomplete, inaccurate or misleading (Fearon, 1995; Powell, 2002). Thus a primary function for any mediator is to facilitate impaired communication and allow parties to better understand the other side's interests, values, capabilities and resolve. While doing that, mediators certainly carry their own biases in how they frame the issue. These preferences are certainly mirrored in the emphasis they endorse in the dialogue. At the same time, they will also bring certain reference points that are primarily aligned with their own normative behaviour. Through a mediated dialogue, mediators may bring new evidence related to a norm in question, indicate the practical implications of certain behaviour and offer creative ways to persuade parties that these norms can be localized and internalized for the betterment of the parties. In fact, these types of processes, as painstaking as they may appear, manage to achieve the most durable solutions and outcomes (Bercovitch and Gartner, 2009) as parties incrementally question the validity of their earlier assumptions, absorb new normative ideas and consequently own the eventual normative change.

While mediators facilitate the dialogue and offer creative formulas for the new and improved normative framework, they may also exercise a form of referent power. Mediators' institutional function and particular reputation may grant them an ability to 'lead by example' (French and Raven, 1959: 266). This can be amplified by mediators' personal characteristics, such as charisma, experience and expertise, which contribute to the mediators' overall attractiveness ability to set standards for appropriate behaviour (Vuković, 2015: 421). As such, mediators may set in motion a process where the norms, which they have already internalized and socially routinized, become *diffused through emulation*. As Gilardi argues, when a norm is emulated the policies are diffused 'because of their normative and socially constructed properties instead of their objective characteristics' (Gilardi, 2012: 470). In these cases mediators highlight appropriateness based on an exogenous experience (which can include their own), so that the parties make their evaluation of appropriateness by evoking a specific identity or role, instead of evaluating likely consequences (March and Olsen, 1998: 949–51). Mediators achieve this objective when parties want to ascertain or aspire to achieve normative identity that characterizes the mediator, through replicating rules and procedures, mirroring particular behaviour, assuming converging principles and allowing mediators to create tailor-made norms that are presented as an emanation of a wanted identity.

Directions for Further Research

As mediators are not passive bystanders that lack the will and skill to assert and diffuse specific norms within a given peacemaking process, future research should pay more attention to *why* certain norms are selected and promoted over others. This may be directly linked to the actual motivations mediators have in the process, which may range from their concerns over detrimental spill-over effects an escalating conflict may have on them, to the establishment of new preference structures that will govern future relations between them and conflicting parties, and their aspiration to assert a normative framework that would limit a rival norm from taking over. Some studies have already pointed out the dilemmas mediators face when choosing between inclusivity and exclusivity, for instance in cases where they have to engage with actors proscribed as terrorist (Palmiano Federer, 2019), or when their mandate does not specify a role for the local civil society groups (Pring, 2017). Yet future studies should expand the purview and explore similar dilemmas on the level of norms related to both the procedure and the content of the peace talks.

Mediation is unequivocally a very practical (foreign) policy tool that can be used to diffuse norms across conflict affected area and incrementally set new standards of behaviour more broadly. Faced with unyielding attitudes of conflicting parties, who are unable or unwilling to settle on a common normative framework, mediators may fill that gap by introducing new interpretations, offering alternatives and providing incentive structures that can support these new perceptions. While the potential is clear and implications are auspicious, norm diffusion through mediation is still an underdeveloped concept both for theory and practice. A nuanced taxonomy of potential strategies for each specific mediator or a coalition of mediators should inspire further research and future policy planning. This chapter aspired to offer the starting ground for that goal.

References

Acharya, A. (2004). How Ideas Spread: Whose Norms Matter? Norm Localization and Institutional Change in Asian Regionalism. *International Organization*, 58(2), 239–75.

Acharya, A. (2011). Norm Subsidiarity and Regional Orders: Sovereignty, Regionalism, and Rule-making in the Third World. *International Studies Quarterly*, 55(1), 95–123.

Axelrod, R. (1984). *The Evolution of Cooperation*. New York, NY: Basic Books.

Axelrod, R. (1986). An Evolutionary Approach to Norms. *American Political Science Review*, 80(4), 1095–111.

Beardsley, K. (2008). Agreement Without Peace? International Mediation and Time Inconsistency Problems. *American Journal of Political Science*, 52(4), 723–40.

Beardsley, K. (2011). *The Mediation Dilemma*. Ithaca, NY: Cornell University Press.

Bercovitch, J. (2009). Mediation and Conflict Resolution. In J. Bercovitch, V. Kremenyuk and I.W. Zartman (eds.) *The SAGE Handbook of Conflict Resolution*. London: SAGE, pp 340–57.

Bercovitch, J. and Gartner, S.S. (2009). *International Conflict Mediation: New Approaches and Findings*. Abingdon: Routledge.

Bercovitch, J. and Jackson, R. (2009). *Conflict Resolution in the Twenty First Century: Principles, Methods and Approaches*. Ann Arbor, MI: Michigan University Press.

Björkdahl, A. (2006). Promoting Norms Through Peacekeeping: UNPREDEP and Conflict Prevention. *International Peacekeeping*, 13(2), 214–28.

Björkdahl, A. (2007). Swedish Norm Entrepreneurship in the UN. *International Peacekeeping*, 14(4), 538–52.

Boesenecker, A.P. and Vinjamuri, L. (2011). Lost in Translation? Civil Society, Faith-based Organizations and the Negotiation of International Norms. *International Journal of Transitional Justice*, 5(3), 345–65.

Brooks, S.M. (2007). When Does Diffusion Matter? Explaining the Spread of Structural Pension Reforms Across Nations. *The Journal of Politics*, 69(3), 701–15.

Buchanan, A. and Keohane, R.O. (2006). The Legitimacy of Global Governance Institutions. *Ethics & International Affairs*, 20(4), 405–37.

Carnevale, P.J. (2002). Mediating from Strength. In Bercovitch, J. (ed.) *Studies in International Mediation*. New York, NY: Palgrave Macmillan, pp 25–40.

Cortell, A.P. and Davis, Jr, J.W. (2000). Understanding the Domestic Impact of International Norms: A Research Agenda. *International Studies Review*, 2(1), 65–87.

Deitelhoff, N. and Zimmermann, L. (2013). *Things We Lost in the Fire: How Different Types of Contestation Affect the Validity of International Norms* (PRIF Working Papers, 18). Frankfurt am Main: Hessische Stiftung Friedens- und Konfliktforschung. Available at: https://nbn-resolving.org/urn:nbn:de:0168-ssoar-455201.

Epstein, C. (2008). *The Power of Words in International Relations: Birth of an Anti-whaling Discourse*. Cambridge, MA: MIT Press.

Evers, M.M. (2017). On Transgression. *International Studies Quarterly*, 61(4), 786–94.

Fearon, J.D. (1995). Rationalist Explanations for War. *International Organization*, 49(3), 379–414.

Finnemore, M. and Sikkink, K. (1998). International Norm Dynamics and Political Change. *International Organization*, 52(4), 887–917.

French, J. and Raven, B. (1959). The Bases of Social Power. In Cartwright, D. (ed.) *Studies in Social Power*. Ann Arbor, MI: Institute for Social Research.

George, A.L. (1988). Incentives for US–Soviet Security Cooperation and Mutual Adjustment. In George, A.L., Farley P.J. and Dallin, A. (eds.) *US–Soviet Security Cooperation: Achievements, Failures, Lessons*. New York, NY: Oxford University Press, pp 641–54.

Gilardi, F. (2012). Transnational Diffusion: Norms, Ideas, and Policies. In Carlsnaes, W., Risse, T. and Simmons, B. (eds.) *Handbook of International Relations*. Thousand Oaks, CA, Sage, pp 453–77.

Hellmüller, S., Federer, J.P. and Pring, J. (2017). *Are Mediators Norm Entrepreneurs?*. Working Paper 3. Swisspeace. Basel.

Hopmann, P.T. (1996). *The Negotiation Process and the Resolution of International Conflicts*. Columbia, SC, University of South Carolina Press.

Hurrell, A. and MacDonald, T. (2013). Ethics and Norms in International Relations. In Simmons, B.A., Carlsnaes W. and Risse T. (eds.) *Handbook of International Relations*. London: Sage, 57–84.

Iklé, F.C. (1967). *How Nations Negotiate*. New York, NY: Praeger.

Jacob, C. (2018). From Norm Contestation to Norm Implementation: Recursivity and the Responsibility to Protect. *Global Governance: A Review of Multilateralism and International Organizations*, 24(3), 391–409.

Kriesberg, L. (2007). *Constructive Conflicts: From Escalation to Resolution*. Lanham, MD: Rowman & Littlefield.

Kurusu, K. (2018). Japan as a Norm Entrepreneur for Human Security. *Routledge Handbook of Japanese Foreign Policy*. Abingdon: Routledge, 321–336.

Mandell, B.S. and Tomlin, B.W. (1991). Mediation in the Development of Norms to Manage Conflict: Kissinger in the Middle East. *Journal of Peace Research*, 28(1), 43–55.

March, J.G. and Olsen, J.P. (1998). The Institutional Dynamics of International Political Orders. *International Organization*, 52(4): 943–69.

Mukherjee, B. and Singer, D.A. (2010). International Institutions and Domestic Compensation: The IMF and the Politics of Capital Account Liberalization. *American Journal of Political Science*, 54(1), 45–60.

Niemann, H. and Schillinger, H. (2017). Contestation 'All the Way Down'? The Grammar of Contestation in Norm Research. *Review of International Studies*, 43(1), 29–49.

Nye, J.S. and Welch, D.A. (2016). *Understanding Global Conflict & Cooperation: An Introduction to Theory and History*. London: Pearson Education.

Palmiano Federer, J. (2019). We Do Negotiate with Terrorists: Navigating Liberal and Illiberal Norms in Peace Mediation. *Critical Studies on Terrorism*, 12(1), 19–39.

Panke, D. and Petersohn, U. (2012). Why International Norms Disappear Sometimes. *European Journal of International Relations*, 18(4), 719–42.

Panke, D. and Petersohn, U. (2016). Norm Challenges and Norm Death: The Inexplicable? *Cooperation and Conflict*, 51(1), 3–19.

Powell, R. (2002). Bargaining Theory and International Conflict. *Annual Review of Political Science*, 5(1), 1–30.

Pring, J. (2017). Including or Excluding Civil Society? The Role of the Mediation Mandate for South Sudan (2013–2015) and Zimbabwe (2008–2009). *African Security*, 10(3–4), 223–38.

Pruitt, D.G. (1983). Strategic Choice in Negotiation. *American Behavioral Scientist*, 27(2), 167–94.

Pruitt, D. and Kim, S.H. (2003). *Social Conflict: Escalation, Stalemate, and Settlement*. New York, NY: McGraw-Hill.

Raven, B.H. (2004). Power, Six Bases of. In Goethals, G.R., Sorenson, G.J. and MacGregor Burns, J. (eds.) *Encyclopedia of Leadership*. Thousand Oaks, CA: Sage Publications.

Risse, T. (2000). 'Let's Argue!': Communicative Action in World Politics. *International Organization*, 54(1), 1–39.

Schimmelfennig, F. (2001). The Community Trap: Liberal Norms, Rhetorical Action, and the Eastern Enlargement of the European Union. *International Organization*, 55(1), 47–80.

Schimmelfennig, F. (2008). EU Political Accession Conditionality after the 2004 Enlargement: Consistency and Effectiveness. *Journal of European Public Policy*, 15(6), 918–37.

Stimmer, A. (2019). Beyond Internalization: Alternate Endings of the Norm Life Cycle. *International Studies Quarterly*, 63(2), 270–80.

Tholens, S. and Groß, L. (2015). Diffusion, Contestation and Localisation in Post-war States: 20 Years of Western Balkans Reconstruction. *Journal of International Relations and Development*, 18(3), 249–64.

Touval, S. and Zartman, I.W. (1985). *International Mediation in Theory and Practice*. Boulder, CO: Westview Press.

Vuković, S. (2014). International Mediation as a Distinct Form of Conflict Management. *International Journal of Conflict Management*, 25(1), 61–80.

Vuković, S. (2015). Soft Power, Bias and Manipulation of International Organizations in International Mediation. *International Negotiation*, 20(3), 414–43.

Vuković, S. (2019). Mediating Closure: Driving toward a MEO. In Zartman, I. (ed.) *How Negotiations End: Negotiating Behavior in the Endgame*. Cambridge: Cambridge University Press, pp 185–200.

Vuković, S. and Hopmann, P. (2019). 'Satisficing in International Mediation: Framing, Justifying, and Creating Outcomes in Peacemaking'. In Wilkenfeld, J., Beardsley K. and Quinn, D. (eds.) *Research Handbook on Mediating International Crises*. Cheltenham, UK: Edward Elgar Publishing, 109–23

Wendt, A. (1999). *Social Theory of International Politics*. Cambridge: Cambridge University Press.

Weyland, K. (2006). *Bounded Rationality and Policy Diffusion: Social Sector Reform in Latin America*. Princeton, NJ, Princeton University Press.

Wiener, A. (2004). Contested Compliance: Interventions on the Normative Structure of World Politics. *European Journal of International Relations*, 10(2), 189–234.

Wiener, A. (2014). *A Theory of Contestation*. Berlin: Springer.

Zartman, I.W. and Touval, S. (1985). International Mediation: Conflict Resolution and Power Politics. *Journal of Social Issues*, 41(2), 27–45.

Zartman, I.W. and Alfredson, T. (2010). Negotiating with Terrorists and the Tactical Question. In Reuveny, R. and Thompson, W.R. (eds.) *Coping with Terrorism: Origins, Escalation, Counterstrategies, and Responses*, Albany, NY: SUNY Press, 247–84.

4

The Emulation of Peace Mediation Practices: Beware of the Jurisgenerative Train

Emmanuel De Groof

Introduction

The recent move towards the professionalization of the peace mediation field has rested on coalescence around certain 'evident' truths surrounding the design and delivery of mediation processes. These truths include the need to see peace mediation as a process rather than an outcome, the need to ensure inclusivity and national ownership of mediation processes, and the embeddedness of mediation within the norms and institutions of the international community. And yet this so-called self-evidence is not always a guarantee of success. It remains necessary to assess 'what really works' in light of the situations where peace mediation, combined with constitutional changes,[1] in the context of a broader transition has not worked, regardless of how one defines peace. Afghanistan, Iraq, Yemen and Central African Republic are among the best examples of where mediation has not worked, whereas South Africa, Tunisia and to a certain extent Kenya have seen more positive results. Reflecting

[1] A combination which became increasingly successful after 'the light footprint approach', with its accent on domestic ownership and inclusivity, was adopted in Afghanistan.

on the differences in outcome, this chapter is concerned with the tension between what is normatively accepted – the self-evident truths of mediation – and 'what works' in practice as well as the long-term implications of such a gap.

There are three normative layers to the discussion. The first concerns the professional deontology – that is the normative canon – of peacemakers and mediators that is considered to guide and constrain their actions. The second concerns the nexus between peace mediation and constitutions, as prime expressions of domestic law and state practice, in the context of broader transitions. The third concerns the progressive development of international law informed by the two other layers. The chapter asks whether there is a connection between deontological and practitioners' guidelines, the reproduction of practices and values, and state practice, and whether emulation and socialization between peacemakers may influence the evolution of international law more broadly in relation to transitional governance. In short, can such a reproduction be jurisgenerative, for example by preparing the terrain for emerging law through custom creation?[2] It could also be argued that a fourth normative reflection may be added. This 'meta-layer' is an assessment of whether the 'bridges' between the three normative layers make for a beneficial cross-fertilization – or not. If one accepts that legality, on the one hand, and morals and political, social and economic desirability, on the other, belong to separate normative registers, such an evaluation may become redundant as it does not necessarily change the legal implications of a cross-fertilization. This is different, however, with regard to the field of public international law, especially in relation to custom creation. Custom formation indeed also depends on *opinio necessatis*, that is the conviction that certain practices are required by political, social or economic exigencies, thus paving the way for *opinio iuris*, the conviction that these practices reflect or amount to law, and eventually transform into custom (Cassese, 2001: 119).

If in this way legality and morality (in turn based on political, social and economic desirability) are somehow intertwined, and this assessment is widely shared, it requires some unpacking of common current practices

[2] From the outset it should be emphasized that the three normative layers are not independent, isolated islands. Deontological obligations can indeed find their way into peace accords, transitional arrangements, interim constitutions or other documents that have a supra-constitutional value and thus define the constitutional order to come after conflict. In turn, supraconstitutional and constitutional texts can contribute to the progressive development of international law.

of how international law currently develops. Through the development of custom power relations are internalized in the law, and the law serves as a tool for re-interpreting these relations. Law is not beyond politics but is itself an intense manifestation of political battle (Salmon, 2002; Klabbers, 2006: 199).[3] Clearly this has implications for the validity and acceptance of core norms in relation to peace mediation.

The argument presented is twofold. First, an observation; second, an interrogation. First, an observation. Communication between the three normative layers finds expression in the jurisgenerative potential of mediation given its increased relationship with constitution making (Berghof Foundation and UN DPPA, forthcoming). Second, an interrogation. How does any disconnection between deontological guidelines on one hand and success in practice on the other impact the credibility of legal outcomes, in terms of both constituent documents, but also the broader development of international law? From a normative standpoint, some distance between the norm and practice constitutes the very essence of normativity, lest norms be reduced to sheer facts. What matters is that violation of norms is recognized as such. Such recognition then actually strengthens the norm rather than weakening it:

> [I]n order to deduce the existence of customary rules, the Court deems it sufficient that the conduct of States should, in general, be consistent with such rules, and that instances of State conduct inconsistent with a given rule should generally have been treated as breaches of that rule, not as indications of the recognition of a new rule. (ICJ, 1986: 98, § 186)[4]

The chapter will now consider the three normative layers in turn, returning to this issue of 'normative disconnect' in the final section.

---

[3] Cassese (1995: 128) remarked in the same sense that legal principles 'are the expression and result of conflicting views of States on matters of crucial importance. When States cannot agree upon definite and specific standards of behaviour because of their principled, opposing attitudes, but need, however, some sort of basic guideline for their conduct, their actions and discussions eventually lead to the formulation of principles.' It is also in this sense that self-determination 'becomes a capacious architecture that accommodates the conflicting powers and fault-lines of the international order' (Bhuta, 2010/11: 17).

[4] There is no perfectly consistent practice, there can be an 'individual deviation [which] may not lead to the conclusion that no rule has crystallised' (Cassese, 2001: 120).

Deontology of Peacemakers, Mediators and Diplomats

What are the recommended practices for the relatively small yet impactful epistemic community of peacemakers, practitioners and diplomats involved in peace negotiations today? In the context of a war–peace 'transition', three strands of practice clearly stand out and contribute to the first normative layer. First, frame the issue as one of governance, requiring fundamental reform. Second, apply the normative framework of international law to the reform process. Third, ensure efforts are as 'inclusive' as possible.

Transitional Governance Fulfilling a Central Role

The first recommended practice is to think in terms of transition and reconstituting the country, using the constitution as a social contract to redefine social relations. In short, think of transitional governance. The very toolbox at the disposal of peace mediators is partly determined by the epistemic community gravitating around peace processes. The community of practitioners engaged in post-war countries and constitution building is indeed relatively small, enabling the reproduction of value systems as highlighted by the United Nations (UN) in its Review of the Peacebuilding Architecture, where it noted that 'over the last couple of decades, a rough template seems to have emerged for international response to post-conflict challenges. First, mediators achieve a peace agreement ... This is followed by a limited "Transition" period' (UNGA and UNSC, 2015: 18). This dominant discourse – which puts transitional governance high on a pedestal – is the result of acculturation catalyzed by a small epistemic community. The re-occurrence of transitional governance can be attributed to phenomena such as the 'migration of constitutional ideas' (Choudry, 2011), 'constitutional borrowing' (Dennis, 2003), 'transnational information networks', acculturation in contact groups,[5] and the use of templates for peacebuilding (Sharp, 2013: 169).

As a result, the epistemic community dealing with these issues creates a habitat favourable to the reproduction of professional practices by emulation, influencing a much bigger community of practitioners including diplomats and mediators. One of these practices concerns how a transition must unfold and must be governed after a non-constitutional

[5] Participants of the contact group 'encouraged countries that have undergone similar processes to share their experiences with the CAR' (African Union, 2014: 2).

rupture. Transitional governance becomes the tool of choice for peace mediators. As its function is now to bring peace, its role has been in a sense aggrandized as compared to the 20th century, during which interim governance fulfilled several functions without also carrying the loaded responsibility of bringing peace.[6] Today, there seems little space to rethink peace mediation if a reassessment runs counter to the *idée fixe*, widely propagated among practitioners, of thinking in terms of transition and of reconstituting a country. Redefining the social contract has become a means to (purportedly) bring peace. I have called this the peace-through-transition paradigm (De Groof, 2020). The very fact that alternative ways are seldom pondered in itself shows how dominant the discourse is.

Incentive to Think in International Legal Terms

A second recommended practice is to think in terms of international law. Ensuring conformity with international law is seen as a deontological obligation. International mediators have the deontological duty to ensure that peace agreements respect international law (UNSC, 2012: 20), including human rights law (Saliternik, 2015). With regard to constitution making, the widely cited 2009 UN Secretary-General (UNSG) Guidance Note on assistance to constitution making provides that 'the UN should consistently promote compliance of constitutions with international human rights and other norms and standards. Thus, it should *speak out* when a draft constitution does not comply with these standards' (Sannerholm, 2012: 237; Saliternik, 2015).[7] The prevalence of international law in transitional governance implies that in post-conflict situations 'public officials have to interpret national law through the lens of international law and standards' (Sannerholm, 2012: 237). The fact that experts should 'speak out' when international norms and standards are not sufficiently integrated in constitutional texts is not a neutral factor. It contributes to the socialization of international norms and their integration into peace processes often through transitional legal orders. The relatively small but powerful epistemic community of peace mediators and constitutional experts has an exponential effect on

[6] As I have described elsewhere, throughout that century, interim institutions were created to deal with matters of regime or personal succession, to overthrow or restore political regimes, to resist foreign occupation or protest against international border settlements, to struggle against domestic repression, to strive for independence (De Groof, 2020), or to indirectly control foreign territory.

[7] Emphasis added.

the internationalization of peace processes and transitional legal orders. The 'rapid internationalisation' of the transitional legal order is seen in several countries (Sannerholm, 2012: 237).[8] States in transition generally express or reaffirm their commitment to international law. Notable examples in this regard are Cambodia, Rwanda and South Africa. After the turn of the century, transitional authorities in Burundi, Afghanistan, Democratic Republic of Congo (DRC), Liberia, Somalia, Haiti, Iraq and Côte d'Ivoire also expressed their deference to international law during transitions or peace processes (De Groof, 2019).

The Deontological Obligation to Include

A third recommended practice and arguably deontological obligation concerns inclusivity, which influences *who* should be included in the peace process, *how* (through representation or direct participation), and *when* (De Groof, 2020). The people, in their various segments, although not all of them (see Kaye, in Chapter 10, this volume) are expected to be involved at various moments of the peace process but in any event during constitution making and towards what is the supposed end of a transition or peace process, generally sealed by a constitutional referendum or general elections.

Inclusivity is mostly seen under a positive light and most often commended in relation to constitution making, where it is seen as catalyzing many good things: '... the more representative and more inclusive constitution building processes resulted in constitutions favouring free and fair elections, greater political equality, more social justice provisions, human rights protections, and stronger accountability mechanisms' (Samuels, 2006: 668).

The question becomes not so much *what* is included in the constitution as *how* it is drafted and to what extent the people are involved, with a subtext that an inclusive approach would have an almost cathartic effect on the society in question. For Samuels, '*how* constitutions are made, particularly following civil conflict or authoritarian rule, impacts the resulting state and its transition to democracy' (Samuels, 2006: 667) while for Brahimi, 'the way a constitution is made in a war-torn country can play a key role in rebuilding or strengthening state and political systems

[8] This author observes that '[t]hrough post-war treaty ratification, the incorporation of international law in constitutions, the establishment of institutions based upon international models, or the employment of standards directly in law-making, *war-torn societies are subject to rapid internationalisation.* This is also evident from the use of international personnel in national institutions' (Sannerholm, 2012: 237; emphasis added).

as well as in securing a durable peace' (Brandt et al, 2011: i). The 'how' almost invariably requires the involvement of the people.

At the same time, inclusivity is often criticized or demands to be qualified, either because, by disrupting the political economy and hierarchical structures of a country, it creates instability (Samuels, 2006: 670–1) or because it is too costly and time consuming (Gluck and Brandt, 2015) or because inclusivity is considered to be applied only in name, for example a checking-the-box Public Relations exercise, as was arguably the case in South Sudan:

> ... one should use terms that are more concrete. This leads to the question of whether the participatory aspects of the constitution-making process were mainly to please international and national actors and to legitimi[z]e the process, and that the function of the participation was what White would term nominal. There are indeed many things that point to a process with high degrees of internal exclusion in the South Sudan Constitution Making. (Storaas, 2015: 8)

Some authors have even suggested that inclusion allows for political recuperation (Partlett, 2012: 4) or paves the way for worst case scenarios (Landau, 2013: 923). Independently of the criticism, inclusivity is seen (at the minimum) as a deontological obligation in official discourse. Are there mediators or practitioners who would openly defend the view that, in order to be effective, state transformation and transitional governance (now mostly seen as essential to effective peace processes) must be predicated on bold, exclusive power (Bhuta, 2010/11)? Such interrogations are rare in spite of the 'needs to be more self-critical of the politics of international intervention in support of inclusive settlements, and more attuned to the local political struggles and dynamics that they seek to affect' (Bell, 2017b: 24).

Constitutions or (Supra-)constitutional Texts Reflecting Practitioners' Deontological Obligations

The triple mantra and deontology that peace mediators should think in terms of transitional governance and reconstitution, should apply international law and should strive for inclusive peace processes also find their way into constitutions – or texts aspiring to having a constitutional or even supraconstitutional value (for example at least provisionally superior to the constitution). This brings us to the second normative layer, and the further question of the link or nexus between 'constitutions' or 'constitutional texts' and peace mediation.

Two issues should be distinguished here. The question of whether the nexus between peace mediation and constitution making should be assessed favourably is *distinct* from the question whether or not the link is already made in practice (see Mubashir et al, in Chapter 16, this volume). Let us here briefly concentrate on the latter question from the perspective of two sorts of texts – UN Security Council (UNSC) resolutions and transition instruments. UNSC resolutions provide in detail how transitions must unfold to favour peace; or endorse transition agendas defined elsewhere.[9] The UNSC has thus adopted resolutions under Chapter VII of the UN Charter with regard to transitions in South Sudan (UNSC, 2014g), Somalia (UNSC, 2014f), Libya (UNSC, 2014e), Mali (UNSC, 2014d), Côte d'Ivoire (UNSC, 2014c),[10] Central African Republic (UNSC, 2014b), Yemen (UNSC, 2014a), Guinea-Bissau (UNSC, 2012), Libya (UNSC, 2011),[11] Haiti (UNSC, 2004) and Afghanistan (UNSC, 2001).[12] The UNSC furthermore reserves the power to take sanctions under the UN Charter against anyone impeding transition. These resolutions systematically concern mediation as well as constitutional issues. Furthermore, and more importantly, instruments triggering transitional governance are themselves often explicit about the peace-through-transition paradigm, connecting peace mediation, transitional governance and constitutional change. Transition instruments in Burundi,[13]

[9] See, for example, resolution S/RES/2118 of 27 September 2013 in which the UNSC endorses the transition agenda of the Geneva Communiqué of 30 June 2012 (UNSC, 2013).

[10] In this resolution, the UNSC refers to the Ouagadougou Agreement and '[d]ecides that the Ivoirian authorities shall submit biannual reports to [a] Committee … on progress achieved in relation to DDR and SSR' (UNSC, 2014c: 4).

[11] In this resolution, the UNSC directly addressed itself to the National Transitional Council on the topic of the transition.

[12] In this resolution, the UNSC refers to the Bonn Agreement, which regulates the transition in Afghanistan. This agreement refers to the UNSC's resolution 1378 on the situation in Afghanistan. For a discussion, see Marauhn (2002: 496).

[13] The 2000 Arusha Agreement mentions the 'institution of a new political, economic, social and judicial order in Burundi' (article 5.1: 17) following the 'speedy establishment of the transitional institutions' (article 5.3: 18) under the chapter 'solutions' (Chapter 2) immediately following the chapter 'nature and historical causes of the conflict' (Chapter 1), leaving no doubt as to the conflict resolution function of transitional governance. Arusha Peace and Reconciliation Agreement for Burundi (2000), [online] 28 August, available from: https://peacemaker.un.org/sites/peacemaker.un.org/files/BI_000828_Arusha%20Peace%20and%20Reconciliation%20Agreement%20for%20Burundi.pdf (accessed 24 July 2019).

Côte d'Ivoire,[14] DRC[15] and Nepal,[16] for instance, enshrine this idea explicitly. The conclusion to be drawn can thus be succinct. Undeniably, and increasingly, in practice a link is drawn between peace mediation and constitution making.

The nexus goes in two directions. In some cases, constitutions take on a pacificatory function. In other cases peace agreements take on a constitutional function. The range of documents, no matter their nomenclature or exact denomination, *used for constitutional purposes* is increasing with time. Fulfilling a transformative and self-*re*determination function, constitutions, broadly understood, have become 'a way by which one social system gives rise to another social system' (Shakhray, 2014: 29). During peace processes and transitions used as avenues to re-determine the social contract, the current deontological practices find their way into documents with constitutional or even supraconstitutional value. The recourse to transitional governance arrangements, the more explicit adherence to (directly applicable) international law, and the insistence on inclusion become part of the DNA of transformative constitutionalism, itself used as a tool in peace processes under the peace-through-transition paradigm.

How Constitutional or Supraconstitutional Practice Shapes International Law

How does constitutional or supraconstitutional practice shape international law? This question relating to the third normative layer is distinct from the deontological obligation already discussed that mediators

---

[14] With respect to the transition in Côte d'Ivoire, the 2003 Linas-Marcoussis Accord provides: 'a Government of National Reconciliation will be set up immediately after the conclusion of the Paris Conference *to ensure a return to peace and stability*' (article 3.a: 2; emphasis added).

[15] The 2002 Pretoria agreement mentions among its 'transition objectives' 'the setting up of structures that will lead to a new political order' in the DRC (II.5: 3). Global and Inclusive Agreement on Transition in the Democratic Republic of Congo (Pretoria agreement) (2002), [online] 16 December, available from: https://peacemaker.un.org/sites/peacemaker.un.org/files/CD_021216_Global%20and%20Inclusive%20Agreement%20on%20Transition%20in%20DRC.pdf (accessed 24 July 2019).

[16] In Nepal the 'progressive restructuring of the state' is a principal component of the 2006 Comprehensive Peace Agreement between the Government of Nepal and the Communist Party of Nepal (Preamble, § 3) [online] 22 November, available from: https://peacemaker.un.org/nepal-comprehensiveagreement2006 (accessed 24 July 2019).

must consider international law including human rights law (and, as the case may be, need to 'speak out') during peace processes. The broader question for the third normative layer is not how international law shapes mediation practice, but how mediation practice in turn shapes international law.

Weber has observed that 'experience reveals a continuous scale of transitions from *norms of conduct guaranteed by mere convention* to those which are regarded as *binding* and guaranteed by law … It should be clear that … the transitions from mere usage to convention and from it to law are fluid' (Weber, 1968: 30–53). In international law, such dynamics form the driver behind custom creation. There should be no doubt that conduct adopted to implement transformative constitutionalism, which goes to the heart of a state's affairs, can reveal practice which, in conjunction with *opinio necessatis* and *opinio iuris*, as previously defined, may contribute to the progressive development of custom.

The following interlinked duties, based on constitutional or supraconstitutional practice inspired by widespread deontological usage, can arguably be requalified as emerging customary obligations incumbent on the state authorities, often *transitional* authorities, tasked with implementing the peace process. First, until the constitution is accepted, transitional authorities have limited powers, not only time-wise but also substantively as durable decisions are to be made only once the state transformation has been completed (De Groof, 2019). Second, the state transformation itself must be progressively inclusive of the people in its various segments of society, including women's groups but usually excluding business (in spite of recent attention to including business in peace processes) (Molloy, 2018; Kaye, in Chapter 10, this volume), diaspora, war- and drug lords (see Van Santen, in Chapter 9, this volume).

The first emerging duty under international law, practice and *opinio iuris* indicates that transitional authorities have fiduciary, caretaking duties which should not pre-empt the future. As Sachs noted, '[t]he ambitions are high but the posture should be humble: the idea of self-effacement is, of course, inherent in the idea of transience' (Sachs, 2020). A second emerging duty relates to inclusivity. As it has currently evolved, inclusivity is best qualified as an *obligation of means*, except when it concerns constitution making. Transitional authorities must apply this requirement throughout the interregnum, must pick one of the approaches for realizing it, and, if it originated from an elite movement, must gradually open up transitional governance to various segments of society. The principle of self-determination emphasizes the importance of *deliberation* during the interregnum. Deliberation allows the people to redefine the social contract, to create a 'political space in which a population can begin a conversation about what kind of country they want to be theirs' (cf Chesterman, 2008) (thus, ultimately, to allow the spirit of constitutionalism to develop) (Chesterman, 2005). During the interregnum, habits of dialogue and compromise are cultivated (Ghai and Galli, 2006: 13).

The allegiance of 'the people' in its various components is instrumental to the participatory and/or representative reformulation of the social contract. Inclusivity imposes a process of deliberation among various segments of society – factions previously at war, political parties, civil society representatives, armed movements, regional entities, women's groups and so on. They all have the right to be taken seriously during the interregnum. This translates into a continuous obligation of means incumbent on transitional authorities. An *obligation of result*, however, imposes itself for the transitional constitution-making process and the approval of the draft constitution towards the end of the interregnum (Thornhill, 2016: 7).

In general, transitional authorities must strike a balance between the power of modification (within the limits imposed by their mandate) and the duty of conservation (regarding all matters not covered by the mandate). Transitional authorities commit both to change (manage the transition) and stability (state continuity; respect of private rights). Enormous procedural powers – the transition as a state-transformation enterprise no less – are combined with few substantive powers. If the argument of emerging custom along these lines can be made, arguably nascent customary obligations also increasingly influence the legal positions of third states and international organizations (for example the prohibition on favouring specific groups during a peace process or on undermining inclusivity otherwise). Any argument about nascent or emerging custom of course comes with a caveat. As with every emerging customary rule, even those who foresee that current trends will probably be confirmed must accept that customs merely germinating at present *may* (and those who are not convinced of their political, social and economic desirability might say *should*) radically change or fade out in the future.

The Risks and Implications of Inter-normative Cross-fertilization

To draw conclusions from this process of normative cross-fertilization a couple of questions serve as a means of recapitulation. These are followed by a different set of questions about the long-term implications of the cross-fertilization between the three layers – deontological, constitutional, international legal – which converge to determine norm germination on the occasion of peace processes and transitional governance, now increasingly seen as twin processes.

First, is there a link between practitioners' and deontological guidelines, the reproduction of practices and values, and state practice? Does emulation between peacemakers influence the evolution of international law in relation to transitional governance, which has become a conflict resolution and peace process tool of choice? Can such a reproduction be jurisgenerative, expressing emerging law through custom creation. The answer to this first set of questions is positive.

Second, is there any causality between the effectiveness, beneficial effect or 'success' of repeated practices and the jurisgenerative character of emulated practices? This is not necessarily the case. In other words, even widespread practices deemed to be obligatory but generating little 'success' or positive outcome can become jurisgenerative. It is not because a rule is poorly designed, poorly applied or even results in disastrous situations, that it does not exist.

From the outset, it has been highlighted that some distance between the norm and practice constitutes the very essence of normativity, lest norms be reduced to facts. Consider the following partly fictitious example. Under the law of the seas, the exclusive economic zone is 200 nautical miles from the baseline. Whether applied or not, and regardless of the commercial results or disasters it may favour, the rule clearly exists. Even if by assumption it would not lead to sustainable and peaceful commerce between nations, this does not, in itself, call into question its existence. The same is in a sense true of deontology-based customary rules. Criticized though they may be for disrupting elite settlements, creating instability, being burdensome or constituting a window-dressing exercise, such rules – for example the inclusivity of the transition – seem to be emerging for being so widespread. This does not come as a surprise in light of the socialization within a small yet powerful specialist epistemic community forming a favourable habitat for norm germination. In a similar vein, the question of whether the nexus between 'mediation' and 'constitution making' is a favourable and commendable one is quite distinct from the question whether, being widely observed in practice, it is jurisgenerative.

This brings us to question the long-term implications of the cross-fertilization between the three – deontological, constitutional, international legal – layers. As long as no conscious choice is made, for example as long as there is no deliberate disruption of the chains linking the three normative layers, the cross-fertilization becomes a necessity in the sense that it simply 'goes on'. But as noted in the introduction, it is necessary to assess the effectiveness of this process. This requires evaluation not only of compliance with the existing deontological frameworks, but of whether or not that results in better mediation outcomes on the ground. It is necessary to examine this trend in light of situations where peace mediation combined with inclusive constitutional changes has not worked by any standard or measure of success. Think, for example, of Afghanistan, Iraq, Yemen and Central African Republic anno 2020.

A similar sense of realism should be applied to the question of inter-normative cross-fertilization on the occasion of peace processes. This should also incentivize thinking and acting in politically smarter ways (Bell, 2017b: 58) in favour of 'principled pragmatic intervention' (Pospisil, 2019: 21). Ineffective deontology can also find its way into international law, especially when there is all but resistance against the *idées reçues* – such as the merits of transitional governance and inclusion – discussed in this chapter. This is where the fourth normative layer mentioned in the introduction, that is, our collective assessment about whether we think the 'bridges' between normative layers make for a beneficial cross-fertilization, should forcefully step in. Such a collective assessment may have to serve as a wake-up call to challenge the common current practices that seem to be deontologically validated and eventually influence the development of international law.

Looking to the future and being conscious of the risks of said cross-fertilization while being appreciative also of its potential, the following questions should be borne in mind. First, and on a general note, should academic and practitioners alike pay more attention to the 'jurisgenerative train' connecting normative layers – is there a need for heightened self-reflection and perhaps concrete readjustments by practitioners should they come to the conclusion that this train is not heading in the right direction? This is particularly important given that some commentators have come to the conclusion that '[a] quarter of a century of investment in transitions … failed to lead to democracy and peace taking hold worldwide' (Bell, 2017a: 15). Then, more specific questions by way of example. How specific must we be about inclusion and what are the dangers of it staying vague? Should the compatibility between constitution making and peacemaking still be assumed (Ludsin, 2011)? If custom is only germinating, are there reasons to bend it, alter it or even stop it? How does progressive development of international law affect the legal position of third states? How to deal with financial incentives to make peace processes inclusive, and with 'external process capture'? As long as such questions are not addressed explicitly by the epistemic community dealing with peace processes and transitional governance, and by the larger group of practitioners including mediators and diplomats serving as a springboard and amplifier for this community, the jurisgenerative train, connecting various normative stations, will steam its way, unabated. If this connection generates norms that are out of tune with reality or even contribute to harming it, this affects the credibility of practitioners' deontology and constitutional practice, which eventually may also leave an imprint on evolving international law and how it relates to peace processes.

References

African Union (2014) *4th Meeting of the International Contact Group on the Central African Republic*, Brazzaville, Republic of the Congo.

Bell, C. (2017a) 'Introduction: Bargaining on Constitutions – Political Settlements and Constitutional State-building', *Global Constitutionalism*, 6(1): 13–32.

Bell, C. (2017b) *Navigating Inclusion in Peace Settlements, Human Rights and the Creation of the Common Good*, London: British Academy.

Berghof Foundation and UN DPPA (United Nations Department of Political and Peacebuilding Affairs) (forthcoming) *Constitutions and Peace Processes: A Primer*.

Bhuta, N. (2010/11) 'New Modes and Orders: The Difficulties of a *Jus Post Bellum* of Constitutional Transformation', International Law and Justice Working Papers, New York: New York University School of Law.

Brandt, M., Cottrell, J., Ghai, Y. and Regan, A. (2011) *Constitution-Making and Reform: Options for the Process*, Geneva: Interpeace.

Cassese, A. (1995) *Self-determination of Peoples*, Cambridge, New York: Cambridge University Press.

Cassese, A. (2001) *International Law*, Oxford and New York: Oxford University Press.

Chesterman, S. (2005) 'Imposed Constitutions, Imposed Constitutionalism, and Ownership', *Connecticut Law Review*, 37(4): 857–90.

Chesterman, S. (2008) 'An International Rule of Law?', *The American Journal of Comparative Politics*, 56(2): 331–61.

Choudry, S. (2011) *The Migration of Constitutional Ideas*, New York: Cambridge University Press.

De Groof, E. (2019) *The Features of Transitional Governance Today* (PA-X Report). Edinburgh: Global Justice Academy, University of Edinburgh. Available from: https://www.politicalsettlements.org/publications-database/features-of-transitional-governance-today/ (accessed 29 June 2020).

De Groof, E. (2020) *State Renaissance for Peace – Transitional Governance under International Law*, Cambridge: Cambridge University Press.

Dennis, D.M. (2003) 'Constitutional Borrowing: The South Africa Experience', *International Journal of Constitutional Law*, 1(2): 181–95.

Ghai, Y. and Galli, G. (2006) 'Constitution Building Processes and Democratisation', *International Institute for Democracy and Electoral Assistance (IDEA)*.

Gluck, J. and Brandt, M. (2015) 'Participatory and Inclusive Constitution Making – Giving Voice to the Demands of Citizens in the Wake of the Arab Spring', United States Institute of Peace (USIP), [online] available from: https://www.files.ethz.ch/isn/188062/PW105-Participatory-and-Inclusive-Constitution-Making.pdf (accessed 24 July 2019).

ICJ (International Court of Justice) (1986) *Case Concerning Military and Paramilitary Activities in and Against Nicaragua* (Nicaragua v. United States of America), 27 June.

Klabbers, J. (2006) 'The Right to Be Taken Seriously: Self-Determination in International Law', *Human Rights Quarterly*, 28(1): 186–206.

Landau, D. (2013) 'Constitution-Making Gone Wrong', *Alabama Law Review*, 64(5): 923–80.

Ludsin, H. (2011) 'Peacemaking and Constitution-drafting: A Dysfunctional Marriage', *University of Pennsylvania Journal of International Law*, 33(1): 239–311.

Marauhn, T. (2002) 'Konfliktbewältigung in Afghanistan zwischen Utopie und Pragmatismus', *Archiv des Völkerrechts*, 40(4): 480–511.

Molloy, S. (2018) 'Business and Peace Agreements', *Political Settlements Research Programme*, [online] available from: http://www.politicalsettlements.org/wp-content/uploads/2018/11/2018_Molloy_Business-Power-Sharing-Report.pdf (accessed 24 July 2019).

Partlett, W. (2012) 'The Dangers of Popular Constitution-Making', *Brookings Journal of International Law*, 38(1): 193–238, [online] available from: https://www.brookings.edu/wp-content/uploads/2016/06/11-constitution-making-partlett.pdf (accessed 24 July 2019).

Pospisil, J. (2019) 'Peacebuilding and Principled Pragmatism' in Conciliation Resources, Political Settlement Research Programme and Accord (eds) *Navigating Inclusion in Peace Processes*, Issue 28, pp 18–22.

Sachs, A. (2020) 'Preface' in E. De Groof and M. Wiebusch (eds.), International Law and Transitional Governance, Critical Perspectives, Routledge Series on Law, Conflict and International Relations.

Saliternik, M. (2015) 'Reducing the Price of Peace: The Human Rights Responsibilities of Third-Party Facilitators', *Vanderbilt Journal of Transnational Law*, 48(1): 179–243.

Salmon, J. (2002) 'Le droit international à l'épreuve au tournant du XXI siècle', *Cours méditérranéens Bancaja de Droit International*, IV: 35–363.

Samuels, K. (2006) 'Post-Conflict Peace-Building and Constitution-Making', *Chicago Journal of International Law*, 6(2): 663–82.

Sannerholm, R.Z. (2012) *Rule of Law after War and Crisis: Ideologies, Norms and Methods*, Cambridge: Intersentia.

Shakhray, S. (2014) 'Basic Law as an Instrument for Legal and Socio-political Transformations', *Russian Law Journal*, 2(1): 29–40.

Sharp, D.N. (2013) 'Beyond the Post-Conflict Checklist: Linking Peacebuilding and Transitional Justice Through the Lens of Critique', *Chicago Journal of International Law*, 14(1): 166–96.

Storaas, G. (2015) 'Participation on Paper but not in Practice? – The South Sudan Constitutional Review Process', Berghof Foundation, *Inclusive Political Settlements* (IPS), Paper 17, [online] available from: https://www.berghof-foundation.org/fileadmin/redaktion/Publications/Other_Resources/IPS/IPS-Paper-17-South-Sudan-vs2.pdf (accessed 24 July 2019).

Thornhill, C. (2016) *Sociology of Transitional Constitutions: Social Foundations of the Post-National Legal Structure*, Cambridge: Cambridge University Press.

UNGA (United Nations General Assembly) and UNSC (United Nations Security Council) (2015) *Resolution A/69/968-S/2015/490 on Integrated and coordinated implementation of and follow-up to the outcomes of the major United Nations conferences and summits in the economic, social and related fields*, [online] 30 June, available from: https://undocs.org/pdf?symbol=en/S/2015/490 (accessed 24 July 2019).

UNSC (United Nations Security Council) (2001) *Resolution 1386*, [online] 20 December, available from: https://www.securitycouncilreport.org/atf/cf/%7B65BFCF9B-6D27-4E9C-8CD3-CF6E4FF96FF9%7D/Afgh%20SRES1386.pdf [accessed 24 July 2019].

UNSC (United Nations Security Council) (2004) *Resolution 1529*, [online] 29 February, available from: https://www.securitycouncilreport.org/atf/cf/%7B65BFCF9B-6D27-4E9C-8CD3-CF6E4FF96FF9%7D/Chap%20VII%20SRES%201529.pdf (accessed 24 July 2019).

UNSC (United Nations Security Council) (2011) *Resolution 2009*, [online] 16 September, available from: https://www.securitycouncilreport.org/atf/cf/%7B65BFCF9B-6D27-4E9C-8CD3-CF6E4FF96FF9%7D/Libya%20S%20RES%202009.pdf (accessed 24 July 2019).

UNSC (United Nations Security Council) (2012) *Resolution 2048*, [online] 18 May, available from: https://www.securitycouncilreport.org/atf/cf/%7B65BFCF9B-6D27-4E9C-8CD3-CF6E4FF96FF9%7D/GB%20SRES%202048.pdf (accessed 24 July 2019).

UNSC (United Nations Security Council) (2013) *Resolution 2118*, [online] 27 September, available from: https://www.securitycouncilreport.org/atf/cf/%7B65BFCF9B-6D27-4E9C-8CD3-CF6E4FF96FF9%7D/s_res_2118.pdf (accessed 24 July 2019).

UNSC (United Nations Security Council) (2014a) *Resolution 2140*, [online] 26 February, available from: https://www.securitycouncilreport.org/atf/cf/%7B65BFCF9B-6D27-4E9C-8CD3-CF6E4FF96FF9%7D/s_res_2140.pdf (accessed 24 July 2019).

UNSC (United Nations Security Council) (2014b) *Resolution 2149*, [online] 10 April, available from: https://www.securitycouncilreport.org/atf/cf/%7B65BFCF9B-6D27-4E9C-8CD3-CF6E4FF96FF9%7D/s_res_2149.pdf (accessed 24 July 2019).

UNSC (United Nations Security Council) (2014c) *Resolution 2153*, [online] 29 April, available from: https://www.securitycouncilreport.org/atf/cf/%7B65BFCF9B-6D27-4E9C-8CD3-CF6E4FF96FF9%7D/s_res_2153.pdf (accessed 24 July 2019).

UNSC (United Nations Security Council) (2014d) *Resolution 2164*, [online] 25 June, available from: https://www.securitycouncilreport.org/atf/cf/%7B65BFCF9B-6D27-4E9C-8CD3-CF6E4FF96FF9%7D/s_res_2164.pdf (accessed 24 July 2019).

UNSC (United Nations Security Council) (2014e) *Resolution 2174*, [online] 27 August, available from: https://www.securitycouncilreport.org/atf/cf/%7B65BFCF9B-6D27-4E9C-8CD3-CF6E4FF96FF9%7D/s_res_2174.pdf (accessed 24 July 2019).

UNSC (United Nations Security Council) (2014f) *Resolution 2182*, [online] 24 October, available from: https://www.securitycouncilreport.org/atf/cf/%7B65BFCF9B-6D27-4E9C-8CD3-CF6E4FF96FF9%7D/S_res_2182.pdf (accessed 24 July 2019).

UNSC (United Nations Security Council) (2014g) *Resolution 2187*, [online] 25 November, available from: https://www.securitycouncilreport.org/atf/cf/%7B65BFCF9B-6D27-4E9C-8CD3-CF6E4FF96FF9%7D/s_res_2187.pdf (accessed 24 July 2019).

Weber, M. (1968) *Economy and Society*, Berkeley and Los Angeles, CA: California University Press.

5

Cowboys or Mavericks? The Normative Agency of NGO Mediators

Julia Palmiano Federer

Introduction

Within the last three decades, non-governmental organizations (NGOs) have become established mediation actors. NGO mediators, understood as private actors taking on discreet or public 'mediative' or facilitative functions among and between the negotiating parties in a peace process, are increasingly invited by negotiating parties to assist in negotiations towards a peace agreement. As private actors, NGO mediators can take on politically sensitive roles without the same accountability mechanisms required by formal mediation actors such as the United Nations (UN), regional organizations or state representatives. For instance, NGO mediators can mediate informally and discreetly in high-stake negotiations without risking the same level of political blowback if things go awry. As private actors, NGO mediators can engage directly with armed actors that are politically sensitive or proscribed as terrorist organizations. As private actors, NGO mediators are not beholden to the same regulations as formal international organizations bound by state or international organization (IO)-sanctioned counter-terrorism regulations. There is little consensus on what the consequences of this phenomenon are for the theory and practice of international peace mediation. NGO mediators have been lauded both as entrepreneurial 'mavericks' redefining the mediation field and as 'cowboys' that disregard the field's normative and political parameters (Martin, 2006).

The rise of NGO mediators coincides with an increasing imperative to promote international norms such as inclusivity, gender equality, human rights and transitional justice in mediation processes (Hellmüller et al, 2015). This normative shift in the mediation field has found mediators increasingly pressured to promote the inclusion of normative parameters at the peace table and in any resulting peace agreements. This chapter is concerned with the normative agency of mediators, or their ability to promote norms to the negotiating parties. While the UN, states and regional organizations are formal entities that wield high amounts of political authority to integrate norms into their mediation interventions, NGO mediators present a more curious puzzle: if NGO mediators do not have high amounts of political leverage, formal mandates and material resources, under what conditions can they promote certain norms to negotiating parties? In other words, what gets them in the negotiating room and what enables them to promote norms to the parties?

An analysis of the normative agency of NGO mediators reveals that their dual identity claims of NGOs *and* mediation actors allow them to both create their own normative parameters and manoeuvre freely within them. This room for manoeuvre affords them a high amount of political flexibility as informal actors. These distinct features translate into forms of agency, especially in terms of promoting certain norms to other mediators and the negotiating parties themselves. NGO mediators act as both norm makers and norm takers simultaneously (Finnemore and Sikkink, 1998), thereby positioning themselves as niche actors with a particular value added to negotiating parties as well as the field of international peace mediation writ large.

Despite the rising prominence of these actors, there is a dearth of research on NGO mediators and their role in the growing normative framework in mediation. This chapter addresses this gap by critically assessing the normative agency of NGO mediators and their effects on norm-driven peace mediation. By providing empirical analysis on how NGO mediators treat their mandates and normative parameters in practice, this chapter also addresses the bias in mediation research that assumes mediators are homogeneous actors. While this chapter's main contribution is a conceptual discussion on the normative agency of NGO mediators, it provides illustrative examples of NGO mediators acting in mediation contexts where informal and discreet mediation is preferred.[1] The chapter

[1] Some empirical examples are drawn from field research conducted in the framework of the author's doctoral research on the role of mediators as norm entrepreneurs.

concludes by discussing the consequences that NGO mediators and their role as norm entrepreneurs have for mediation theory and practice.

The Rise of NGO Mediators

Private diplomacy was not always viewed as an accepted or common form of mediation in contemporary mediation literature. Mediation is commonly understood as a 'process of conflict management, related to but distinct from the parties' own negotiations, where those in conflict seek the assistance of, or accept an offer of help from, an outsider [to change their perceptions or behaviour, and to do so without resorting to physical force or invoking the authority of law]' (Bercovitch, 2009: 343). While mediation has been used as a tool of dispute settlement since antiquity (Kriesberg, 1997), it rose to prominence as a form of conflict resolution after the end of the Cold War. In the context of post-Cold War intra- or inter-state armed conflict, third-party 'outsiders' (Kriesberg, 1997) who were tasked with bringing negotiating parties towards a political settlement or agreement were normally officially mandated by the UN, states, and regional organizations (Greig and Diehl, 2012). UN envoys or embassy diplomats who were mandated to mediate in conflicts reflected the state-focused nature of international diplomacy. Consequently, mediation literature at this time focused heavily on analysing the role of a mediator from a strategic bargaining and rationalist perspective (Zartman and Touval, 1985; Bercovitch et al, 1991; Walter, 1997; Beardsley, 2009; Kydd, 2010). While mediation literature focused on the role of mediators in bringing parties towards a ceasefire or peace agreement and the behavioural tactics and strategies they used to do so, the comparative advantages and disadvantages of different types of mediators were addressed in a wave of literature assessing the effects of globalization on the peace and conflict landscape (Crocker et al, 2004; Crocker et al, 2015). While UN envoys, state diplomats and official representatives of international organizations acting as mediators have been studied in mediation literature (Bercovitch et al, 1991), the role that NGO mediators play in conflict resolution has not been studied as closely.[2]

Two factors related to the wave of globalization around the turn of the millennium facilitated the rise of NGO mediators. First, global politics shifted its focus away from the state and towards non-state actors. Civil society actors and NGOs played an increasingly large decision-making

[2] Save for a few notable exceptions, for example the work of Pamela Aall (2000: 121–41) and Taulbee and Creekmore (2003: 156–71).

role in politics. Consequently, the number of NGOs addressing a vast array of environmental, health, political and social issues has proliferated exponentially in the post-Cold War period. Second, the peacemaking field became embedded within the liberal peacebuilding paradigm and, as a result, became increasingly normative in nature. The advent of the liberal peacebuilding paradigm after the Cold War redefined mediation from a vehicle for strategic bargaining for mutually beneficial outcomes towards a norm-laden vehicle for peaceful and just societies (Richmond, 2018). Liberal peacebuilding aims to imbue conflict and post-conflict societies with functioning and legitimate governance, security and judicial institutions that are supported by a market economy. Peace was no longer understood as the absence of war, but the presence of democracy (Paris, 2004; Hsieh and Shannon, 2005; Campbell et al, 2011). While the liberal peacebuilding paradigm has been criticized by scholars for its unintended negative effects on local populations in conflict affected areas (Paris, 2002; Chetail, 2009; Mac Ginty, 2011), liberal peacebuilding has become the dominant paradigm in which peace mediation occurs.

The Shift Towards Non-state Actors in Conflict Resolution

The shift towards non-state actors as actors with agency in global politics (Josselin and Wallace, 2001) was mirrored in international peace mediation (Hellmüller et al, 2017). When literature on civil war began to study the role of non-state armed groups (Fearon and Laitin, 2003) in the context of intra-state conflict (Kaldor, 1999; Kalyvas, 2001), the 'supply' side of conflict resolution also began to consider 'non-state' alternatives to mediation (Hare, 1992). While official mediation conducted by states still dominated the number of mediation interventions since the cold war (Greig and Diehl, 2012), non-state actors played leading mediation roles in resolving armed conflict. The Vatican's role in mediating the 1978–79 Beagle Channel Dispute between Chile and Argentina (Princen, 1992) and the Quaker religious community's involvement in a number of conflicts (Yarrow, 1978; Bailey, 1985) highlights the experiences of religious transnational organizations in mediating between conflict parties. Accounts of eminent individuals such as former presidents and national leaders leading mediations through their own NGOs (Taulbee and Creekmore, 2003) also signal the shift towards private diplomacy. The turning point towards pure NGO mediation was the mediation of Catholic-lay organization Community d'Sant Egidio in the early 1990s in Mozambique. Community d'Sant Egidio took a leading role in brokering the 1992 Rome General Peace Accords between conflict parties FRELIMO and RENAMO in Mozambique's bitter civil war. It was one of the first times that mediators acting in a private capacity took the lead mediation role over official, formal actors (Crocker et al, 1999). As previously mentioned, Community d'Sant Egidio's experience took place in a shifting context where civil society organizations and NGOs were also taking a more prominent role in global politics (Babbitt, 2009; Zanker, 2014). The increasing role of non-governmental actors taking on conflict resolution roles is also illustrated in the development of 'Track II' diplomacy (Lederach, 1997), a level of negotiations in which unofficial peacemaking initiatives could be convened and supported by NGOs as well as religious leaders, eminent persons and, increasingly, 'professional' conflict resolution organizations (Aall, 1996).

In the 1990s a rising number of NGOs focused their activities on conflict resolution; NGOs which engaged primarily in humanitarian or development activities began to engage actively as mediators (Aall, 1996; Taulbee and Creekmore, 2003). In the early 2000s NGOs such as the Centre for Humanitarian Dialogue (HD Centre) and the Crisis Management Initiative (CMI) took leading mediation roles in conflicts, most prominently brokering the agreement between the government of Indonesia and the Free Aceh Movement (GAM) insurgents (Shea, 2016) in 2005. Their involvement propelled the realization among other mediation actors that private diplomacy within an NGO structure was a model of engagement that was quickly gaining ground. Within the next decade or so, the number of NGO mediators actively engaging in armed conflict contexts steadily increased and changed the way mediation was conducted (Lehti, 2018).

The Normative Turn of the Mediation Field

The second shift that has facilitated the rise of NGO mediators is the 'normative turn' (Cortell and Davis, 2000) of the mediation field. The advent of liberal peacebuilding has shifted the role of mediators from peace brokers to peacebuilders. Mediators are now expected to promote norms in their mediation interventions (Hellmüller et al, 2015).

NGO mediators have played a significant role in this normative turn in mediation. As Convergne (2016a: 135) describes, classical mediation actors such as the UN '[rely] on knowledge produced by an epistemic community of peace and conflict scholars …, embedded in a network of nongovernmental mediators with which it exchanges know-how, following the logic of communities of practice'. This exchange and the production of expertise between classical and NGO mediators (formal and informal) has resulted in a corpus of policy directives, written guidelines, manuals, guidance notes, workshops and training that promote international norms, culminating in the UN 'Guidance for Effective Mediation' (UN, 2012). This seminal document outlines different norms and standards for effective mediation, ranging from national ownership to inclusivity, and was developed through an in-depth collaboration with the UN and different NGO mediators. This phenomenon has led to an emerging discourse on why normative considerations matter in mediation interventions, as a growing number of academic studies assess the impact of the promotion of different international norms in mediation such as inclusivity (Paffenholz, 2014; Donais and McCandless, 2016; Pring, 2017), gender equality (Anderlini, 2007; Cohn, 2013), transitional justice (Davis, 2014; Hayner, 2018), human rights (Julio and Drummond, 2017) and democracy (Doyle, 2005).

The growth of the normative framework in mediation resulted in part from 'expertise-focused cooperation' (Convergne, 2016a) between mediators and non-state actors (NGOs, academics, research institutions) that produce knowledge and guidance on mediation. This exchange often occurs in the framework of 'mediation support' in which individuals, organizations and bespoke structures provide technical expertise to mediators. The first mediation support unit (MSU) was created in 2006 to support UN mediators to 'offer technical and operational support to peace processes, to strengthen mediation capacity within and outside the UN … and to produce and spread knowledge materials on mediation' (Convergne, 2016b: 182). NGO mediators constitute a central part of mediation support structures as mandated mediators rely on them as additional 'layers of expertise' after core headquarters staff in the respective organizations[3] and other mediators involved in a given process (Convergne, 2016b). The UN's MSU, for instance, draws assistance and expertise from non-governmental actors, including a roster of about 200 non-governmental mediation specialists and thematic experts as well as numerous think tanks and NGOs (Convergne, 2016a). Thus, the emergence of mediation support has created a whole new set of actors who engage in a given mediation process. This trend has created space for non-state actors such as NGOs to play central roles in mediation, setting standards for policy and practice.

[3] Many mediation support structures are being developed to support regional organizations such as the European Union, the African Union and the Organization for Security and Cooperation in Europe. For more information, see Stenner (2017) and Lanz et al (2017).

NGO Mediators as Norm Entrepreneurs?

The rise of NGO mediators due to the shift towards non-state actors and the shift towards norms in mediation begets a set of important questions. First, given that NGO mediators are increasingly pressured by the mediation community of practice to promote norms in mediation processes, can NGO mediators promote norms? Second, if NGO mediators do not wield high amounts of political leverage and material resources like more formal actors such as the UN, under what conditions can they promote norms to the negotiating parties? Third, how do NGO mediators promote norms as both knowledge producers and peacemaking practitioners?

Norm diffusion theories in international relations that seek to explain how norms transfer from one context to another can elucidate to what extent NGO mediators act as norm entrepreneurs. Norm entrepreneurs are actors who try to convince actors to take on a certain norm (Finnemore and Sikkink, 1998). These norm entrepreneurs can be individuals or groups that try to change social understandings through different tools such as the 'strategic use of information, symbolic politics, leverage politics and accountability politics, issue framing, and shaming' (Finnemore and Sikkink, 2001). Many of these theories take an 'agentic' approach to norm diffusion, highlighting the role of an agent over structure in determining how norms are spread, contested, localized and internalized (Acharya, 2004; Wiener, 2014). Adapting these theories to mediation highlights how mediators draw agency from their ability to interpret their environment; act strategically based on their interpretation; and use their position to act based on their intention (Hellmüller et al, 2017). Mediators with high amounts of agency may be better placed to promote norms to the negotiating parties. In this vein, the normative agency of mediators relates to their ability to promote norms to the negotiating parties and other mediators, as well as navigate between different normative frameworks in global politics (Palmiano Federer, 2018). While formal mediators such as the UN and state actors have clear mandates, high amounts of political leverage and abundant material resources that contribute to their normative agency, the same is not the case for NGO mediators.

Thus, understanding the dual identity of NGO mediators as NGOs *and* mediators sheds light on their normative agency. NGO mediators' self-conception relies on these two identity claims. In other words, they take on the role of mediators *within* an NGO structure. First, NGO mediators are NGOs in the sense that they are non-governmental actors that act in an unofficial or private function and partner with other actors addressing a social or political issue through projects and programming (De Mars and Dijkzeul, 2015). Furthermore, NGOs conceive of themselves as global moral compasses that can make representative claims about a social issue at the grassroots level. NGO mediators also make this claim when they can capitalize on moral claims of representing a 'global civil society', especially in environments where governmental actors or international organizations suffer from crises of legitimacy. Second, NGO mediators can also take on mediation activities as mediators, mediation support actors or a combination of both. NGO mediators can send individuals to engage directly with negotiating parties in a given mediation process, conduct back channel negotiations or even convene negotiating parties in a dialogue process. NGOs can take on these roles at all mediation tracks. NGO mediators can facilitate Track 1 negotiations with official negotiating parties; provide mediation support to Track 1 mediators; facilitate parallel, informal processes between individual representatives from conflict parties (often referred to as Track 1.5); engage locally based influential persons to strengthen peace constituencies in conflict contexts on a Track 2 level; and work with grassroots community members on a Track 3 level to build broad-based public support for the process (Lanz et al, 2009). NGO mediators can concurrently take on mediation support roles that include providing technical expertise and support to other mediation actors and the mediation community of practice writ large (Haas, 1992).

Thus, NGO mediators occupy a niche space as both 'norm makers' (knowledge producers and norm setters of the normative framework in mediation) and 'norm takers', mediators who must act within certain normative parameters when they engage in a mediation process. These identity claims as both norm makers and norm takers constitute an alternative form of normative agency that relies less on political leverage and material resources and more on soft power and legitimated authority in the eyes of the negotiating parties (Vuković, 2015).

NGO Mediators as Norm Makers

NGO mediators conduct mediation activities within an NGO structure. This structure affords them agency in terms of their ability to act based on an intent or, in other words, acting through a strategy rather than a reaction (Hellmüller et al, 2017). NGO mediators conduct mediation activities via two central NGO strategies: partnering with a range of actors and producing knowledge as non-governmental, grassroots, civil society actors. This format allows NGO mediators to act as norm makers by setting norms or creating the content of the normative framework (in other words, what norms constitute the normative framework) itself. NGO mediators engage in norm-setting behaviour. NGO mediators contribute to norm setting through knowledge production practices such as conducting practice-oriented research about the practice of mediation, conducting 'lessons learned' exercises with mediators or documenting best practices, and forming networks of mediation actors to exchange lessons learned through their experiences. A primary way that NGO mediators contribute to norm setting is through writing guidance documents for the mediation community of practice. These guidance documents outline prescriptive guidelines, 'tips' and imperatives for mediation actors and clearly illustrate NGO mediators' roles in norm setting. Furthermore, NGO mediators disseminate these norms by partnering with key players within the mediation community of practice, such as the UN.

In regard to the first strategy, NGO mediators partner with a range of actors (De Mars and Dijkzeul, 2015), which facilitates their role as norm makers. The practice of partnering allows NGO mediators to draw on access to the UN, insider mediators or hard-to-reach actors, or politically unsavoury actors. Partnering gives NGOs knowledge and access on a high level that can render them legitimate in the eyes of the negotiating parties. For instance, NGO mediators often use their identity as private actors to set a norm around engaging with all actors, no matter how politically sensitive this may be (Powell, 2014; Garrigues, 2015). NGOs can act as a gateway for excluded armed groups to enter into dialogue processes with lower political risks. NGOs can also create a connection between the parties and states, as many NGOs are funded by states (Bandarage, 2011). NGOs are appealing to armed groups as interlocutors because the armed group might be open to having greater access to the outside world but cannot get through to states or the UN because of security concerns or questions surrounding political legitimacy. Another norm that NGO mediators espouse through partnerships is the norm of effective peacemaking. For instance, one of the core values underlying the German NGO mediator Berghof Foundation's approach is the belief that 'partnerships lead to better results' (Berghof Foundation, n.d.) as it allows them to create higher levels of synergy and effectiveness. The British NGO mediator Inter Mediate also refer to the increase in effectiveness that cultivating partnerships yield: '[w]herever possible Inter Mediate will draw on and leverage the resources of larger organisations – governments and international institutions that spend billions of dollars annually to deal with the effects of conflict from peacekeeping to humanitarian intervention. Our aim is to increase the effectiveness of some of that spending' (Inter Mediate, n.d.).

In regard to the second strategy, NGOs use these partnerships to disseminate the knowledge that they create. NGO mediators are also appealing to the UN and states as a source of expertise. Scholars have studied the production of expertise by the UN and its reliance on NGOs to produce it, prompting some to call NGOs the 'third UN' (Weiss et al, 2009). The UN often draws on expertise from NGO mediators in conducting research, capacity building and other activities that contribute jointly to the institutionalization and development of the mediation field (Cooper and Hocking, 2000). The growth of the normative framework in mediation is no exception: NGO mediators have contributed to the development of the field by providing input to seminal documents such as the UN 'Guidance for Effective Mediation', which promotes and formalizes the role of certain international norms in international peace mediation. For instance, the inclusivity norm, outlined in the UN 'Guidance for Effective Mediation' as the 'extent and manner in which the views and needs of conflict parties and other stakeholders are represented and integrated into the process and outcome of a mediation effort' (UN, 2012: 11) has been explicitly integrated into the mandates and policies of UN and state-level mediators. For example, the Office of the Special Envoy for Syria established the Civil Society Support Room in 2016 to incorporate the perspectives of Syrian civil society actors (Hellmüller and Zahar, 2018) in a way to foster greater civil society inclusion. Similarly, the African regional organization the Intergovernmental Authority on Development explicitly mandated the inclusion of civil society in the ongoing peace process in South Sudan (Pring, 2017). The ongoing peace processes in Colombia, Myanmar, Ukraine and many others showcase how mediators grapple with incorporating the inclusivity norm in their respective contexts. Despite these developments in practice, there is little existing empirical analysis on how NGO mediators actually promote the inclusivity norm and other norms that they have set within the normative framework in mediation.

Furthermore, NGO mediators are also characterized by their moral authority as a source of agency. Intentional or not, NGO mediators are associated with characteristics such as 'virtue' or 'moral authority' due to the nature of NGOs. Moral authority is a common identity claim among NGOs as moral global compasses (De Mars and Dijkzeul, 2015). As NGOs are relied on to monitor the ethical practices of governments and undertake humanitarian challenges (Gourevitch et al, 2012) much of their credibility stems from this reputational virtue. Their image as neutral and reliable actors contributes to this type of 'moral legitimacy' (Lehrs, 2016). While NGOs writ large claim moral legitimacy because they are broadly seen as value-based organizations, faith-based NGOs active in mediation have an even higher amount of moral authority. For instance, Indonesian-based NGO Muhammadiyah was part of the International Contact Group in the Philippines, and precisely for being faith based was important for the Moro Islamic Liberation Front to have as part of the mediation team; for them, an Islamic, faith-based NGO was chosen for observing and supporting negotiations because they wielded moral authority as a faith-based organization. However, NGO mediators do not necessarily espouse cosmopolitan norms. In fact, they may interpret international norms differently and design their mediation interventions based on pragmatism and politics rather than ethics and virtue. As norm takers, NGO mediators ironically do not always promote the norms that they create in the normative framework of mediation. While this creates complexity in mediation practice, the following explains why this nevertheless displays normative agency.

NGO Mediators as Norm Takers

NGO mediators are also norm takers in the sense that they can be constrained by certain norms. However, due to their nature as private and, in many cases, informal actors, a central element of an actor's agency is the ability to interpret the environment that they are in. This can result in NGO mediators being less constrained by different political and international norms than their formal counterparts. In the mediation field, a central part of their environment, which determines the parameters of their engagement in a mediation process, is their mandate. NGO mediators demonstrate agency in reinterpreting the concept of mandate and, in particular, normative mandates. Their redefinition of mandates into entry points creates political room for manoeuvre and political flexibility. A mandate is a set of instructions issued to a mediator by a multilateral organization that outlines the parameters of their engagement and the outcome of the process (Nathan, 2017). Mandates can range in form and function, and can be constitutional, political or normative. Mandates can also come from donors and/or the parties themselves (Nathan, 2017).

In regard to normative agency, the normative mandate, or the normative parameters of engagement, are important to consider. As previously discussed, the normative framework in mediation that constitutes the normative mandate has grown in the last 25 years (Hellmüller et al, 2015). It consists of both legal and non-legal instruments that delineate the parameters for mediators' behaviour in mediation processes. While compliance and international law has been the subject of rich study by international legal scholars and political scientists (Kastner, 2015), there is considerably less interaction around legal rules, legal norms and political norms in mediation processes because of the blurred boundaries between them, especially when legal institutions and rule of law are challenged or defunct.

While legal obligations can be distinguished between hard and soft law, a more useful way to see how legal obligations apply to mediators is to focus on their *room for manoeuvre* in mediators' implementation of applicable rules of international law. The characteristics of this room for manoeuvre stem largely from the specificity of the mandate given to the mediator. For mediators mandated by the UN, while they have the most explicit legal obligations, room for manoeuvre arises within the broad guidelines and instructions directly given to them. It results from the anarchic nature of the international system and the associated issues that arise when attempting to apply international law in conflict and post-conflict settings. For example, the dimension of criminal accountability in a mediator's mandate is often present at the formal level, but commonly broad and inaccurate, pragmatically allowing for some space for engaging with actors. There are also guidelines for mediators relating to amnesties that provide room for manoeuvre. While this may be extremely difficult, there are no hard law rules on the nature of the appendage outlining the reservation, therefore leaving the mediator with room for manoeuvre. International human rights law and international humanitarian law also offer some flexibility in specific instances. As part of customary international law, some covenants and treaties allow for some degree of derogation (for example, if a state declares a state of emergency).[4] In this vein, legal rules prohibit and create certain red lines and boundaries for mediators, depending on the context and the legal rule in question.

Despite the growth of the normative framework in mediation, little has been done to distinguish between and among these norms and to whom they apply at a given time. The UN 'Guidance for Effective Mediation' acknowledges that 'mediation takes place between normative and legal frameworks, which may have different implications for different mediators' (UN, 2012: 16). Where does the guidance lie on the conduct of NGO mediators? It is unclear if such guidance does not exist or merely remains tacit. For instance, in terms of the politically charged and sensitive issue on amnesties, there is no distinction on what type of mediators the obligation to prosecute and for criminal accountability applies to. This constructive ambiguity means that NGO mediators can have a different normative

[4] However, there are also 'serious breaches' with the obligation to investigate and prosecute, even with international customary law that does not have hard law conventions like the Genocide Convention.

framework than more formal types of mediators, such as representatives of the UN, states or regional organizations.

NGO mediators take advantage of this constructive ambiguity around mandates. They challenge the very necessity of formal mandates by placing more emphasis on the parties' mandate and entry points into a mediation context. NGO mediators do not necessarily vie for official mandates (creating competition between official and private actors) but focus rather on *entry points*, or an invitation to mediate or get involved, given by a local actor – or what Nathan calls a mandate from the parties (Nathan, 2017). This view challenges the notion of official mandate as the only approach to enter into a mediation, and further enables access to conflicts that are not yet declared or in contexts resistant to international intervention.

As NGO mediators do not have any political authority to impose conditions on the negotiating parties, to elicit this mandate from the parties, they have to sell themselves through advertising their comparative advantage over other types of mediators. This is a largely entrepreneurial approach in a political context – to a certain extent, it depends on access, contacts and entry points at a given point in time. Therefore, the *entry point* into a mediation space is a large part of the normative socialization of NGO mediators. NGO mediators can create entry points through national contacts who can sell the notion of allowing international support on less political, more technical issues. The NGO mediator would then be there to fulfil this request. Therefore, an entry point can be made without normative or political strings attached (Mediation actor, 2017a). NGO mediators will conduct different activities that may not be their biggest priority but that are important to gain access and build trust of the parties, as "we need to be seen that we are useful and valuable to them" (Mediation actor, 2017b). This constitutes another departure from classical mandates: starting from entry points, mandates from the parties can be *built*. To many NGO mediators, a mandate is a "product of what the parties want to achieve", something that is developmental, iterative and earned (Mediation actor, 2016a).

Redefining mandates as entry points consequently creates more room for manoeuvre and political flexibility around norms. NGOs are not state or UN actors bound by rigid normative and legal frameworks and conceive of themselves as "on the same level" of grassroots organizations or the non-state actors themselves. NGOs may be "extremely informal and ad hoc" with an anarchical and organic way of working (Mediation actor, 2016b), which is why a key practice of NGOs is engaging with actors with whom more formal actors like the UN do not have the time or ability to engage for political reasons (Mediation actor, 2016c). This is why NGOs often work with armed groups that are too hard-line, too sensitive for the more formal actors to engage with, or because they are not pressing on the mediation agenda of these formal actors. This informality also secures what Lehrs (2016: 391) calls 'the power of deniability', where NGO mediators can test out new things or ideas, and more powerful actors can distance themselves if things go awry. NGO mediators who can navigate their own organization and institution have a lot of room for manoeuvre in promoting or not promoting certain norms because of this political flexibility that comes with being a private or informal actor.

The Consequences of NGO Mediation

NGO mediators have been called both mavericks redefining the field and cowboys that ignore the normative and political parameters of the mediation field: 'private actors tend to operate in a judicial haze and answer only to their financial backers' (Convergne, 2016a: 140). This binary is not helpful in understanding the consequences of NGO mediation on the field. On responding to the disparaging comment of NGO mediators as cowboys, which insinuates that NGO mediators operate without consideration of rules, Martin Griffiths, the founder of the HD Centre, argues that NGO mediators *do* have a robust normative framework, it is just not as explicit as other mediators' and more self-conceptualized. In fact, because NGO mediators operate 'outside the formal diplomatic framework, they have to be "fastidious" in examining the moral dilemmas, legal obligations and operational requirements' (Martin, 2006: 68) of each scenario or situation. 'If you have to make up your own rules it tends to make you more cognizant of ethics and more disciplined … we are not cowboys at all' (Martin, 2006: 68). Especially in terms of normative agency, it is more helpful to understand NGO mediators as both norm takers and norm makers rather than rule breakers. Understanding the identity claims that NGO mediators make as both NGOs and mediators allows for richer analysis and understanding of how the rise of NGO mediators relates to norm-driven mediation interventions. NGO mediators acting as norm entrepreneurs has important implications for both mediation policy and practice.

First, while the normative turn in mediation is discussed in a growing number of studies, many mediation policymakers and practitioners are not fully cognizant of their role as norm entrepreneurs and the mechanisms through which norms are promoted. Furthermore, many actors mandated to promote norms are not aware of the outcomes of norm diffusion and what consequences norm diffusion or displacement have on a given peace process. It is especially confusing when NGO mediators simultaneously act as norm makers and norm takers without official mandates. There are clear limits to norm-driven mediation, and more empirical work needs to be done tracing the effects of norm promotion in mediation processes.

Second, understanding the specific forms of agency that NGO mediators have to promote norms sheds light on the increasing heterogeneity of mediators and the distinct sources of agency that they draw on to forward an intent (in this case, promoting norms). The emergence of NGO mediators as both mediation actors convening negotiating parties in dialogue processes as well as mediation support actors providing assistance to other mediators can create confusion and coordination issues about role clarity in practice. Understanding the different sources of agency among different kinds of mediators can offer new types of coordination, such as outsourcing and risk sharing (Palmiano Federer, 2018) between formal and informal actors. However, when multiparty mediation takes place (Crocker et al, 2015) the consequences of multiple norm entrepreneurs on a given peace process are not clear.

Third, the link between knowledge production via the increasing professionalization of the mediation field and the shift to norm-driven mediation must be better understood. NGO mediators play a significant role in both fields, both as knowledge producers and mediators. Both norm-driven mediation and the professionalization of the field are viewed as a vehicle towards more effective mediation practice. However, as other chapters in this volume suggest, this may not always be the case. Assuming that effective mediation can be achieved through greater professionalization of the field or an increasingly robust normative framework risks undermining contextual and local knowledge and experience of the conflict context. Normative or technical approaches to mediation may not always result in effective outcomes.

Conclusion

This chapter discussed the normative agency of NGO mediators. By understanding the conditions under which NGO mediators can promote norms both to other mediators and the negotiating parties, this chapter provides a more nuanced analytical take on the impact these types of mediators have on mediation. NGO mediators are neither mavericks nor cowboys, but complex actors that occupy niche spaces as both NGOs and mediators. They are both mediators and mediation support actors. They are both norm shapers and norm takers. These multiple identity claims and self-conceptions provide the basis of their normative agency: their ability to interpret and redefine the notion of mandate for greater political flexibility in practice as well as their ability to conduct mediation activities within NGO structures. These alternate sources of agency provide legitimacy for NGO mediators to engage directly with negotiating parties and also promote certain norms. The limits of normative agency become clear when NGO mediators are not cognizant of their role as norm entrepreneurs and do not have the agency to control the outcome of the norm diffusion process. This can have negative effects on peace processes. The normative agency of different types of mediators must be studied respectively as the mediation field continues to become increasingly normative in nature.

References

Aall, P. (1996) 'NGOs and Conflict Management', *United States Institute of Peace*, [online], available from: https://www.usip.org/sites/default/files/pwks5.pdf (accessed 28 July 2019).

Aall, P. (2000) 'NGOs, Conflict Management, and Peacekeeping', *International Peacekeeping*, 7(1), 121–41

Acharya, A. (2004) 'How Ideas Spread: Whose Norms Matter? Norm Localization and Institutional Change in Asian Regionalism', *International Organization*, 58, 239–57.

Anderlini, S.N. (2007) *Women Building Peace: What They Do, Why It Matters*, Boulder, CO: Lynne Reinner Publishers.

Babbitt, E.F. (2009) 'The Evolution of International Conflict Resolution: From Cold War to Peacebuilding', *Negotiation Journal*, 25(4), 539–49.

Bailey, S.D. (1985) 'Non-official Mediation in Disputes: Reflections on Quaker Experiences', *International Affairs*, 61(2), 205–22.

Bandarage, A. (2011) 'The "Norwegian Model": Political Economy of NGO Peacemaking', *The Brown Journal of World Affairs*, 17(2), 221–42.

Beardsley, K. (2009) 'Intervention Without Leverage: Explaining the Prevalence of Weak Mediators', *International Interactions*, 35(3), 272–97.

Bercovitch, J. (2009), 'Mediation and Conflict Resolution' in Bercovitch, J., Kremenyuk, V. and Zartman, W.I. (eds.) *The Sage Handbook of Conflict Resolution*, London: Sage.

Bercovitch, J., Anagnoson, T. and Wille, D. (1991) 'Some Conceptual Issues and Empirical Trends in the Study of Successful Mediation in International Relations', *Journal of Peace Research*, 28(1), 7–17.

Berghof Foundation (n.d.) 'How We Work', [online], available from: https://www.berghof-foundation.org/en/about-us/how-we-work/ (accessed 26 July 2019).

Campbell, S., Chandler, D. and Shabaratnam, M. (2011) *A Liberal Peace? The Problems and Practices of Peacebuilding*, London: Zed Books Ltd.

Chetail, V. (2009) *Post-Conflict Peacebuilding: A Lexicon*, Oxford: Oxford University Press.

Cohn, C. (2013) *Women and Wars: Contested Histories, Uncertain Futures*, Cambridge: Polity Press.

Cooper, A.F. and Hocking, B. (2000) 'Governments, Non-Governmental Organisations and the Re-Calibration of Diplomacy', *Global Society*, 14(3), 361–76.

Convergne, E. (2016a) 'UN Mediators' Collaboration with Scholars and Expert NGOs: Explaining the Need for Knowledge-based Communities in Today's Conflicts', *International Negotiation*, 21(1), 135–64.

Convergne, E. (2016b) 'Learning to Mediate? The Mediation Support Unit and the Production of Expertise by the UN', *Journal of Intervention and Statebuilding*, 10(2), 181–99.

Cortell, A. and Davis, J.W. (2000) 'Understanding the Domestic Impact of International Norms: A Research Agenda', *International Studies Association*, 2(1), 65–87.

Crocker, C., Hampson, F.O. and Aall, P. (1999) *Herding Cats: Multiparty Mediation in a Complex World*, Washington, DC: United States Institute of Peace Press.

Crocker, C., Hampson, F.O. and Aall, P. (2004) *Taming Intractable Conflicts: Mediation in the Hardest Cases*, Washington, DC: United States Institute of Peace.

Crocker, C., Hampson, F.O. and Aall, P. (2015) 'The Shifting Sands of Peacemaking: Challenges of Multiparty Mediation', *International Negotiation*, 20(3), 363–88.

Davis, L. (2014) *EU Foreign Policy, Transitional Justice and Mediation: Principle, Policy and Practice*, Abingdon: Routledge.

De Mars, W.E. and Dijkzeul, D. (2015) *The NGO Challenge for International Relations Theory*, Abingdon: Routledge.

Donais, T. and McCandless, E. (2016) 'International Peacebuilding and the Emerging Inclusivity Norm', *Third World Quarterly*, 38(2), 291–310.

Doyle, M. (2005) 'Three Pillars of Liberal Peace', *American Political Science Review*, 99(3), 463–6.

Fearon, J.D. and Laitin, D.D. (2003) 'Ethnicity, Insurgency, and Civil War', *American Political Science Review*, 97(1), 75–90.

Finnemore, M. and Sikkink, K. (1998) 'International Norm Dynamics and Political Change', *International Organization*, 52(4), 887–917.

Finnemore, M. and Sikkink, K. (2001) 'Taking Stock: The Constructivist Research Program in International Relations and Comparative Politics', *Annual Review of Political Science*, 4, 391–416.

Garrigues, J. (2015) *The Case for Contact: Overcoming the Challenges and Dilemmas of Official and Non-official Mediation with Armed Groups*, Oslo: The Norwegian Peacebuilding Resources Centre.

Greig, M. and Diehl, P. (2012) *International Mediation*, Cambridge: Polity Press.

Haas, P.M. (1992) 'Introduction: Epistemic Communities and International Policy Coordination', *International Organization*, 46(1), 1–35.

Hare, P. (1992) 'Informal Mediation by Private Individuals' in Bercovitch, J. and Rubin, J.Z. (eds.) *Mediation in International Relations: Multiple Approaches to Conflict Management*, Basingstoke: Macmillan.

Hayner, P. (2018) *The Peacemaker's Paradox: Pursuing Justice in the Shadow of Conflict*, Abingdon: Routledge.

Hellmüller, S., Palmiano Federer, J. and Pring, J. (2017) 'Are Mediators Norm Entrepreneurs?', *swisspeace Working Paper*, [online] March, available from: https://www.swisspeace.ch/assets/publications/downloads/Working-Papers/b59c7cb279/Are-Mediators-Norm-Entrepreneurs-17-swisspeace-sara_hellmueller-julia_palmiano_federer-jamie_pring.pdf (accessed 26 July 2019).

Hellmüller, S., Palmiano Federer, J. and Zeller, M. (2015) 'The Role of Norms in International Peace Mediation' *swisspeace and NOREF*, [online] April, available from: https://www.swisspeace.ch/fileadmin/user_upload/Media/Publications/The_Role_of_Norms_in_International_Peace_Mediation.pdf (accessed 9 August 2019).

Hellmüller, S. and Zahar, M. (2018) *Against the Odds: Civil Society in the Intra-Syrian Talks*, New York, NY: International Peace Institute.

Hsieh, H.F. and Shannon, S.E. (2005) 'Three Approaches to Qualitative Content Analysis', *Qualitative Health Research*, 15(9), 1277–88.

Gourevitch, P.A., Lake, D.A. and Stein, J.G. (2012) *The Credibility of Transnational NGOs: When Virtue Is Not Enough*, New York, NY: Cambridge University Press.

Inter Mediate (n.d.) 'Mission', [online], available from: http://www.inter-mediate.org/mission.html (accessed 26 July 2019).

Josselin, D. and Wallace, W. (2001) *Non-state Actors in World Politics*, New York, NY: Palgrave.

Julio, C.F. and Drummond, P. (eds.) (2017) *Human Rights and Conflict Resolution: Bridging the Theoretical and Practical Divide*, New York, NY: Routledge.

Kaldor, M. (1999) *New and Old Wars*, Palo Alto, CA: Stanford University Press.

Kalyvas, S. (2001) '"New" and "Old" Civil Wars: A Valid Distinction?', *World Politics*, 54, 99–118.

Kastner, P. (2015) *Legal Normativity in the Resolution of Internal Armed Conflict*, Cambridge: Cambridge University Press.

Kriesberg, L. (1997), 'The Development of the Conflict Resolution Field' in Zartman, W.I. and Rasmussen, J.L. (eds.) *Peacemaking in International Conflict: Methods and Techniques*, Washington, DC: United States Institute of Peace Press.

Kydd, A. (2010) 'Rationalist Approaches to Conflict Prevention and Resolution', *Annual Review of Political Science*, 13, 101–21.

Lanz, D., Pring, J., Von Burg, C. and Zeller, M. (2017) 'Understanding Mediation Support Structures', *swisspeace*, [online], October, available from: https://www.swisspeace.ch/assets/publications/downloads/Reports/589fa0b148/swisspeace-MSS-study.pdf (accessed 28 July 2019).

Lanz, D., Sguaitamatti, D. and Siegfried, M. (2009) 'Towards Realizing the Strengths and Mitigating the Challenges of NGO Mediators', *swisspeace and Center for Security Studies, ETH Zurich*, [online], February, available from: https://www.swisspeace.ch/fileadmin/user_upload/Media/Topics/Mediation/Resources/Lanz__David__Damiano_Sguaitamatti_and_Matthias_Siegfried_Towards_Realizing_the_Strengths_and_Mitigating_the_Challenges_of_NGO_Mediators.pdf (accessed 26 July 2019).

Lederach, J.P. (1997) *Building Peace: Sustainable Reconciliation in Divided Societies*, Washington, DC: United States Institute of Peace.

Lehrs, L. (2016) 'Private Peace Entrepreneurs in Conflict Resolution Processes', *International Negotiation*, 21(3), 381–408.

Lehti, M. (2018) *The Era of Private Peacemakers: A New Dialogic Approach to Mediation*, Berlin: Springer.

Mac Ginty, R. (2011) *International Peacebuilding and Local Resistance: Hybrid Forms of Peace*, Basingstoke: Palgrave Macmillan.

Martin, H. (2006) *Kings of Peace, Pawns of War: The Untold Story of Peacemaking*, London: Continuum.

Mediation actor (2017a), interviewed by telephone in Mawlamyine, Myanmar by Julia Palmiano Federer, October 2017.

Mediation actor (2017b), interviewed in Yangon, Myanmar by Julia Palmiano Federer, March 2017.

Mediation actor (2016a), interviewed by Skype in Bern, Switzerland by Julia Palmiano Federer, October 2016.

Mediation actor (2016b), interviewed by Skype in Bern, Switzerland by Julia Palmiano Federer, October 2016.

Mediation actor (2016c), interviewed in Bern, Switzerland by Julia Palmiano Federer, November 2016.

Nathan, L. (2017) 'Marching Orders: Exploring the Mediation Mandate', *African Security*, 3–4, 155–75.

Paffenholz, T. (2014) 'Civil Society and Peace Negotiations: Beyond the Inclusion-Exclusion Dichotomy', *Negotiation Journal*, 30(1), 69–91.

Palmiano Federer, J. (2018) 'We Do Negotiate With Terrorists: Navigating Liberal and Illiberal Norms in Peace Mediation', *Critical Studies on Terrorism*, 12(1), 19–39.

Paris, R. (2004) *At War's End: Building Peace After Civil Conflict*, Cambridge: Cambridge University Press.

Paris, R. (2002) 'International Peacebuilding and the "Mission Civilisatrice"', *Review of International Studies*, 28, 637–56.

Powell, J. (2014) *Talking to Terrorists: How to End Armed Conflicts*, New York, NY: Random House.

Princen, T. (1992) 'Mediation by a Transnational Organization: The Case of the Vatican'. In Bercovitch, J. and Rubin, J.Z. (eds.) *Mediation in International Relations: Multiple Approaches to Conflict Management*, Basingstoke: Macmillan.

Pring, J. (2017) 'Including or Excluding Civil Society? The Role of the Mediation Mandate for South Sudan (2013–2015) and Zimbabwe (2008–2009)', *African Security*, 1–16.

Richmond, O.P. (2018) 'A Genealogy of Mediation in International Relations: From "Analogue" to "Digital" Forms of Global Justice or Managed War?' *Cooperation and Conflict*, 53(3), 301–19.

Shea, N. (2016) 'Nongovernmental Organisations as Mediators: Making Peace in Aceh, Indonesia', *Global Change, Peace & Security*, 28(2), 177–96.

Stenner, C. (2017) 'The Institutionalization of Mediation Support: Are Mediation Support Entities There Yet?', *Berghof Foundation*, [online] available from: https://www.berghof-foundation.org/fileadmin/redaktion/Publications/Other_Resources/Stenner_TheInstitutionalizationOfMediationSupport.pdf (accessed 28 July 2019).

Taulbee, J.L. and Creekmore, M.V. (2003) 'NGO Mediation: The Carter Center', *International Peacekeeping*, 10(1), 156–71.

UN (2012) 'Guidance for Effective Mediation', [online], available from: https://peacemaker.un.org/sites/peacemaker.un.org/files/GuidanceEffectiveMediation_UNDPA2012%28english%29_0.pdf (accessed 25 July 2019).

Vuković, S. (2015) 'Soft Power, Bias and Manipulation of International Negotiations in International Mediation', *International Negotiation*, 20, 414–43.

Walter, B. (1997) 'The Critical Barrier to Civil War Settlement', *International Organization*, 51(3), 335–64.

Weiss, T.G., Carayannis, T. and Jolly, R. (2009) 'The "Third" United Nations', *Global Governance: A Review of Multilateralism and International Organizations*, 15(1), 123–42.

Wiener, A. (2014) *A Theory of Contestation*, Heidelberg: Springer.
Yarrow, C.H.M. (1978) *Quaker Experiences in International Conciliation*, New Haven CT: Yale University Press.
Zanker, F. (2014) 'Legitimate Representation: Civil Society Actors in Peace Negotiations Revisited', *International Negotiation*, 19, 62–88.
Zartman, W.I. and Touval, S. (1985) 'International Mediation: Conflict Resolution and Power Politics', *Journal of Social Issues*, 41(2), 27–45.

6

The Challenges of Legalized Peacemaking: The Case of the 2012–16 Peace Negotiations in Colombia

Asli Ozcelik

Introduction

The normativization of peace mediation, particularly by reference to international law, has shaped the field significantly in the 21st century. The United Nations (UN), regional organizations, international financial institutions, states active in the field of mediation, and non-governmental organizations have all adopted codes of conduct, guidelines and policies to provide their mediators with normative and operational guidance (see, for example, UN, 2012; ACCORD and AU, 2014; OSCE, 2014). In addition to articulating new norms of peacemaking, these documents increasingly urge compliance with international law in peace mediation. For example, the UN Guidance for Effective Mediation (UN, 2012: 16) states that peace agreements should 'respect international humanitarian, human rights and refugee laws' and that mediation takes place 'within the framework constituted by … global and regional conventions, international humanitarian law, human rights and refugee laws and international criminal law, including, where applicable, the Rome Statute of the International Criminal Court'. Consequently, as noted by the European External Action Service (2016: 2), 'those mediating in conflicts today are faced with clearer, more comprehensive, but also more complex, international legal and normative frameworks that attempt to define what is (and what is not) acceptable in negotiations to end armed violence'.

The increasing role attached to international law in peace mediation is driven by the assumption in international policy that conformity with international law and norms contributes to the 'legitimacy' of the negotiation process and 'durability' of the resultant peace agreements (UN, 2012; ACCORD and AU, 2014). The existence of a normative framework, the assumption goes, provides negotiating parties with a common, objective language to frame their demands and stipulates outer limits that render certain issues non-negotiable. Although they bind and guide the mediators affiliated to the respective organization, the guidelines and policy documents laying out normative parameters for peace mediation indirectly create a normative framework for peace negotiations as the ultimate aim is compliance by the negotiating parties. The availability of normative parameters thus facilitates negotiations that take place in the shadow of violence and in an atmosphere of mutual distrust between states and armed opposition groups.

This chapter challenges these assumptions circulated in international policy and scholarship by probing into the contingency and complexity of the roles international law plays in peace negotiations. Despite some of its advantages, the norm-driven approach to peace mediation, particularly as it pertains to international law, should be tempered with caution when mediation policy and practices are determined. To date, calls for caution and humility as to what laws and norms can achieve and risk in negotiated transitions have predominantly focused on their constraining effect for pragmatic peacemaking solutions and on the tension between the global and local norms and practices. Building on these lines of criticisms, two further reasons that warrant caution towards the legalization of peacemaking are explored in this chapter, drawing on lessons from the highly legalized peace negotiations between the Colombian government and the Fuerzas Armadas Revolucionarias de Colombia (FARC-EP) during 2012–16, particularly in relation to the negotiation of the transitional justice component of the resultant Final Agreement to End the Armed Conflict and Build a Stable and Lasting Peace (2016, hereinafter the Final Peace Agreement): (i) the discrepancy between arguments made in the name of law and *lex lata* (the law as it currently stands), and (ii) the malleability of international law to interpretation and strategic instrumentalization.

The 2012–16 Colombian negotiation episode provides a useful case study for three main reasons. First, the 'legal cultural propensity to formal legalised documentation of each piece-meal peace process' in Colombia (Bell et al, 2015: 1) makes it possible to have access to such documents and has led to the characterization of negotiations by legal argumentation.

Connected to this, secondly, are the ample references to international law during both the negotiations and the resultant agreements. Lastly, the process has been judicialized at both domestic and international levels with the actual or potential future involvement of the Colombian Constitutional Court, Inter-American Court of Human Rights (IACtHR) and the International Criminal Court (ICC). This has amplified the role of legal norms in the negotiations and thus enables an analysis of how various domestic and international actors strategically interpreted international law under the shadow of three courts (Hillebrecht et al, 2018). The case study is introduced in the third section, following the explanation of the roles of international law in peace mediation in the second section. The fourth section then discusses the challenges of legalized peace mediation in light of the Colombian episode.

The Prescriptive and Functional Roles of International Law in Peace Mediation

In the context of peace mediation and negotiation, international law is first and foremost seen as a source of normative prescriptions (Wählisch, 2016). A distinction commonly made in this regard is between process-related and content-related norms (see, for example, Hellmüller et al, 2015). The former pertains to inclusion and exclusion of certain actors in peace processes and the impartiality and neutrality of mediators. It is argued in particular that international legal norms require in a peace process the inclusion of civil society, women, and the affected minority and indigenous groups or the exclusion of certain actors such as (alleged) perpetrators of international crimes or 'coupists' involved in an unconstitutional change of government (see, for example, Levitt, 2012; Saliternik, 2016). As to content, it is suggested both in policy and scholarship that international law proscribes certain compromise arrangements such as amnesties for international crimes and serious violations of human rights or exclusionary power sharing, while prescribing certain substantive guarantees such as the inclusion of human rights guarantees in a peace agreement. Moreover, although the Rome Statute does not impose obligations on states, except for obligations of cooperation with the ICC, the complementarity test creates an imperative of compliance with its requirements for those who desire to avoid an investigation. Negotiating peace in the shadow of the ICC also affects the process of negotiations; the duty of the states parties to cooperate with the Court and hand in persons subject to arrest warrants means that peace talks with such persons cannot be held in the territory of states parties and where they are held elsewhere, mediators affiliated to states parties to the Statute or to the UN are to avoid non-essential contacts with persons subject to arrest warrants.

Examining the extent to which the ascertained roles of international law are borne out by *lex lata*, or remain 'normative expectations' as opposed to international legal obligations as the UN Guidance for Effective Mediation acknowledges (UN, 2012), is beyond the scope of this chapter. What is important for the purposes of this chapter is to point out the prescriptive role attached to international law in the policy and scholarship of peace mediation. In this respect, it should also be added that, in addition to the negotiation process and content of peace agreements, international law bears relevance to agreement implementation; for example, the Security Council may demand compliance where violations of a peace agreement threaten international peace and security, and international actors, particularly the UN, undertake significant roles in the implementation of peace agreements. Consistency with international law is therefore also presented as a potential requirement for international support to the implementation of an agreement (UN, 2017).

Beyond the prescriptive role of international law in peace mediation, some scholars point out its constitutive, symbolic or functional roles. The scholarly emphasis on the non-prescriptive roles of international law dovetails with the policy assumption that international law promises to bring legitimacy and certainty to peace negotiations. First, law can provide certainty through its normative prescriptions and delineate the bargaining zone (Dajani, 2007). For example, blanket amnesties that foreclose any form of accountability for certain international crimes and serious violations of human rights or certain political power-sharing arrangements that restrict individual human rights unjustifiably may amount to a violation of the negotiating state's relevant international obligations. Although, as will be argued in the fourth section, the prescriptive reach of international law relevant to peacemaking is far more limited than it is often purported to be, to the extent that it is relevant, applicable and sufficiently specified, international law provides clarity as to the legal confines of the peacemaking space by constraining the arrangements available to mediators and negotiators.

More broadly, international law is believed to bring certainty to peace processes by functioning as an enduring normative framework, while everything else, including the constitutional order, political and military power structures, control over wealth sources, and even political identities, is subject to negotiation. Sriram (2017) thus suggests, in a critical vein, that international policymakers employ international law as a 'tool' to overcome the indeterminacies of transitions. Peace negotiations take place between actors that do not trust each other, where either there is no respect for the domestic legal system as it is seen as one of the root causes of the conflict, or the existing rules and institutions are too weak and ineffective. In such conditions, especially when peacemaking requires departures from the existing constitutional order, scholars argue that international law may function as the 'law of laws', that is a 'source of normative transcendence' (Teitel, 1997; Kastner, 2015). Writing in the broader context of political transitions, this is one of the roles Teitel (1997) attaches to the 'transformative' international law that can mediate legal and political tensions and transcend domestic law and politics.

Secondly, at the intersection of certainty and legitimacy concerns, there is an emphasis on the function of international law as a common language and framework in which mediators, negotiating parties and other affected actors can frame their positions (Dajani, 2007; Turner, 2016). Particularly, international human rights law and humanitarian law provide peacemaking actors with a framework for the negotiation of various issues, ranging from ceasefires to elections and political parties. In this respect, it is claimed that using law to frame peace negotiations also enables rational bargaining despite the 'cognitive and emotional barriers' both between the negotiating parties and among the broader public (Saliternik, 2016). Furthermore, it may help mediators retain their neutrality and impartiality by framing their normative ambitions in relation to the adoption of certain procedural or substantive peacemaking modalities as rooted in international law and escape the accusation of interventionist mediation (Mediation Support Network, 2013).

This section identified the prescriptive roles of international law in peace mediation and negotiation, as well as the functional roles commonly attached to it in peacemaking policy and scholarship. Against this background and focusing on the transitional justice chapter of the Agreement, the next section introduces the 2016 Final Peace Agreement concluded in Colombia and its negotiation process, with a view to testing in the fourth section the extent to which international law fulfilled the prescriptive and functional roles attached to it and examining where and why it failed to do so.

The 2012–16 Peace Negotiations between the Colombian Government and the FARC-EP

Background to the Conclusion of the 2016 Final Peace Agreement: a Legalized Negotiation Process

The armed conflict between the government and the FARC-EP, which marred Colombia for over five decades with a staggering toll of victims, was brought to an end with the conclusion of the Final Peace Agreement on 24 August 2016 and the resulting transformation of the FARC-EP to a political party. The Agreement, a substantial document consisting of six main chapters on (i) rural reform, (ii) political participation of former guerrillas, (iii) ceasefire and disarmament, (iv) illicit crops, (v) victims, and (vi) implementation and verification, was the outcome of the peace negotiations of 2012–16, which were highly internationalized, legalized and judicialized. As will be explored later, these dynamics had both benefits and drawbacks for the conclusion of the Agreement by the parties and its subsequent reception by other groups in Colombian society.

The internationalization of the process had various dimensions, ranging from the location of the talks to the involvement of third state guarantors and international mediators in the negotiations, and from the references to international instruments in the Agreement to the envisaged role of the Security Council in the Agreement's implementation. The Track 1 negotiations between the teams of the government and the FARC-EP took place predominantly in Havana, facilitated by guarantor countries Cuba and Norway, observer countries Venezuela and Chile, and Special Envoys of the UN, European Union (EU), United States (US) and Germany (Final Peace Agreement, 2016). As international actors, particularly the UN, often act as 'norm entrepreneurs' in peace negotiations (Kastner, 2015), their involvement also influences the design of negotiation processes and resultant peace agreements. For example, the official negotiations in Colombia were supplemented by a broader, inclusive process that involved victims, women, Lesbian, Gay, Bisexual, Transgender and Intersex (LGBTI), and indigenous groups, in accordance with (but not necessarily merely because of) the inclusivity norm promoted in international peacemaking policy. The resultant Agreement was welcomed by the Security Council in Resolution 2307 (2016) and cautiously endorsed by the Prosecutor of the ICC.

In addition to being internationalized as such, the negotiations were also heavily legalized. Domestic and international actors used the vocabulary of international law during the negotiations to frame their positions, either in support of or in opposition to the agreement that was being negotiated, in televised debates or published documents. Particularly, the discussions on the legal status and legality of the transitional justice system were infused with references to international law both by the negotiating parties and by other domestic and international actors. Furthermore, the Agreement, as a rare example in intra-state peacemaking instruments, claims 'international standing'; it is signed expressly as a Special Agreement under Common Article 3 of the Geneva Conventions and deposited before the Swiss Federal Council in Bern, as well as including a request to be incorporated in a Security Council Resolution. As a simplistic yet helpful indicator of the role of international law in the negotiations, the Agreement also contains several references to international legal instruments; for example, it refers to the Rome Statute alone 12 times (Preamble, Final Peace Agreement, 2016).

Legalization of the negotiation process, particularly by reference to international law, may be attributed to many reasons, including the legal culture in Colombia and the involvement of international actors in the negotiations. It was also a result of the judicialized nature of the process as the negotiations took place in the shadow of three courts: the Colombian Constitutional Court, the ICC and the IACtHR. First, the Colombian Constitutional Court has pronounced on the constitutionality of the (renegotiated) 2016 Final Peace Agreement, implementing laws, and laws enacted throughout the peace negotiations in a series of decisions. Article 93 (1993) of the Colombian Constitution gives 'domestic priority' to international human rights treaties and stipulates that the rights enshrined will be interpreted in accordance with such treaties. Due to this status of international law within the Colombian constitutional system, the decisions of the Constitutional Court relating to the peace process involved pronouncements on the relevant international law as part of the constitutionality review of the implementing laws and contributed to the legalization of the negotiations by reference to international law. The role of the Court in legalizing the negotiations was heightened particularly as the Court reviewed the constitutionality of the laws, which aimed to create a legal space for the peace negotiations or implement some of the interim agreements piecemeal, simultaneously with the negotiations.

Secondly, as Colombia has been under preliminary examination by the ICC Office of the Prosecutor (OTP) since 2004, the OTP has had an influential role in the negotiation and implementation processes of the Agreement. In addition to commenting on the negotiations through its official reports on the state of the preliminary examination, the OTP officials had meetings with government officials and civil society groups, made press statements signalling the OTP position in relation to issues that were negotiated by the parties at the given time, and even submitted an amicus curiae brief (a brief filed with the court by someone who is not a party to the case, literally a 'friend of the court') in relation to the review of the law implementing the transitional justice chapter of the Agreement by the Colombian Constitutional Court (Hillebrecht et al, 2018). Such indirect involvement of the ICC in peace processes, for example in Uganda and Kenya as well as in Colombia, positions the ICC as 'a third-party actor' in peace negotiations 'in an abstract sense' (Gissel, 2017). Accordingly, as will be explained in the next section, the involvement of the OTP in the peace process and the threat of investigation by the ICC significantly shaped the negotiations and the resulting Agreement in Colombia.

Lastly, the IACtHR also played an important, albeit much more indirect, role in the negotiations, particularly due to its case law on the issue of amnesties for serious violations of human rights. Establishing a duty to investigate and to punish under the Convention, the Court consistently rejected the compatibility of general and unconditional amnesties with the Convention, which cover serious human rights violations and aim to prevent their investigation and punishment (see, for example, *Barrios Altos v Peru*, 2001; *Gomes Lund et al v Brazil*, 2010; *El Mozote v El Salvador*, 2012). However, the Court acknowledged the compatibility with the Convention of limited amnesties that exclude serious human rights violations from their scope and the exceptional application of reduced or alternative yet proportionate criminal sanctions in transitions (*Rochela Massacre v Colombia*, 2005). Furthermore, in his concurring opinion in *El Mozote v El Salvador*, Judge Garcia-Sayán indicated that the selective prosecution of those most responsible for serious human rights violations may also be justified 'in the context of a process aimed at ending, through negotiations, a non-international armed conflict', given the 'enormous legal and ethical requirements in the search to harmonize criminal justice and negotiated peace' (*El Mozote v El Salvador*, 2012). The fact that the parties cited this Concurring Opinion in Chapter 5.1.2 of the Agreement clearly attests to the fact that they were mindful of the case law of the IACtHR during the negotiations.

Although the Agreement was adopted as a result of an internationalized, legalized and judicialized negotiation process, its conclusion and ratification into Colombian law have faced several obstacles, not least with the rejection of the Agreement by a plebiscite on 2 October 2016, albeit by a narrow margin of 0.4 per cent. The Agreement was eventually renegotiated by the parties and ratified by the Congress without a further public vote. However, its implementation continues to face challenges under a new government elected after the conclusion of the Agreement and with an express campaign promise to reverse certain aspects of its implementation, especially in relation to the transitional justice system put in place as per the Agreement. Several issues proved to be controversial during the negotiation and implementation of the Agreement, including the legal status of the Peace Agreement, its gender inclusivity, the tension between land reform and private rights, and most notably the transitional justice system envisaged by the Agreement. Various domestic and international actors and groups, ranging from the right wing 'No' campaign of former President Uribe to the Americas

Division of Human Rights Watch, and from the OTP to the religious groups in society, voiced concerns about these aspects of the Agreement, referencing international law or the international normative agendas in peacemaking. What is notable for the purposes of this chapter is that the two most legalized aspects of the negotiations and the resultant Agreement, that is, its legal status and transitional justice component, were identified by commentators as the main reasons behind the opposition to the Agreement and the plebiscite defeat (Huneeus and Urueña, 2016). The next section zeroes in on the transitional justice component of the Agreement, that is, the Victims' Agreement, and the debate surrounding its legal status, with a particular focus on the role of international law.

Negotiated Justice: the Victims' Agreement

Chapter Five of the Final Peace Agreement, titled the Victims' Agreement, lays out the 'Comprehensive System for Truth, Justice, Reparations and Non-Recurrence' adopted by the parties and was incorporated into Colombian law through a constitutional amendment, namely Legislative Act 01 of 4 April 2017. Considerations of compliance with international law, particularly with the Rome Statute, have permeated various aspects of the negotiation of the Victims' Agreement. This is evidenced by the explicit references to international law both in the text of the Agreement and in the statements of the domestic and international actors involved in the peace negotiations and the post-plebiscite renegotiation process. The references to international law, however, did not translate into widely accepted normative parameters or an enhanced perceived legitimacy of the Agreement. Instead, they added fuel to the transitional justice debate, with a plethora of differing, and at times contradictory, interpretations of the relevant law.

At the core of the Victims' Agreement are the provision of an amnesty for political and related crimes, by explicit reference to Article 6(5) of the 1977 Additional Protocol II to the Geneva Conventions of 12 August 1949, and the establishment of a judicial mechanism as part of the Colombian legal system, the Special Jurisdiction for Peace (JEP), to deal with the most serious crimes committed in the context and by reason of the armed conflict. Article 40 of the Agreement (2016) guarantees that

> [c]rimes against humanity, genocide, serious war crimes – that is, any violation of international humanitarian law committed as part of a systematic attack – hostage taking or other serious deprivations of freedom, torture, extrajudicial executions,

> forced disappearances, rape and other forms of sexual violence, child abduction, forced displacement and the recruitment of minors will all be ineligible for an amnesty or pardon, in every case as established in the Rome Statute.

As to these crimes, the JEP may impose alternative criminal sanctions in the form of restraint of liberty for five to eight years to perpetrators who confess to their crimes in an early fashion and prison sentences of up to eight years for those who confess later but before a judgment. Those who fail to admit responsibility for the crimes committed will be subject to prison sentences of up to 20 years. The crimes will be deemed more serious by the JEP when committed against women or persons belonging to vulnerable groups that are subject to special protection, such as indigenous peoples, internally displaced persons and refugees, minors, LGBTI and elderly people. The Tribunal can also order reparations and guarantees of non-recurrence and operates alongside a truth commission, and the Comprehensive System is to operate with 'an equity-based and gender-based approach' (Part 5.1., Final Peace Agreement, 2016).

During the negotiations, two aspects of the Agreement's complex transitional justice system proved to be particularly controversial from an international law perspective, namely, case prioritization and alternative criminal sanctions. Some domestic actors, international lawyers, Amnesty International (AI) and Human Rights Watch (HRW) asserted that the alternative sanctions that will be imposed by the JEP do not reflect the gravity of the crimes committed during the conflict (see, for example, AI, 2016; HRW, 2017). During the renegotiation of the Agreement, former President Uribe published a counter-proposal (2016) laying out what could be the bases for an acceptable peace agreement in his view. Referencing international law, particularly the Rome Statute, several times, this document sets out Uribe's interpretation of the relevant law and rejects the legality of the alternative criminal sanctions. This line of criticism is also pursued by the incumbent President Duque in his attempts to undo some aspects of the Agreement's implementation. In addition to the issues of case prioritization and alternative criminal sanctions, the scope of the political crimes that would benefit from the amnesty was also unsatisfactory to the opposition groups, despite excluding international crimes and serious violations of human rights and gaining the ICC Prosecutor's approval. For example, Uribe expressed his concern that the crimes of drug trafficking and kidnapping could be pardoned as 'related offences' to political crimes (Uribe, 2016), although this is in violation of neither Colombian nor international law. In addition to providing an example of the differing views on the legality of the transitional justice system of the Agreement, as will be explored in the next section, Uribe's position also demonstrates how international law may be instrumentalized by actors, regardless of whether they are in fact driven by legality concerns in their opposition to a peace agreement.

The OTP also weighed in on the issues of case prioritization and alternative criminal sanctions. Contrary to the actors mentioned earlier, however, the OTP's opposition to the negotiating parties' approaches on these issues evolved over time. As to case prioritization, the OTP had raised concerns about the selection and prioritization of cases concerning those most responsible for conflict-related crimes as part of the envisaged transitional justice framework, when the Colombian Congress approved a constitutional amendment, known as the Legal Framework for Peace (LFP), at the outset of the negotiations in 2012 (ICC-OTP, 2012). Due to this focus of the legislation, according to the OTP, it appeared to shield perpetrators who committed crimes within the jurisdiction of the Court but were not among those most responsible for these crimes, that is the low-level offenders, from criminal accountability. As to alternative criminal sanctions, it was reported that the ICC Prosecutor rejected outright the adequacy of alternative criminal sanctions without prison time for compliance with the Rome Statute (Seils, 2015: 5).

The OTP changed its position on both issues over the course of the negotiations. By 2014 the OTP had seemingly departed from its earlier position on case prioritization and confined its examination to whether the domestic judgments delivered thus far focused on those most responsible for the most serious crimes committed (ICC-OTP, 2014). As to alternative criminal sanctions, in a speech he gave in Colombia, the Deputy Prosecutor Stewart (2015) offered a less assertive interpretation of the Rome Statute that sanctions that are proportionate to the gravity of the crimes committed would suffice for the purposes of complementarity regardless of whether imprisonment was foreseen. Despite the change of position in relation to the two issues, the OTP remains concerned regarding the 'consistency or compatibility with customary international law and the Rome Statute' of four aspects of the JEP legislative framework: 'the definition of command responsibility, the definition of "grave" war crimes, the determination of "active or determinative" participation in the crimes, and the implementation of sentences involving "effective restrictions of freedoms and rights"' (ICC-OTP, 2017: para 144, pp 32–3). Despite the OTP amicus intervention before the Colombian Constitutional Court communicating these concerns, the JEP legislative framework has been unanimously approved by the Court, except for a few of its articles.

Another controversial aspect, which is distinct from the transitional justice issue yet relates to its legal implementation, was the parties' attempt to attach 'international standing' to the Agreement. This strategy stemmed from the parties' desire for the Agreement, particularly its transitional justice component, to become part of the Colombian constitutional block, a doctrine adopted by the Colombian Constitutional Court to incorporate international law into domestic constitutional law (Betancur Restrepo, 2016). Therefore, the parties sought to attach international and thus constitutional status to the Agreement, which would supposedly shield the implementing transitional justice legislation from international judicial and domestic political challenges. The Colombian Constitutional Court, however, forestalled this strategy. Conditionally upholding a 2016 law on the submission of the Agreement to plebiscite, the Court added the proviso that the Peace Agreement would not automatically be included in the constitution and the result of the plebiscite would only be binding for the President. In the renegotiated Agreement, the parties clarified that it would not be part of the constitution or the constitutionality block but only a parameter for the interpretation of the implementing laws for three presidential terms, to the extent that the contents of the Agreement correspond to the norms of international humanitarian law or fundamental rights. The parties still refer to the Agreement as a Special Agreement but, having done away with the claim of constitutional status, this reference remains largely symbolic. The parties' attempt to fashion the Agreement as of international and thus constitutional status was perceived both by the opposition and the public as an attempt to subvert the established means of constitutional change, and judicial and democratic oversight (Huneeus and Urueña, 2016).

Overall, the negotiation of the Victims' Agreement has been the most legalized and controversial episode of the process. Rather than replacing political contestation and pragmatic bargaining with objective and clear red lines and normative guidance, the role attached to international law in the process by domestic and international actors led to a complex negotiation process in the language of law. On the one hand, this ensured that some form of accountability was to be guaranteed for international crimes and human rights violations and could not be done away with for the sake of a negotiated settlement. Internalization of international accountability norms, victims' rights, and a gender perspective by the parties are also notable in this respect, arguably as the achievements of a norm-driven approach, understood broadly to extend beyond *legal* norms. Yet, the manifold references to international legal norms have led to confusion as to law's content and stigmatization of certain positions either as externally imposed or illegal. The following section elaborates on the roles international law played in the Colombian peace negotiations, with a view to understanding the challenges and limitations of an international law-based approach in peace mediation.

The Challenges of Legalized Peace Mediation and Negotiation

One of the main criticisms directed at the legalization of peace mediation and negotiation concerns the role of law, and norms in general, in diminishing the space for pragmatic bargaining necessary to achieve a negotiated end to an armed conflict (Anonymous, 1996; Menthe, 2007; Arnault, 2014). International law and courts have been seen as unduly constraining negotiations, for example through the commitment to the principle of territorial integrity at the expense of secessionist solutions to conflicts or to individual human rights over group rights (Menthe, 2007; McCrudden and O'Leary, 2013). Furthermore, the tension between the law's demands, often enlisted for the 'justice' side of the equation, and the requirements of negotiated peace has been particularly well explored in the literature on the so-called peace versus justice debate. International law, or to be more precise, a certain interpretation of it that prioritizes a retributive approach even in the context of a negotiated transition from conflict, and the OTP's insistence on criminal accountability for domestic cases to fulfil the requirements of the complementarity test strain peace negotiations, where non-criminal accountability mechanisms or strategic silence may be favoured by the parties, or even by the affected communities. In Colombia, although the parties were eventually able to agree on a transitional justice arrangement, unlike, for example, the fate of the peace negotiations in Uganda, the insistence of certain domestic and international actors on criminal accountability and imprisonment for international crimes and serious violations of human rights put pressure on the negotiations and led to the marginalization of certain issues that were of significance to the affected communities, such as land reform and socio-economic justice (García and Engle, 2016). Therefore, by laying red lines, if and where it does so, international law may constrain, complicate and unduly shape the 'peacemaking space' while fulfilling its function of providing certainty to negotiators and mediators.

Notwithstanding the merit of the criticism regarding the tension between law and negotiation, it is important to point out that the prescriptive reach of international law in general is not as extensive as is often assumed in peacemaking policy and scholarship by either the critics or the proponents of the legalization of the field. Some of the norms cited in peacemaking policy or practice may not exist as positive (or even soft) legal rules, may not be applicable to peace negotiations in general or in the specific jurisdiction, or may be under-specified to provide any precise normative guidance for negotiations (Ozcelik, 2018). For example, although most peacemaking guidelines contain assertions regarding the prohibition of amnesties for international crimes and serious violations of human rights and the purported requirement of including criminal accountability mechanisms in peace agreements, the relevant international law provides for a normative framework that is much more nuanced and flexible (Ozcelik, 2018). As such, the negotiating parties in Colombia were able to devise a complex and innovative transitional justice system that married the requirements of justice and negotiated peace, and which in principle complies with the relevant international law (Cassel, 2015). Another example from the Colombian peace negotiations regarding the limited prescriptive reach of international law relates to the debate surrounding the legal status of the Agreement. Despite the contested nature of peace agreements between governments and armed opposition groups as internationally binding instruments, the parties attempted to attach international status to the Final Peace Agreement to protect it from future amendments and shield it from judicial challenges before domestic and international courts (Ozcelik, 2020). The strategy was not only prone to failure on legal grounds, but also had the adverse effect of discouraging the public from supporting what was partly seen as an attempt to escape democratic and judicial scrutiny. Excessive reliance on international law in peacemaking faces the challenge of 'spreading itself too thin' (Turner, 2016), particularly when arguments made in the name of law do not correspond to *lex lata*. This, then, raises false hopes, makes it difficult for the parties to identify what the law says, and contradicts the legal certainty function of international law. After all, the functional roles of international law are predetermined by its normative reach.

In addition to the risks of far-reaching assumptions regarding the prescriptive role of international law, legalized peace mediation should more openly recognize the malleability of international law to interpretation and strategic instrumentalization. International law is often considered as a static framework of determinate legal norms in the peacemaking guidelines. However, international law may itself become the subject of negotiations through the process of law ascertainment and interpretation, particularly where there is excessive reliance on international law, as was the case in Colombia. While the OTP originally presented the Rome Statute as a non-negotiable framework for any transitional justice arrangement in Colombia and insisted on the requirement of criminal sanctions within that framework, the negotiating parties challenged this through their own legal interpretations of the requirements of the complementarity test, as well as of Colombia's relevant obligations under international law. As a result, the OTP's position evolved over time to accept the overall compliance of the Comprehensive System with the Rome Statute. As international law itself becomes the subject of negotiations through legal interpretation as such, it becomes harder to draw a stark distinction between law and political negotiation; the openness and discretion required for bargaining and compromise creep into the sphere of law rather than being replaced by it. This nature of legal argumentation is not necessarily a challenge in itself; to the contrary, it allows contestation in the ascertainment and interpretation of law. However, it becomes a challenge for those actors in the field of peacemaking, who use the language of law to delineate what is (not) negotiable in absolute terms.

The openness of law to negotiation resonates with its malleability to strategic instrumentalization. Although it is often seized as a 'tool' to overcome the indeterminacy of political transitions and to provide clarity as to what transitions require, international law can be, and has been in Colombia, instrumentalized for competing political agendas. Although it provides a common vocabulary and framework for negotiations, international law cannot in and of itself resolve fundamental disagreements that exist among domestic actors regarding the nature and purpose of a transition. For the 'No' campaign, the FARC-EP represented criminals that had to be punished and removed from the political scene, whereas the Agreement envisaged a transitional justice system constructing accountability within a broader framework of truth, reparations and reconciliation and the transformation of the FARC-EP into a political party. Shadowing the political economy behind the opposition of the rural elites to the Agreement and the competing interests of criminal groups engaged in illicit trafficking (Pospisil, 2016), the transitional justice agreement became the channel through which opposition to the peace process was expressed and legal argumentation became the language of that expression. Therefore, it needs to be acknowledged that law's authority is often instrumentalized by various actors in peace processes to avoid political contestation, and mediators should be wary of what underlying issues the use of the language of law is intended to mask.

Conclusion

The increasing references to international law in peace negotiations and resultant agreements, the review of peace agreement-based laws and practices by domestic and international courts, and most notably the proliferation of normative guidelines adopted by the UN, regional organizations, international financial institutions, peace facilitator third states, and non-governmental organizations all point to the increasing normativization and legalization of peace mediation and negotiation. Although there is undoubtedly an awareness in peacemaking policy and scholarship about the risks of over-legalization, new guidelines and calls for the clarification and codification of normative directions in peacemaking abound. There is, however, also a simultaneously emerging concern about the erosion of the peacemaking principles of independence, openness, discretion and agility, which is partly linked to the normativization of peace mediation and the effect of this on the declining success of peace mediation, especially of UN mediation, and agreements over the past decade (Harland, 2018). Drawing on this warning, the aim of this chapter has been to demonstrate the challenges and limitations of a norm-driven approach to peace mediation and negotiation to the extent that international law is the source, or part of, the normative framework. In addition to the tensions between law and negotiation and between the global and the local that are explored in the existing literature, the chapter has highlighted two further challenging aspects of legalized approaches to peace mediation and negotiation, relating to international law's limited prescriptive reach in providing clear and specified normative parameters and to its openness to negotiation and instrumentalization.

These reservations are put forward neither to denounce the relevance of international law in peace negotiations altogether nor to advance a project of increasing its relevance through progressive codification, but to emphasize the need to recognize the politics of international law and to nuance the claims of causality between compliance with international law in peacemaking and the legitimacy, or durability, of peace negotiations and agreements. Therefore, this is a call first for a more rigorous examination of what international law requires in peacemaking. It is important to point out the leeway international law leaves for political decision making and local practices vis-à-vis the more aspirational pronouncements in policy and scholarship. The second call is for an acknowledgement that law in and of itself cannot supersede negotiation and the various languages employed during negotiation. Nor can international law avoid instrumentalization merely by virtue of its normative authority. The sober perspective that international law is not a source of determinate answers to the multifaceted and historically, politically and socio-economically contingent questions of transitions would allow peace mediators to sustain the relevance of international law in peacemaking as but one framework for negotiation. Mediators can refer to law in opening up a space for the inclusion of issues and actors that are often disregarded by negotiating parties in negotiation, as well as for the avenues international law offers in support of the conclusion and implementation of peace agreements, particularly relating to the tools at the disposal of the Security Council to exhort conflict parties to agree on a negotiated settlement and comply with it. Beyond this, instead of assuming that the legalization, and broader normativization, of peacemaking is good or effective per se, arguments in favour of further legalization, and thus normativization, need to be tempered with caution. As the Special Representative of the Secretary-General and Head of the UN Mission in Colombia contends, 'current international demands ["in the field of normative peacemaking today"] need evidence-based validation before they need further advocacy' (Arnault, 2014).

References

ACCORD and AU (2014) *African Union Mediation Support Handbook* (South Africa: ACCORD). Available at: https://www.accord.org.za/publication/african-union-mediation-support-handbook/ (last accessed: 25 July 2019).

AI (Amnesty International) (2016) 'Colombia: Historic Peace Deal Must Ensure Justice and an End to Human Rights Abuses'. Available at: https://www.amnesty.org/en/latest/news/2016/09/colombia-historic-peace-deal-must-ensure-justice-and-an-end-to-human-rights-abuses/ (last accessed: 25 July 2019).

Anonymous (1996) 'Human Rights in Peace Negotiations', *Human Rights Quarterly* 18(2), 249–58.

Arnault, J. (2014) 'Legitimacy and Peace Processes: International Norms and Local Realities', *Accord: An International Review of Peace Initiatives* 21, 21–5.

Bell, C., O'Rourke, C. and Matzner, S. (2015) 'A Chronology of Colombian Peace Processes and Peace Agreements', *PSRP Briefing Paper No. 1*. Available at: http://www.politicalsettlements.org/publications-database/a-chronology-of-colombian-peace-processes-and-peace-agreements/ (last accessed 10 May 2019).

Betancur Restrepo, L. (2016) 'The Legal Status of the Colombian Peace Agreement', *AJIL Unbound* 110, 188–92.

Cassel, D. (2015) 'Untitled Letter to the President of the Republic of Colombia, 25 September 2015'. Available at: https://klau.nd.edu/assets/177163/spec_jurisd_peace_legal_ltr_9.25.15.pdf (last accessed 10 May 2019).

Colombia-FARC-EP (2016) 'Final Agreement to End the Armed Conflict and Build a Stable and Lasting Peace'. Available at: http://especiales.presidencia.gov.co/Documents/20170620-dejacion-armas/acuerdos/acuerdo-final-ingles.pdf (last accessed: 10 May 2019).

Dajani, O.M. (2007) 'Shadow or Shade? The Roles of International Law in Palestinian-Israeli Peace Talks', *Yale Journal of International Law* 32, 61–124.

European External Action Service (2016) 'Global Challenges and Trends in International Peace Mediation and Diplomacy: A Background Note'. Available at: http://eeas.europa.eu/archives/docs/cfsp/conflict_prevention/docs/20160519-global-challenges-and-trends_final_en.pdf (last accessed: 10 May 2019).

García, H.A. and Engle, K. (2016) 'The Distributive Politics of Impunity and Anti-Impunity: Lessons from Four Decades of Colombian Peace Negotiations' in Engle, K., Miller, Z. and Davis, D. (eds), *Anti-Impunity and the Human Rights Agenda* (Cambridge: Cambridge University Press).

Gissel, L.E. (2017) 'Legitimising the Juba peace Agreement on Accountability and Reconciliation: the International Criminal Court as a third-party actor?', *Journal of Eastern African Studies* 11(2), 367–87.

Harland D. (2018) 'The Lost Art of Peacemaking', *The Centre for Humanitarian Dialogue Oslo Forum Background Paper*. Available at: https://www.hdcentre.org/publications/the-lost-art-of-peacemaking/ (last accessed: 10 May 2019).

Hellmüller, S., Palmiano Federer, J. and Zeller, M. (2015) 'The Role of Norms in International Peace Mediation', *swisspeace and NOREF*. Available at: https://www.swisspeace.ch/fileadmin/user_upload/Media/Publications/The_Role_of_Norms_in_International_Peace_Mediation.pdf (last accessed: 25 July 2019).

Hillebrecht, C., Huneeus, A. and Borda, S. (2018) 'The Judicialization of Peace', *Harvard International Law Journal* 59(2), 279–330.

HRW (Human Rights Watch) (2017) 'Colombia: Fix Flaws in Transitional Justice Law'. Available at: https://www.hrw.org/news/2017/10/09/colombia-fix-flaws-transitional-justice-law (last accessed: 10 May 2019).

Huneeus, A. and Urueña, R. (2016) 'Introduction to the Symposium on the Colombian Peace Talks and International Law', *AJIL Unbound* 110, 161–4.

ICC-OTP (2012) 'Interim Report on the Situation in Colombia'. Available at: https://www.fidh.org/IMG/pdf/otp_-_colombia_-_public_interim_report_-_november_2012.pdf (last accessed: 10 May 2019).

ICC-OTP (2014) 'Report on Preliminary Examination Activities 2014'. Available at: https://www.icc-cpi.int/iccdocs/otp/OTP-Pre-Exam-2014.pdf (last accessed: 10 May 2019).

ICC-OTP (2017) 'Report on Preliminary Examination Activities 2017'. Available at: https://www.icc-cpi.int/itemsDocuments/2017-PE-rep/2017-otp-rep-PE_ENG.pdf (last accessed: 10 May 2019).

Kastner, P. (2015) *Legal Normativity in the Resolution of Internal Armed Conflict* (Cambridge: Cambridge University Press).

Levitt, J. (2012) *Illegal Peace in Africa: An Inquiry into the Legality of Power Sharing with Warlords, Rebels, and Junta* (Cambridge: Cambridge University Press).

McCrudden, C. and O'Leary, B. (2013) 'Courts and Consociations, or How Human Rights Courts May De-stabilize Power-sharing Settlements', *The European Journal of International Law* 24(2), 477–501.

Mediation Support Network (2013) 'Translating Mediation Guidance into Practice: Commentary on the UN Guidance for Effective Mediation by the Mediation Support Network'. Available at: www.mediationsupportnetwork.net (last accessed 10 May 2019).

Menthe, D. (2007) 'Legalization and the Mediation of International Disputes: The Balkan Experience', *Connecticut Journal of International Law* 23, 83–121.

OSCE (2014) 'Mediation and Dialogue Facilitation in the OSCE: Reference Guide'. Available at: http://www.osce.org/secretariat/126646 (last accessed 10 May 2019).

Ozcelik, A. (2018) *The Role of International Law in the Negotiation of Peace Agreements* (Unpublished PhD Thesis, University of Glasgow). Available at: http://theses.gla.ac.uk/id/eprint/70976 (last accessed 10 May 2019).

Ozcelik, A. (2020) 'Entrenching Peace in Law: Do Peace Agreements Possess International Legal Status?', *Melbourne Journal of International Law* 21(1). Available at: https://papers.ssrn.com/sol3/papers.cfm?abstract_id=3700001 (last accessed 4 October 2020).

Pospisil, J. (2016) 'Colombia: Don't They Want Peace?', *Political Settlements Research Programme Opinion*. Available at: https://www.politicalsettlements.org/2016/10/04/colombia-dont-they-want-peace/ (last accessed 4 October 2020).

Saliternik, M. (2016) 'Perpetuating Democratic Peace: Procedural Justice in Peace Negotiations', *European Journal of International Law* 27(3), 617–42.

Seils, P. (2015) 'Squaring Colombia's Circle: The Objectives of Punishment and the Pursuit of Peace' *The International Centre for Transitional Justice Briefing Paper.* Available at: https://www.ictj.org/publication/squaring-colombia-circle-objectives-punishment-peace (last accessed 10 May 2019)

Sriram, C.L. (2017) 'Beyond Transitional Justice: Peace, Governance, and Rule of Law', *International Studies Review* 19, 53–69.

Stewart, J. (2015) 'Transitional Justice in Colombia and the Role of the International Criminal Court'. Available at: https://www.icc-cpi.int/iccdocs/otp/otp-stat-13-05-2015-ENG.pdf (last accessed: 10 May 2019).

Teitel, R. (1997) 'Transitional Jurisprudence: The Role of Law in Political Transformation', *The Yale Law Journal* 106, 2009–80.
Turner, C. (2016) 'Editorial Comment: Law and Negotiation in Conflict: Theory, Policy and Practice', *Global Policy* 7(2), 256–60.
UN (2012) Guidance for Effective Mediation. Available at: https://peacemaker.un.org/sites/peacemaker.un.org/files/GuidanceEffectiveMediation_UNDPA2012%28english%29_0.pdf (last accessed: 25 July 2019).
UN (2017) Guidance on Gender and Inclusive Mediation Strategies. Available at: https://peacemaker.un.org/node/2940 (last accessed: 10 May 2019).
Uribe, A. (2016) 'Bases de Un Acuerdo Nacional de Paz'. Available at: http://static.iris.net.co/semana/upload/documents/bases-de-un-acuerdo-nacional-de-paz.pdf (last accessed: 10 May 2019).
Wählisch, M. (2016) 'Normative Limits of Peace Negotiations: Questions, Guidance and Prospects', *Global Policy* 7(2), 261–6.

Cases and Legislation

Constitution of Colombia (1991).
IACtHR, Case of Barrios Altos v Peru, Merits Judgment, March 14, 2001 Series C No 75.
IACtHR, Case of Gomes Lund et al ('Guerrilha do Araguaia') v Brazil, Preliminary Objections, Merits, Reparations, and Costs Judgment of November 24, 2010 Series C No 219.
IACtHR, Case of the Massacres of El Mozote and nearby places v El Salvador, Merits, Reparations and Costs Judgment of October 25, 2012 Series C No 252.
IACtHR, Case of the Rochela Massacre v Colombia Merits, Reparations and Costs Judgment of May 11, 2007 Series C No 163.

PART II
Inclusion in Theory and Practice

7

Inclusive of Whom, and for What Purpose? Strategies of Inclusion in Peacemaking*

Andreas T. Hirblinger and Dana M. Landau

Introduction

Inclusion has emerged as a prominent theme at the heart of peacemaking across theory, policy and practice. Mediation scholars, policy makers, and practitioners have argued that inclusion is critical for ending armed conflicts (Nilsson, 2012; Krause et al, 2018; Yousuf, 2018) and building peaceful states and societies (Castillejo, 2014; Bell and Pospisil, 2017; International IDEA, 2017; Pospisil and Rocha Menocal, 2017; World Bank Group and United Nations, 2018). These insights have been accompanied by efforts to promote inclusive peacemaking through stronger international policy frameworks (de Waal, 2017; Turner, 2020). However, despite its recent ubiquity, inclusion has remained an ill-defined term (Hellmüller, 2019). Calling for *inclusive* peace processes inevitably raises the questions of *whom* to include, *how* and *why*. Since peacemaking commonly entails the (re)negotiation of core features of state and society, discourses and practices of inclusion can be critical. Inclusion raises a

* This chapter is an early version of an article published as 'Daring to Differ? Strategies of Inclusion in Peacemaking', *Security Dialogue*, 51(4): 305–22. We thank SAGE for granting the right to reuse these materials.

host of issues that are at the heart of violent conflict and its resolution, pertaining not only to political voice and representation, but to questions of the identity of the included, their relationships and the political community they are part of. It thus appears that the seemingly benign and consensual idea of inclusion is, in fact, highly political.

This chapter seeks to problematize the research, policy and practice of inclusion by situating it in larger debates about what peace means and how it can be achieved. The idea of inclusion, if not the exact term, has long played an important role in the study of peace. We therefore aim to bring the epistemic dimension of the term – theories of peacebuilding that stipulate the relationship between inclusion and peace – into conversation with the emerging international policy framework on inclusive peacemaking, as well as with the practical efforts of mediation actors to promote inclusion in peace processes. We identify three main rationales put forth for inclusion that can be derived from peacemaking theory, and argue that these correspond with specific strategies of inclusion in peacemaking policy and practice. Importantly, these strategies also have implications for how the included are framed and this lastly effects the kind of peace that can be achieved. The chapter thus highlights important tensions in the conceptualization and use of inclusion and offers ways forward for a reflexive research and practice of inclusion.

The chapter first discusses the rationales for inclusion put forward in peacemaking theory by asking how scholars have viewed the relationship between inclusion and peace. It discusses three broad rationales for inclusion: to increase the legitimacy of processes, to protect or empower specific groups, or to transform relationships. We then turn to policy. The second section discusses how three corresponding inclusion strategies are represented in key United Nations (UN) documents that provide guidance on inclusive peacemaking, and demonstrates how these rely on framing the included in open, closed or relational terms. In a final section, we ask how this is affecting practice. While efforts to foster inclusion are commonly associated with promoting broader participation of an openly defined public in order to increase the legitimacy of a given peace process, international inclusion policy and practice have also been shaped by essentializing discourses that aim to protect or empower specific groups. While this leads to trade-offs and contradictions in current peacemaking practice, we suggest that a relational inclusion strategy may help advance a peace that is both more contextually grounded and more focused on long-term conflict transformation. The conclusion sketches out the cornerstones of a research agenda that could contribute to a more critical and more relevant study of inclusion in peacemaking.

Rationales for Inclusion in Peacemaking Theory

Why should inclusion matter in peacemaking? What relationships have scholars found between inclusion and peace? In this section, we identify three major rationales for inclusion emerging from peacemaking and peacebuilding theory, which contain assumptions about the relationship between inclusion and peace. Each of these rationales corresponds with different framings of the included. First, inclusion is advanced to build a more legitimate peace through broader participation, secondly, to empower and protect specific, closely defined actor groups, promoting them as champions of peace, and thirdly to transform the social and political structures that underlie conflict. The first rationale frames the included in open terms that can accommodate a heterogeneity of characteristics and interests, the second in closed terms pertaining to specific identity traits, and the third frames the included in relational terms emerging within a specific social, cultural or political context. In the following, we briefly map these three rationales and corresponding framings in the peacemaking and peacebuilding literature.[1]

Inclusion to Build Legitimacy

The first rationale for inclusion is based on the assumption that broadening participation in a peace process will make resulting peace agreements more legitimate by ensuring the process is representative of a broader set of interests. A version of this rationale is already evident in the literature on power sharing, focusing on ending violence by including major conflict parties and distributing power among them (Malmin Binningsbø, 2013). Power-sharing research initially focused narrowly on the role of armed actors and political elites, seeing elite cooperation and elite bargains as an important precondition for peace (Lindemann, 2008; Norris, 2008; Mehler, 2009; Lindemann, 2011). The question of inclusion further focused on so-called 'spoilers', actors that can derail agreements if excluded (Nilsson, 2008; Blaydes and de Maio, 2010; Nilsson and Söderberg Kovacs, 2011; Reiter, 2016). From this perspective, horizontal inclusion of all, usually armed, actors ensures that incentives are not created for those left out to destabilize an agreement (Raffoul, 2019).

[1] This brief review of rationales for inclusion does not purport to be comprehensive. Rather, it serves to highlight that different rationales require different framings and assumptions about the included. The subsequent sections demonstrate the analytical utility of this perspective.

Beyond ending violence, power-sharing agreements also aim to build more legitimate political arrangements by distributing power among and between conflict parties and their constituencies (Spears, 2000; Hartzell and Hoddie, 2003; Hoddie, 2014; Hartzell and Hoddie, 2015). Therefore, the scope of inclusion is usually extended beyond armed elite actors, as evidenced in research on the role of civil society in peace processes (Bell and O'Rourke, 2007; Wanis-St. John, 2008; Paffenholz, 2010; Nilsson, 2012). For instance, scholars have argued that participation of actors beyond the main armed conflict parties makes peace processes more legitimate and agreements more likely to be implemented. Civil society can play an important role in increasing the transparency of peace process and holding conflict parties to account (Nilsson, 2012; Zanker, 2014) and can enable inclusive settlements beyond formal institutions and outside the capital (Heitz, 2009). It has also been suggested that civil society inclusion in negotiations increases the durability of peace, particularly in non-democratic societies (Nilsson, 2012).

Inclusion as a means to build legitimacy also features in debates about the importance of national or local ownership in peacebuilding and political transitions (Reich, 2006; Chesterman, 2007). The principle of ownership builds on the assumption that the 'success of any reform process depends on the extent to which it is perceived as legitimate by those who have to live with the outcomes' (Donais, 2009: 121) and seeks to reconcile international peacebuilding agendas with the participation of local actors in order to build a legitimate, 'popular peace' (Roberts, 2011). For mediators, this raises the practical question of which actors need to be included in order to reach legitimate agreements (Goldmann et al, 2013). In contrast, more critical scholars argue that the discourse of ownership is largely used as a tool to legitimize international activities in conflict-affected contexts, pointing to the largely symbolic and discursive value of calls for broader inclusion and participation (Kappler and Lemay-Hérbert, 2015; von Billerbeck, 2016). Importantly, calls for inclusion that aim to build legitimacy through broad participation generally use vague framings of the included, leaving their translation into tangible policy options open. Given the fact that seats at the negotiation table are limited, any efforts to make peace processes more broadly inclusive will face the challenge of reconciling the interests of more narrowly defined actor groups.

Inclusion to Empower and Protect

Inclusion is also advanced in order to empower and protect particular groups. In this case, the assumption is that building peace requires strengthening the position of specific actors that have suffered in conflict or who can be champions of peace. Their inclusion aims at protecting their rights, enhancing their political voice or addressing previous harms. This rationale frames the included in closed terms, as specific groups with a common identity trait, such as gender, language or ethnicity, and as such accentuates and fixes these, particularly where they are linked to vulnerabilities that emerge in conflict. As Turner has argued, 'negotiating a settlement between elites and armed actors perpetuates the marginalisation of vulnerable groups who may have suffered the most as the result of conflict' (Turner, 2020). The inclusion of these groups thus serves as a counter-strategy.

In relation to ethnic, linguistic or religious groups, scholars have argued for their inclusion in peace processes and in favour of provisions for group rights in peace agreements as crucial for conflict resolution (Kempin Reuter, 2012; Wise, 2018), building on broader debates about the politics of recognition (Taylor, 1994) and minority rights (Kymlicka, 1996). Critics have argued that these approaches overlook groups' nature as mutable social formations, noting that measures aimed at empowerment can entrench identities and conflict cleavages, thus potentially perpetuating conflict (Bose, 2002). However, empowerment and protection have been particularly prominent rationales in the context of the inclusion of women in peacemaking, as outlined in the UN's Women, Peace and Security (WPS) agenda. Here too, scholars have highlighted the agenda's implicit essentialization of women as both vulnerable and peaceful (Davies and True, 2019). However, essentialized framings can also be used to advance changes in the distribution of power in post-conflict contexts (Porter, 2007, 2013). As such, the case for women's, and other marginalized actors', inclusion in peace processes can be made by drawing on Spivak's concept of 'strategic essentialism', whereby differences within a group are strategically downplayed for the sake of an emancipatory political project (Spivak, 1988). In fact, much of the women's empowerment discourse has focused on vulnerabilities to sexual and gender-based violence. Women have been portrayed as victims of war in need of protection. The rationale of inclusion then is to counteract women's vulnerability by increasing their role in peace processes (Väyrynen, 2010: 147). While the view of women as peaceful victims, often reproduced in arguments for their inclusion in peacemaking, has empowered women to mobilize politically, it also reaffirms traditional gender roles that marginalize women in political life (Väyrynen, 2010; Aharoni, 2017: 311–12), with possible disempowering effects (Porter, 2007: 74).

Inclusion to Transform Relationships and Build Community

Inclusion can also be advanced to transform relations between groups, framing the included neither in broad and open, nor in essentialized and closed, but rather in relational terms. This rationale for inclusion is occupied with the relations between conflict stakeholders, and with transforming and rebuilding those in line with insights from the conflict transformation literature (Lederach, 1997, 2005). The latter views conflict as a consequence of contradictions in the structure of society that can be transcended through a change in relationships. Inclusive processes thus aim to build a community 'in which the past division of winners versus losers, victims versus perpetrators, "us" and "them" are overcome', however, without 'erasing or evading differences between people' (Mani, 2005: 511–12).

As captured in Galtung's 'triangle of violence', this approach is interested in the interaction between direct, cultural and structural forms of violence (Chetail, 2009: 1). It also builds on development research and 'dependency-thinking', which advances concepts of positive peace that focus on the material and social relationships between conflict stakeholders (Götschel, 2009: 92–3) and rejects fixed understandings of conflict party identities and interests. Instead, scholars highlight how interests depend on social relationships and focus on changing the parties 'from adversaries to something else' (Mitchell, 2002: 16), arguing for peacebuilding to be 'responsive to the experiential and subjective realities shaping people's perspectives and needs' (Lederach, 1997: 24). Lederach's integrated framework for peacebuilding considers the visible *issue* in the context of the wider *relationship* among conflict parties, as well as the systems and sub-systems in which these relationships are located. For instance, conflicts underpinned by a relationship of prejudice or bias should be analysed and tackled as part of a broader system of social structures which create and perpetuate racism (Lederach, 1997: 24). Peace can thus be understood as a 'dynamic social construct' and peacebuilding should aim at 'transform(ing) conflict towards more sustainable and peaceful relationships' (Lederach, 1997: 20).

This approach requires peacemakers to make sense of the web of relationships in which conflict occurs, before aiming at social change through rebuilding the social spaces that give people a sense of identity (Lederach, 2005). For the question of inclusion in peacemaking, this implies a focus on the relationships between included actors. While not radically deconstructing actor categories, inclusion can nonetheless address cultures of domination and oppressive power structures by working on 'culturally sanctioned forms of oppression, whether related to caste, ethnic identity, sexuality or ability' (Francis, 2004: 7). The emphasis on relationality is chosen in order to facilitate a change of the social and cultural structures that underpin conflict. From this point of view, inclusion can only play a meaningful role in peace processes if practised in a way that accounts for the constructedness of identities through relationships and aims at their transformation.

Strategies of Inclusion in International Peacemaking Policy

Following the discussion of the rationales for inclusion in peacemaking theory, this section discusses how these correspond with strategies of inclusion on the international policy level. To this end, we studied how different framings of inclusion are manifested in key UN documents. The documents are either guidance material produced by the UN's Mediation Support Unit (MSU) and its partners, or form part of the UN's normative framework on mediation, which include statements and reports by the UN Secretary-General (UNSG), and resolutions by the UN Security Council (UNSC) and the UN General Assembly (UNGA).[2] The document analysis was complemented by interviews with practitioners engaged in UN mediation and mediation support, whom we asked about their practices of fostering inclusion in peace processes, and their reflections on the purpose(s) of inclusion in peacemaking.[3] Our analysis was guided by two questions: which referent object of inclusion do the policy documents identify, and for what purpose?[4] In a first step,

[2] Most of these documents were retrieved from the UN's *Peacemaker* Website, [online] available from: www.peacemaker.un.org (accessed March 2018), which aims to provide 'actors involved in peace processes and the negotiation of peace agreements with key knowledge material to support their work effectively'. In addition, we retrieved further sources relevant for mediation from the Official Document System of the United Nations. These included UNSC and UNGA resolutions related to peacemaking without specific country focus, as well as UNSC Presidential statements and reports by the Secretary-General that discuss peace and security issues and mediation. In total, we analysed 108 documents.

[3] We conducted nine expert interviews. In order to enable frank conversations about politically sensitive processes, we offered full anonymity to the respondents.

[4] To this end, we screened more than 500 text segments that contain references to inclusion or participation. The basic unit of analysis was a paragraph. Using Qualitative Data Analysis (QDA) software, we conducted an automated search for references to inclusion and participation, in either nominal or verbal constructions. The text segments were then qualitatively analysed, with the reading scope limited to the respective paragraph.

we descriptively coded the identified objects of inclusion. In most cases, these are specific actor types, such as women, youth or civil society, while sometimes reference is made to territorial, scalar or social dimensions, such as regions, marginalized groups, or minorities. Against the backdrop of the literature discussed earlier, we inferred that references to the object of inclusion can be grouped according to at least three main categories of framings: *open* references, such as to 'stakeholders', 'communities' or 'citizens', which are ambiguous in meaning and provide room for interpretation; *closed* references, such as to 'women' or 'youth', referring to an actor group that is identifiable according to relatively clear criteria; and *relational* references, such as to 'powerful' or 'marginalised actors', which derive their meaning from being situated in a specific socio-political context. Of course, it can be argued that all terms are ultimately relational as they form part of a system of signification in which no single signifier can independently convey meaning. However, the division into categories of framings serves to illustrate that these correspond with the three rationales for inclusion identified in the preceding section, variously shaping the view on the included and their role in peacemaking.[5]

A birds-eye view on the body of documents reveals a pattern in the distribution of framings of inclusion, with considerable variation between guidance documents and the normative framework. For example, UNSC resolutions predominantly use closed formulations that fix actor identities, with references to women making up the majority of these, while mediation guidance relies more on open and relational terminology. Reports by the Secretary-General use both relational and open terminology but are dominated by closed terms, which are used at least once in every report. The use of relational terminology is strongest in UN mediation guidance, where almost a third of all mentions of inclusion use a relational framing, occurring in two thirds of all documents. The relevance of these findings lies in the different purposes of these documents in practice. While the normative framework, and in particular UNSC resolutions, are in principle binding documents, mediation guidance notes are suggestive, rather than authoritative, and reflect UN best practice.

[5] Some terms also fit more than one of these categories. For instance, the term 'stakeholder' has a strongly relational dimension as membership of this group depends on an interest in the peace process in question. On the other hand, the term provides room for interpretation since it could potentially extend more broadly to everyone affected by a conflict, whether domestically or abroad. In those cases, terms were added to both categories.

Open Framings: Voices, Stakeholders and Civil Society

The UN Guidance for Effective Mediation (2012), the UN's cornerstone document on mediation, defines 'inclusivity' as referring to 'the extent and manner in which the views and needs of conflict parties and other stakeholders are represented and integrated into the process and outcome of a mediation effort' (UNSG, 2012: 11). The emphasis is on inclusion beyond the conflict parties, and the argument is grounded in inclusion as a path to broad-based buy-in to peace. The guidance stresses that 'it cannot be assumed that conflict parties have legitimacy with, or represent, the wider public'; mediation efforts limited to the main conflict parties may thus create perverse incentives for violence, while civil society actors can increase the legitimacy of a peace process (UNSG, 2012: 11).

References to inclusion with the aim of increasing the legitimacy of peace processes predominantly employ open framings, for instance when reference is made to the participation of 'stakeholders', 'voices' or 'perspectives'. References to civil society inclusion are often grounded in arguments about strengthening a peace process's legitimacy (UNGA, 2012: 25–6), or local ownership (UNGA, 2012: 50), as a means of including a variety of perspectives (UNGA, 2012: 48), ensuring that grievances are addressed (UNGA, 2012: 101), or exerting influence on conflict parties (UNSC, 2014: 6). Alongside 'civil society', the term 'stakeholders' is also dominant. The UNSG Report on *Strengthening the Role of Mediation*, for instance, makes several references to stakeholder inclusion, arguing that it 'creates mechanisms to include all perspectives along the process' (UNGA, 2012: 20), and for 'cultivating and exercising ownership' (UNGA, 2012: 50). Interestingly, reference to 'stakeholders' is largely absent from UNSC and UNGA resolutions. Reference to stakeholders is much more pronounced in mediation guidance documents, which establish a link between stakeholder inclusion and more sustainable and legitimate processes based on national or local ownership (UNSG, 2012: 12; Mason, 2013: 2; UNDPA and UNEP, 2015: 10), establishing broader buy-in (UNDPA and UNEP, 2015: 11), creating room for a diversity of ideas (Mason, 2013: 77), including all or different perspectives (UNSG, 2012: 4, 10), and a greater likelihood of conflict causes being addressed (UNDPA and UNEP, 2015: 6). Open terminology that refers to the need for broad-based inclusion of stakeholders, voices, and perspectives is thus mainly based on instrumental arguments, which claim that broad-based inclusion will increase the legitimacy of the process and will lead to more sustainable results.

Closed Framings: Women, Youth and Religious Actors

The dominant framings across all document types, however, are closed framings, and among these, references to women. This is unsurprising given the number of UNSC resolutions that were adopted in the past two decades as part of the UN's WPS agenda, which has been accompanied by significant international advocacy efforts to promote women's inclusion in peacemaking (Martin de Almagro, 2018; True and Wiener, 2019). Our interviews with practitioners similarly suggest a widespread equation of 'inclusion' with 'women's inclusion' among mediation professionals, indicating that the inclusion agenda has been decidedly shaped by the WPS agenda.

The most well-known resolution on women's inclusion, UNSC resolution 1325, establishes a relationship between the 'maintenance and promotion of international peace security' and the 'protection and full participation' of women and girls (UNSC, 2000). Based on the claim that 'civilians, particularly women and children, account for the vast majority of those adversely affected by armed conflict', the resolution suggests a range of measures aimed at the increased participation of women in conflict prevention, management and resolution. At the same time, the resolution explicitly cites international law applicable to the rights and protection of women and girls, while repeatedly stressing their 'special needs', and calls on all parties to armed conflict to protect women and girls from gender-based violence and on states to prosecute respective crimes. The provisions for increased participation are thus closely tied to the protection of women's rights.

A strong emphasis on women's participation is also visible in reports by the UNSG. The *Strengthening the Role of Mediation* (2012) report discusses UN-led mediation activities, and documents how mediators have aimed to include women therein, including through the employment of gender advisers (UNGA, 2012: 33), the provision of funds to support women's participation in peace panels, and consultations with women (UNGA, 2012: 122). These efforts are built on the assumption that it requires women to address the gendered dimensions of conflict, as 'women' and 'gender expertise' are almost always mentioned jointly without differentiation. Importantly, this essentialism is not strategic in its effort to empower women as a social group, but seems to associate gender expertise with women as a fixed category. Our interviews with mediation practitioners similarly suggest that the inclusion of women in peace processes is often driven by assumptions about their roles and interests that leave little room for their empowerment through inclusion, and in fact may cement their marginalization in public life.

In addition to women, other closed terms, such as 'youth' or 'religious groups' also feature in the policy documents, albeit far less prominently. These are more strongly represented in the mediation guidance documents than in the international normative framework. In contrast to women, the participation of these groups is not justified by protection or empowerment rationales, but rather on functional grounds. While 'youth' and 'religious groups' are often subsumed under civil society (UNSG, 2017: 28), in some cases they are singled out as actors with a distinct role, for instance when 'youth' are identified as possible spoilers to an agreement (Mason, 2013: 47). As the interviews discussed later illustrate, references to different closed categories in policy documents can lead to competing claims for inclusion in light of the ultimately limited seats available at a negotiation table.

Relational Framings: the Marginalized and Vulnerable, Versus Powerful Actors

Finally, relational framings feature relatively weakly in the policy documents. Their use is largely confined to mediation guidance and a few sections of UNSG reports. One plausible explanation for this pattern is that relational thinking stems mainly from the practice of mediation and gains its entry through the reporting on best practices and lessons learned. The most striking examples of the use of a relational term are references to 'marginalised' groups or actors, sometimes in relation with the more open term 'stakeholder' (UNDPA and UNEP, 2015: 9). Other relational terms, such as 'minorities', 'powerful actors' or 'vulnerable groups', are largely absent from UNSC and UNGA resolutions, while featuring strongly in mediation guidance. The latter discuss marginalization, for example in relation to decision-making in negotiation processes, which should safeguard marginalized interests vis-à-vis 'the most powerful stakeholders' (Mason, 2013: 76; UNDPA and UNEP, 2015: 34). While sometimes reference is broadly made to 'social, demographic, religious and regional minority identities' (UNDPA, 2017: 10), some statements limit the focus to specific groups such as women (UNITAR and UNDPA, 2010: 14; UNDPA, 2017: 10), indigenous people (UNDPA and UNEP, 2015: 8, 36), or youth (UNDPA and UNEP, 2015: 8, 36; UNDPA, 2017: 10), thus merging relational and closed terms.

Relational framings of inclusion situate the object of inclusion within their social and political relationships and thus hint at structural inequalities and power imbalances as underlying causes of conflict. This reflects the underlying assumptions of the conflict transformation school, resulting in the combination of closed and relational terminology employed with a view to transforming conflict. The focus on the relationship between conflict parties is complemented by an open conception of the community in which conflict transformation has to take place. This reason can also take instrumental forms: inclusive mediation is portrayed as a prerequisite to prevent 'marginalised groups … [from] end[ing] up with the desire to undermine any agreements reached' (Mason, 2013: 75). This is particularly visible in statements about the necessity to include marginalized regions in which armed conflict has occurred, such as Darfur (Mason, 2013: 50).

Complementary or Conflicting Framings of Inclusion?

The review of international peacemaking policy demonstrates a tension between efforts to empower and protect specific groups, which requires naming and defining them, and the urge to stress their socio-political construction and thus malleability. The latter would allow for a context-sensitive and dynamic practice of inclusion that avoids the pitfalls of essentialization, while the former may be necessary to combat the long-standing exclusion of certain actors from peacemaking. The policy documents at times acknowledge this tension. For instance, the UN Guidance on Gender and Inclusive Mediation Strategies recognizes that 'it may be difficult to engage interest groups that are not easily defined or lack clear leadership, such as social movements, youth, and women's groups' while at the same time asking mediators to 'put a premium on stakeholder mapping, planning and management of the process' (UNDPA, 2017: 21). Interviews with mediation practitioners indicate that such stakeholder mapping is often beyond their capacities, leading them to fall back on inclusion strategies that rely on closed terms and a 'box-ticking' mentality. Efforts to avoid essentializing understandings of the included are also evident in the guidance, which stresses that the 'call for inclusion … is not limited to women, but applies to social, demographic, religious and regional minority identities as well as to youth and to organised civil society and professional organisations' (UNDPA, 2017: 6). However, the document justifies the focus on the 'gender dimension' by reference to the fact that 'women and girls tend to be identified first and foremost as victims of violence', therefore 'rights-based attention to their needs is of paramount importance' (UNDPA, 2017: 6–7). It also argues that while 'women are frequently part of movements demanding change', they 'tend to be excluded from peace and transition processes', and further makes the case that women's inclusion can have broader positive effects as it is 'more likely to generate broad national ownership and support' by expanding 'the range of domestic constituencies engaged in a peace processes' (UNDPA, 2017: 8).

This and other policy documents are thus characterized by an intermingling of two functional arguments: on the one hand, specific groups such as women merit particular protection, which their inclusion in peacemaking is posited to enhance. On the other hand, these groups are included for their substantive contributions to peacemaking and in order to contribute to broader participation. In practice, however, promoting broad-based inclusion through closed categories comes with trade-offs, as will be argued in the next section. In contrast, relational framings that focus on the material, social and cultural relations between groups may transcend this tension and offer an avenue for context-sensitive and transformative inclusion practices.

Strategies of Inclusion in Peacemaking Practice

This final section explores how mediation professionals directly involved in peace process design make practical decisions about inclusion and how their choices relate to the rationales and framings found in peacemaking theory and policy.[6] To this end, we asked professionals with experience in UN mediation and mediation support about their practices of fostering inclusion in peace processes and the role of policy and guidance documents therein.[7] Overall, the focus on inclusion in policy discourses is mirrored in peacemaking practice. However, the normative framework and guidance

[6] This section builds on nine expert interviews with current and former UN mediators, mediation support actors, and members of UN mediation teams. The interviewees included current and former staff at MSU, who were involved both in drafting guidance documents and in supporting UN Special Envoys and their teams, as well as former senior members of UN Special Envoy teams and political missions. Jointly, the interviewees have experience working directly on over a dozen peace processes on behalf of the UN in the past two decades, including in Afghanistan, Somalia, Colombia, Syria, Yemen and Cyprus. All interviews were conducted between July 2018 and April 2019. One interview was conducted in person, and the remainder via phone or video call, and all but two interviews were conducted jointly by the two authors.

[7] This reflection was inspired by two years of engagement in research–policy transfer in the field of peace process design and mediation, during which the authors were able to observe first-hand the prevailing discourses and practices of inclusion. These experiences additionally fed into the analysis. Unless otherwise noted, the statements made in this section are based on the expert interviews conducted. To protect their anonymity we do not attribute any findings to specific interviewees.

on inclusion stands in tension with the pragmatic choices of mediators and their often limited influence in a given peace process. Inclusive peacemaking is easier prescribed than done. In fact, for practitioners, there exist significant trade-offs and dilemmas when operationalizing inclusion. While inclusion discourse has led to a heightening of demands for participation in peace processes and has thus fuelled the game of 'enlarging the table' – which had traditionally been both exclusive and elitist – seats at the negotiation table are inevitably limited. This problem is augmented by the increasing fragmentation of armed groups and conflict stakeholders in contemporary armed conflicts.[8]

The previously mentioned policy documents affect peacemaking practice in various ways, ranging from directive to suggestive. UNSC resolutions inform the mandates of UN peace operations and political missions, thus providing clear prescriptions for how to practise inclusion. While UNSC resolutions provide 'a floor, not a ceiling' for inclusion, as one high-level mediator put it, they certainly shape the menu of options by putting political weight behind the inclusion of specific actors. Resolutions by the UNSC and UNGA also shape the discourse on inclusion more broadly, by rallying member states behind particular inclusion agendas that highlight specific conflict stakeholders. UN guidance documents, on the other hand, originate with the MSU's mission to professionalize mediation (Convergne, 2016), signalling that mediation is not an intuitive practice, but a principled and structured one. While not binding, they provide advice and principles that serve as a foundation for mediation practice. However, for practitioners these documents often appear too broadly worded to be readily implementable. Moreover, several interviewees mentioned that the ambitious nature of international policy on inclusion overstates the actual influence that mediators exercise at the negotiation table. Mediators may shape the process by suggesting specific designs and making arguments for inclusion on normative or pragmatic grounds. However, they cannot impose any inclusive arrangements against the will of the conflict parties or influential stakeholders.

[8] This is certainly the case for seats at the formal negotiation table, but practically also applies to other inclusion formats such as consultations. Even internet-based consultations remain limitedly inclusive in practice due to challenges in processing large numbers of responses.

Operationalizing an Inclusive Peace for All?

While conflict parties tend to understand inclusion as confined to those who bear arms, for mediators, inclusion beyond armed actors aims at securing a more lasting peace, by avoiding elite deals that create incentives for future violence. Some mediators also consider the purpose of broadening inclusion as fostering public support for a peace process, in which case they concede that often a merely symbolic form of inclusion is practised, culminating in the 'photo opportunity' with members of religious groups, civil society, or women. This is because the political realities of peace processes make broad-based inclusion an ideal, rather than a realistic objective. Some mediators bemoan the fact that the UN normative framework and guidance documents ignore these realities, making inclusion appear like a largely rhetorical aspiration by the UN, rather than a method employed strategically to make peace according to one of the earlier-mentioned rationales.

While mediators' long-term goal may be to build legitimate peace and inclusive governance, these matter less in the short-term politics of peacemaking, and might even impede mediators' priority to end violence, requiring first and foremost getting armed actors to the negotiation table. In this reading, 'open term' inclusion suffers additionally from the weakening of liberal approaches and the space for civil society shrinking across the world. Recent attempts at broadening inclusion to women and civil society in UN-mediated peace processes for Syria and Yemen have demonstrated that little room exists for ambitious normative projects. Nonetheless, a common mediator strategy to foster inclusion is to present pragmatic arguments to conflict parties, focusing on how enlarging representation at the table beyond the conflict parties, or diversifying their own delegations, can enhance their legitimacy and strengthen ties to their constituents, increase public support for the talks, and strengthen the legacy of the process. These considerations are particularly pressing in light of the increased fragmentation of armed groups in contemporary conflicts.

However, the inherently context-specific nature of peacemaking is in tension with generic formulations in policy documents that frame the included in open terms, such as 'stakeholders' or 'civil society', leaving mediators with difficult choices in operationalizing inclusion. In practice, stakeholders need to be mapped out – a task that requires time, resources and deep context knowledge, none of which are guaranteed features in mediation. And while the term 'civil society' continues to convey a sense of impartiality, in practice, included civil society actors have political opinions that do not correspond with a neutral, umbrella-like perspective of the needs and interests of a broader population. In the end, political and operational pressures on mediation teams often lead to inclusion efforts following a 'standard formula' of consultations and 'photo opportunities', giving voice predominantly to representatives of urban-based, professionalized civil society organizations.

Box-ticking Exercises: an Inclusive Peace for Few?

Mediation professionals commonly invoke closed framings of the included, most prominently in relation to a prioritization of women's inclusion, and to a lesser extent of youth. This reflects the significant emphasis there has been on women's participation in peace processes since the passing of UNSC resolution 1325. The ready association of 'inclusion' with 'women' among practitioners is also facilitated by institutionalized UN mechanisms, including the MSU's Standby Team of Senior Mediation Advisers, which includes an expert on 'Gender and Inclusion', or the direct support provided by UN Women to women's inclusion in various ongoing peace processes.

However, the reverting to closed terms is also a fallback option in light of the difficulties of operationalizing an open framing of the included. This is because without in-depth knowledge of a given context, as one interviewee put it, 'it is impossible to see who is missing from the table'. Predefined actor groups based on gender or age simplify this intricate task. Women are an identifiable group: outsiders can easily count the number of women in a process, which then serves as a proxy for its inclusiveness. Several interviewees noted the danger of developing a 'box-ticking' mentality around inclusion, which reduces sensitivity to the conflict context, potentially obscures important fault lines, and can turn inclusion into a tokenistic exercise.

Inclusion strategies that apply closed framings also presume an essentialized group interest. For mediation practitioners, the rationale for women's inclusion corresponds with arguments presented in UN policy: to enhance women's voices and foster more diverse participation in order to advance women's rights and combat sexual and gender-based violence. Concrete UN mediation support activities in the realm of women's inclusion have empowerment at their core, typically involving capacity building and networking to prepare women for upcoming negotiations. However, respondents noted that the empowerment rhetoric often falls short: the mere presence of a small number of traditionally excluded individuals at the negotiation table can backfire as they are unlikely to make their contributions heard.

Furthermore, mediators' experiences demonstrate that concerns about essentializing women's (and other) identities are warranted. The earlier-mentioned interventions in support of women's inclusion obscure women's heterogeneous identities and create erroneous assumptions about their apolitical and 'independent' nature. Conflict parties may strategically exploit the inclusion discourse to place loyal women representatives at the table, a problem mentioned by several interviewees who spoke of 'regime women' or 'proxy women' included in negotiations. Moreover, inclusion by fixed actor category tends to deny the included the choice to speak on matters unrelated to their group membership. The resulting dynamic was described in interviews as one where, for example, included women 'fail to perform' the role expected of them by inclusion advocates since they sometimes even take 'regressive' positions on women's rights. The same can be said for those included by ethnicity or region: identity traits can be co-opted in order to occupy seats on a minority ticket, while advancing other agendas. This suggests that a strategic essentialism 'from the top' is likely to fail as it typically overlooks the complex interplay of the identities and interests of those included or excluded from a given process.

Finally, the use of closed framings can lead to competition for inclusion between fragmented interest groups that complicates peacemaking efforts. For instance, the latest trend to highlight the inclusion of youth has raised fears that representatives of 'quota' civil society groups may no longer engage in joint agendas, but rather compete in a struggle for seats at the table. Similarly, in contexts such as the UN-mediated Syria talks, calls for a separate women's delegation were met with fears that this could undermine other civil society representatives (Kapur, 2017). In sum, peacemaking strategies that frame the included in closed terms may help to fulfil international demands for inclusion, however they also contain the risks and trade-offs explored previously.

Towards Relational Inclusion

In contrast, a relational approach aims to account for the complexity, fluidity and intersectionality of actors' multiple interests and identities. Relationality requires thinking about the included not as homogeneous actor groups with clearly defined identities and interests, but moving the focus to the space between actors, asking how their multiple relationships can be transformed through peacemaking. It is less concerned with who has a voice at the table than with what this voice expresses, and for what purpose. This perspective may not produce easy answers. Unsurprisingly, we note that the practice of relational inclusion is less established among mediation professionals. Nonetheless, many acknowledge its potential to address the tensions arising from open and closed framings of inclusion, and aspire to more tailored, context-sensitive inclusion strategies built on thorough conflict and context analyses that can account for the cleavages and exclusionary fault lines of a particular conflict, be they regional, linguistic, ethnic, age or gender related.

Such an approach not only considers gender relations, for example, but includes a woman's position in existing power relations related to class, race and ethnicity. Relational inclusion therefore requires embracing the ontological complexity of social relationships that underpin both conflict and peace when studying and practising inclusion. It means asking less about who should be included, than what relations need to be transformed. This may require moving away from a notion of formal inclusion at the table that puts emphasis on the physical presence of a group representative voicing the seemingly homogeneous interests of a bounded constituency, towards a notion of substantive inclusion that focuses on the themes, narratives and interests that underpin relationships and therefore need to be brought to the table.

The outcome-oriented nature of mediation processes means the negotiation table may not be the obvious venue for conflict transformation. In fact, in discussions on sequencing, interviewees referred to the need to combine mediation with longer-term dialogue processes. Nonetheless, the decision on which relationships need to be discussed at the table should ideally itself be taken through a participatory, relational process in which mediators map out the web of relationships, including conflict fault lines and power relations. This means bringing perceptions and assumptions to the table as well so that conflict parties' and stakeholders' views on the conflict, and the inclusive arrangements through which the conflict can be transformed, can be co-constituted. Relationality thus invites us to think beyond the ideal-typical peace table constituted by single actors with bounded identities that define their interests, rights and needs, and move towards complex, dynamic mechanisms of negotiation that put those relationships on the table that are in need of transformation.

Conclusion and Outlook

Inclusion is currently omnipresent in international peacemaking agendas and discourses. As a concept it is deeply intertwined with many questions that are at the heart of the pursuit of peace. Inclusion may be promoted with the implicit aims of empowerment and protection of rights, the transformation of society or to increase the legitimacy of processes and outcomes. This points to the more fundamental question of what, ultimately, makes a good peace. In its current popularity however, inclusion risks becoming an empty buzzword, added as a qualifier to 'peace' in policy discourses, advocacy campaigns and diplomatic statements. We argue that if inclusion is to avoid this fate and make a meaningful contribution to peacemaking practice, scholars, policy makers, and practitioners must examine and make explicit its unspoken assumptions, theoretical groundings and political uses.

The analysis of key UN documents revealed a tension between the international normative framework, which exhibits a strong emphasis on closed terms with the aim of protecting and empowering included groups, and mediation guidance documents, which emphasize the merit of open and relational framings and ask for a deeper engagement with the conflict contexts. The predominant use of open and closed, as opposed to relational, framings leads to limitations in mediation practice: while open framings require operationalization if they are to transcend a merely symbolic function, closed framings can have essentializing and disempowering effects and can pitch actors with seemingly fixed identities against one another. In contrast, a transformative approach to inclusion, which engages with the relationships between actors, seems better placed to account for the intersectional, complex and fluid nature of their identities and interests. Relational inclusion thus focuses less on who has a seat at the table, and more on which relationships are brought to, and transformed, at the table.

Further research can contribute to the articulation of such an approach. A future research agenda on inclusion should focus more explicitly on the relational dimension of inclusion by conceiving of actors at the table not as representatives of static group interests, but rather as part of a dynamic web of relationships. This would shift the focus of current inclusion practice to how mediation efforts can support deeper social and political transformation. To better understand the merits and risks of relational inclusion, such research should employ an intersectional lens and critically reflect on claims about the interests and identities of the included. Relational inclusion should also be studied in its temporal and socio-spatial dimensions, asking how mediation efforts at the negotiation table interact with and can be complemented by broader conflict transformation efforts, and in what sequence this occurs. Building on the problematization of inclusion in peacemaking presented in this chapter, this emerging research agenda can ultimately contribute to a more critical, reflexive and relevant discourse and practice of inclusion.

References

Aharoni, S.B. (2017) 'Who Needs the Women and Peace Hypothesis? Rethinking Modes of Inquiry on Gender and Conflict in Israel/Palestine', *International Feminist Journal of Politics*, 19(3): 311–12.

Bell, C. and O'Rourke, C. (2007) 'The People's Peace? Peace Agreements, Civil Society, and Participatory Democracy', *International Political Science Review*, 28(3): 293–324.

Bell, C. and Pospisil, J. (2017) 'Navigating Inclusion in Transitions from Conflict: The Formalised Political Unsettlement', *Journal of International Development*, 29(5): 576–93.

Blaydes, L. and de Maio, J. (2010) 'Spoiling the Peace? Peace Process Exclusivity and Political Violence in North-Central Africa', *Civil Wars*, 12(1–2): 3–28.

Bose, S. (2002) *Bosnia after Dayton: Nationalist Partition and International Intervention*, London: Hurst & Co.

Castillejo, C. (2014) 'Promoting Inclusion in Political Settlements: A Priority for International Actors?', *The Norwegian Peacebuilding Resource Centre*.

Chesterman, S. (2007) 'Ownership in Theory and in Practice: Transfer of Authority in UN Statebuilding Operations', *Journal of Intervention and Statebuilding*, 1(1): 3–26.

Chetail, V. (ed) (2009) *Post-Conflict Peacebuilding: A Lexicon*. Oxford: Oxford University Press.

Convergne, E. (2016) 'UN Mediators' Collaboration with Scholars and Expert NGOs: Explaining the Need for Knowledge-Based Communities in Today's Conflicts', *International Negotiation*, 21(1): 135–64.

Davies, S.E. and True, J. (eds) (2019), *The Oxford Handbook of Women, Peace and Security*, Oxford: Oxford University Press.

de Waal, A. (2017) 'Inclusion in Peacemaking: From Moral Claim to Political Fact' in P. Aal and C.A. Crocker (eds), *The Fabric of Peace in Africa: Looking beyond the State*, Waterloo: Centre for International Governance Innovation, pp 165–86.

Donais, T. (2009) 'Inclusion or Exclusion? Local Ownership and Security Sector Reform', *Studies in Social Justice*, 3(1): 117–31.

Francis, D. (2004) 'Culture, Power Asymmetries and Gender in Conflict Transformation', *Berghof Research Center for Constructive Conflict Management*.

Goldmann, J., Kraus, A.I., Mason, S., Sticher, V. and Unger, B. (eds) (2013) 'Mind the Gap: How Mediation Support Can Better Respond to the Needs of Local Societies', *Discussion Points of the Mediation Support Network (MSN)*, No. 4.

Götschel, L. (2009) 'Conflict Transformation' in V. Chetail (ed), *Post-conflict Peacebuilding: A Lexicon*, Oxford: Oxford University Press, pp 92–104.

Hartzell, C. and Hoddie, M. (2003) 'Institutionalizing Peace: Power Sharing and Post-Civil War Conflict Management', *American Journal of Political Science*, 47(2): 318–32.

Hartzell, C. and Hoddie, M. (2015) 'The Art of the Possible: Power Sharing and Post-Civil War Democracy', *World Politics*, 67(1): 37–71.

Heitz, K. (2009) 'Power-Sharing in the Local Arena: A Rebel-Held Town in Western Côte d'Ivoire', *Africa Spectrum*, 44(3): 109–31.

Hellmüller, S. (2019) 'Beyond Buzzwords: Civil Society Inclusion in Mediation' in H-W. Jeong (ed), *Conflict Intervention and Transformation: Theory and Practice*, London and Lanham, MD: Rowman & Littlefield, pp 47–65.

Hoddie, M. (2014) 'Managing Conflict After Civil War: the Power-sharing and Power-dividing Approaches', *The Finnish Institute of International Affairs*: 1–14. Available at: https://www.fiia.fi/wp-content/uploads/2017/01/ a2.pdf.

Kappler, S. and Lemay-Hérbert, N. (2015) 'Hybrid Local Ownership in Bosnia-Herzegovina and Kosovo: From Discursive to Material Aspects of Ownership' in S.Y. Lee and A. Özerdem (eds), *Local Ownership in International Peacebuilding: Key Theoretical and Practical Issues*, London: Routledge, pp 74–92.

Kapur, B. (2017) 'Syrian Women in Political Processes 2012–2016, Literature Review', *The Kvinna till Kvinna Foundation*.

Kempin Reuter, T. (2012) 'Including Minority Rights in Peace Agreements: A Benefit or Obstacle to Peace Processes after Ethnic Conflicts?' *International Journal on Minority and Group Rights*, 19(4): 359–97.

Krause, J., Krause, W. and Bränfors, P. (2018) 'Women's Participation in Peace Negotiations and the Durability of Peace', *International Interactions*, 44(6): 985–1016.

Kymlicka, W. (1996) *Multicultural Citizenship: A Liberal Theory of Minority Rights*, Oxford: Clarendon Press.

International Institute of Democracy and Electoral Assistance (IDEA) (2017) *The Global State of Democracy: Exploring Democracy's Resilience.*

Lederach, J.P. (1997) *Building Peace: Sustainable Reconciliation in Divided Societies*, Washington, DC: United States Institute of Peace Press.

Lederach, J.P. (2005) *The Moral Imagination: The Art and Soul of Building Peace*, Oxford: Oxford University Press.

Lindemann, S. (2008) 'Do Inclusive Elite Bargains Matter? A Research Framework for Understanding the Causes of Civil War in Sub-Saharan Africa', *Crisis States Discussion Papers*, London: London School of Economics and Political Science.

Lindemann, S. (2011) 'Inclusive Elite Bargains and the Dilemma of Unproductive Peace: A Zambian Case Study', *Third World Quarterly*, 32(10): 1843–69.

Malmin Binningsbø, H. (2013) 'Power Sharing, Peace and Democracy: Any Obvious Relationships?' *International Area Studies Review*, 16(1): 89–112.

Mani, R. (2005) 'Rebuilding an Inclusive Political Community After War', *Security Dialogue*, 36(4): 511–12.

Martin de Almagro, M. (2018) 'Lost Boomerangs, the Rebound Effect and Transnational Advocacy Networks: A Discursive Approach to Norm Diffusion', *Review of International Studies*, 44(4): 672–93.

Mason, S. (ed) (2013) 'Translating Mediation Guidance into Practice: Commentary on the UN Guidance for Effective Mediation by the Mediation Support Network', *Discussion Points of the Mediation Support Network (MSN)*, No. 2.

Mehler, A. (2009) 'Introduction: Power-Sharing in Africa', *Africa Spectrum*, 44(3): 2–10.

Mitchell, C. (2002) 'Beyond Resolution: What Does Conflict Transformation Actually Transform?', *Peace and Conflict Studies*, 9(1): article 1.

Nilsson, D. (2008) 'Partial Peace: Rebel Groups Inside and Outside of Civil War Settlements', *Journal of Peace Research*, 45(4): 479–95.

Nilsson, D. (2012) 'Anchoring the Peace: Civil Society Actors in Peace Accords and Durable Peace', *International Interactions*, 38(2): 243–66.

Nilsson, D. and Söderberg Kovacs, M. (2011) 'Revisiting an Elusive Concept: A Review of the Debate on Spoilers in Peace Processes', *International Studies Review*, 13(4): 606–26.

Norris, P. (2008) *Driving Democracy: Do Power-Sharing Institutions Work?* Cambridge: Cambridge University Press.

Paffenholz, T. (2010) 'Civil Society and Peacebuilding' in T. Paffenholz (ed), *Civil Society and Peacebuilding. A Critical Assessment*, Boulder, CO: Lynne Rienner Publishers, pp 43–64.

Porter, E.J. (2007) *Peacebuilding: Women in International Perspective*, London and New York: Routledge.

Porter, E.J. (2013) 'Rethinking Women's Empowerment', *Journal of Peacebuilding & Development*, 8(1): 1–14.

Pospisil J. and Rocha Menocal, A. (2017) 'Why Political Settlements Matter: Navigating Inclusion in Processes of Institutional Transformation: Introduction to Special Issue', *Journal of International Development*, 29(5): 551–8.

Raffoul, A.W. (2019) 'Tackling the Power-Sharing Dilemma? The Role of Mediation', *swisspeace report*.

Reich, H. (2006) 'Local Ownership in Conflict Transformation Projects. Partnership, Participation or Patronage?', *Berghof Occasional Paper No. 27*, Berlin: Berghof Research Center for Constructive Conflict Management.

Reiter, A.G. (2016) *Fighting over Peace: Spoilers, Peace Agreements, and the Strategic Use of Violence*, New York, NY: Palgrave Macmillan.

Roberts, D.W. (2011) 'Post-Conflict Peacebuilding, Liberal Irrelevance and the Locus of Legitimacy', *International Peacekeeping*, 18(4): 410–24.

Spears, I.S. (2000) 'Understanding Inclusive Peace Agreements in Africa: The Problems of Sharing Power', *Third World Quarterly*, 21(1): 105–18.

Spivak, G.C. (1988) 'Can the Subaltern Speak?' in C. Nelson and L. Grossberg (eds), *Marxism and the Interpretation of Culture*, Urbana and Chicago, IL: University of Illinois Press, pp 271–313.

Taylor, C. (1994) *Multiculturalism: Examining the Politics of Recognition*, Princeton, NJ: Princeton University Press.

True, J. and Wiener, A. (2019) 'Everyone Wants (a) Peace: The Dynamics of Rhetoric and Practice on "Women, Peace and Security"', *International Affairs*, 95(3): 553–74.

Turner, C. (2020) 'Mapping a Norm of Inclusion in the Jus Post Bellum' in C. Stahn and J. Iverson (eds), *Just Peace After Conflict: Jus Post Bellum and the Justice of Peace*, Oxford: Oxford University Press.

UNDPA (United Nations Department of Political Affairs) (2017) *Guidance on Gender and Inclusive Mediation Strategies*, Nairobi: UNON Publication Section.

UNDPA (United Nations Department of Political Affairs) and UNEP (United Nations Environment Programme) (2015) *Natural Resources and Conflict: A Guide for Mediation Practitioners*.

UNGA (United Nations General Assembly) (2012) *Resolution A/66/811 on Strengthening the Role of Mediation in the Peaceful Settlement of Disputes, Conflict Prevention and Resolution*, 25 June.

UNITAR (United Nations Institute for Training and Research) and UNDPA (United Nations Department of Political Affairs) (2010) *A Manual for UN Mediators: Advice from UN Representatives and Envoys*.

UNSG (United Nations Secretary-General) (2012) 'Guidance for Effective Mediation' in United Nations General Assembly (UNGA), *Resolution A/66/811 on Strengthening the role of mediation in the peaceful settlement of disputes, conflict prevention and resolution*, 25 June.

United Nations Secretary-General (UNSG) (2017) *Resolution A/72/115 on the United Nations Activities in Support of Mediation*, 27 June.

United Nations Security Council (UNSC) (2000) *Resolution S/RES/1325 on Women and Peace and Security*, 31 October.

United Nations Security Council (UNSC) (2014) *Resolution S/RES/2171 on the Use of System-Wide Approach to Conflict Prevention*, 21 August.

Väyrynen, T. (2010) 'Gender and Peacebuilding' in O.P. Richmond (ed), *Peacebuilding. Critical Developments and Approaches*, New York, NY: Palgrave Macmillan, pp 137–53.

von Billerbeck S.B.K. (2016) *Whose Peace? Local Ownership and United Nations Peacekeeping*, Oxford: Oxford University Press.

Wanis-St. John, A. (2008) 'Peace Processes, Secret Negotiations and Civil Society: Dynamics of Inclusion and Exclusion', *International Negotiation*, 13(1): 1–9.

Wise, L. (2018) 'Setting Aside the "Others": Exclusion amid Inclusion of Non-Dominant Minorities in Peace Agreements', *Nationalism and Ethnic Politics*, 24(3): 311–23.

World Bank Group and United Nations (UN) (2018) *Pathways for Peace. Inclusive Approaches for Preventing Violent Conflict.*

Yousuf, Z. (2018) 'Navigating Inclusion in Peace Transitions. Beyond Elite Bargains', *Political Settlements Research Programme Report and Accord Spotlight*, London: Conciliation Resources.

Zanker, F. (2014) 'Legitimate Representation: Civil Society Actors in Peace Negotiations Revisited', *International Negotiation*, 19(1): 62–88.

8

Rethinking Mediation During Contested Regime Transformation and Episodes of Mobilization

Elisa Tarnaala

Introduction

Mediation scholarship focusing on international diplomacy and formal processes has paid little attention to the interplay between contested political processes at regime level and the collective action of ordinary people in demonstrations, protests and revolutions. Yet both regime type and previous patterns of mobilization and protest impact the space for manoeuvre in mediation. Structural conditions such as political institutions, historical legacies and economic realities shape the limits of what is possible in mediation and resulting peace processes. In other words, both pre-existing configurations of political contestation, as well as unexpected or spontaneous manifestations of political agency affect what is deemed possible by the regime and its outside contenders. It is therefore important to pay closer attention to these dynamics.

This chapter focuses on peace mediation from the perspective of political transitions and social mobilization. Most peace and transitional processes today from Tunisia to Burundi, Colombia to Libya have remained protracted and highly contested for years. It is possible to affirm that important mediation and conflict resolution efforts in these countries, as well as in several others, are taking place away from formal negotiation tables – parallel, independent or in opposition to the official process. In this context, the crucial questions for mediation theory and practice evolve around understanding the role and political reach of mediation to prevent and resolve crises originating from intra-regime division and conflict during regime transformation on the one hand, and extra-regime contentious claim making by actors that wish to challenge the status quo on the other hand. Street mobilizations to affect public opinion during the transition and ongoing negotiations are part of the repertoire of collective action in conflicted transitions and contested peace processes. Today both organized and spontaneous manifestations of protest have become increasingly visible. As a result it has become critical to understand how these forms of mobilization and pressure seek to transform the regime by influencing the negotiating parties from outside the formal peace table. This means recognizing and re-evaluating how mediation can positively engage with conflicted transitions, when regimes with long-term authoritarian legacies clash with domestic opposition and local participatory agendas, including contested and politicized peace initiatives. It also means better comprehending the link between conjectural political unrest in a given country and its historical experience of protest and repression. One way of understanding these dynamics is through the lens of inclusion.

Recently, mediation research and policy has converged around the idea of inclusion. Inclusion has become a buzzword for peace processes to the extent that authors have referred to the inclusion confusion (de Waal, 2017) or the new inclusion project (Bell, 2018). Others have shown through UN materials and interviews how inclusion is recommended from building legitimacy to the process to including 'voices and stakeholders' in negotiations. Equally, inclusion has stretched from protecting the marginalized, to the inclusion of women among mediation professionals (Hirblinger and Landau, 2020). This converging of growing normativity on inclusion with calls for its practical implementation have gradually developed into inclusion becoming a preferred method and a goal in itself in peace processes. Strategic inclusivity advice to mediators has become commonplace, and encounters with local actors as well as with marginalized and victimized groups have been facilitated by third parties to persuade elite negotiators at the peace table of the benefits of inclusion. These efforts by multiple international actors to render peace processes and their designs more inclusive by incorporating claims of new agents into negotiations should not be underestimated. In many cases, creating fora and listening to those who were excluded from the formal peace negotiation has increased public and international legitimacy of the process and provided strength for movements and organizations to continue their struggle for representation.

However, what has been largely excluded from this analysis is the relationship between models of process-centred inclusion and political agency and social transformation that is exercised outside the formal process. These forms of mobilization are increasingly important in questioning and challenging existing regimes and yet are not easily incorporated into existing inclusion practices. Within the crowded field of international mediation, state representatives and elites, oppositions and social movements interact with international entities, all intensely mandated to support inclusion. Inclusion has become a sought-after outcome that represents normatively all the good things – it has become simultaneously a condition for future democracy, peace and a just society, and a vehicle towards these goals. This has led to optical errors in over-evaluating and confusing the normative context and technical solutions of an inclusive peace process with the political realities outside the process. In this sense, a growing consensus over technical inclusive peace process design risks silencing more radical political demands for reform and inclusion manifested in socio-political processes that demand transformative change in state–society relations (Acemoglu and Robinson, 2017).

To rethink mediation from the perspective of political transitions and social mobilizations, two academic traditions of understanding political conflict, and their key conceptual categories, are highlighted: the literature on regime change, and research on mobilization and social conflict. These interrelated fields have rarely been examined together from the perspective of mediation theory and practice. Mediation theory based on models related to individual actors and their choices has tended to sideline the essential question of the significance of regime type when setting expectations for short-term political change. Similarly, the historical space for civil society as an indicator of what type of change can be imagined, and what is deemed possible by the regime and its contenders (in the longer term) is another topic that has interested sociologists but has been unexplored in the mediation literature. These two macro-societal, structural characteristics have a decisive impact on what peace processes can achieve in terms of socio-political change more broadly, and including previously excluded groups in peace processes in particular.

To illustrate the argument on inclusion, political agency and structural conditions, the issue of women's participation in peace processes is given a specific emphasis. The chapter highlights that a greater historical sensibility to contextual particularities of women's movements and their political demands is needed in order to better understand how change happens and what can be built on earlier legacies. Without a willingness from the regime's representatives and the negotiating elites to engage at a strategic moment in questions of structural reform that would respond to claims for a more inclusive state, simply including women in mediation and peace processes risks becoming a tick-box exercise. If the process looks overwhelmingly inwards, to its own effectiveness and not outwards towards historically and contextually constructed demands about participation and representation, efforts by international diplomatic actors, funders and professional peace mediation organizations to include women in peace processes as negotiators, mediators or civil society participants can result in disillusionment. Transitions from war to peace, and particularly the institutional change that is often associated with them, are long-term processes. Changing political attitudes takes longer than dismantling the power structures of the previous regime. Women's inclusion in this political scene cannot be regarded as a separate sphere of activity where easy outcomes can be expected. In the context of mediation, efforts to include women are fundamentally dependent on regime type and transformation, and on the availability of political space for collective claim making as a means of challenging the status quo.

Transitions from War to Peace: Understanding the Dynamics of Regime Change

After the Cold War, mediation as an international instrument for settling political disputes became closely associated with the concept of liberal peace and its normative political and economic framework within the boundaries of the existing state system (Paris, 2004). Mediation was seen more broadly as a way of settling, resolving or pacifying differences through diplomacy, law, institutional reform, and state-centric design (Richmond, 2018). Peacebuilding operations were named second generation or post-Westphalian since they aimed not merely to ensure the continued existence of the state, but also to feature parliamentary democracy, protection for minority rights, and free-market capitalism. The standard post-war package aimed at facilitating the transition to liberal democracy included constitution making, elections within two years of war's end, civil society funding and extensive state building (Anderson, 2016).

Within this framework it was believed that if peace negotiations broadened democratic agendas by providing political opportunities for excluded groups, then comprehensive peace agreements could remake the state as a liberal democracy. Transition studies in the 1990s that mostly focused on elites and decisions made at the formal political level (O'Donnell et al, 1991; Rueschemeyer et al, 1992) influenced this vision as they concentrated on how the political regime changes through a 'pact' that allows leaders to settle disputes and share power within the framework of democracy. Emphasizing the trajectories from dictatorship to democracy or from war to peace, these transformations were understood through a lens of political science and sociology and as an exercise in domestic politics where state institutions changed from closed and authoritarian to liberal democratic, with limited and controlled external influence. This had an impact on the field of mediation studies, which adopted a similar understanding of regime change, albeit through the lens of international diplomacy, great power politics and the role of the United Nations. Common to these approaches was a focus on concerted political will, effective leadership and governable states as ideal types of liberal peace.

Focusing on ideal types, however, overshadowed the fact that most transitioning states continued being hybrid regimes. It was noted that hybrid regimes – those between dictatorship and democracy – were statistically more prone to violence and instability. It was deemed unrealistic to expect the creation of new, democratic institutions in response to a peace agreement, especially in states that had barely enough resources to support the survival of their populations (Osterud, 2004). In response, others argued that in order to advance democracy in conditions of fragility, the focus of developing state institutions should be directed to strengthening civil society and the private sector at the expense of the state (Barnett, 2011). Moreover, research on African peace processes noted that, to date, there had been no concrete cases but only a few positive developments from war-autocracy to peace-democracy. Truly inclusive peace processes still remain a normative ideal rather than empirically validated experiences as almost all African states experiencing full-scale civil war have been, and continue to be, autocracies (Maina and Melander, 2016: 288–92). The most interesting angle for both research and policy in these cases consists of shifting the focus from straightforward regime change to understanding what non-linear transitions and transformations below the level of the state would allow mediation to achieve, and what could be expected from the resulting peace process.

Understanding the political dynamics of conflicted and occasionally violent transformations of post-war hybrid regimes might cast more light on the future role of mediation than models based on inclusive peace processes that implicitly expect authoritarian regimes to transition towards democracy once an agreement has been reached following an inclusive process. The second decade of 2000 saw cases such as Libya, where an internationally assisted constitutional and political process has reverted to open civil war, and Burundi, where, after an inclusive peace agreement and years of relative stability, violent political competition through the electoral system is pushing the country back into conflict and authoritarianism. Even in countries that were not deemed fragile, but with relatively stable institutions and considerable middle class populations – countries such as Colombia and Ukraine – the regime itself is constantly being contested in the midst of prolonged crisis. Looking at the discrepancy between negotiations and political regimes from an international angle, scholars have emphasized that across the Middle East, peace initiatives have avoided deep structural and geopolitical problems in the state or international system, and merely searched for the mitigation, but not ending, of violence. Mediation has operated on existing and unquestioned relations between geopolitics, regimes, technology and capital. It has included accepting power balances between the state and various violent and non-violent non-state actors (Duffield, 2002; Chandler and Richmond, 2015). This inconsistency between the liberal democratic norms and political realities around peace processes understood as political marketplaces where complex local and regional interests are negotiated in the midst of conflict seems not to be changing (Carothers and Samet-Marram, 2015). Neither the international mediation community, nor indeed the theoretical literature on mediation, has yet developed any new tools for understanding the impact of these situations that evolve outside the peace table but are closely associated to decisions made around it.

Within the more practice-oriented policy literature on peace mediation, some authors converge on the claim that an elite pact is required for a transition to take place, but for inclusion mechanisms to be introduced, some degree of openness of the regime towards broadening participation needs to exist (Paffenholz et al, 2016; Whitfield, 2019). In concrete cases where a participatory process was lacking – including failure to accept claims made through citizen mobilization – a peace process could not be implemented beyond an agreement on paper. If an elite agreement on participation was missing from an earlier phase of political settlement, any inclusive national dialogue process that followed to collectively deliberate over a common future could not independently alter or even question existing power balances and lead to inclusive transitions (Papagianni, 2014). Willingness to be open to the demands for reform through participatory processes is therefore a key requirement for inclusion to be successful.

However, the risk of this approach, as seen in cases as different as the Central African Republic, Libya and Colombia, where pressures for deeper change were truncated, is that enabling participation beyond the technical process may also enable social and political mobilization that challenges the existing power balance between state and society. This type of inclusive transition has a high risk of dividing the elites. Negotiating elites therefore accept broadening participation only if it entails no risk to them or it caters to their needs – that is, if the probability of change outside the process itself is very low. This creates incentives to maintain an inwards-focused approach to inclusion in mediation to avoid the risks of engaging with external forces that cannot be controlled. However, it also undermines the value of inclusion as a form of participation in mediation.

As a result, it may be more relevant to examine the reform and participatory pressures on political systems as indicators of regime transformation and therefore on the likelihood of success in mediation. For example, it is difficult to assess how Colombia, despite its perfectly inclusive peace table, will settle the problem of continuing violence against local social movement leaders demanding the implementation of the peace agreement; or how Burundi, after a successful peace process in the 1990s, can avoid its current spiral into authoritarianism. These cases remind us of the long-term consequences of peace mediation and of reaching short-term agreements that do not adequately engage with the external factors of regime type that will limit the possibility for change. As Christine Bell has noted, radical disagreement over the state's project of inclusion, and the incapacity of democratic institutions to adequately address it, is fast becoming the global dilemma of our time (Bell, 2018: 16), and it is a dilemma that has particular relevance for the work of peace mediation.

Movements, Mobilizations and the Limits of Civil Society Participation

Most studies of social movements have focused on fully mature democratic systems or examined agency that played a role in successful transitions to democracy (Tarrow, 1994; Bosi et al, 2016). As with the regime change literature, these studies have often ignored the mobilization cycles that place the question of democratization on the agenda and drive the struggle for either democratic consolidation or defeat (della Porta, 2014). In transitions involving conflict or post-conflict situations, directing attention to episodes of mobilization that illuminate the dynamics of transitions from below can provide important insights for studying mediation and peace processes. Even in cases where transition was unsuccessful, these moments of agency highlight diverse paths to regime transformation. Organizational and institutional structures, forms of action, and dynamics of past episodes of mobilization can offer essential information for future change (della

Porta et al, 2018). In this light, it is crucial to make sense both of how movements with organizational resources can influence peace processes in a more structured way, and of how moments of popular and often spontaneous mobilization can have an impact on the political context and public opinion during various phases of the process. Both these aspects of mobilization can shape the prospects of success in mediation but are often overlooked in the literature on inclusion as it looks inwards at the process rather than outwards to what is happening outside the talks. Yet to understand the contribution of movements and mobilizations to mediation it is necessary to understand the context in which civil society operates, including understanding the history of social mobilization and the political space within which it happens. There are two key themes to be explored. The first is the depoliticizing effect of the inclusion of civil society in formal peace processes. The second is the risk to social and political movements in engaging in mobilization.

Recent mediation literature that has focused on the inclusion of civil society in peace mediation has focused on the benefits of this participation for ensuring both the inclusivity of the agenda, and the legitimacy of the outcome. Civil society participation has been widely discussed as a means of democratizing peace processes (Paffenholz et al, 2016; Yousuf, 2018). Inclusive representation is believed to have beneficial impacts on the resulting peace agreement in relation to matters such as respect for human rights and democracy. Further, inclusive processes are believed to lead to more sustainable agreements (Nilsson, 2012; Krause et al, 2018). However, such studies implicitly assume that 'civil society' supports peace processes, does not attempt to challenge or radically question the premise of representation, and stays uninvolved in the power politics of mediation. In these terms, inclusion co-opts social and political movements as civil society and mainstreams their demands into the language of mediation and liberal peacebuilding.

An inclusive mediation process is often expected to produce more sustainable peace not only nationally, but also locally. International interventions tend to see the local population in idealistic terms and assume a shared understanding of the aims of the post-war reconstruction process between international actors and the local population (Carayannis et al, 2014; Paffenholz, 2015). Indeed, some scholars have argued that the discourse of local ownership is largely used as a tool to legitimize international activities in conflict-affected contexts (see Hirblinger and Landau, 2020: 4). Yet empirical studies examining the relationship between internationally led peacebuilding efforts and local contexts have noted how local civil societies are tied in numerous ways to the politics that drive other national actors (Björkdahl and Höglund, 2013).

Grassroots participation is part of the political dynamics in conflict-affected countries. Social movements and activists were a vital component of most independence struggles in Africa. Labour, youth and women's movements fought for the end of authoritarianism and headed demands for democracy in Latin America and Asia. In all these contexts, organized movements were decisive actors in contentious politics that pushed for state formation, state building and broadening citizenship (Lewis, 2002: 569–86; Bermeo and Yashar, 2016).

These examples lead to the second theme related to civil society participation, which is the lack of acknowledgement of the risks of mobilization in states where the regime is unwilling to engage with demands for more radical social or political transformation. With the focus on civil society inclusion as an unquestioned and unproblematized benefit for the process, mediation research has not fully recognized the threats involved in more radical mobilization and protest during peace processes nor considered how these dynamics impact on the likelihood of success of mediation. Emphasizing inclusivity and participation can become challenging if security and political space are lacking. For example, in the case of Colombia, despite a comprehensive peace agreement and an inclusive peace process involving the international community as well as representatives of civil society, ongoing political tensions and violence threaten the transition. Less an outcome of an inclusive peace, this shows a continuum with the country's historical patterns of crushing movements violently, especially those outside the capital, in particular in the regions with a history of protest, subversion and poverty. An inclusive process that implicitly or explicitly opens the space for civil society to challenge current institutions in a political context where the government is not open to demands for deeper or more transformative change creates risks and will be unlikely to lead to a sustainable agreement. Understanding the history of social and political mobilization within the country in question is therefore crucial to understanding the likely effect of inclusion in mediation.

Many organizations across the globe today have less space within which to operate as governments characterize civil society more as political opponents than organizations contributing to democracy and social change. This is a challenging situation for mediation as the same governments that negotiate peace also control civic space with an iron fist. Moreover, within regimes that prioritize political cohesion and economic progress over human rights and democratic governance, patterns are emerging where neighbouring states apply similar legislation and tactics, learning from one another about how to control civic space. In countries such as Rwanda, Burundi and South Sudan (all conflict or transitioning states) this type of transnational learning is taking place (Oxfam, 2016). This is evidenced in the fact that some of the recent high-profile protests have failed to deliver significant near-term results despite their international visibility and ongoing internationally sponsored peace processes in the region. The broader picture is more complex than these processes reveal. Research on mediation and mediation frameworks has a lot to gain from merging contextual analysis with theoretical reflection on the balance between peace agreements involving intra-process participation, and social and political mobilization outside the process. In the early works on democratization, movements and mobilizations were either ignored altogether or regarded with suspicion as dangers to democracy and stability (Huntington, 1965). The works on contentious politics brought many new empirical studies and theoretical reflection about the relationship between the state, political parties and movements to better understand the logic of social change during political mobilization (Goldstone, 2003; Tarrow, 1994). Recently, researchers have pointed out that overlooking the impressive heterogeneity of today's protests can cause observers to underestimate the significance of the protest events and overestimate how easy it will be for governments to shut them down (Carothers and Wong, 2020). This creates a potential political blind spot for mediators.

Not all mobilization will bring about a transition, but intense grassroots mobilization can be a moment of critical juncture towards change. Even when demands are silenced, the next attempt to break with the past might be louder and with today's hybrid regimes where the pressure from below is often crushed, a repertoire for future cycles of mobilization will remain. By taking into account the regime's past and the previous space for civil society it becomes easier to understand how the issue of inclusion is negotiated, co-opted or left aside in a peace process, as regimes try to control the interests of both local and transnational actors in order to manage instability and maintain power.

Women's Participation in Peace Negotiations and Women's Movements

These dynamics relating to regime change and social and political mobilization are particularly evident in the literature on women's participation in peace processes. The Women, Peace and Security Agenda has mirrored the drive towards co-option of political protest and managing it within the parameters of a mediation process. And yet this overlooks much of the contribution of women's political activism and grassroots mobilization in demanding social and political reform outside of formal processes.

Women's rights scholars and activists have emphasized how women's rights as international normative frameworks in peace and security were not born within the liberal democratic paradigm. They preceded historically and were constructed theoretically in their time as arguments for radical equality. According to research these were outcomes of the joint efforts of domestic, transnational and international feminist advocacy groups who demanded the inclusion of women's rights specifically (Htun and Weldon, 2018). Many women's movements and activists who led these early initiatives had participated in revolutionary or liberation movements in their respective countries. They later led activities pushing for the recognition of human rights and women's rights and have headed demonstrations for political renovation, democratic participation and social justice (El Said et al, 2015). Gender-sensitive security approaches, and justice and equality as bases for governance, health and education, were at the centre of this feminist agenda that placed the state at the core of its demands, along with a claim for global justice as part of its narrative. The Women, Peace and Security Agenda, which started to develop in the 2000s, built strongly on this legacy but also developed in sync with the liberal peace norm diffusion where a supporting civil society, local participatory mechanisms and women at the peace table were seen as non-political and non-regime-questioning options towards peace.

The current literature on women, peace and security provides much empirical information on women's peace activism and involvement in peace processes (Ellerby, 2013). Recently, a body of policy literature has emerged that has argued how women's participation in peace negotiations is beneficial to the process in particular, and to the sustainability of peace in general (UN Women, 2012; Palmiano Federer and Gasser, 2016). The international community has been called to act on the low numbers of women signatories of peace agreements or women lead mediators as successful outcomes in peace processes are argued to depend on the participation of women and girls, while excluding women contributes to the failure of peacebuilding (UN Women, 2012; Dayal, 2018). More cautious observers have remarked that, especially when complemented by other forms of outreach and engagement, women's potential to broaden the base of a political process – if it advances – is significant (Whitfield, 2019: 6). The benefit of women's participation in peace processes (beyond a normative conviction that female participation ought to be supported), however, still tends to be based on the notion of female 'soft skills', such as the trust- and community-building skills of women and women's organizations that are portrayed as fundamentally non-political. Women have to appeal to the dominant individuals controlling the negotiations, casting themselves as non-threatening and occupying consultative roles in the processes. There is no information why in some countries, in certain cases, this type of soft-skill participation has failed to work, or how the political context, such as other civil society groups and their agendas, can make women's participation difficult.

Several authors have highlighted, from the perspective of comparative peace processes, how, in numerous documented cases, women advocated for peace and security but also sought to advance demands to reform the post-conflict state (McWilliams and Kilmurray, 1997; Nakaya, 2003; Daley, 2007; Meertens and Zambrano, 2010). It is widely acknowledged that women should participate in and influence peace negotiations not only in terms of representation or general peace advocacy, but also through seeking to influence the post-conflict state by introducing issues of structural reform and gender justice to the agenda of negotiations (Anderson, 2016). The literature, both policy oriented and theoretical, however, places a much stronger emphasis on advocating for peace than demanding reforms. Women are advised to build alliances and enter the process early on in order to gain a seat at the table or ensure channels of communication with the mediators. There is strikingly little knowledge available on women's struggles for agenda setting – which issues competed in entering the agenda of the negotiations, and how those themes that were chosen were included and others rejected.

Protection and participation of women are recognized as important elements of international mediation practice at the level of international, regional and sub-regional organizations. The preference of international organizations in promoting women's participation and advocacy for peace through civil society and directing the voice of women towards the international community might result in less interest in promoting women's interaction with state actors. Overlooking the power holders of the regime risks excluding future demands for political and social transformation promoted by women's organizations. The important focus on local and informal peacebuilding, and the increasing calls to enforce women's national and international peace networks, should not disconnect mediators from the national-level political and social realities in supporting women's movements in the framing of issues of structural reform and political participation. Mediation and post-conflict contexts present an important window of opportunity for women to promote institutional change (Hughes, 2009). They create opportunities to participate in social, political and economic transformation and the struggle to include women's rights in these efforts is one of the first ways to create this change (Ní Aoláin et al, 2011; Tripp et al, 2009).

Focusing on peace agreements between 1975 and 2011, Miriam Anderson (2016) finds that the conflict length, the cohesiveness of the local women's groups involved, and women's presence at the peace table were instrumental in determining whether women's rights were included in the texts of peace agreements.[1] According to Anderson, women's rights clauses in peace agreements are framed in human rights language and reflect international norms on women. Due to the links between the women representatives and transitional feminist advocacy networks, the language reflects less specific national or regional cultural norms and emphasizes international norms of protection of women and rights to participate. Anderson argues that peace processes are important sites for norm diffusion. From the 195 peace agreements surveyed and relating to 58 conflicts, 40 per cent (23) contain references to women. These agreements try to include women's rights; they mostly reflect international norms on women's rights, but they seek also to alter women's role in the state. The study reveals that women activists use human rights language because of their socialization in transnational feminist networks. The use of the language does not appear to be a conscious choice, but through socialization processes women activists have come to identify with human rights language and use it by default (Anderson, 2016: 2–13, 50).

In this direction, UN resolution 1325 has been criticized because it assumes that women's victimization in conflict and absence in peacebuilding institutions can be remedied by drawing international attention to the issue. For the critics it is unrealistic to assume that the power of advocacy and better technical instruments could overcome greater structural factors that create and promote inequality. Supposing that international frameworks will be adopted and implemented despite power asymmetry is highly unlikely (Kuttab, 2014). In real-life conflicts, an engagement with the broader opening of the post-agreement polity has continued to be difficult or impossible for excluded groups. Once the peace table is over and the formal process has closed, it is in the juncture of inter-regime political competition; battles between ex-regime, deep state, and criminal enterprises; and episodes of street protests where women's movements need to survive and be supported.

[1] Peace agreements reviewed in the study containing provisions on women's rights (23 in total) set out certain parameters for a formal transition such as gender quota in the administration, or pursued to change women's status in the long term, supporting gender-role transformation. Other agreements did not specify legislative change but called for awareness in women's rights and participation generally. Several mentioned electoral quotas or mandated the creation of institutions and offices devoted to women's rights (Anderson, 2016: 6, 14–19). All the agreements referred to common principles of human rights and specific instruments, but most framed their goals in a remarkably vague way: the relationship between women and the state ought to be changed, but without saying how.

Conclusion

In the peace mediation literature the issue of political will and regime character have central roles in the success and failure of peace negotiations. The leadership of the different opposing factions is critical to the advancing of the dialogue, as the thinking and ideology that guides particular leaders is likely to have influence over the setting of the agenda and posterior enforcement of the agreement. In many contexts, the conflict parties and their leaders have not been primarily concerned in the social conditions of their countries, and promoting social and political change by demanding rights related to political participation, development, health and education has been in the hands of other actors. In these cases political parties and social movements have been the most critical agents pushing for regime transformation and an inclusive state. In a transitional setting, intra-regime and ex-regime hidden tensions, and outside mobilization claiming for inclusion, play a critical role in stabilizing or destabilizing the process. Many current peace processes and transitions that have extended in time or relapsed in conflict are examples of these dynamics at play. The key to understanding today's post-Westphalian processes characterized by enduring transitions is perhaps to accept that the outcomes of mediation cannot be fixed, at least in the short or medium term.

The chapter has suggested that the obstacles in advancing political agendas that could address issues of rights and state reform during peace processes might result not only from a lack of political will of states or power players, but also from an incapacity to conceive mediation in broader terms, where not only the formal actors at the table and those 'included' need to be taken into account, but also the mobilizations within society and the domestic political competition associated with regime transformation. Inclusion should not be understood in an instrumentalist or simplistic way as part of a toolkit equalling an inclusive process with an inclusive list of participants or consultations involving like-minded actors. From a perspective of political transitions and social mobilization, claims over inclusion are elements of time-bound and contentious agendas, inherently linked to the disputes over the state's project of rights, participation and justice, and thus essentially part of the political process of democratization. Seen from this angle, in mediation settings inclusion as part of a socio-political process needs to be contextualized in the political past and shifting power balances within a regime. It should entail critical debates about structural reforms and a long-term approach to political change, and include political parties and other social forces. Otherwise, an inclusive process can become merely a technical exercise benefitting external process designers and operational frameworks for development aid implementation (Richmond, 2018).

Understanding the centrality of the regime type and the political tensions and divisions entailed in it, as well as the historical trajectories and current dynamics of civil society mobilizations, can provide a more accurate picture for international and domestic mediation actors in peace processes. It is expected that the agency of social forces other than the negotiating elites can be important in introducing specific civil, political and social rights and pushing for regime transformation – if the context is right. Political organizing and claim making, including by women's movements, shapes the context and impacts regime dynamics, but change will not be fast or linear. Rethinking mediation should involve understanding these multiple political time frames and their impacts. During the critical junctures that peace processes can be, the recognition of citizens' right to protest; creation of channels of institutional access; and public sensitivity to social justice could advance remarkably, instead of being just distant ideals.

References

Acemoglu, D. and Robinson, J.A. (2017) *The Emergence of Weak, Despotic and Inclusive States*. NBER Working Paper No. 23657.

Anderson, M. (2016) *Windows of Opportunity: How Women Seize Peace Negotiations for Political Change*, Oxford: Oxford University Press.

Barnett, M. (2011) *Empire of Humanity: A History of Humanitarianism*, Ithaca, NY: Cornell University Press.

Bell, C. (2019) 'New Inclusion Project: Building Inclusive Peace Settlements' in A. Carl (ed) *Accord Issue 28, Navigating Inclusion in Peace Processes*, London: Conciliation Resources, pp 11–17.

Bermeo, N. and Yashar D. (eds) (2016) *Parties, Movements, and Democracy in the Developing World*, Cambridge Studies in Contentious Politics, Cambridge: Cambridge University Press.

Björkdahl A. and Höglund K. (2013) 'Precarious Peacebuilding: Friction in Global-Local Encounters', *Peacebuilding*, 1(3), 289–99.

Bosi, L., Giugni, M. and Uba, K. (eds) (2016) *The Consequences of Social Movements*, Cambridge: Cambridge University Press.

Carayannis, T., Bojicic-Dzelilovic, V., Olin, N., Rigterink, A. and Schomerus, M. (2014) 'Practice Without Evidence: Interrogating Conflict Resolution Approaches and Assumptions', *Justice and Security Research Programme (JSRP) Paper 11*, London: International Development Department, London School of Economics.

Carothers, T. and Samet-Marram, O. (2015) *The New Global Marketplace of Political Change*, Washington, DC: Carnegie Endowment for Peace.

Carothers, T. and Wong, D. (2020) 'Misunderstanding Global Protests', Commentary, Carnegie Endowment for International Peace, 1 April.

Chandler, D. and Richmond, O.P. (2015) 'Contesting Post-liberalism: Governmentality or Emancipation?', *Journal of International Relations and Development*, 18, 1–24.

Daley, P. (2007) 'The Burundi Peace Negotiations: An African Experience of Peace-Making', *Review of African Political Economy*, 34(112), 333.

Dayal, A. (2018) *Connecting Informal and Formal Peace Talks: From Movements to Mediators*, Washington, DC: Georgetown Institute for Women, Peace and Security.

de Waal, A. (2017) 'Inclusion in Peacemaking: From Moral Claim to Political Fact' in P. Aall and C. Crocker (eds) *The Fabric of Peace in Africa: Looking Beyond the State*, Waterloo, ON, Canada: Centre for International Governance Innovation, pp 165–86.

della Porta, D. (2014) *Mobilizing for Democracy. Comparing 1989 and 2011*, Oxford: Oxford University Press.

della Porta, D., Hidde Donker, T., Hall, B., Poljarevic, E. and Ritter, D.P. (2018) *Social Movements and Civil War. When Protests for Democratization Fail*, London: Routledge.

Duffield, M. (2002) *Global Governance and the New Wars: The Merging of Development and Security*, London: Zed Books.

El Said, M., Meari, D.L. and Pratt, D.N. (eds) (2015) *Rethinking Gender in Revolutions and Resistance: Lessons from the Arab World*, London: Zed Books.

Ellerby K. (2013) '(En)gendered Security? The Complexities of Women's Inclusion in Peace Processes', *International Interactions*, 39(4), 435–60.

Goldstone, J. (ed) (2003) *States, Parties, and Social Movements. Cambridge Studies in Contentious Politics*, Cambridge: Cambridge University Press.

Hirblinger, A. and Landau, D. (2020) 'Daring to Differ? Strategies of Inclusion in Peacemaking', *Security Dialogue*, Online First.

Htun M. and Weldon L. (2018) *The Logics of Gender Justice: State Action on Women's Rights Around the World*, New York: Cambridge University Press.

Hughes, M. (2009) 'Armed Conflict, International Linkages, and Women's Parliamentary Representation in Developing Nations', *Social Problems*, 56(1), 174–204.

Huntington, S. (1965) 'Political Development and Political Decay', *World Politics*, 17(3), 386–430.

Krause, J., Krause, W. and Bränfors, P. (2018) 'Women's Participation in Peace Negotiations and the Durability of Peace', *International Interactions*, 44(6), 985–1016.

Kuttab, E. (2014) 'The Many Faces of Feminism. Palestinian Women's Movements Finding a Voice', in S. Nazneen and M. Sultan (eds) *Voicing Demands: Feminist Activism in Transnational Contexts*, London: Zed Books, pp 219–87.

Lewis, D. (2002) 'Civil Society in African Contexts: Reflections on the Usefulness of a Concept', *Development and Change*, 33(4): 569–86.

Maina, G. and Melander, E. (2016) *Peace Agreements and Durable Peace in Africa*, Scottsville: University of Kwa-Zulu-Natal Press.

McWilliams, M. and Kilmurray, A. (1997) 'Athene on the Loose; the Origins of the Northern Ireland Women's Coalition', *Irish Journal of Feminist Studies*, 2(1), 1–21.

Meertens, D. and Zambrano, M. (2010) 'Citizenship Deferred: The Politics of Victimhood, Land Restitution and Gender Justice in the Colombian (Post?) Conflict', *International Journal of Transitional Justice*, 4(2): 189–206, July.

Nakaya, S. (2003) 'Women and Gender Equality in Peace-building: From Women at the Negotiation Table to Postwar Structural Reforms in Guatemala and Somalia', *Global Governance*, 9, 459–76.

Ní Aoláin, F., Haynes, D.F. and Cahn, N. (2011) *On the Frontlines: Gender, War and the Post-Conflict Process*, Oxford: Oxford University Press.

Nilsson, D. (2012) 'Anchoring the Peace: Civil Society Actors in Peace Accords and Durable Peace', *International Interactions: Empirical and Theoretical Research in International Relations*, 38(2), 243–66.

O'Donnell, G., Schmitter, P. and Whitehead, L. (eds) (1991) *Transitions from Authoritarian Rule: Comparative Perspectives*, Volume 3, Baltimore, MD: Johns Hopkins University Press.

Osterud O. (2004) *Power and Democracy: Critical Interventions*, Aldershot: Ashgate.

Oxfam (2016) 'Putting Citizens' Voice at the Centre of Development: Challenging Shrinking Civic Space across Africa', *Pan African Policy Brief*, [online] November, available from: https://www.oxfam.org/sites/www.oxfam.org/files/file_attachments/oxfam-policy-brief-civil-society-nov16_en.pdf (accessed 29 August 2019).

Paffenholz, T. (2015) 'Unpacking the Local Turn in Peacebuilding: A Critical Assessment Towards an Agenda for Future Research', *Third World Quarterly*, 36(5): 857–74.

Paffenholz, T., Ross, N., Dixon, S., Schluchter, A.-L. and True, T. (2016) *Making Women Count – Not Just Counting Women: Assessing Women's Inclusion and Influence on Peace Negotiations*, Geneva: Inclusive Peace & Transition Initiative/The Graduate Institute of International and Development Studies and UN Women.

Palmiano Federer, J. and Gasser, R. (2016) 'International Peace Mediation and Gender: Bridging the Divide', *BPC Policy Brief*, Vol 6(5), November/16.

Papagianni, K. (2014) *National Dialogue Processes in Political Transitions*. Civil Society Dialogue Network Discussion Paper No. 3.

Paris, R. (2004) *At War's End*, Cambridge: Cambridge University Press.

Richmond, O.P. (2018) 'A Genealogy of Mediation in International Relations: From "Analogue" to "Digital" Forms of Global Justice or Managed War?', *Cooperation and Conflict*, 53(3), [online], available from: https://journals.sagepub.com/doi/full/10.1177/0010836717750198 (accessed 29 August 2019).

Rueschemeyer, D., Stephens, E.H. and Stephens, J.D. (1992) *Capitalist Development and Democracy*, Chicago, IL: University of Chicago Press.

Tarrow, S. (1994) *Power in Movement. Social Movements, Collective Action and Politics*, Cambridge and New York: Cambridge University Press.

Tripp, A., Caimiro, I. and Kwesiga, K. (2009) *African Women's Movements: Transforming Political Landscapes*, New York: Cambridge University Press.

UN Women (2012) *Women's Participation in Peace Negotiations: Connections between Presence and Influence*, New York: UN Women.

Whitfield, T. (2019) 'Mediating in a Complex World', *Oslo Forum Background Paper*, Geneva: The Centre for Humanitarian Dialogue, [online], available from: https://www.hdcentre.org/wp-content/uploads/2019/07/Mediating-in-a-complex-world.pdf (accessed 29 August 2019).

Yousuf, Z. (2018) *Navigating Inclusion in Peace Transitions: Beyond Elite Bargains*, London: Conciliation Resources.

9

From Normative to Social Approaches to Inclusion: Supporting Multi-scalar Peace Process Design

Emma Van Santen

Introduction

The conflict environment in which peace mediators operate has changed considerably since the end of the Cold War. The discrete Cold War conflicts between a state and a major ethno-nationalist rebel group, each backed by a Cold War power, have fragmented into complex multi-layered and intersecting local communal and national civil struggles. Modern conflict is also characterized by a proliferation of different types of armed groups, including organized crime, rebel groups, gangs and global Islamist groups. The complexity of contemporary intra-state conflicts poses fundamental questions regarding the relevance of the dominant liberal inclusion strategies for peace mediation. 'Inclusion' is a major pillar of peace process design. It encompasses the selection of actors to be included at the negotiating table. The term inclusion also refers to issues and themes that should be included in the negotiating agenda to ensure that the grievances that caused the conflict are addressed (Paffenholz, 2015). The traditional inclusion/exclusion framework views violent non-state actor inclusion strategy as a trade-off between liberal norms and pragmatic considerations of power. Norm-driven peace process design aims to include as many state-level representatives in dialogue in accordance with the norm of political participation and excludes criminal actors from political dialogue on the basis of their illegality. Pragmatic peace process design permits the inclusion of criminal actors necessary for efficient conflict resolution and promotes the pragmatic exclusion of extraneous political actors who may prevent a speedy settlement (Lanz, 2011: 275). Both liberal and pragmatic inclusion strategies are based on the liberal normative binary between legitimate political actors and illegitimate criminal actors.

This chapter argues that the traditional inclusion/exclusion framework, derived from the norm of political participation in state institutions and the norm of legality, and based on an analytical distinction between the 'political' and 'criminal' methods or motives of armed groups, is inadequate to manage the complex array of actors and national and local grievances that inform modern conflicts. To overcome the limitations of norm-driven inclusion strategies in addressing micro local governance drivers of conflict, this chapter sets out a sociology of inclusion strategies – liberal, pragmatic and social – deployed by different mediators to manage the conflict. The analysis suggests that in addition to the traditional categories of liberal and pragmatic strategies, the peace mediation profession has developed a third context-driven 'social' approach to inclusion based on the concept of inclusive peace process design. Encapsulated in the UN 'Guidance for Effective Mediation' (UN, 2012: 3) as a fundamental principle of peace mediation, 'inclusivity' mandates engagement with a broad range of local actors and local socio-economic issues to increase the social legitimacy of the peace process, without normative restrictions on inclusion of actors or the negotiating agenda.

It suggests an emerging peace mediation profession plays a key role in adapting inclusion strategies to changing conflict contexts. The professionalization of peace mediation is characterized by the entrance of a body of third-party non-state international non-governmental organizations (INGOs) into the peace mediation space (Lanz, 2011). These 'new' mediators are not constrained by the liberal, normative peacebuilding architecture or international security agendas. They are therefore uniquely placed to develop pragmatic responses to the gaps in the dominant norm-driven inclusion practice, which currently excludes many local actors as external 'criminal' or illiberal security threats to society and as a consequence leaves the local micro-conflicts in conflict zones off the negotiating agenda (Peace mediation professional, 2018a).

The connection between the two elements of inclusion – who gets a seat at the table and what issues get placed on the negotiating agenda – are underexplored in the academic and policy literature. This chapter focuses on the impact of the politics of inclusion regarding violent non-state actors on the negotiating agendas of peace processes. It shows how the conflict analysis that underpins inclusion of violent non-state actors shapes and limits understandings of the causes of conflict and, in turn, the scope of issues that are placed on the negotiating agenda. To adapt peace mediation to fragmented, multi-scalar contemporary intra-state conflicts, a general shift is required from traditional inclusion strategies focused on normative legitimacy, efficiency and narrow armed-group analysis towards 'inclusivity' aimed at social legitimacy, local-level engagement and a detailed analysis of the complex social context of conflict zones.

This chapter argues that sociological concepts and methods can support the shift towards 'social' inclusion. The value of a sociological approach to conflict analysis and inclusive peace process design has not been explored in the peace mediation literature. The key difference between traditional conflict analysis and new sociological approaches to conflict zones is that the sociologists view violent non-state actors not as ancillary challengers to the state but as socially embedded within local power structures. It understands armed violence not as an external security threat but as a community-based response to the poor local governance and social injustices associated with the neoliberal state. The sociological approach differentiates and defines armed groups not according to their political or criminal motives and methods but on the social legitimacy of their governance strategies. The socio-centric analytical framework for violent non-state actors as governors of territory can bring the weaknesses of state local governance into the analytical frame and onto the negotiating agenda.

The chapter makes these arguments by tracing the manifestation of the three types of inclusion – liberal, pragmatic and social – in the Mali peace process. The Mali case was selected because it reflects changing conflict dynamics since the end of the Cold War. Mali has suffered three waves of civil war since gaining independence in 1960, with each wave sparked by ethnic Arab-Tuareg rebellion against the black African government in the South. Since the fourth rebellion in 2012, historical communal conflicts over drug-trafficking routes and land have fused with ethno-nationalist and global Islamist struggles against the Malian state, producing a complex and overlapping array of violent non-state actors and local and national grievances. To resolve the conflict, peace processes must address the local governance issues that promote the emergence of organized crime and community alliances with armed groups for security of land tenure and livelihoods. After outlining the historical development of the traditional inclusion/exclusion framework, it focuses on the 2015 Bamako national peace process, which adopted a liberal normative approach to inclusion; the pragmatic realist criminal pacts of the Anefis processes in

Northern Mali; and the socially inclusive local mediation networks to resolve communal conflict in Central Mali.

The Traditional Framework of Inclusion and Exclusion

The following section places the evolution of the traditional framework for inclusion in peace negotiations in historical perspective to highlight the limits of liberal norm-driven inclusion in contemporary peace mediation environments. It argues that inclusion strategies developed for peace mediation to support post-Cold War democratic transitions under an overarching international liberal architecture have declining relevance in post-9/11 era peace mediation. Peace mediation is currently conducted under the international security paradigm that manages the violent consequences of the neoliberal policies and democratization mandated by the liberal peace framework. Peace mediation became the cornerstone of the post-Cold War international liberal architecture which made a connection between peace and the political and economic freedom of democratic societies. In the 1990s, Cold War-era ideological proxy wars between left wing and right wing warring factions in Africa and Latin America and the ethnically driven self-determination disputes that arose from the breakdown of the Soviet Union and decolonization in Africa were subject to comprehensive peace mediation processes. These discrete two-party conflicts were fought over the form and substance of state political institutions and their resolution involved a widespread transition to post-conflict neoliberal democracies.

The traditional framework for inclusion in peace mediation reflects these objectives of liberal peacemaking to achieve post-conflict democratic transitions and the empirical realities of two-party political military conflicts in the immediate post-Cold War era. It depicts the politics of inclusion as a dynamic interplay between the broad liberal norm of political participation, mandating the inclusion of as many non-armed political actors as possible in dialogue to foster a democratic culture in society, and pragmatic inclusion strategies to achieve efficient conflict resolution by limiting negotiations to the strongest one or two military players in the conflict (Lanz, 2011: 275). The emphasis of the traditional framework on the liberal transformation of state institutions on the one hand, and armed groups on the other, is supported by the greed vs. grievance framework of conflict analysis. This framework classifies armed groups in terms of their political or economic motivations for rebellion against the state and frames conflict as a symptom of the exclusion of rebel groups and the ethnic, ideological or religious communities they represent from state political institutions or economic resources (Ballentine and Nitzschke, 2003). The constructivist literature in international relations and sociology is critical of the 'grievance' paradigm of conflict analysis, highlighting that socially constructed ethnic and religious identities are instrumentalized and mobilized by elites to drive wars that serve elite political objectives (Fearon and Laitin, 2000). The focus on armed groups is also promoted by the pragmatic 'spoiler' and 'ripeness of conflict' tools of conflict analysis. Zartman's ripeness of conflict concept indicates that armed conflicts can only be resolved when two armed groups face a mutually hurting stalemate, that is, a situation in which neither side can win militarily and negotiated settlement is the only way out (Lanz, 2011). Stedman (1997) defines 'spoilers' as non-state actors who believe that peace emerging from negotiations threatens their power, worldview and interests and who use violence to undermine attempts to achieve peace. Stedman's 'limited spoilers' can be managed by recognition and redress of specific political grievances. 'Total' spoilers such as global 'terrorist' groups commit to radical political or religious ideologies and offer little hope of settlement. 'Greedy' spoilers change their goals in accordance with a cost-benefit analysis of making peace or continuing with war (Stedman, 1997: 5).

The traditional 'exclusion' framework for violent non-state actors obtained salience in peace mediation in the post-9/11 international security environment in which the objectives of the liberal peace were diluted in favour of state security. The traditional exclusion framework for violent non-state actors indicates that exclusion from peace mediation involves a trade-off between the liberal norm of legality, which mandates the exclusion of illegal 'criminal' actors from political dialogue as external security threats to liberal society, and the pragmatic necessity of including 'criminal' actors in order to cease hostilities and achieve a settlement (Lanz, 2011). The exclusion framework defines violent non-state actors in terms of an abstract political–criminal binary. The shift in the focus of peace mediation from liberal democracy to liberal security accompanied the violent consequences of the political and economic liberalization associated with the international liberal architecture of the 1990s. The post-war processes of neoliberalism, leading to a reduction of the resources available to the state, democratization and decentralization, and involving the withdrawal of the state security apparatus, provided the socio-economic conditions for the emergence of a myriad of new unconventional violent non-state actors in the Global South, including gangs, organized crime and Islamist groups, to provide governance and security for poor communities in the absence of the state (Davis, 2010).

These new violent non-state actors sparked new complex, localized and fragmented forms of conflict that flow more from the gaps in neoliberal state local governance than broad religious or ideological differences (Mets, 2007).

As liberal security discourse delineates the boundaries of and protects neoliberal polities from the violent consequences of the socio-economic marginalization produced by neoliberal policies (Samara, 2007), inclusion strategies in post-9/11 peace processes are informed by security classifications of violent non-state actors that divide conflict zones and the actors within them into political, terrorist and criminal realms. The latter two are excluded from dialogue as illiberal or illegal and subject to security measures. As with the greed/grievance analytical and 'spoiler' framework for 'political' actors, 'terrorist' and 'criminal' actors are defined in accordance with their methods and motives for challenging and undermining the state (Picarelli, 2006: 1). The UN defines terrorism as a politically motivated action that is intended to cause death or serious bodily harm to civilians or non-combatants with the purpose of intimidating a population or compelling a government or an international organization to do or abstain from doing any act (UN, 2004a; UN, 2004b). In the context of the 'war on terror' and in the absence of a clear legal definition of terrorism in times of war, 'terrorist' actors have shifted from 'political' actors to 'criminal' actors. War on terror discourse focuses on the 'new terrorism', which is distinguished by its willingness to utilize global networks, cause large numbers of civilian casualties, and challenge the values of the liberal international system with an alternative universalist religious/Islamist ideology (Ressa, 2011). This is juxtaposed with the 'old terrorism', which challenges the political and territorial hegemony of nation states for an ethno-nationalist cause (Helgesen, 2007). 'New' terrorist groups are said to harbour an intractable illiberal ideology and so cannot be transformed into legitimate social groups through peace mediation but must be contained through security measures prescribed in peace agreements. The 'criminalization' of new terrorists and the close association made between 'new terrorism' and Islamic ideology has rendered negotiation with armed groups that employ Islamist discourse almost obsolete as they now fall squarely on the wrong side of the liberal politics–crime dichotomy (Verhoeven, 2009: 405). Ethno-nationalist struggles that use terrorist strategies are understood to be completely subsumed by the new global terrorism.

The UN Convention against Transnational Organized Crime enshrines the economic motivations behind organized crime by defining organized crime as 'a structured group of three or more persons, existing for a period of time and acting in concert with the aim of committing one or more serious offences in order to obtain, directly or indirectly, financial or other material benefit' (UN, 2000). Because the drug economy is a major source of funding for armed groups in the post-Cold War neoliberal era, the global 'war on drugs' discourse permeates and undermines peace processes with the assumption that insurgencies will be weakened if their criminal support base is eradicated (Felbab-Brown, 2009: 100). 'War on drugs' discourse promotes a focus on criminal law enforcement strategies in peace agreements to eliminate the financial source of conflict instead of political dialogue to manage the root causes of violence and organized crime in state neoliberal governance practices.

Peace mediation driven by the liberal inclusion norms of political participation in state institutions and liberal exclusion norms based on legality have promoted an emphasis in peace processes on elite power-sharing in state institutions and state security. The weakness of traditional norm-driven inclusion strategies for developing long-term local governance solutions to contemporary conflicts promoted by neoliberal governance is connected to the analytical tools that define rebel groups, criminals and terrorists in terms of their methods and motives for challenging the state. The abstract analysis removes armed groups from their social context and deflects the attention of mediators away from the socio-economic and local governance root causes of conflict. The focus on distinct methods and motives also has little basis in the empirical reality of conflict zones in neoliberal polities, where armed groups employ a variety of overlapping political, criminal and terrorist strategies and objectives.

An alternative political discourse defining the causes of violence and conflict in terms of the socio-economic injustices of neoliberal governance has developed in neoliberal societies to challenge the dominant liberal security discourse regarding new violent non-state actors (Samara, 2007). Social justice narratives, prevalent in social protest and media campaigns, highlight armed violence not as an external security threat or as a product of elite armed actor exclusion from state institutions but as a community-based response to poor state and local governance. They advocate the social inclusion of marginalized groups in neoliberal society through just land and property distribution and the development of livelihoods instead of political inclusion in state institutions or state security solutions to violence. This chapter argues that social inclusion narratives have influenced peace process design through an emerging peace mediation profession, the concept of inclusivity and new forms of conflict analysis based on sociological concepts and methods. The remainder of the chapter sets out a sociology of inclusion strategies – liberal, pragmatic and social – deployed by different mediators to manage the conflict in Mali. By highlighting the limitations of norm-driven traditional inclusion strategies based on narrow armed-group analysis, it argues that a shift to social inclusion strategies aimed at social legitimacy and analysis of the social context of conflict to capture the local governance drivers of conflict is required to adapt peace process design to an era of neoliberalism.

Liberal Security Approaches to Inclusion: the Politics of Inclusion in the Bamako Peace Process

The failure of the 2015 Bamako peace process demonstrated the weaknesses of the inclusion norm of political participation in state institutions and the exclusion norm of legality in the Malian context. The Bamako peace process was the main elite political settlement following the 2012 rebellion. The 2012 rebellion was sparked by the National Movement for the Liberation of the Azawad (MNLA), which was established in October 2010 following the return of Tuareg fighters to Mali after the fall of Muammar al-Gaddafi in Libya. The MNLA is part of a long history of secular Tuareg rebel movements in Mali dating back to the decolonization process which left the Tuareg people split across five countries: Mali, Libya, Algeria, Burkino Faso and Niger. The MNLA never claimed any link to Tuareg ethnicity, indicating they stood for the independence of all the regions of the North of Mali, which they call the Azawad.[1]

The 2012 rebellion differed from previous Tuareg rebellions because of the influence of international Jihadist-Salafist movements in Mali and the intrusion of the war on terror into the Bamako peace process. In launching the rebellion, the MNLA forged an alliance with 'Anṣār ad-Dīn, the other Tuareg-dominated group led by a former Tuareg separatist leader from the 1990s. The 'Anṣār ad-Dīn have an Islamist agenda to introduce shari'a law throughout Mali. After taking vast tracts of territory in Northern and Central Mali, the MNLA were soon militarily overpowered and displaced by three Islamist groups: 'Anṣār ad-Dīn (who broke their alliance with MNLA), al-Qā'idah in the Islamic Mahgreb (AQIM), and its off-shoot, the Movement for Oneness and Jihad in West Africa (MUJAO). AQIM is an Algerian off-shoot of al-Qā'idah and MUJAO is an AQIM splinter group comprised of Malians and Mauritanians. The Macina Liberation

[1] The details of the timeline of the conflict and the armed groups involved provided in these opening paragraphs were obtained through interviews conducted by the author in Bamako, Mali in August 2018 (Local notable, 2018; Local notables, 2018; Local official, 2018; Peace mediation professional, 2018c; UN official, 2018b).

Front (MLF), led by an ethnic Fulani Islamic preacher, also emerged in Central Malian communities at this time. A French-led counter-terrorism operation recovered much of Central and Northern Mali in 2013, which provided space for the Bamako peace process between the state and the secular Tuareg movements. The rise in Islamist and ethno-nationalist armed groups in the North also took place in a context of the rapid expansion of the drug-trafficking economy, which had deep historical roots in Northern communities. The MNLA, AQIM and 'Anṣār ad-Dīn gained increasing control of drug-trafficking routes that finance the local governance of Northern communities, displacing customary clan chiefs and other traditional local leaders. As the state withdrew completely from Central Mali after 2012, the MNLA and MUJAO also gained a stronghold in Central Mali by forming alliances and providing governance, weapons and security for rival ethnic farmer (Dogon) and nomadic herder (Fulani) communities engaged in long-running communal conflicts over pasture land and water. It is in this complex context of intersecting local populations, international Islamist organizations, ethno-nationalist armed groups, and criminal organizations that mediators attempted to apply inclusion norms developed for a simplistic two-party civil war.

Following the norm of state-level political participation and the norm of legality, the peace mediators divided the armed groups into 'political', 'criminal' and 'terrorist' categories, with the latter two excluded from the peace process. Although Northern and Central Mali is comprised of numerous ethnic groups and clans, traditional two-party 'grievance' conflict analysis informed the dominant international framing of the Malian conflict as a two-party ethnically driven conflict between the Tuareg ethnic group in the North and the black African government in the South that could be solved through a political power-sharing deal. The peace process began with the MNLA and the High Council for the Unity of Azawad (HCUA), both of which desired independence for the North. The weaknesses of context-independent greed vs. grievance 'spoiler' and 'balance of power' analysis, which assumes rebel groups are the legitimate representatives of the ethnic communities they claim to negotiate for and implicitly provides guidance for the management of only two primary combatants (a rebel group and the state) with monolithic objectives, became apparent during the Bamako negotiations. Many local communities, clans and ethnic groups in the North did not feel adequately represented by the MNLA or the HCUA, which were comprised of combatants from Libya who had not lived in Mali for some time. Echoing constructivist critiques of the grievance literature, some local notables believed the MNLA were 'hijacking' the Tuareg identity to gain state political power (Local notable, 2018). As a result, the number of 'political' armed groups in Mali increased steadily during the peace process from two (MNLA and HCUA) to eight. The armed groups were established either just before or in reaction to the peace talks and their creation was motivated by the need for representation in the peace talks as these groups desired the maintenance of national unity rather than independence for the North (Local notable, 2018). The extra armed groups were also created along ethnic and clan-based lines. The Co-ordination of the Movements of Patriotic and Resistance Fronts (CMFPR) is a conglomeration of self-defence movements made up of Songhai and Peul in the Gao and Mopti regions. The Movement of Arab Azawad (MAA) was established to protect Arab interests of the North. The GATIA were made up of pro-government militia with links to the Malian army. Despite the evidence of political tensions among local communities in the North, mediators grouped the 'political' ethno-nationalist armed groups into two broad negotiating coalitions, reflecting the analytical and normative bias towards two-party structured negotiations between armed groups and the state on national issues.

The exclusion norm of legality is also of limited practical value in the Malian context, given the 'hidden' involvement of 'compliant' or 'political' actors in drug-trafficking activities and the fusion of ethno-nationalist, global 'terrorist' and ethnic communal struggles. Any one of the armed groups or communities could have fallen on the wrong side of the politics-crime dichotomy by virtue of their association with Islamist groups or their criminal or terrorist methods or motives of challenging the state. The signatories of the Bamako agreement harboured deep ethnic and community-based rivalries over access to drug-trafficking routes (Local notable, 2018), which erupted into local armed struggles immediately after the Bamako agreement was signed. The inability of conflict analysis based on the politics–crime dichotomy and the methods and motives of armed groups to capture local power politics and the criminal agendas of 'political' actors resulted in the fragmentation of the two negotiating coalitions around the armed clashes and the breakdown of the power-sharing deal in the 2015 agreement.

The willingness of the international community to 'turn a blind eye' to the criminal activities of 'compliant' groups is connected to the national, democratic nature of their political demands (Local notable, 2018), which reflected international understandings of the conflict in Mali as a monolithic two-party ethno-nationalist rebellion against the state. The 'compliant' groups could also speak the international language of norm-driven inclusion. Because armed groups in Mali do not fit neatly into the abstract and artificial politics–crime dichotomy, the supposedly objective and universal norm-driven inclusion labels were manipulated by these powerful and internationally acceptable elite players to further their political or security interests at the expense of the interests of local communities (Peace mediation professional, 2018c). Inclusion decisions were also made at the political discretion of the French and Algerian mediators, who had close links to the international counter-terrorism operation in Mali and ensured that inclusion strategies aligned with international security priorities (Peace mediation professional, 2018b).

The 'compliant' groups made efforts to exclude their clan-based and inter-ethnic rivals of the North by denouncing them as criminals, while denying involvement in the criminal activities they pursued in private (Local notable, 2018). The rebel coalitions also made public statements distancing themselves from the 'terrorist' groups they were now seeking to displace in Central Mali even though they had joined forces to overthrow the state in 2012 (Local notable, 2018). Because the 'compliant' groups and their allies in the Dogon farmer communities in Central Mali did not employ the discourse of the global Islamist struggle, they escaped the international label of 'terrorist' even though they frequently used 'terrorist' strategies against their ethnic rivals for water and pasture land (Peace mediation professional, 2018a). The 'terrorist' label was applied to entire ethnic Fulani nomadic herder communities in Central Mali, which had aligned themselves with the Islamist groups 'Anṣār ad-Dīn, AQIM, MUJAO and the home-grown MLF. The region of Mopti in Central Mali was excluded from the Bamako process as a 'terrorist' hotspot even though the Islamist struggle in the region is closely linked to intensive communal conflict over land and drug trafficking (Peace mediation professional, 2018a). In a context where 'terrorist' groups operating in Mali are now primarily led by a group of Malians rather than global actors, the Malian government expressed a willingness to talk to the 'jihadists'. The government, however, changed its position due to pressure from France, illustrating the influence of international security agendas on the peace process in Mali (Boutellis and Zahar, 2017). The elite-driven politics of inclusion demonstrates the weaknesses of the normative structure and abstract analytical categories underpinning orthodox inclusion strategies in complex conflict contexts. It resulted in the exclusion of the majority of Central Mali and many Northern local leaders from the negotiating table and, as a result, the question of land governance and drug trafficking from the negotiating agenda. Given the dominance of the norm of legality and liberal security discourse throughout the peace process, state security issues were the priority negotiating agenda item for the state and the international community (UN official, 2018a). The Bamako agreement bolstered international and state counter-terrorism capacity to confront Islamist groups, which exacerbated grievances regarding state oppression in Northern and Central Mali. The emphasis on the norm of political participation in democratic state institutions resulted in the transfer of key positions in national political and security institutions to a narrow Arab-Tuareg elite which had little connection to many Northern and Central communities and which were known to persecute Fulani nomadic herder communities in Central Mali. The disjuncture between the Bamako agreement, which served international and elite priorities, and the local drivers of conflict indicates a need to rethink inclusion strategies in fragmented, localized conflicts of the kind in Mali. New inclusion strategies must involve analysis and engagement at the local as well as the national levels. The following two sections discuss the departure from liberal normative approaches to mediation at the local level in order to resolve communal conflicts in Mali.

Pragmatic Approaches to Inclusion: Criminal Elite Pacts

The Anefis peace processes of 2015 and 2017 demonstrate the shortcomings of armed group-centric mediation in managing local organized crime-driven conflict in Northern Mali. The Anefis processes adhered to the pragmatic side of the exclusion framework, which allows engagement with criminal actors in order to achieve efficient conflict resolution. Given the realities of local governance in modern conflict zones, where organized crime has the monopoly on violence and social service provision in vast tracts of territory, pragmatic dialogue with 'criminals' to manage, rather than eradicate, criminal violence has become inevitable (UN official, 2018a). The trend in international civil war peace processes is to employ a combination of law enforcement measures that adhere to liberal legality norms by treating criminal actors as an external threat to society and pragmatic negotiations with criminal actors. Negotiation with 'criminals' has been facilitated by the fragmentation and expansion of the peace mediation profession, with INGO mediators conducting the Anefis process in parallel to but completely separate from the Bamako Accord, which was the main political settlement governed by liberal security norms.

The influx of returned Tuareg fighters from Libya and the formation of the MNLA in 2010 upset the delicate alliances between the armed groups AQIM and 'Anṣār ad-Dīn and the clan-based patronage networks that controlled Northern drug-trafficking routes (Local official, 2018). As the MNLA and other emerging armed groups sought to insert themselves into local drug-trafficking networks, fighting around key nodes of the drug-trafficking routes increased during and after the Bamako process. The implementation of the Bamako agreement has been hindered by the lack of cohesive and consistent local dispute-resolution processes regarding these drug-trafficking disputes, which have traditionally supported national peace processes in Mali. Local mediations were run by local political elites steeped in knowledge of how drug trafficking informed local governance and local politics. The 1995 Bourem process, which was credited with saving the 1995 national peace accord, was initiated and pushed forward by village chiefs and civilians who understood the destructive impact of the militarization of drug-trafficking routes on local governance (Boutellis and Zahar, 2017: 30). The increasing connection between armed groups, drug trafficking and the provision of local governance has reduced the influence of customary chiefs and other local community members. As a result, Northern communities lack the leadership required to pursue peaceful resolution of drug-trafficking disputes.

Third-party non-state mediators stepped in to orchestrate a series of local mediations to defuse communal conflicts over drug-trafficking routes in Northern Mali. The first Anefis process in 2015 resulted in a 'roadmap comprising a series of measures, including the cessation of hostilities, joint initiatives for intercommunal and intracommunal reconciliation, the exchange of prisoners, and the free movement of people and goods' (Boutellis and Zahar, 2017: 30). The second process in 2017 focused on the inclusion of armed groups, resulting in a narrow negotiating agenda to keep routes for drug trafficking open to diminish armed competition and theft (Peace mediation professional, 2018a). The second more exclusive process is indicative of the increased militarization of the Northern drug-trafficking routes, with armed groups displacing the historical social networks on which the drug-trafficking trade is based.

Critics of the Anefis process argue its efforts to accommodate organized crime have only produced another layer of exclusive elite pacts between armed groups with questionable social legitimacy at the expense of broad-based inclusion of the local leaders, youth and women who have a stake in the resolution of drug-trafficking disputes and improved local governance (Peace mediation professional, 2018a). The weakness of the Anefis process is related to the reliance of mediators on the traditional abstract classifications of violent non-state actors in terms of their methods and motives. By ignoring the broader context of local governance, internationally led efforts to revitalize local mediation processes have merely transferred the apolitical, liberal security analytical lens to the local level.

Stamping out drug trafficking through law enforcement interdiction or quelling crime-related violence through the regulation of drug-trafficking routes are only short-term solutions to a problem that is entrenched in the governance of local communities in Northern Mali. Without the development of local governance, communities will continue to support and rely on armed groups, funded by criminal activity, to provide basic services. The agendas and stakeholder-engagement strategies of local mediation must evolve from the mere accommodation of armed groups to support the transformation of local governance in Northern communities. This involves a shift in focus on armed groups and the treatment of organized crime as a security issue. To address issues of criminal governance, crime-related violence must be treated as an issue of governance and social justice that is included in the main political peace process. Although the Anefis process represented a departure from the traditional normative basis of liberal peace mediation, its design still reflected the politics–crime dichotomy on which traditional peace mediation is based. It was not a political process as state local political and civil society actors were never party to the negotiations. Instead, the negotiations were conducted between elite armed criminal actors in the criminal realm, reinforcing the view of crime-related violence as an external security threat rather than as a part of a general conflict that stems from poor state governance.

Mediation agendas that address local governance issues require rethinking the conceptual basis of inclusion strategies to allow an understanding of armed groups as socially embedded actors capable of holding legitimacy and power in the territories they control. Understanding armed groups in terms of their role in local governance shifts attention away from the armed groups and their criminal methods towards the weaknesses in state local governance that promote alliances between local populations and armed groups. By placing armed groups in their social context, local issues come to the fore. The concept of inclusive peace process design has provided a basis for rethinking traditional inclusion strategies in light of the social connections of armed groups and their role in providing governance in the absence of the neoliberal state.

Social Approaches to Inclusion: Inclusive Peace Process Design

This section argues that inclusion to achieve social, rather than normative, legitimacy based on 'inclusivity' provides a path forward to address micro-drivers of conflict based on sociological analysis of the social context of conflict zones. The approach of 'inclusive' peace process design towards the selection and engagement of violent non-state actors represents a departure from normative approaches to inclusion which determines the legitimacy of violent non-state actors as peace negotiators in terms of their adherence to liberal norms. Inclusivity is encapsulated in the UN 'Guidance for Effective Mediation' (UN, 2012: 3) as one of the 'fundamentals' of peace process design. Inclusivity refers to the extent to which the needs and views of conflict parties and other stakeholders are represented and integrated into the process and outcome of the mediation effort.

'Inclusivity' demands that 'the conflict parties have legitimacy with, or represent, the wider public' (UN, 2012: 11). This is a sociological definition of legitimacy, focusing on the empirical social acceptance of parties to negotiate on behalf of the community. It moves the analytical gaze to the local level, opening up space for consideration of the role that armed groups play in the governance of local communities. The dominant view among UN officials and peace mediation professionals interviewed by the author is that there should be no normative restrictions on mediator engagement with as many armed and non-armed stakeholders as possible, with the only prohibition being placed by UN officials and some peace mediation professionals on dialogue with violent non-state actors indicted by the International Criminal Court (interviews with UN officials and peace mediation professionals (UN official, 2018a)). UN member states and academic literature have tended to equate inclusive peace process design with the inclusion of local non-armed actors, such as civil society and women. The peace mediation profession has, however, continued to highlight that, in order to achieve sustainable outcomes, inclusivity in peace processes must encompass all relevant actors that matter for reaching agreements (interviews with UN officials and peace mediation professionals (UN official, 2018a)). The rationale behind 'inclusivity' is that a process that includes the views of a wide range of local stakeholders is more likely to address the root causes of conflict and have legitimacy at the local level (UN, 2015). 'Inclusive' negotiating agendas are also driven by the objective of social legitimacy, which is achieved by ensuring that processes capture local as well as national issues. Addressing the range of grievances in fragmented conflict zones involves a shift from an excessive focus on the national-level negotiating table as the locus of inclusion (Paffenholz, 2015). Inclusive peace process design demands that mediators embrace multi-layered, ongoing inclusion modalities, including local mediation, consultations, inclusive commissions, public referenda and dialogues at the national and local level (Peace mediation professional, 2018a).

There are shortcomings in the conceptual basis for 'inclusive' engagement with local actors and grievances. Sociological methods and analytical frameworks for conflict and violent non-state actors can give conceptual content to the concept of inclusive peace process design, informing negotiating agendas and actor selection driven by the objective of social legitimacy. The literature on civil war, terrorism and organized crime respectively has moved beyond motives, strategies and methods of violence to sociological analysis of how violent non-state actors govern the territories they control.[2] The key difference between traditional conflict and security analysis and new sociological approaches is that the sociologists view violent non-state actors not as ancillary challengers to the state but as socially embedded within local power structures. It understands armed violence not as an external security threat or as the result of exclusion from state institutions but as a community-based response to poor local governance in the neoliberal state. The sociological approach differentiates and defines armed groups not according to their political, economic or criminal motives or their terrorist strategies but according to the social legitimacy of their governance strategies. Kalyvas (2006), Picarelli (2006) and Podder (2013) have all argued that a focus on the micro-dynamics of armed-group governance of territories can overcome the limits of the artificial politics–crime binary in conflict and security analysis. By understanding violence as a mode of governance, rebel groups, 'criminal' groups and 'terrorist' groups can all be classified according to their *predatory* or *protective* governance strategies in local communities rather than using artificial political–criminal binaries. Some armed groups, particularly those that are more transnational or networked in nature, have weak local, social ties and therefore have a *predatory* relationship with communities and low levels of legitimacy. The national and global economic or ideological objectives of these groups outweigh any connection they may have to local grievances and local micro-conflicts. These groups use violence against communities in an arbitrary manner and do not invest in the welfare and public services of local communities. Other armed groups are entwined with existing local power structures through ethnic, tribal or religious linkages and obtain strong social legitimacy through their protective governance strategies. They use violence sparingly in accordance with social norms and provide security, livelihoods, welfare and justice in a relatively fair manner. These analytical categories avoid essentializing the local by revealing that governance strategies and levels of legitimacy are influenced by local connections with global orders and ideologies.

[2] See, for example, Péclard and Mechoulan (2015) for rebel governance literature; Davis (2009) for violent non-state actors; and Locke (2012) for organized crime.

The predatory/protective governance distinction can help mediators distinguish which armed actors are socially legitimate representatives of communities within the context of inclusive peace process design. Local armed groups with protective governance strategies are strong candidates for inclusion in peace processes that are attentive to local priorities for peace. Armed groups with *predatory* or non-existent local governance strategies are candidates for law enforcement approaches. In Central Mali, key armed stakeholders include the ethno-nationalist MNLA and the Islamist groups AQIM, which migrated to Mali from Algeria; the MUJAO, which pursues a broader Islamist agenda across West Africa, and 'Anṣār ad-Dīn, which promotes shari'a law in Mali and includes Arab minorities threatened by the Tuareg-dominated MNLA in the North (Local official, 2018). The Islamist MLF, led by an Islamic Fulani preacher, has also emerged in Fulani communities to provide security against Malian state persecution of Fulani communities (Local official, 2018). The perceived arbitrary nature of the state, manifest through its security forces and corrupt judicial system, contrasted with the effectiveness of Islamist groups under whose rule corruption and local banditry was drastically reduced (UN official, 2018b). The Fulani are routinely subject to mass detentions and extrajudicial executions by state-sanctioned Dogon and Tuareg militias aligned with the MNLA, one of the signatories of the Bamako agreement. State forestry and water officials also arbitrarily deprive them of them property with impunity. With their grievances excluded from successive national peace agreements, the Fulani are turning to Islamist groups for assistance.

The Islamist groups MUJAO and 'Anṣār ad-Dīn exhibit some protective behaviour towards Fulani communities and can claim some level of social legitimacy due to the security they provide from the predatory behaviours of the Malian state. Their decisions regarding land disputes, sometimes in accordance with shari'a law, are viewed as more just than those delivered by the state. However, the global nature of their ideological goals does not reflect the grievances of the local communities regarding land tenure and state corruption and predation. 'Anṣār ad-Dīn and MUJAO 'protection' is transactional in nature, with security and governance provided in exchange for recruits for their global struggle (UN official, 2018b). Because of their role in Central Malian communities, these groups warrant careful inclusion in select dialogue for pragmatic purposes but should not be taken to be the legitimate representatives of all herder communities. The MLF is a home-grown Central Malian Islamist organization that is deeply entrenched in Fulani governance structures and uses Islamist discourse to express local grievances. Given the high levels of social legitimacy of the MLF, it can make a strong claim to represent Fulani communities in negotiations that prioritize local grievances. As many Fulani youth and lower classes disgruntled with the corruption of their elders joined MUJAO or 'Anṣār ad-Dīn instead of the MLF, inclusion strategies should reflect inter-generational and class divides within Fulani communities.

A sociological analysis of Northern communal conflicts could facilitate the inclusion of the excluded local non-armed leaders in the Anefis processes. The social legitimacy of Northern local leaders stems from measured control of deep, socially embedded historical drug-trafficking networks. These leaders have converted financial profits from drug trafficking into social capital, with communities paying for mosques and buying herds of cattle (Local notables, 2018). Although their authority is increasingly challenged by armed actors and younger members of their communities, they still play a legitimate role in local governance. Their inclusion, together with a broad selection of youth, women, ethnic and clan-based representatives, would facilitate an agenda focused on the local governance issues giving rise to organized crime in addition to pragmatic ceasefire agendas.

Inclusive peace process design must also encompass a range of local non-armed actors. The 'local' is often treated by analysts and peace mediators as an undifferentiated field of uniform actors and interests, leading to the assumption that all Fulani monadic herders are 'terrorists' and that the armed groups of Northern Mali are the legitimate representatives of all Northern communities. A sociological empirical analysis, which places conflict in its social and political context, can facilitate the identification and inclusion of a diverse range of armed and non-armed actors who have an interest in peace and the improvement of local governance. This includes customary leaders, civil society, women and youth. Sociological analysis exposes unequal local power structures and grievances along class, gender and inter-generational lines that must be addressed if local governance is to improve. Although the engagement of armed groups as socially legitimate actors opens up peace processes to considerations of local governance and grievances, the risk remains that armed groups will simply assume the privileged role normally afforded to customary elites in communities, displacing the interests of more marginalized members of the community, including women and youth. The Anefis process is an example of this phenomenon, where armed groups were negotiated with in place of old customary elites. Professional mediators avoided this issue in Central Mali by basing peace process design on the inclusion of non-armed community members first and adding members of armed groups as they were necessary to the community-led process.

The 'bottom-up' approach to mediator selection and armed-group actor selection for local agro-pastoralist mediations in Central Mali reflected inclusive peace process design and many of the insights from the sociological analysis of the Malian conflict (Peace mediation professionals, 2019). The international mediators did not assume that Islamist armed groups represented the interests and objectives of local communities. They facilitated community exchanges to identify community leaders with the necessary social legitimacy and competence to negotiate the resolution of communal conflicts. They ensured that all social groups – pastoralists, farmers, fishermen, youth, elders, men and women – were equally represented in community mediation teams. The community mediators are familiar with the geography of pasture lands in dispute. They have proficient knowledge of customs and traditions and the community sense of justice. Because of the community links of the mediators, they focus agendas on the origins of the conflict in old disputes over natural resources rather than Islamist or ethnic armed conflict. The INGO mediators replaced community mediators when armed groups exerted influence over communal conflicts, using its networks with the national government and armed groups to negotiate ceasefires. Local and national authorities were also included in communal agreement implementation.

New sociological approaches to mediation and conflict analysis should be supported by the introduction of new professional actors into the peace process. The appointment of a third-party non-state mediator, who does not have ties to international security agendas, is important to open the peace process up to new analytical frameworks, actors and methods of conflict analysis. Sociologists should be included in mediation teams to support new modes of stakeholder engagement and agenda setting.

Although local mediation is an effective conflict resolution tool in the Malian context, local governance cannot be developed without the funding, policy support and inclusion of state actors in the process. Experts in sociology could be a useful link between local mediation and national peace processes by providing missing information on local power structures and interests at both levels. Community mediators, selected using sociological analysis and social inclusion practices, are also strong candidates for inclusion in national dialogues and implementation plans to connect local to national mediation. Their inclusion at the national level would shift national negotiating agendas away from state security reform and national power sharing towards local police reform, justice, education, livelihoods, natural resources management and other governance issues.

Conclusion

The management of fragmented intra-state conflicts driven by intersecting global, national and local grievances and armed groups requires multi-layered peace process design that supports inclusion modalities at the community and national level. In Mali, an ad hoc, multi-layered peace process is supported by three distinct inclusion strategies developed by different state and non-state mediators at the national and local levels. The international liberal Bamako peace process and the pragmatic realist criminal pacts of the Anefis process were underpinned by inclusion strategies based on the normative distinction between political and criminal actors, with the latter excluded from liberal peacemaking. The normative approach to inclusion was inadequate in addressing local governance drivers of conflict because the analytical framework focused the analytical gaze at the national level, removed armed actors from their socio-political context and had little practical value in the Malian context where 'politics', 'crime' and 'terrorism' overlap.

The concept of inclusive peace process design informed the third inclusion strategy in Mali driven by the social, and not the normative, legitimacy of the actors selected and the negotiating agenda. Inclusion in Central Mali agro-pastoralist local mediations was 'bottom-up', with professional international peace mediators facilitating community exchanges to select socially legitimate community mediators to conduct mediation that prioritized local grievances regarding natural resources governance.

Given the success of social approaches to inclusion in capturing and addressing the complexity of the Malian conflict, social approaches to inclusion have the potential to connect the national and local elements of multi-scalar peace processes. New sociological conceptual frameworks, which define conflict as a product of poor state governance and armed groups in terms of their local governance strategies, can support the formalization of social approaches to inclusion at the national level, uniting local and national actors and grievances under the analysis of governance of conflict societies as a whole.

References

Ballentine, K. and Nitzschke, H. (2003) 'Beyond Greed and Grievance: Policy Lessons from Studies in the Political-economy of Conflict', *International Peace Academy Policy Report* [online] October, available from: https://reliefweb.int/sites/reliefweb.int/files/resources/6765C3D3477FE91C8525742400689BD7-IPA_ArmedCoflict_Oct03.pdf (accessed 20 August 2019).

Boutellis, A. and Zahar, M. (2017) 'A Process in Search of Peace: Lessons from the Inter-Malian Agreement', *International Peace Institute* [online] available from: https://www.ipinst.org/wp-content/uploads/2017/06/IPI-Rpt-Inter-Malian-AgreementFinalRev.pdf (accessed 25 July 2019).

Davis, D.E. (2009) 'Non-state Armed actors, New Imagined Communities, and Shifting Patterns of Sovereignty and Insecurity in the Modern World', *Contemporary Security Policy*, 30(2), 221–45.

Davis, D.E. (2010) 'Irregular Armed Forces, Shifting Patterns of Commitment, and Fragmented Sovereignty in the Developing World', *Theory and Society*, 39, 397–413.

Fearon, J. and Laitin, D. (2000) 'Violence and the Social Construction of Ethnic Identity', *International Organization*, 54(4), 845–77.

Felbab-Brown, V. (2009) 'Peacekeepers Among Poppies: Afghanistan, Illicit Economies and Intervention', *International Peacekeeping*, 16(1), 100–14.

Helgesen, V. (2007) 'How Peace Diplomacy Lost Post 9/11: What Implications Are There for Norway?', *Oslo Files on Defence and Security*, 3 [online] available from: https://forsvaret.no/ifs/Oslo-Files-32007-Peace-diplomacy-post-911 (accessed 23 August 2019).

Kalyvas, S. (2006) *The Logic of Violence in Civil Wars*, Cambridge: Cambridge University Press.

Lanz, D. (2011) 'Who Gets a Seat at the Table? A Framework for Understanding the Dynamics of Inclusion and Exclusion in Peace Negotiations', *International Negotiation*, 16, 275–95.

Local notable (2018), interviewed in Bamako, Mali by Emma van Santen, August.

Local notables (2018), interviewed collectively in Bamako, Mali by Emma van Santen, August.

Locke, R. (2012) 'Organised Crime, Conflict and Fragility: A New Approach', International Peace Institute.

Mets, S. (2007) 'New Challenges and Old Concepts: Understanding 21st Century Insurgency', *Parameters* [online] available from: https://ssi.armywarcollege.edu/pubs/parameters/articles/2011winter/Metz.pdf (accessed 25 July 2019).

Paffenholz, T. (2015) 'Inclusivity in Peace Process', *United Nations University Centre for Policy Research* [online] available from: https://pdfs.semanticscholar.org/ecc7/37a5c9dd6bc25285cf859dfb571c85320bc6.pdf (accessed 25 July 2019).

Peace mediation professional (2018a), interviewed in Geneva, Switzerland by Emma van Santen, April.

Peace mediation professional (2018b), interviewed in New York, United States by Emma van Santen, April.

Peace mediation professional (2018c), interviewed in Bamako, Mali by Emma van Santen, August.

Peace mediation professionals (2019), interviewed in Geneva, Switzerland by Emma van Santen, January.

Péclard, D. and Mechoulan, D. (2015) 'Rebel Governance and the Politics of Civil War', swisspeace Working Paper.

Picarelli, J.T. (2006) 'The Turbulent Nexus of Transnational Organized Crime and Terrorism: A Theory of Malevolent International Relations', *Global Crime*, 7(1), 1–24.

Podder, S. (2013) 'Non-state Armed Groups and Stability: Reconsidering Legitimacy and Inclusion', *Contemporary Security Policy*, 34(1), 16–39.

Ressa, M. (2011) *Seeds of Terror: An Eyewitness Account of Al-Qaeda's Newest Center of Operations in Southeast Asia*, New York, NY: Free Press.

Samara, T.R. (2007) 'Development, Social Justice and Global Governance: Challenges to Implementing Restorative and Criminal Justice Reforms in South Africa', *Acta Juridica*, 113, 113–33.

Stedman, S.J. (1997) 'Spoiler Problems in Peace Processes', *International Security*, 22(2), 5–53.

UN (2000) 'Convention against Transnational Organized Crime and the Protocols Thereto' [online] 15 November, available from: https://www.unodc.org/unodc/en/organized-crime/intro/UNTOC.html#Fulltext (accessed 20 August 2019).

UN (2004a) 'United Nations Security Council Resolution 1566 (2004) on Threats to International Peace and Security Caused by Terrorist Acts' [online] 8 October, available from: https://www.un.org/ruleoflaw/files/n0454282.pdf (accessed 26 August 2019).

UN (2004b) 'Report of the High-level Panel on Threats, Challenges and Change' [online] 2 December, available from: https://www.un.org/ruleoflaw/blog/document/the-secretary-generals-high-level-panel-report-on-threats-challenges-and-change-a-more-secure-world-our-shared-responsibility/ (accessed 26 August 2019).

UN (2012) 'Guidance for Effective Mediation' [online] available from: https://peacemaker.un.org/sites/peacemaker.un.org/files/GuidanceEffectiveMediation_UNDPA2012%28english%29_0.pdf (accessed 25 July 2019).

UN (2015) 'High Level Panel on Peace Mediation', Report obtained from the UN Mediation Support Unit by Emma van Santen in April 2018.

UN official (2018a), interviewed in New York, United States by Emma van Santen, April.

UN official (2018b), interviewed in Bamako, Mali by Emma van Santen, August.

Verhoeven, H. (2009) 'The Self-fulfilling Prophecy of Failed States: Somalia, State Collapse and the Global War on Terror', *Journal of Eastern African Studies*, 3(3), 405–25.

10

The Business of Peace and the Politics of Inclusion: The Role of Local Business Actors in Yemen (2011–16)*

Josie Lianna Kaye

Introduction

Business actors in zones of conflict – especially but not only those in the natural resources sector – have often been conceived of in negative terms: as entities requiring either significant regulation, as epitomized by the Extractive Industries Transparency Initiative (EITI),[1] the Kimberley Process,[2] and Publish What You Pay Us,[3] or significant amounts of 'hand-holding', encapsulated in various 'do no harm' initiatives such as the United Nations (UN) *Guiding Principles on Business and Human Rights*

* This chapter is based on the author's DPhil thesis: see Josie L. Kaye (2019) 'The business of peace and the politics of inclusion: what role for local "licit" and "illicit" business actors in peace mediation?', DPhil thesis, University of Oxford, available at: https://ora.ox.ac.uk/objects/uuid:3003288e-8dee-47e3-b860-8d7a21b5d077.

[1] The Extractive Industries Transparency Initiative's website is available from: https://eiti.org/ (accessed 15 September 2018).

[2] The Kimberley Process's website is available from: http://www.kimberleyprocess.com/ (accessed 15 September 2018).

[3] The Publish What You Pay Us website is available from: http://www.pwypusa.org/ (accessed 15 September 2018).

(OHCHR, 2011), and the Organisation for Economic Co-operation and Development (OECD) *Guidelines for Multinational Enterprises on Conducting Business in Weak Governance Zones* (OECD, 2006). Slowly but surely, however, the notion that business is an actor requiring a degree of *control* to mitigate its nefarious impacts has given way to the idea that businesses can serve as 'active agents of peace, stability and long-term development' (Miklian and Schouten, 2014: 2). This shift away from businesses as purely negative actors towards their discursive recasting as peacemakers and peacebuilders has been shepherded by the UN ever since former Secretary-General Kofi Annan's speech at Davos (UNSG, 1999) in 1999, where he called for a 'new partnership among governments, the private sector, and the international community' (Tesner and Kell, 2000: xxii).

Since then, businesses have featured prominently on the international stage. In 2004 the UN Security Council established a working group on 'the role of business in conflict prevention, peacekeeping and post-conflict peacebuilding' (Deitelhoff and Wolf, 2010: 3); in 2011 a private sector focal point was appointed to the UN Peacebuilding Office (Ford, 2015: ix); in 2012, the UN Secretary-General's annual report on post-conflict peacebuilding explicitly underscored the need to engage business in the process of sustainable peace for the first time (Ford, 2015: 4); and, John Ruggie's 'Protect, Respect, Remedy' framework focused almost exclusively on the role of businesses operating in conflict-affected and fragile states (Ford, 2015: 67). More recently, in 2017 the Global Alliance for Reporting on Peaceful, Just and Inclusive Societies hosted an event at the General Assembly entitled 'Better Business for a Better World' to discuss how the private sector can engage with Sustainable Development Goal (SDG) Goal 16 (Conroy, 2017). Similarly, the UN-World Bank report on 'Pathways for Peace' outlined a role for the private sector in conflict prevention and, in September 2018, Secretary-General Guterres convened the 'UN Private Sector Forum', which emphasized the role businesses play in 'contributing to and investing in sustainable development and peace' (United Nations Global Compact, 2018).

These efforts appear designed to make the 'business case for peace', that is, to articulate why the notion that the 'business of business is business' (Friedman, 1970) – as stated famously by Milton Friedman in 1970 – is false, misplaced or outdated. The rationales – as articulated by policy makers and academics alike – have taken the form of economic consequentialism ('economic development is good for peace'), appeals to morality ('it is the right or "ethical" thing to do'), and commercialism ('peace is good for business'), among others. Over the years, 'Business for Peace' (or B4P) – a termed coined by the UN Global Compact's platform for businesses operating in countries in conflict (United Nations Global

Compact, nd) – has become shorthand for the myriad of expectations placed on business actors operating in countries in conflict, ranging from 'do no harm' to 'do something', and, ideally, 'do good'.

Conversely, the 'peace case for business' is comparatively weak and has yet to translate into any meaningful change on the ground. The double standards in this regard are therefore quite stark: the onus is on businesses to incorporate 'peace' into their operations, but peacemaking actors are not required to incorporate business actors into theirs, despite the fact that business actors may be actively hampering, or may be well positioned to actually ameliorate, the achievement of mandates. On the contrary, international peacemaking actors, at the UN especially, appear to have a well-entrenched 'blind spot' when it comes to business actors in countries in conflict, a blind spot which often extends more generally to economic dynamics, issues and processes. As underscored by Jolyon Ford in his book *Regulating Business for Peace*, published in 2015, business goes 'unmentioned in almost all peace operations periodic reports' and operations have 'largely neglected business relative to other peace stakeholders or spoilers' (Ford, 2015: 16).

This 'blind spot' is surprising – and harmful – and provides further evidence of the failure of UN peacemakers and peacebuilders to engage meaningfully with local power dynamics, leading some to conclude that international peacemakers have 'been only too happy to embrace the language, though rarely the spirit, of the local turn' in peacebuilding (Mac Ginty and Richmond, 2013: 779). When viewed through the lens of peace mediation, the 'local turn' has inevitably given rise to a discourse on 'inclusion':[4] who gets a seat around the table? Whose views – and on what – are consulted and/or reflected on in the peacemaking process? More than just a discourse, however, the inclusion narrative takes on the form of a 'political practice' since it constructs meaning, empowers and fixes 'the limits of socially recognised modes of objectivity, subjectivity and conduct in the peacemaking realm' (Ashley, 1989: 282).

The UN Guidance on Effective Mediation defines inclusion as 'the extent and manner in which the views and needs of conflict parties and other stakeholders are represented and integrated into the process and outcome of a mediation effort', a definition which allows for some degree of 'constructive ambiguity' (UNSG, 2012). The Guidance goes on to

---

[4] Interestingly, analysis of this discourse has been under-represented in academic literature and has been covered predominantly by those we might consider as falling into the narrow 'academic-practitioner' category, including those at the Berghof Foundation, swisspeace, the International Peace Institute, the Inclusive Peace and Transitions Initiative and the Mediation Support Network.

link inclusivity with effectiveness, legitimacy, national ownership, and the tension that exists between inclusivity and efficiency, including the well-versed notion that the more complex mediation processes become, the more difficult it is to reach an agreement. The discourse around inclusion, however, is less black and white than it may at first seem.

Indeed, while not made explicit, the UN practice and discourse of inclusion generally falls into two categories, as outlined by David Lanz (2011): those that should be included on normative grounds, and those that should be included on pragmatic grounds. Some actors, he argues, are included on the basis of *international norms*, including the belief that broad inclusion fosters democratic culture, and that including civil society actors builds popular support for peace; similarly, actors may be excluded on normative grounds if including perpetrators of mass atrocities prevents accountability, and in the framework of the war on terror, whereby exclusion of terrorist groups is a tool of delegitimization. Similarly, groups may be included on the basis of *practical requirements*, including realpolitik, such as actors who could undermine peace; and, from the perspective of implementation, that is those actors whose support is necessary for long-term peace consolidation. Furthermore, actors can be excluded for practical reasons, including the belief that peacemaking processes should be 'kept simple', and/or to exclude hardliners who may undermine peace from the 'inside' (Lanz, 2011). As will be explored throughout the rest of this chapter, what is striking is the silence and exclusion of businesses from both rationales, despite the normative and pragmatic grounds for including them.

Using the example of Yemen from 2011 to 2016, this chapter demonstrates that business actors play four instrumental, overlapping roles in war-to-peace transitions that tend to be ignored by UN envoys and their teams: as supporters and/or humanitarian aid providers (or 'benefactors'); as beneficiaries of the government and the war economy ('profiteers'); as mediators and peacemakers ('intermediaries'); and as conflict actors or spoilers ('agitators'). Whereas the UN and partners have developed frameworks, mechanisms and processes designed to bring armed groups – who often play comparable roles – to the negotiation table or to minimize their negative impacts on peace processes, such thinking has yet to be extended to business actors who wield a deceptively less violent form of economic and, indeed, political power. These roles underscore the need for a *local business lens in peace mediation* to inform the process, structure and content of mediation processes, and are based on the four roles played by local business actors. So what role did local business actors play during the Yemen transition in 2011–16, and to what extent were these roles taken into consideration by the UN Special Envoy for Yemen and his team? Are such UN–business dynamics the exception or the rule?

Yemen in Crisis

In 2010, on the eve of the 'Arab Spring', small-scale protests began increasing in both frequency and intensity (Lackner, 2017: 35). Echoing and drawing both hope and inspiration from the success of the movements simultaneously unfolding in Tunisia and Egypt, by 2011 large-scale sit-ins were underway at Sana'a University's own 'Change Square' – drawing tens of thousands of 'tribesmen, students, Houthis and others' (International Crisis Group, 2011: 4). Demonstrations spread quickly to other governorates, with support from Yemen's leading opposition party, the Joint Meeting Parties (JMP). What began as a disparate collection of critiques of government-led actions – ranging from land appropriation, to media-related injustices (Lackner, 2017: 35) to economic grievances – increasingly escalated into broader and more unified condemnation of the regime. Exacerbated by Saleh's attempts to make constitutional changes to remain in power, calls for him to step down underscored frustration with endemic corruption, nepotism, mismanagement and poverty as a result of his reign since 1999 – as Yemen's first and only directly elected president. The conflict intensified when, as tens of thousands finished praying near the epicentre of the protest movement on 18 March, snipers stationed on rooftops and inside buildings opened fire indiscriminately, killing almost 50 protestors and wounding hundreds (Brandt, 2017: 332). Remembered as the 'Friday of Dignity', the violence marked a turning point, including a 'declaration of a state of emergency and international condemnation, and ultimately culminat[ing] in mass defections and resignations of formerly loyalist politicians and military officers' (Brandt, 2017: 332).

The Gulf Cooperation Council (GCC) – with support from the UN and the European Union (EU) – stepped in to negotiate an exit for Saleh. The 'Transition Agreement' – also known as the GCC Agreement (GCCA) initiated the transfer of power and established a Government of National Unity composed of 50 per cent of nominees for each party, with due consideration given to the representation of women (Agreement on the implementation mechanism for the transition process in Yemen in according with the initiative of the GCC, 2011). The GCCA had two major phases: the first phase included an early presidential election, which took place on 21 February 2012 and saw the election of Hadi; and the second, covering the remaining period until 2014, envisioned the National Dialogue Conference (NDC), constitutional reform, a constitutional referendum, the reform of political and electoral laws, parliamentary and local council elections, and presidential elections, if required (UNGA, 2013). After several delays, the NDC began in March 2013, bringing together 565 delegates from across the country; it was designed to help resolve some of the country's internal conflicts and to seek consensus on the future structure of the state.

Despite progress made in the context of the NDC, Yemen's fragile peace unravelled in August 2014, when, in reaction to the government's decision to remove fuel subsidies in line with International Monetary Fund (IMF) requirements, protests re-erupted. After their arrival in the city in September 2014 – incensed by Hadi's failure to deliver on diverse commitments, capitalizing upon increasing discontent with the government and with behind-the-scenes support from former 'enemy' Saleh[5] – the Houthis decided to seize the moment: in January 2015 they formed a new executive body (the Supreme Revolutionary Committee) and declared themselves in control of the government (Hill, 2017: 271). Hadi, who manage to escape[6] from his 'house arrest', then declared Aden the temporary capital of the 'legitimate government'. Violence between Houthi militants and government forces escalated in March 2015, when, at Hadi's request, a Saudi-led coalition began a military campaign, including airstrikes and naval blockades. During this period, two rounds of UN-led peace talks were held under the auspices of Special Envoy Ismail Ould Cheikh Ahmed, in Geneva in mid-2015, and Kuwait in 2016, but yielded few meaningful or sustainable results.

The Role of Businesses: Yemen in Transition 2011–16

An oft-quoted estimate suggests that in 2011 approximately ten families controlled more than 80 per cent of business activity in Yemen, including imports, manufacturing, processing, banking and telecommunications (Salisbury, 2011: 11); the economy, therefore, has traditionally been dominated by a system of patronage 'that is both close to and suspicious of the government' (el Taraboulsi-McCarthy et al, 2017: 4). According to a 2015 census, large enterprises (over 25 employees) account for only 0.3 per cent of all enterprises, and larger businesses established prior to

[5] Because, as Ginny Hill explained simply, the ascendency of the Houthis 'also contributed to the rout of his own opponents'; the Houthis and Saleh found common cause 'in wanting to humiliate Hamid [al-Ahmar] and Ali Mohsin' (Hill, 2017).

[6] Disguised as a woman (Hill, 2017: 271)

2011 were pressured to partner with prominent political, military and tribal elites (World Bank, 2015: 8). The families tend to be local, regional and international since many of the biggest firms are run by foreign-based Yemenis (el Taraboulsi-McCarthy et al, 2017: 4) with regional and/or global business ties. The business elite can – according to Peter Salisbury – be divided into five key categories (Salisbury, 2011: 10–11): first, a small traditional merchant elite which pre-dates Saleh's rule composed of a few commercial families/business actors with close relationships to the president; second, 'tribal capitalists' such as the al-Ahmar family, who use their social position to obtain business-related 'favours'; third, 'bureaucrats in business' or politicians from the General People's Congress (GPC) and JMP, who behave in tribe-like fashion; fourth, security services, dominated by Saleh's family/clan, including Ali Mohsin, who controls state-based military companies and engages in illicit activities (referred to here as 'businessmen in arms'); and, fifth, a small group of technocrats, or 'young reformers' constrained by their relative lack of power and the need to play by the rules of the patronage 'game'.[7] Business actors from each of these categories played four roles during the 2011–16 period.

First, business actors served as 'benefactors' (or 'humanitarians'). In 2011 the tribal groups and the traditional merchant elite found themselves in the same 'camp' when both – for different reasons – provided support to the demonstrators. Traditional merchant elites such as the *Hayal Saeed* Group,[8] the *Thabet* Group[9] – labelled the 'Ta'iz-Boys' (Albrecht, 2002: 143) – and many others provided the protestors with food, medicines and generators (Anonymous business leader, 2018a); some of these business

[7] Research for this chapter indicated that many 'young reformers' are sons of the traditional merchant elite, who have chosen to take different political positions from those of their families.

[8] The Hayal Saeed Group is made up of approximately 40 businesses, including, for example, The National Trading Company (NATCO); Pharma for Trading and Marketing Company; Artix for Trading Company; Marooj for International Technology; Yemen Company for Industry and Trading; Yemen Flour Mills Company; National Company for the manufacture of sponge and plastic; Yemeni Company for the Manufacture of Dairy Products; United Insurance Company; Yemeni Company for Sugar Refining; Hascan Co Limited; Arab Factories; Yemen International Hospital; Al Saeed Hotel (Mercure); Hadramaut Industrial Complex; East Start Company; Somalia Telecom, among many others.

[9] The Thabet Brothers Group is made up of around ten businesses, including but not limited to: National Oil Manufacturing Company; Modern Good Products Company; Yemen Stores for Fruits and Meat; Red Sea Contracting and Construction Company; Albaria Yemeni Company Limited; Yemen Dairy Manufacturing Company; Tuhama Trading Company; International Company for Packaging Industry, amongst others.

actors went one step further and brought university professors to work with the youth "to discuss what kind of change they wanted to see and how to protest in the right way" (Anonymous business leader, 2018a). Others provided the protestors with head cameras to enable them to document the violence inflicted on them, predominantly by regime forces (Anonymous business leader, 2018b). The al-Ahmar family, a long-standing political rival of Saleh, with extensive business interests, also supported the protestors, providing them with a large tent and a kitchen and publicizing their cause through their media channel (Anonymous Yemeni expert, 2018c). Furthermore, grappling with the absence of the state and poor infrastructure, business actors contributed their services in ways that were instrumental to the Yemeni people; referring to the largest business entity in Yemen, the *Hayal Saeed* Group, one expert underscored the manner in which businesses began "fixing roads, and carrying out infrastructure projects that the Government should have carried out" (Anonymous Yemeni expert, 2018b). In the face of a failing national grid and fuel shortages, for example, business actors facilitated a transition to solar power and, in 2017, a survey found that four out of five considered themselves involved in the relief effort (Nasser, 2018: 31). "When everything was collapsing," stated one businessman, "the private sector never gave up in providing the services and food that society needed" (Anonymous businessman, 2018a).

Second, business actors played the role of 'beneficiary', reaping the benefits of their roles, and/or in expanding the war economy and, therefore, playing the role of 'profiteer'. All the major business actors in Yemen benefited from the system due to the patronage networks in place and the fact that it was impossible to do business without being 'close' to the government. However, some business actors benefited more than others. Businessman Ahmed Saleh al-Essi,[10] for example, was appointed as Deputy Director for Economic Affairs in the President's Office in the Hadi Government. Several of those interviewed indicated that he made his fortune through legal and illegal means as controller of fuel imports through the port of Aden; he now serves as 'gatekeeper': "Everyone in the business community has to work through him or Hadi's son, or they can work through the Central Bank, but they cannot go beyond these three" (Noman, 2018).[11] According to a journalist writing for *Le Monde* (Imbert, 2018), al-Essi has a monopoly on the import of fuel into Aden,

[10] The al-Essi Group, a family-run business, is based in Dubai.

[11] Mustapha Noman is a former Ambassador, a former Deputy Foreign Minister of Yemen, and an opinion writer.

for which the government gives him between 30 and 40 million dollars each month.

Furthermore, since 2015, fuel smuggling has become the largest illicit business in Yemen; it is estimated that there are 25 new companies working in this sector from Dubai; Mohammed Saleh, the brother of the Houthi spokesperson, for example, established three companies between 2015 and 2016.[12] While many business actors have profited from smuggling, the collapse of the banking sector and the erosion of the Central Bank of Yemen's supervisory and regulatory functions have provided new opportunities for international money transfers: "A network of currency exchangers with links to the warring parties operate this black market, sharing their gains with the different parties in return for protection and permission to operate" (Anonymous Yemeni expert, 2018a). When so many business actors are involved in both licit and illicit transactions, the line between business actors, militias and warlords becomes quite fuzzy: many business actors are smuggling fuel, drugs and weapons that benefit such armed groups; similarly, many militias act like businesses, earning income through taxing trade, border fees and duties paid on goods at checkpoints (Salisbury, 2018: 24).

Third, businesses served as mediators and peacemakers, acting more broadly therefore as 'intermediaries'. In 2011, when the protestors were calling for President Saleh to step down, a group of business actors established a 'Mediation Committee' made up of around ten representatives of the largest families in the Chamber of Commerce. "Not everybody was interested in participating," recounted one member: "some left the group as they didn't want to be involved in politics, while others feared it could be judged as working against the President" (Anonymous businessman, 2018a). The group, however, was not necessarily 'anti-Saleh', but wanted to prevent an escalation of conflict, and "to protect the thousands of people that work for us", as one businessman stated (Anonymous businessman, 2018a). The Committee met with all relevant political stakeholders and, after several rounds of consultation, decided to propose that the President should resign one year later, cutting his remaining term in half, but leaving enough time for an orderly transition; the Committee planned to announce the proposal in the context of a press conference. However,

[12] The international community said that the Yemeni bank accounts were closed as they did not follow the Yemeni money laundering regulations. But if one wanted to stop this, one would focus on Dubai. Ninety-nine per cent of the fuel comes from Dubai. The Hadi government and the coalition are involved in this process and benefiting from it. Houthis benefit – they control the local markets, the areas where there is more consumption.

the killing of protestors on 18 March led to a complete abandonment of the initiative as business actors no longer believed there was a decent exit option for the President. A similar mediation initiative was launched in August 2014 in response to an escalation of the conflict with the Houthis; the group of business actors 'shuttled' between Hadi, the Houthis and other political figures but to no avail.

Therefore, when the National Dialogue began, business actors were hopeful they would regain influence over the peaceful trajectory of the country. However, given that the NDC allocated the 'private sector' only three out of 565 seats[13] – compared to 120 seats allocated to civil society, youth and women – the Chamber of Commerce consulted with a broader set of business actors to elaborate private sector priorities, which were presented to the NDC Secretariat and the formal private sector representatives. After all, as one businessman stated, "what could three individuals do amongst all these people?" (Anonymous businessman, 2018b). Efforts to work from outside the NDC included consultations, producing policy papers, lobbying and other initiatives. Moreover, during the UN-led talks in Kuwait, under the auspices of the International Finance Cooperation (IFC) and on the initiative of a business leader, members of the business community gathered in Dubai to launch a new discussion group called 'the New Yemen', which explored federalism and prospects for the business community in Dubai in the reconstruction of Yemen.

Lastly, business actors also played the role of agitator and 'conflict-maker' – sometimes also serving as 'spoilers'. Businesses affiliated with the military such as the Yemeni Economic Corporation (YECO, formerly the Military Economic Corporation, MECO), a government entity headed by a close Saleh ally, is accused of financing attacks on the 2011 protestors; witnesses claim he sent gunmen to use live bullets to disperse demonstrators (Gordon, 2018). Former President Saleh and Hamid al-Ahmar[14] – the family's most successful entrepreneur (Hill, 2017: 221) – furthermore, have used their extensive business wealth to support and

[13] Three official seats were allocated to the private sector (Ahmad Bazarah, Najat Jomaan and Yousif Alkuriimi), and two other businessmen also participated in another capacity (Yousef Alkuremee and Khlaed Abdulwahed).

[14] The al-Ahmar family owns a number of business entities, including but not limited to: Prospects for printing and publishing; ATICO Oil Company; Apollo Travel Co; the Yemeni Company for Public Telephones; Al Salam Trading and Agencies Est; Petroleum Technology Gas; National Travel Agency, Arab Horizons Services; United Medical Company; and the Yemeni Corporation for Equipment. Hamid is the son of the former Speaker of Parliament, paramount leader of the Hashed tribal grouping and head Islamist-tribal *Islah* movement, Shaykhs Abdullah Bin Hussain al-Ahmar.

influence the Houthis and the 'anti-Houthis' respectively, by providing weapons and financial support. One well-established trade and contracting company is said to have provided extensive financial and logistical aid to the Houthis (Anonymous Yemeni expert, 2018c); some business actors have provided support in kind, through use of their hotels, transport facilities and communication while others have been 'obliged' to provide support through taxes and levies in order to either protect their factories or to be able to travel and/or operate through certain areas. Other armed groups have also behaved as 'businesses', seeking to accrue finances in exchange for services. Terrorist groups, such as al-Qaida in the Arabian Peninsula (AQAP), for example, capitalized upon the widely supported demonstrations of 2011 to create 'Ansar al-Sharia', thereby attempting to re-orient itself locally as a populist movement (UNSC, 2015). According to Yemeni officials interviewed by the UN Panel of Experts, AQAP is mainly funded through the payment of ransom for kidnapped foreigners and the looting of banks' (UNSC, 2015).

What is evident from an analysis of Yemen's political economy at the local, regional and international levels is the manner in which the aforementioned roles of businesses are informed, shaped and constrained by political, social and cultural forces anchored in the long-standing history of the conflict, and Yemen's place in the region and the world. Contrary to international relations literature broadly speaking and to *mainstream* (*American*) International Political Economy specifically, therefore, businesses do not perceive themselves – and nor do they behave – as traditional economic theory has suggested, according to the logic of purely rational actors motivated by material gains calculated on a 'cost-benefit' analysis, but play decidedly political *and* economic roles, often on the basis of political *and* economic motivations, and most certainly with political *and* economic ramifications that both sustain and undermine peacemaking efforts. To what extent were these dynamics taken into consideration by UN peacemaking actors? And does this represent the exception or the rule?

The UN Approach to Businesses in Yemen

According to those UN officials and Yemeni business actors interviewed during the period 2011–16: no political economy analyses were undertaken by the Special Envoy(s) and his team; the main conflicting parties aside (some of which, as outlined previously, wore business 'hats'), business actors did not participate formally or informally in the negotiations around the GCCA; they played only a marginal role in the

NDC; they played no formal or informal role in the negotiations held in Kuwait or Geneva; and business leaders were not included deliberately in any outreach strategies – with one exception in 2016. As one UN official stated, "Business actors are so important and it is one of the huge gaps in our engagement and our approach" (United Nations official, 2018c). But to argue that business actors played little or no role in the UN peacemaking strategy would be misleading; an analysis, however, of *the way* in which business actors were included and, indeed, excluded, from the peacemaking process is revealing.

First, the Headquarters-based entities reporting on Yemen during the period from 2011 to 2016, including the Human Rights Council, the Security Council and the Secretary-General, for example, feature a long list of stakeholders in their resolutions and reports – 'stakeholders' being actors with a stake in the conflict, that is, those who are assumed to have agency. These include: the government of Yemen, armed opposition groups, *al Hirak*, Southern leaders, youth, the al Houthi movement, Salafists, the *Islah* party, the JMP, the GPC, armed tribesmen, Yemeni armed forces, al-Qaida, assailants, diplomats, Ministers, security officers, the GCC, the League of Arab states, civil society representatives, sheikhs, notables, battalions, armoured brigades, the Yemeni coastguard, and the Revolutionary Committee (in no particular order). These are all what one might – through a narrow reading – term 'political actors', in one shape or form. Generally speaking, the private sector, business actors and the economy – formal or informal – go largely unmentioned.

Second, on the rare occasions when businesses *are* included by Head Quarters entities it is generally through two lenses. The first is largely humanitarian, whereby economic and business-related dynamics are discursively tied to humanitarian rather than political dynamics. For example, in 2013, the Human Rights Council discussed the increasing food prices, decreased access to water, and the doubling of transportation costs, indicating that these dynamics made 'health care and other basic services even more difficult to access' (UNGA, 2014); similarly, the President of the Security Council notes the need to expedite economic reforms to achieve 'macroeconomic stability, fight poverty, and address the chronic humanitarian consequences in a sustainable manner' (UNSC, 2014). The second lens through which the economy and businesses are viewed is through the sanctions regime. The report of the Panel of Experts, responsible for overseeing the sanctions measures imposed in resolution 2140 (UNSC, 2015) extensively discusses Yemen's economy and focuses predominantly on the illicit economy, arms dealers and the financing of terrorist groups such as AQAP and business actors responsible for helping former President Saleh hide his assets. The three individuals who were subjected to targeted sanctions can all be considered political and/or security actors: (i) Abd al-Khaliq al-Huthi; (ii) Abdullah Yahya al Hakim; and (iii) Ali Abdullah Saleh (the first two being rebel leaders, and the last the former President).

Third, at the country level, there is strong evidence that economic issues and actors *were* fully appreciated by some UN actors and often incorporated into analyses; but this knowledge did not translate into a different way of doing peacemaking and often failed to make its way from the development side of 'the house' to the political. The UN Common Country Assessment of 2011 (UNDP, 2011), for example, discusses patronage networks and the links between political leadership and prominent business families but, in programmatic terms, the UN Development Assistance Framework (UNDAF) only mentions the private sector once in the Results and Resources Framework; similarly, the Joint United Nations Framework to support the transition in Yemen in 2012–14 (2012) analyses the root causes of the conflict through a lens of unequal access to power and resources, and goes on to envision a role for the private sector in the transitional process – albeit as a single reference and in terms of 'partnerships' among a long list of other stakeholders. Several UN officials interviewed lamented the management style of Special Envoy Benomar, which they maintain undermined the possibility for greater cross-pollination between the work being undertaken by United Nations Development Programme (UNDP), for example, on such issues and the Office of the Special Envoy (OSE); as Steven Zyck suggested, animosity between the UN Special Envoy and senior UN development figures 'ultimately prevented the OSE from drawing fully upon other UN agencies in country', and especially from providing 'more robust and frequent technical inputs' for the NDC (Zyck, 2011: 8–9).

Fourth, the concept of 'inclusivity' did not apply to business actors or to the private sector. In the GCCA, for example, which was supported by the UN, a number of groups were cited as requiring a seat at the NDC table, including 'youth, the Southern Movement, the Houthis, other political parties, civil society representatives and women' – a narrow list considering that participation was meant to reflect 'all segments of Yemeni society' (Republic of Yemen, 2012: 16). Francesco Mancini and Jose Vericat, furthermore, underscored how Benomar was credited for 'going out of his way to be inclusive and to reach out to a wide range of stakeholders' and go on to argue that the 'ultimate example of this was the NDC, where he made it his personal mission to ensure that a significant number of women and youth were included' (Mancini and Vericat, 2016: 11). As previously mentioned, only three out of 565 seats at the NDC were allocated specifically to the private sector compared to 140 seats allocated to women, youth and civil society. Similarly, while Ismail Ould Cheikh Ahmed appointed seven Yemeni women to participate in consultations during the Kuwait negotiations (Bilqis, 2018), the same cannot be said for business actors (Anonymous businessman, 2018b). Interestingly, Mancini and Vericat also state that 'a mediation process should be considered inclusive enough when it does not exclude parties that could disrupt an agreement from the outside or include parties that could prevent an agreement internally' (Mancini and Vericat, 2016: 14–15) on the one hand, and that, for peace processes to endure, 'they should also include those who did not take up arms but were working for peace' (Mancini and Vericat, 2016: 15). Business actors and economic actors are, it seems, excluded therefore both from an understanding of inclusivity, as well as from the definition of actors 'working for peace'.

Fifth, despite an understanding of the complexity of conflict landscapes and the interrelated nature of politics and economics, on the rare occasions when the economic dimensions of peacemaking were considered, a bifurcated approach dominated. UN officials, for example, underscore that they did meet with business actors, but that they met with them in their capacity as political leaders – and here they refer most prominently to members of the Saleh and al-Ahmar family. This separation of the political and economic is underscored by the rather unique deployment of an economist seconded from the World Bank to the Special Envoy's Office. While she was well placed to infuse a political economy approach into the work of the Special Envoy, her primary task consisted of setting up a joint trust fund to be managed by the OSE; one individual alone could not be expected, however, to be able to counter-balance the absence of a political economy-infused approach, which was catastrophic on two counts. The first concerned the 'regions issue' under discussion in the NDC, where two 'federal visions' were presented: one which proposed two regions (north and south), and another made of six regions – both highly contentious since 'Southern lands are wealthier, and more than twice the size of northern lands; yet the northern population is more than four times the southern population' (Day, 2014: 27). The Houthis objected to the federal plan entirely, arguing that it divided the country into poor and wealthy regions, and the region 'that included the Houthi heartland had neither access to the Red Sea nor to the natural resources (oil and gas) of al-Jawf and Mareb' (Lackner, 2017: 43). Second, in early 2014, following the conclusion of the NDC, the issue of reforming fuel subsides was under discussion; the World Bank and the IMF were pushing for a reduction in subsidies and, despite efforts to ensure it would be undertaken in a conflict-sensitive manner, President Hadi ended up issuing a circular to cut all subsidies overnight – a decision which sparked extensive demonstrations and gave significant 'ammunition' to the Houthis, who used the event to insist that the political elite were out of touch with the needs of real people.

The only exception to the otherwise endemic exclusion of local business actors came in 2016, when the OSE can be credited with "trying to develop an economic strategy" (United Nations official, 2018a). These efforts were undertaken in partnership with the World Bank, the IMF and the Berghof Foundation, although many would argue that – with the conflict then under way – it was too little too late. The strategy was designed to ensure basic state functioning through the preservation of the Central Bank's functions. In this capacity, the OSE engaged with the leaders of the main commercial families in Yemen – aligned with different 'factions' of the conflict – with a view to seeking consensus on what was required on the part of the Central Bank in order for businesses to continue import and expert, and to therefore to ensure "basic economic survival" (United Nations official, 2018a). This involved direct negotiations with political and business figures and representatives from the Central Bank, as well as a Track II process. As one UN official stated, this was, unfortunately, an exception: "I've never heard of something like this in a UN process" (United Nations official, 2018a). It is interesting that such an approach emerged so late in the UN strategy and that, when it did, it focused on leveraging largely 'licit' business actors for issues perceived as 'economic' issues, thereby ring-fencing those issues perceived as being more 'political' in nature and maintaining a sanctions-dominant approach to those businesses perceived as 'illicit'.

The Exception or the Rule?

Engagement with UN officials as well as with many of its mediation-oriented partners – including the Centre for Humanitarian Dialogue (HD Centre), the Crisis Management Initiative (CMI) in Helsinki, the European Institute of Peace (EIP), swisspeace and many others off the record – indicates that, while there are indeed exceptions to this rule, the Yemen case is a robust example of the way in which mediation practitioners have a blind spot when it comes to local business actors. What was striking from these interviews was the degree of surprise and, indeed, exasperation among practitioners: "it is so obvious that [local business engagement] is what we should be doing, but we don't do it" was a common refrain. As former Special Representative of the Secretary-General (SRSG) Keating, who is most certainly in the 'exception category', underscored: in the context of peacemaking "you ignore political economy and the role of business at your peril" (Keating, 2018). Engagements with UN and non-UN mediators alike give rise to five key arguments for why businesses *are not* or, indeed, *should not* be included in peace processes, arguments which will be rejected here before exploring a more structured analysis of this exclusion. These 'anti-business' arguments are revelatory; they confirm the manner in which the 'political practice' of peace mediation is deeply entrenched in socio-historical power configurations in which 'who and what' gets included and excluded from peace mediation discourses and practice is not only taken for granted, but that attempts to question and reform the practice are resisted.

The first argument concerns *necessity*: businesses are not needed around the table because they are represented by government figures with business interests. This is, of course, true, but this invariably concerns state-led businesses and the notion that the only businesses that matter in-country are state-led ones is not only false, but also implicitly promotes a questionable intertwining between contentious politics and business actors. The second argument concerns *impracticability*: a mediator cannot include everyone around the table. This is, of course, also true; but there are many more women, civil society and youth in the world than there are businesses, so numerically speaking it is less complex to include businesses than it is other actors. This argument also assumes that businesses can *only* be included via a seat at the table, whereas the discourse on normative inclusion demonstrates the multiple forums through which businesses can be engaged. The third argument concerns *motivations*: businesses are, it is argued, profit-seeking entities and mediators cannot be seen to legitimize economic motives. The implication of this argument is that the 'usual' political actors have non-profit-seeking motivations, an argument which is certainly not borne out by reality; moreover, the notion that businesses *only* seek profit is reductionist and also disproven – not least in the context of the Yemen example analysed in this chapter. Even if we assume that businesses *do* have economic motives, if these economically motivated actors undermine prospects for peace surely it would be pragmatic to include them? The fourth argument revolves around *legitimacy*: who do business actors 'represent'? Again, this question is logically dubious based on our understanding of the inclusion discourse. It could be argued, for example, that they represent the thousands of workers employed by them, or the country's economic future; on the other hand, if this is an argument for non-engagement, it can also be asked: who do so-called 'pariah groups' represent? The last argument concerns *status*: business actors are 'elites', they do not represent the 'local'. Almost all those who participate in Track I negotiations are in some shape or form elites; as the circle of inclusion has been extended to civil society actors, women and youth many also have become 'co-opted elites' since peacemakers tend to reach out to a certain sub-section of well-educated, urban-dwelling actors who speak the 'language' of peacebuilding and who have an interest in 'being included'. Consequently, like many other stakeholder groups, many business actors are elite, others may not be. These arguments do not justify or explain their exclusion.

So what explains the exclusion of businesses from peacemaking? Actors from the political side of the UN underscore three key factors: the structure of the system, the 'culture' of the organization, and the skill set/toolkit available to them. Concerning organizational structure, many suggested that the UN is simply not set up to engage with businesses, underscoring its preference for the (so-called) 'formal' over the 'informal', and the state over non-state actors: the daily work of UN staff is, therefore, related to formal, largely state-based interactions (Anonymous academic, 2018). As one UN official stated, "we are not very good at understanding the underworld; we understand where the fault-lines are but not with any level of granularity that would help us to formulate strategies that would be effective" (United Nations official, 2018b). The focus remains on those entities labelled as national 'political' or 'security' actors – and at the national level. Businesses are only engaged with through the lens of post-conflict actors that can create jobs and assist with economic rejuvenation. The UN, it is argued, was set up to deal with 'politics'. But, as one UN official conceded, "the UN was established when functional lines were clearer, when inter-state conflict predominated", and the inter-linkages between and among actors were less complex (United Nations official, 2018b). Part of the challenge of dealing with businesses, therefore, stems from the need to adapt to 21st-century realities.

Others emphasized the cultural bias of the organization, which prevents it from acknowledging, let alone engaging, with business actors. As Gerald Pachoud, the former focal point for the private sector at the UN Peacebuilding Support Office confirmed, "people at the UN understand that you can only make peace with your enemies, but those same people won't engage with businesses because they are profit-making entities" (Pachoud, 2018).[15] This is, he argues, based on a reductive binary, whereby the UN, non-profit 'white-knights' are juxtaposed with the profit-seeking, inherently 'bad' commercially minded business actors. It is a type of basic, anti-capitalist mindset, he suggested, which is extremely limiting from the perspective of conflict resolution: "why," he asked, "would someone planting bombs have more legitimacy to be included

[15] Gerald Pachoud is a former Special Advisor to Special Representative of the Secretary-General, John Ruggie, and an expert on business and human rights.

than someone who provides livelihoods?" (Pachoud, 2018). Many among UN staff are insulated from so-called 'new actors' and change can be slow; it took decades, for example, to accept NGOs as key stakeholders and businesses have a long way to go before they can be perceived to be on an equal footing. This leads UN actors, whether in the context of the SDGs, sustaining peace and other important policy contexts, to perceive the private sector as a 'cash-cow' rather than a partner for peace, a conflict actor to be leveraged, a spoiler or quite simply a stakeholder. "This," Pachoud argued, "is pure short-sightedness"; international actors should, he underscored, "be looking beyond contribution to participation" (Pachoud, 2018).

For some, the key failure to consistently include business actors relates to skills, tools and working methods at the UN. As one academic suggested,

> 'an understanding of local power dynamics within the UN does not prevail as they don't hire using these optics – it is simply information that is difficult to absorb as an international organisation; people tend to be lawyers, or political scientists, they have a sort of "barcode" and can't think outside "the UN"'. (Anonymous academic, 2018)

This leads staff to focus on political and security institutions and it is the "luck of the draw" to have people with political economy "know-how" on mediation teams (United Nations official, 2018b). Even when such analyses are developed by others, it does not make its 'way up' the decision-making tree; and, on the rare occasion that political economy issues *are* reflected in UN analyses, such considerations are left behind as the process of elaborating a strategy unfolds. As the process goes on, "it increasingly becomes about the party dynamics at the table, the intransigence of certain groups, the fragmentation of others, and the whole political economy angle of things gets pushed to the background instead of going towards a proper political economy-style engagement" (Government official, 2018). Another senior UN official suggested that SRSGs do not have the sort of "instinct or inclination to look at a political economy approach to conflict or violence reduction or promoting peace" (United Nations official, 2018d).

The marginalization, and in some cases exclusion, of businesses from peace mediation is not, however, unique to the UN System. David Harland, Director of the HD Centre, for example, when describing his experience suggested that "it has forever been seen as important and a good thing to engage with the private sector, but it never quite happens – either due to perceptions of impartiality, or problems on their end related to the potential for legal liability." As mediators, he continued, "we are considerably more comfortable in dealing with the political and military expression of interests than with business interests" (Harland, 2018). Similarly, Tuija Talvitie, Director of CMI, suggested that, as people who work in conflict prevention and resolution, mediators "understand politics and political processes rather well, but are less adept at dealing with economic dynamics – not to mention powerful business people" (Talvitie, 2018). Laurent Goetschel, Director of swisspeace, one of the pioneers of the (international) 'business for peace' mediation space, said that progress to include businesses in peace lags behind the inclusion of business participation in human rights and development realms due to the prevailing notion that politics and economics are two different spheres (Goetschel, 2018). So if the exclusion of businesses is not unique to the UN, it can be argued that peace mediation broadly speaking, and the discourse on 'inclusion' in particular, have been constructed in a manner that implicitly and explicitly excludes local business actors.

Conclusion

Peacemaking practice has evolved on the basis of 'institutionalised structures, conventions, or background understandings' (Ashley, 1989: 272) that mistakenly preclude and exclude business actors from the realm of peace mediation. Peace processes have taken on a specific form, a certain essence, a way of being in which business actors seemingly have no place; however, as argued by Richard Ashley, the 'structure of collective experience does not fall from heaven as a pure, unambiguous, already differentiated presence' (Ashley, 1989: 272), but is the result of the intertwining of historical processes, practices and power which has the effect of legitimizing certain actors and delegitimizing others. A business lens in peace mediation is a way to overcome one of the 'blind spots' mediation actors have towards local power dynamics. Indeed, a business lens in peace mediation recognizes the four roles businesses play in local contexts as benefactors, profiteers, intermediaries and agitators, roles which underscore the imperative of extending the discourse and political practice of inclusion to include local business actors. This lens can be applied in three key 'areas': first, in terms of mediation strategy/ process by leveraging the relationships of power and influence business actors have over political actors and armed groups; second, in terms of mediation content/agreements, by building upon the knowledge and expertise of business actors of transnational socio-economic dynamics and licit and illicit economies; and, third, with regard to mediation 'structure'/

format by recognizing local business actors as entry-points for addressing the sub-optimal coordination between economic and political actors on the international stage, particularly in overcoming the 'gap' between peacemaking and post-conflict-related processes.

References

Anonymous academic (2018), interviewed in person by Josie L. Kaye, 9 September, Geneva.

Anonymous business leader (2018a), interviewed by phone by Josie L. Kaye, 24 October.

Anonymous business leader (2018b), interviewed by phone by Josie L. Kaye, 28 November.

Anonymous businessman (2018a), interviewed by phone by Josie L. Kaye, 12 October.

Anonymous businessman (2018b), interviewed by phone by Josie L. Kaye, 2 November.

Anonymous Yemeni expert (2018a), interviewed by phone by Josie L. Kaye, 22 June.

Anonymous Yemeni expert (2018b), interviewed by phone by Josie L. Kaye, 14 September.

Anonymous Yemeni expert (2018c), interviewed by phone and in person by Josie L. Kaye, September–November.

Agreement on the implementation mechanism for the transition process in Yemen in according with the initiative of the Gulf Cooperation Council (GCC) (2011), 5 December.

Albrecht, H. (2002) 'The Political Economy of Reform in Yemen: Privatisation, Investment, and the Yemeni Business Climate', *Asien Afrika Latinamerika*, 30(2): 131–50.

Ashley, R.K. (1989) 'Living on Border Lines: Man, Poststructuralism, and War' in J. Der Derian and M.J. Shapiro (eds) *International/Intertextual Relations: Postmodern Readings of World Politics*, Lexington MA: Lexington Books, pp 259–322.

Bilqis, A.O. (2018), interviewed by phone by Josie L. Kaye, 2 November.

Brandt, M. (2017) *Tribes and Politics in Yemen, A History of the Houthis Conflict*, London: Hurst & Co.

Conroy, S. (2017) 'Peace and the Private Sector: The Business Role for Goal 16', *Alliance for Peacebuilding*, [online] 19 October, available from: https://allianceforpeacebuilding.org/2017/10/peace-and-the-private-sector-the-business-role-for-goal-16/ (accessed 25 July 2019).

Day, S.W. (2014) 'The 'Non-conclusion' of Yemen's National Dialogue', *Foreign Policy*, 27 January.

Deitelhoff, N. and Wolf, D.K. (2010) *Corporate Social Responsibility? Corporate Governance Contributions to Peace and Security in Zones of Conflict*, New York, NY: Palgrave Macmillan.

el Taraboulsi-McCarthy, S., Najid, N. and Willitts-King, B. (2017) 'Private Sector Engagement in Complex Emergencies: Case Studies from Yemen and Southern Somalia', *HPG Report*.

Ford, J. (2015) *Regulating Business for Peace: The United Nations, the Private Sector and Post-Conflict Recovery*, Cambridge: Cambridge University Press.

Friedman, M. (1970) 'The Social Responsibility of Business Is to Increase Its Profit', *The New York Times Magazine*, 13 September.

Goetschel, L. (2018), interviewed by phone by Josie L. Kaye, 19 October.

Gordon, S. (2018) 'The Parallel Revolution in Yemen', *Critical Thinking*, [online] 6 March, available from: https://www.criticalthreats.org/analysis/the-parallel-revolution-in-yemen (accessed 19 September 2018).

Government official (2018), interviewed by phone by Josie L. Kaye, 16 October.

Harland, D. (2018), interviewed in person by Josie L. Kaye, 25 September, Geneva.

Hill, G. (2017) *Yemen Endures: Civil War, Saudi Adventurism and the Future of Arabia*, Oxford: Oxford University Press.

Imbert, L. (2018) 'Ahmed Saleh al-Essi, Portrait d'un profiteur de guerre au Yemen', *Le Monde*, [online] 12 December, available from: https://www.lemonde.fr/international/article/2018/12/12/ahmed-saleh-al-essi-un-profiteur-dans-la-guerre-au-yemen_5396360_3210.html (accessed 25 July 2018).

International Crisis Group (ICG) (2011) 'Popular Protest in North Africa and the Middle East (II): Yemen Between Reform and Revolution', *Middle East/North Africa Report*, No. 102, 10 March.

Joint United Nations Framework to support the transition in Yemen 2012–2014 (2012) *A Multi-dimensional Framework to Support a Peaceful and Inclusive Transition*, 30 March.

Keating, M. (2018), interviewed by phone by Josie L. Kaye, 9 November.

Lackner, H. (2017) *Yemen in Crisis – Autocracy, Neo-Liberalism and the Disintegration of a State*, London: Saqi Books.

Lanz, D. (2011) 'Who Gets a Seat at the Table? A Framework for Understanding the Dynamics of Inclusion and Exclusion in Peace Negotiations', *International Negotiation*, 16(2): 275–95.

Mac Ginty R. and Richmond, O.P. (2013) 'The Local Turn in Peace Building: A Critical Agenda for Peace', *Third World Quarterly*, 34(5): 763–83.

Mancini, F. and Vericat, J. (2016) 'Lost in Transition: Mediation in Libya, Syria, and Yemen', International Peace Institute (IPI).

Miklian, J. and Schouten, P. (2014) 'Business for Peace: The New Paradigm of International Peacebuilding and Development', SSRN Working Paper.

Nasser, A. (2018) 'Beyond the Business as Usual Approach, Private Sector Engagement in Post-Conflict Yemen', Sana'a Centre for Strategic Studies, August.

Noman, M. (2018), interviewed by phone by Josie L. Kaye, 26 September.

Office of the United Nations High Commissioner for Human Rights (OHCHR) (2011) *Guiding Principles on Business and Human Rights: Implementing the United Nations 'Protect, Respect and Remedy' Framework.*

Organisation for Economic Co-Operation and Development (OECD) (2006) *OECD Risk Awareness Tool for Multinational Enterprises in Weak Governance Zones.*

Pachoud, G. (2018), interviewed by phone and in person by Josie L. Kaye, 10 and 18 September, Geneva.

Republic of Yemen (2012) *Final Report of the Technical Committee to Prepare for the Comprehensive National Dialogue Conference (Technical Committee Report)*, 12 December, Sana'a, Yemen, Annex 2.

Salisbury, P. (2011) 'Yemen's Economy: Oil, Imports and Elites', *Middle East and North Africa Programme Paper*, Chatham House.

Salisbury, P. (2018) 'Building Peace in Yemen from the Ground Up: How to End the Conflict', *Foreign Affairs*, 28 February.

Talvitie, T. (2018), interviewed by phone by Josie L. Kaye, 18 October.

Tesner, S. and Kell, G. (2000) *The United Nations and Business, A Partnership Recovered*, Basingstoke: Palgrave Macmillan.

UNDP (United Nations Development Programme) (2011) *United Nations Common Country Assessment (UNCCA). Republic of Yemen.*

UNGA (United Nations General Assembly) Human Rights Council (HRC) (2013) *Resolution A/HRC/24/34 on the Situation of Human Rights in Yemen*, [online] 25 July, available from: https://undocs.org/en/A/HRC/24/34 (accessed 25 July 2019).

UNGA Human Rights Council (HRC) (2014) *Resolution A/HRC/27/44 on the Situation of Human Rights in Yemen*, [online] 27 August, available from: https://undocs.org/A/HRC/27/44 (accessed 25 July 2019).

United Nations Global Compact (2018) *UN Private Sector Forum – Building and Investing in Peace for All*, 24 September.

United Nations Global Compact (nd) *Work with a Local Network to Advance Peace*, [online] 27 August, available from: https://www.unglobalcompact.org/take-action/action/peace-local-activities (accessed 25 July 2019).

United Nations official (2018a), interviewed by phone by Josie L. Kaye, 17 July.

United Nations official (2018b), interviewed by phone by Josie L. Kaye, 11 October.

United Nations official (2018c), interviewed by phone by Josie L. Kaye, 1 November.

United Nations official (2018d), interviewed by phone by Josie L. Kaye, 9 November.

UNSC (United Nations Security Council) (2014) *Resolution S/PV.7255*, [online] 29 August, available from: https://undocs.org/en/S/PV.7255 (accessed 25 August 2019).

UNSC (United Nations Security Council) (2015) *Resolution S/2015/125 Letter dated 20 February 2015 from the Panel of Experts on Yemen Established Pursuant to Security Council Resolution 2140 (2014) Addressed to the President of the Security Council*, [online] 20 February, available from: https://www.securitycouncilreport.org/atf/cf/%7B65BFCF9B-6D27-4E9C-8CD3-CF6E4FF96FF9%7D/s_2015_125.pdf (accessed 25 July 2019).

UNSG (United Nations Secretary-General) (1999) *Press Release SG/SM/6881 Secretary-General Proposes Global Compact on Human Rights, Labour, Environment, in Address to World Economic Forum in Davos*, [online] 1 February, available from: https://www.un.org/press/en/1999/19990201.sgsm6881.html (accessed 25 July 2019).

UNSG (United Nations Secretary-General) (2012) 'Guidance for Effective Mediation' in United Nations General Assembly, *Resolution A/66/811 on Strengthening the Role of Mediation in the Peaceful Settlement of Disputes, Conflict Prevention and Resolution*, [online] 25 June, available from: https://undocs.org/A/66/811 (accessed 24 July 2019).

World Bank (2015) 'The Republic of Yemen, Unlocking the Potential for Economic Growth, A Country Economic Memorandum', *Middle East and North Africa Region, Macroeconomics and Fiscal Management Global Practice*, October.

Zyck, S.A. (2011) 'Mediating Transitions in Yemen: Achievements and Lessons', *International Peace Institute*, May.

11

Mediating Across Worldviews

Jeffrey R. Seul

Introduction

The default mechanisms, practices and mindsets we have relied upon for decades in our efforts to manage and resolve violent intra-state and international conflict, including common modes of peace mediation, may no longer be fully up to the task – if, indeed, they ever were. They often seem inadequately attuned to the drivers of our most persistent conflicts; unresponsive to the core motivations and aspirations of conflict stakeholders. This is because many of our most persistent and challenging conflicts are, and always have been, propelled by contending worldviews[1] and their normative dictates.

Worldview conflict is not new, but the role worldviews play in conflict has not been sufficiently understood and accepted, nor have our approaches to dealing with worldview conflict met its driving logic head on. During the Cold War, and in the years following it when the conceptual and methodological foundations of the contemporary conflict

[1] Within the disciplines of religious studies and theology, the term 'worldview' has become associated with the Christian evangelical tradition, perhaps complicating my use of it from the perspective of those working primarily within those disciplines. The term has a longer and more varied history, however, and it has been embraced more broadly, both by those in other academic disciplines and in common usage. I use it precisely because it has this broader appeal and a common meaning that many people seem to grasp readily. For an intellectual history of the term and its usage across disciplines, see Naugle (2002).

resolution field were being laid, worldview differences tended to get filed either under the heading of 'ideology'[2] (for example, Communism as ideology) or of 'identity' (see, for example, Kelman, 1997).[3] Ideology often implies a certain misguided dogmatism, if not irrational fanaticism, rather than genuine, legitimate disagreement about a vision of the world, how it works, and principles for flourishing within it. It also has a political connotation, obscuring the fact that there are many types of worldviews which arguably are not concerned with politics in the first instance. Identity is a more fundamental and useful concept that is entwined and symbiotic with the notion of worldview, but it alone does too little to help us understand and work within and across the normative orders in which conflict stakeholders' identities are forged and expressed, and which constrain (and also can create) opportunities for conflict resolution. As we rethink peace mediation today – in an era when the liberal worldview that gave rise to contemporary conflict resolution theory and practice, including its multilateralist (see, for example, Palacio, 2019) and 'free world' (Taylor, 2019) aspirations, is itself increasingly questioned – we would be wise to consider more fully how worldview collisions contribute to conflict and how we might adapt peace mediation theory and practice in order to mediate across worldviews more effectively. I believe this is one of today's most important frontiers in the field of peace mediation.

In this chapter, I argue that prevailing approaches to peace mediation have largely sidestepped and sought to avoid differences in the worldview

[2] Juan Ugarriza (2009) has reviewed the embrace and rejection of the concept of ideology in conflict theory, ultimately arguing for re-embrace of a transformed definition of the term that is closely related to the notion of worldview as I use it: '[I]deology could be defined as a set of beliefs based on ideals (i.e. equality, power, justice), which is turned into a project aimed at achieving social perfection by managing social relations. Ideologies are considered here as overarching cultural systems that nevertheless may be influenced or shaped by power and economic relations' (citations omitted) (Ugarriza, 2009: 84).

[3] We could think of identity as a broader and more fundamental concept than worldview, encompassing elements of individual and group life, like language, attachment to place, and even very individual characteristics, that are not always components of one's worldview. In this sense, identity is the foundational concept, and one's worldview is a subset of one's identity. In my experience, however, many of the greatest challenges in conflict resolution work exist at the 'level' of worldviews, and the felt constraints they impose. We too seldom 'work up' at this level systematically enough when using approaches to conflict resolution that are focused on identity needs and related conflict dynamics. Attending systematically, and effectively, to parties' worldview orientations requires theoretical and methodological shifts in our approach to conflict resolution work.

(and associated normative) lenses through which parties view, and seek to resolve, their conflicts. They have focused instead on social scientific concepts, such as needs and interests, in hope of helping parties find common ground. While there likely is a small set of universally shared basic human needs (Tay and Diener, 2011), one's understanding of how one's needs and related interests can be satisfied, and therefore the ways in which one goes about trying to satisfy them, are influenced by the worldview one holds and shares with others. We all seek to resolve conflict in ways that comport with our worldviews, because contravening their tenets and dictates risks upsetting the normative order through which our needs and interests are fulfilled. Unless and until our approaches to peace mediation take all stakeholders' normative orientations seriously, and on their own terms, we have little hope of finding durable solutions to these conflicts.

The theory and practice of mediating across worldviews is a vast, complex topic that cannot be explored comprehensively in this chapter. I briefly explain what I mean when I use the term worldview; discuss some of the reasons why worldview conflicts can be so intense and difficult to resolve; consider some ways in which liberal institutions, and approaches to peace mediation that follow from them, seem inadequate for addressing worldview conflict; and highlight six key tasks (among others) that likely must be taken up in order to mediate across worldviews successfully, many of which seem to be largely neglected in most peace mediation practice today.

Worldviews

Human beings are meaning makers. We seek and make meaning, individually and collectively, about mundane matters and about the very nature of reality.[4] Worldviews are the mental models we hold, more and less consciously, about how the natural and social worlds cohere, what makes them cohere, what is valued and what is not, and even what we can know and how we know it.[5] Our individual and collective identities

[4] This dimension of human experience has been identified and studied from diverse humanistic and scientific perspectives. For two contemporary social scientific perspectives on the forces propelling our meaning making and the mechanics of it, see Routledge (2018) and Kegan (1982).

[5] Conflict resolution scholar Jayne Docherty (2001: 51) helpfully defines a worldview as any system that attempts to answer the following five questions, however explicitly, completely or compellingly it does so: (a) What is real or true? (Ontology); (b) How is 'the real' organized? (Logic); (c) What is valuable or important? (Axiology); (d) How do we know about what is? (Epistemology); (e) How should I or we act? (Ethic).

– our sense of self and who we identify with and are most inclined to trust – are entwined with and substantially defined by our worldviews.

For many of us, our worldviews overlap considerably with others' worldviews. Different worldviews sometimes even have common, though often differently interpreted, elements. Christianity appropriates elements of Jewish tradition. Islam appropriates Jewish and Christian prophets. Religious nationalist movements, whether Religious Zionists in Israel or Christian Evangelicals in the United States, mix religion with political perspectives held by some who do not share their religious orientation. Many religious people the world over embrace scientific understandings as part of their worldviews; some scientists are religious.

In the WEIRD (western, educated, industrialized, rich and democratic) world, many of us tend to think of religion as the primary, if not sole, source of worldviews. If we are atheists or not particularly religious, we may not see our perspectives and values (whether right leaning, left leaning or centrist) as worldviews. We may consider a scientific materialist perspective to be an indisputably judgement-free orientation, rather than a perspective that requires its own inferential leaps – at least if we believe science puts all the big questions about the universe, and life within it, to rest, or that it undoubtedly will do so in time. Through science, we seek a grand, synthetic theory of everything, built upon propositions that have been tested extensively and not disproven, yet fundamental gaps in our scientific understanding of the universe and our own experience remain, and some of them may be impossible to fill.[6] Religious worldviews are not the only worldviews, and many worldview conflicts – from partisan disagreements between conservative and liberal citizens in the United States to the trade wars between that country and China – either do not involve parties who think of themselves as religious or do not consistently implicate all parties' religious beliefs, whatever they may (or may not) be.

Though worldviews tend to develop through group-level interactions – we send signals to each other about our respective beliefs, with communal beliefs and bonds of trust developing in tandem in the process – a given person's worldview also will be anchored partially in individual experience. Each of us filters what we experience in the present through a unique prism that has been shaped and tempered, in part, by our personal physiology and temperament, our family history, the imprints left by difficult experiences (for example, coping with a disability or a

[6] Sceptics should read Du Sautoy (2017), a work which explores the boundaries of scientific knowledge, written by an atheist mathematician who is Simonyi Professor for the Public Understanding of Science at the University of Oxford.

traumatic event), our differing patterns of membership in multiple affinity groups, and other factors, many of which influence us unconsciously. Intense conflict sometimes arises between members of the same moral community, despite the broader worldview they largely share, in part because of such individual differences.

Worldviews, Decision Making and Conflict

Most of us, much of the time, try to make decisions and act in ways that are consistent with the expectations of others with whom we share a worldview; indeed, our worldviews either supply or imply norms about how one should and should not behave. As conflict resolution scholar Jayne Docherty explains, our worldviews generate 'coherent structures of expectations' (Docherty, 2001: 108) that communicate both permissions and constraints. In other words, our worldviews order our social lives, helping construct the perceptual, conceptual, emotional and relational 'field' in which we figure, rank and seek to satisfy our needs and interests. A given individual's or group's worldview and associated values may stem from one or more of many sources within our evolutionary and cultural heritages, including humanistic traditions, civic systems (such as law) and religion. The worldview-dependent and -defining norms one embraces often are fundamental and so cannot be deviated from lightly, like driving a few miles over the speed limit.

Our worldviews mostly operate in the background, before conscious perception, much as we are unaware of the physical features and processes by which we see – until we brush up against others' worldviews (or, in the case of our vision, have a grain of sand in an eye). When our worldviews collide, many of us, much of the time, reflexively defend the rightness of our perspectives. We regard them as self-evident, or at least more securely justifiable – as they undoubtedly are, almost by definition, from within our own worldview (see Haidt, 2012; Greene, 2013).

Sometimes the normative mandates of one's worldviews are clear. Much of the time, however, our worldviews have fuzzy boundaries. New situations require us to weigh and prioritize competing values within them. Worldviews do evolve, though usually very slowly. Even so, a range of interpretive flexibility presently exists within most worldviews, including conservative religious worldviews – though, as an outsider, we may not see or be inclined to accept this. Members of moral communities are constantly negotiating over norms and how to apply them. This is why Docherty prefers to speak of 'worldviewing' (a verb, something that we are always doing), rather than 'worldviews' as such (Docherty, 2001: 50).

Disputes driven by worldview differences can be particularly intense and challenging to resolve, in part because they threaten the moral and social order on which satisfaction of our needs and interests appears to depend. When a worldview conflict can be brought before a court or arbitrator, the 'resolution' we can expect is a judicial decision that disregards one party's favoured norms or attempts to balance competing norms in a way the litigants may not recognize as compatible with any of their respective worldviews (see Seul, 2004). This seldom is possible, nor would it likely be effective, in intra-state or international armed conflicts. In any event, negotiation and mediation hold greater promise for achieving outcomes that are consistent with all the parties' worldviews – at least in theory. Needless to say, this is more easily said than done. The key, as discussed later, is to embrace and work within parties' seemingly incompatible worldviews, helping them explore and understand each other's normative frames and search for agreements that can fit into those frames.

Because the core issues in a worldview conflict often have sacred value (see, for example, Atran et al, 2007), parties cannot realistically hope to coerce each other into their own conceptual reality (Docherty, 2001: 112). Interpersonal communication practices such as active listening and demonstrating empathy for the other's perspective and experience sometimes can be immensely helpful in a worldview conflict, but they will not mechanistically assure a smooth process when negotiating across worldviews. An intense emotional response is natural when we perceive identity-anchoring values to be threatened, but we must do more than attend to emotions wisely and sensitively.[7] Essential as that may be, emotions alone do not tell us enough about the normative contexts we inhabit and how to achieve resolution in keeping with them. Nor can we expect to appeal to reason from a position outside another's worldview, because the other is acting rationally within his or her worldview.[8] Finally, in the typical dispute in which parties have a common worldview, a resolution can be achieved if one party is willing to pay enough money or transfer something else of material value, because money can sufficiently address the other party's underlying concerns within that worldview context. Indeed, in a traditional dispute we might see it as 'progress' if one party offered to buy the other out, trading dollars or some other thing of mundane value (land

[7] For example, Daniel Shapiro (2016) places great emphasis on transforming emotional dynamics, yet also emphasizes the need for other types of work, like the structural transformation of divisive relationships.

[8] Susan Hunter (1989) observed three decades ago that the essential tension in contentious public policy disputes is not between emotion and reason, but between different meaning (reason) systems. Many violent intrastate and international conflicts share this characteristic.

or other property, a legal right, or some endowment or entitlement). In a worldview conflict, however, the latest social science research suggests that even making an offer like this can backfire, causing the conflict to intensify, rather than move toward resolution (Ginges et al, 2007).

In a nutshell, the conceptual frame of standard-issue interest-based bargaining and many of the prescriptions that flow from it are insufficient for addressing worldview conflict. This is likewise true for approaches based upon human needs theory, at least to the extent such approaches, perhaps in practice more than in theory, sidestep or minimize the salience of the parties' differing *worldview*-generated constraints, as opposed to political and resource constraints. Some of the concepts, process features, and skills associated with interest-based bargaining and human needs theory approaches to conflict resolution may prove useful in efforts to negotiate across worldviews, but they must be adapted to the context of worldview conflict and augmented with tools and methods they do not always employ.

Liberal Institutions, Worldview Conflict and Peace Mediation

Many modern national and international norms and institutions can be seen as mechanisms for mediating among contending worldviews and groups' understandings of their respective interests in light of their worldviews. Notions of statehood and state sovereignty, often traced to the Peace of Westphalia, emerged to help mediate among sectarian divisions resulting to a great extent from competing religious worldviews. Our various forms of democratic governance and their operational principles and mechanisms, like citizen voting and the notion of church–state separation that exists in some countries, attempt to mediate among diverse intra-state stakeholders and their contending visions. International treaty regimes and organizations, such as the United Nations (UN), provide norms and procedures that help prevent or address frictions among states which (through their officials) understand and act upon their interests, at least in part, through the lens of a mainstream worldview that holds sway within each. Ethnic, racial and linguistic affinities obviously remain salient for many people and so remain a major influence in international affairs. Nonetheless, the lines of communities bound by a shared worldview, whether religious or non-religious, often cut across these and other group affinities with equal or greater force, binding otherwise diverse groups of people together through the power of a shared perspective – not just within states, but, increasingly, irrespective of borders.

These modern, liberal norms and institutions have been remarkably effective in some ways. For example, while other factors undoubtedly played a role, the European Union has, for decades, contributed significantly 'to the advancement of peace and reconciliation, democracy and human rights in Europe', as the Nobel Committee observed when announcing the 2012 Nobel Peace Prize. The UN, its agencies, and its representatives have been awarded the Nobel Peace Prize 11 times in recognition of similar contributions to global cooperation, peace, security, and economic, social and environmental well-being (See UN, n.d.). Over this same period, however, we also increasingly have begun to see the limits of liberal institutions' capacity to serve some important human needs and desires, at least as these institutions presently tend to operate (see, for example, Sandel, 2018). Much has been gained by putting relatively greater emphasis upon the individual (over the group) and the material (over the symbolic), as liberal democratic institutions, and their companion, capitalism, arguably have come to do. Still, much is lost. The pervasive sense of isolation and loneliness reported in many western societies may be partially attributable to a progressive shift in how we find ourselves situated in relation to others: a shift from knowing ourselves primarily as members of groups bound tightly by thick, overlapping, tangled normative fibres, on the one hand, and, on the other hand, knowing ourselves as members of much larger, more diverse groups, loosely bound by comparatively thin and formal political and legal norms and procedures and impersonal networks of economic exchange, much of it with distant strangers. Even if it can be said that, for many people, modern, liberal institutions have contributed relatively more to the satisfaction of basic (food and shelter) and security (safety) needs than have the contending normative orders they were designed to tame and relativize, it is not clear that they contribute more to satisfaction of our higher-order, psychosocial needs – for love and social support, respect and pride, agency and self-mastery.

If many of our most challenging intra-state and international conflicts today – from the conflict in Afghanistan to the populist uprisings destabilizing some western democracies – seem to involve contending worldviews, then we also should recognize and accept that one of these worldviews is the liberal ideal itself. By one telling, liberal norms and institutions were designed and expected to subordinate and orchestrate the conflicting demands emanating from those worldviews that architects of the liberal order considered illiberal; they were designed to dominate illiberal worldviews benevolently, keeping them on an equal footing with one another, so none could dominate the others. But those who embrace the liberal ideal have tended to see both its procedural and substantive norms largely as *neutral* or *self-evidently right and just* mediating mechanisms – obvious guarantors of equality and fairness in the highest sense – rather than as features of yet another worldview, as others are more inclined to see liberalism, or at least some features of it.[9]

During much of the 20th century it appeared the liberal project largely was succeeding, at least with respect to modern domestic and international institutions' taming of religious institutions and sentiments as a rival force (Mavelli and Petito, 2012; Desch, n.d.). Some declared – quite prematurely, it now seems, based upon recent projections (Pew Research Center, 2015) – that religious commitment was in rapid decline globally and would one day disappear. In reality, the competition among secular worldviews (for example, democratic capitalism versus communism) tended to overshadow, and keep in check, religious, ethnic and other cultural tensions teeming beneath the surface layer cast by the major geopolitical rivalries.

The Israeli–Palestinian conflict can be seen as a leading example of a conflict fuelled by tensions between liberal and so-called illiberal worldviews (see Zalzberg, 2019). Some astute analysts believe on good evidence, including first-hand accounts of those involved in the negotiations, that the 2000 Camp David process unwound over issues related to the disposition of the Temple Mount/Al-Aqsa Mosque compound and the surrounding areas of Jerusalem. While many sets of options for resolving these issues reportedly were entertained, none satisfied religious leaders sufficiently. They had largely been excluded from the process and were not greatly involved in preparations for it. Consequently, the proposals developed and entertained by the secular-political leaders and their negotiation teams did not sufficiently account

[9] To be sure, liberal norms are one of my own primary reference points. I believe they are of immense past, present and future importance and value. Yet, I also understand that notions of equality and justice develop, are applied and evolve (often very slowly) within particular, overarching cultural contexts and worldviews, some of which may seem as foreign and questionable to me as they seem familiar and legitimate to the vast majority of sensible people who inhabit them. This chapter obviously raises serious questions about normativity and relativism that cannot be addressed sufficiently within its scope. For present purposes, I simply acknowledge that, however 'woke' I may consider myself to be, none of us is ever 'fully woke'. I also maintain that acknowledging this requires both that I be willing to interrogate my own worldview, with an eye towards uncovering and addressing its blind spots and shortcomings (and perhaps even some wilfully malicious tendencies), and that I be willing to explore others' worldviews with genuine curiosity and openness to what they may get right that mine gets wrong. I must do this even when others' worldviews seem backward from my perspective and even when these others seem unwilling or unable to reciprocate fully.

for the varied ways in which diverse religious actors make meaning about this important holy site, which is the physical and symbolic epicentre of the conflict, and the many complicated issues associated with it from the perspective of religious actors, especially religious nationalists (see, for example, Hassner, 2009: 78–88).

While secular-political leaders in the Camp David era failed to see or accept that the Israeli–Palestinian conflict has an undeniable and unavoidable religious dimension, this certainly is not the only worldview chasm that contributes to the conflict's seeming intractability. The conflict is enacted upon—or, rather, *is*—a collage of contending worldviews, not just regionally, but also in its geopolitical dimension (for example, in the ways in which tensions between the United States and Russia impinge upon the conflict). We see secular versus religious (Jewish, Muslim and Christian) worldviews; religious versus non-religious worldviews; politically conservative versus progressive worldviews; democratic versus autocratic worldviews; and so on.

The core of the Camp David process was typical of Track I negotiation as it is still widely understood and practised. Current office holders and their designates engaged in interest-based bargaining with the help and good offices of a third party. The talks focused on finding packages of mostly material trades thought to address the stakeholders' respective interests – interests conceived of mostly in mundane, rather than symbolic, terms. Consequently, the negotiators sought to permanently distribute some things (for example, the land of Israel and Palestine, including the Temple Mount/Al-Aqsa) that many people in each community regard as fundamentally indivisible, particularly if any division is to be declared permanent. Track II initiatives that helped lay a foundation for the Camp David process, and the Oslo process before it, focused more explicitly on the underlying needs, fears and concerns of members of each community, but they still largely sought solutions from within a liberal, secular, democratic worldview and the constraints such a worldview imposes from the perspective of those who do not share it to the same degree. They sought solutions that would comport with – and *primarily* with – the liberal mindset and narrative. Even the most open and free-ranging Track II processes tended not to explore, let alone seek to accommodate, normative considerations associated with religious worldviews, and especially not religious nationalist worldviews, which were deemed too radical (or even retrograde).

Contemporary approaches to religious peacebuilding that have begun to emerge over the past 20 years have done relatively little to advance the state of the art in conflicts with a religious dimension, like the Israeli–Palestinian conflict. They have tended to emphasize values and stories that are *shared* by two or more religions (for example, the Abrahamic traditions). Unfortunately, they do not sufficiently correct for blind spots in mainstream, secular, social scientific approaches to conflict resolution as they generally have not helped parties take up serious differences between religions, and their respective claims and dictates, as they relate to a protracted conflict. These differences cannot be dismissed or overcome so easily.

When peace mediation processes, at whatever stage and by whatever name (Track I, Track II, national dialogues, and so on), minimize or systematically avoid stakeholders' differing worldview orientations and the genuine normative constraints they impose, trying instead to focus attention more or less exclusively on universal needs and shared or compatible interests, or even on shared *values*, the prospects for resolving a conflict involving contending worldviews are greatly diminished.[10] Difficult as it may be for mediators to attempt to work within stakeholders' normative frames and find what (often slim) possibilities for conflict resolution may lie within and across them, the alternative likely is futile. I believe one of the biggest challenges and urgent priorities in the field today is the development of approaches to peace mediation that help us – both stakeholders and those who wish to support their conflict

[10] Neuroscientist and philosopher Joshua Greene views utilitarianism as the meta-ethical system best able to guide us toward resolution of worldview conflicts (Greene, 2013: 254–353). On the one hand, it is hard to disagree with this idea, which floats above our problem space at a very high level of abstraction. Almost by definition, those interested in achieving a genuinely consensual resolution of a worldview conflict will seek, and, if successful, converge upon, an outcome they believe Pareto optimizes for stakeholder utility (in other words, well-being). On the other hand, Greene is rather vague, at best, about how to deal with the very real difficulties presented by competing worldview constraints in the process. In the context of a worldview conflict, in which background norms are not universally shared, parties have divergent notions of what constitutes well-being, and therefore about how to achieve and maintain their own well-being in the face of worldview differences. If Greene is suggesting that people should, and easily can, abandon or override constraints imposed by their worldviews, in service of universally shared notions of what does, or should, 'make everyone happy', then this seems rather fanciful, at least at this point in history. If he is suggesting (as I am) that negotiators should seek the best outcomes available *within their worldview constraints* as they exist today, or as they reasonably may be amenable to revision in the near future, then this is much easier said than done. In this case, what we need, more than abstract insights and general prescriptions that cut against the grain of at least some parties' worldviews – their 'priors', in social scientific parlance – are *methods* for putting this aspiration into practice. In essence, we need approaches for achieving outcomes that maximise joint utility *across*, not in spite of, deontological ethical systems that are, at least partially, incongruent.

resolution efforts – explore and mediate across multiple worldviews. The goal of peace mediators must be solutions that work within each of several worldviews, even if stakeholders ultimately tell different stories within their communities about what makes the outcome of a mediation process acceptable from a normative perspective.

Mediating Across Worldviews

Peace mediators who wish to help conflict stakeholders negotiate effectively across worldviews should support modes of analysis, individual and joint reflection, dialogue and other work that can be exceptionally challenging, but which, done thoroughly and well, have genuine potential to contribute to conflict transformation. The following activities and practices are among those they should consider utilizing.

Map the Worldviews

Conflict mapping is a common element of most pre-mediation and ongoing conflict assessment work (see, for example, Schirch, 2013) but conflict analysts and peace mediators seldom give sufficient attention to stakeholders' worldviews, including the constraints they impose and the permissions they afford. Robust worldview mapping requires much more than merely identifying shared pro-peace values that might be of use in mediation efforts. Some variant of the principle 'love thy neighbour' exists within all religions, for example, and there is evidence that reminders of these principles incline people to be more tolerant of members of other groups, at least temporarily (Rothschild et al, 2009). Nonetheless, general appeals to abstract, conciliation-promoting values that exist within stakeholders' normative traditions tend not to be much help in resolving worldview conflict. Ultimately, the parties will need more complete and granular images of the normative landscapes they and others inhabit – images that, among other things, reveal the fences and other boundaries that place limits on how reconciliation-promoting values may be applied, as well as the gates and sections of fence (in other words, normative constraints) that have begun to collapse, without a communal will to rebuild them.

Peace mediators should work with each stakeholder group and other experts to map the contours of each group's worldview, particularly their features that are most directly implicated in the conflict. The parties need a bird's-eye view of the terrain they occupy – the ground from which their perspectives on the conflict, their perceived needs and interests, and options for resolution spring. Worldview mapping work can look a lot like other conflict mapping work, which often consists of information and data-gathering activities such as interviews, documentary research and surveys. The focus, however, should be on communal narratives and norms, rather than solely on positions, interests, needs and the like. There are various social scientific instruments that can be useful, in some contexts, for helping parties articulate and/or examine their own and others' worldviews.[11] These tools can be illuminating but they generally are no substitute for defining the precise features and boundaries of the moral order to which a group adheres and which makes it cohere.

It is critical to map differences, on an issue-by-issue basis, among subgroups within each stakeholder group, in order to understand intra-group dynamics that affect peace mediation efforts. Stakeholder groups with differing worldviews often can identify some common values, but those values do not exist in a vacuum. In practice, they have to be balanced and prioritized against other values to which a group subscribes, all as understood in light of the group's shifting history, institutions, economic realities and the like. Stakeholders and peace mediators need to understand more than the litany of features of each relevant worldview; they also must understand the importance of each feature in relation to others from the perspective of each key subgroup within a broader stakeholder group. This sort of subgroup analysis will be useful in the intra-party work that is often necessary when mediating across worldviews (on which more later in the chapter).

A principal goal of worldview mapping is development and continual refinement of ever-evolving, reasonably balanced, detailed narrative descriptions of the parties' respective worldviews, as they pertain to any matter any party considers to be an issue at play in a conflict. Another goal is creation of a comprehensive stakeholder map that includes the perspectives of individuals and subgroups who must be persuaded and/or who have, or may have, sufficient moral authority to help alter the normative landscape. Relationship visualization tools, like Kumu (n.d.), can be immensely helpful for assembling and organizing data and making them comprehensible.

Peace mediators also must map their own worldviews if they hope to be effective. In other contexts, in which the disputants share a worldview, it is

[11] See, for example, the various instruments at https://moralfoundations.org (Moral Foundations, n.d.) that have been developed to support Moral Foundations Theory research, as well as the survey questions used in the World Values Survey, which are accessible at http://www.worldvaluessurvey.org/WVSOnline.jsp (World Values Survey, n.d.).

natural and wise to use a mediator with the same worldview orientation. In worldview conflict, however, a single mediator may struggle to relate to the worldviews of one or both parties. Using a team of co-mediators that mirrors the parties' differing worldviews, or that at least includes one person who has a deep understanding of and appreciation for each party's worldview, can be a good approach.

Arrange a Guided Tour of Each Worldview

Once each party is clear about which features of its worldview are implicated in the conflict, and how they are implicated, the parties should take turns offering tours of how things look from inside their respective worldviews. 'Speak to be understood', Herbert Kelman, professor emeritus of social psychology at Harvard University (and one of my mentors), is fond of saying to parties in conflict. This means trying as best one can to present one's inside perspective in ways that help outsiders relate to it; for example, by anticipating what might seem surprising to others and making tentative analogies to features of others' worldviews. 'Listen to understand' is the second half of Kelman's formula, by which he means that we should be attentive, curious and respectful visitors. Setting aside the question of whether it is wise even to try to do this, a party is not likely to change others' worldviews by debating with them during a conflict resolution process. The goal should be to understand where others are coming from; where they can go and how they can get there; and where they are unlikely to be able to go, at least in the near term. A party should ask genuinely curious questions designed to serve that goal. If one party can express appreciation for features of others' worldviews (or at least demonstrate understanding of them as their inhabitants see them), all the better.

Stack the Worldview Maps to Identify Overlapping Terrain and Gaps to Be Bridged

One of the key prescriptions of standard interest-based bargaining is to identify 'objective criteria' (see, for example, Fisher et al, 1981) the parties can reference to converge upon and legitimize an agreed outcome on an issue. Most negotiation theorists likely envision a single legitimating standard that all parties can embrace to justify an agreement. In a worldview conflict, however, this may prove exceptionally difficult or impossible. Advice like this assumes parties share a more or less identical set of background norms, or that they merely use different vocabularies to express the same concepts and commitments. When this is not true, however, they must develop a better understanding of their own and others' worldviews and seek a resolution that is legitimate within each of them – even if each element of their agreement cannot be justified by pointing to a single principle that all parties can embrace.

Imagine the worldview maps the parties have created and shared could be drawn on clear plastic sheets. If mediators were to place one map on top of the other(s) to see where they line up and where they do not, everyone might spot common features that already exist within each worldview. Shared values generally are easy to see, but it can be as or more helpful to identify regions of hospitable terrain on which new, shared understandings can be built, compatible ideas and practical realities can stand side by side, or seeds of possible future agreements can be planted and expected to grow. Perhaps everyone at the table can see that something one party wants is permitted by the others' worldview – within certain parameters. The careful mediator also will look for regions in each map that do not meet, but which are close enough that it might be possible to construct new bridges to join them. If each party could envision taking a small step in the other's direction, could they meet on that bridge?

One practical way to 'stack the maps' is to create a chart in which each issue in the conflict gets a row, with columns for narrative description of each party's worldview as it relates to that issue and an additional column for options that comport with each worldview. Peace mediator(s) can use a chart like this to help the parties brainstorm options that could address each issue in a way which is consistent with the permissions and constraints of each worldview. This sort of exercise can produce a useful 'gap analysis' that clarifies which issues require the most attention and which worldview constraints need to be reframed, relaxed or revised, to whatever extent may be possible, in order to reach agreement.

My map analogy is limited in a number of ways, including the missing dimension of (historical and future) time. Can exploring ways in which landscapes have shifted over time help everyone envision new present-day options? Can time-bounding elements of an agreement help parties accept a change to the status quo, at least for some time, because they need not concede that they have altered the landscape indefinitely?

Attend to Symbolic Dimensions of the Conflict and Persuade Skilfully in Light of Them

Much conflict resolution theory is premised upon the hypothetical *rational actor* model that dominates modern economic theory. This model has been tempered by findings from psychology about the actual mechanics of human perception, cognition and judgement, but this tempered view of rationality still assumes individuals always seek to achieve outcomes that maximize net personal, *worldly* gains; sometimes, according to this perspective, we simply are prone to errors in perception, cognition and judgement that prevent us from optimally serving our self-interest (see, for example, Bazerman and Shonk, 2005).

Some conduct, like suicide attacks or forgone opportunities to resolve a conflict on terms widely judged by others to be beneficial, seems so to defy self-interest, however, that it strains the rational actor model to breaking point. This sort of conduct makes more sense when viewed from the perspective of a *devoted actor* model, in which one is willing to defend what is at stake in the conflict at great, and even ultimate, this-worldly personal cost (Atran, 2003). Devoted actors do not seek outcomes that maximize individual self-interest in mundane or material terms; they act to preserve and defend a moral order with which they and their compatriots identify completely (see Atran et al, 2007; Ginges and Atran, 2009; Fiske and Rai, 2015). The devoted actor can, of course, be seen as an absolutely resolute rational actor; as a person who values one thing (like resistance to foreign occupation) much more than other things (like the prospect of continued this-worldly existence with family and friends) that most of us give more weight when making decisions. In this sense, the devoted actor who resorts to violence is acting to maximize personal gain. S/he simply ascribes much higher value to outcomes that others either consider immoral or as entailing unacceptable costs.

Some suggest that (religious or secular) sacred values may not really be incommensurable (non-tradable) with more mundane interests. Some values that are deeply-held by some people may well be more subject to compromise when one's alternatives to negotiation are unattractive (see Hoffman et al, 1999; Tetlock, 2003; Tenbrunsel et al, 2009). Studies by experimental anthropologist Scott Atran, political scientist Robert Axelrod and their colleagues indicate, however, that many conflicts with devoted actors are likely to remain immune to negotiation so long as efforts to resolve them solely employ methods that treat sacred values as if they were readily tradable. From a practical perspective, we would be wise to assume in these situations that concessions involving sacred values cannot be bought with concessions on more mundane matters, even though, with careful attention to process, including the sequencing of moves, a package deal in which all parties to a conflict realize gains and losses on both sacred and mundane matters ultimately may be possible 'within an overarching moral frame of social duties and (material) attempts to balance duties', rather than through trades that ask devoted actors to disregard or minimize felt duties imposed by sacred values (Atran and Axelrod, 2008: 229).

In one study, social psychologist Jeremy Ginges, Atran and other researchers assessed Israelis' and Palestinians' and other combatants' willingness to end their conflict through material concessions and compromises on issues to which one or both of the communities attached sacred values (for example, territory, the right of return and the status of Jerusalem). They found that proposed trades in which one side would concede something to which it attached sacred value in exchange for material benefits (for example, money) generated a 'backfire effect', increasing resistance to resolution of the conflict. However, even the most hawkish members of each community were open to proposals in which each side made concessions involving sacred values (Ginges et al, 2007; Atran et al, 2007). The conventional thinking among conflict resolution theorists and practitioners is that incremental progress on resolution of more mundane issues eventually can lead to willingness to compromise on major issues of symbolic importance, but this research suggests instead that symbolic gestures (like demonstrations of recognition and respect or an apology) may pave the way for negotiation of more mundane issues (Atran and Axelrod, 2008). The implication, of course, is that peace mediators should invest at least as much energy in efforts to achieve early symbolic concessions as they invest in efforts to achieve material concessions.

Atran and Axelrod also suggest numerous strategies for reframing sacred values to make trades involving them more tenable, including updating how sacred values are expressed to signal retreat from or revision of claims or demands one knows are inaccurate or out of step with current realities; expressing or operationalizing sacred values in ways that are creatively ambiguous; and changing the context or time horizon for full realization of a group's vision, without foreclosing it altogether, so the stakes are lowered here and now; among others (Atran and Axelrod, 2008; and Atran, 2010). These reframing strategies (and others we can imagine) all have a common logic and objective: they enable a party to enter and negotiate within the other's frame of reference without leaving one's own frame of reference, and they permit parties to retain (sometimes in a refigured way) the symbolic value associated with what they hold sacred, while enabling them to divide the mundane or material value associated with what they hold sacred.

Neuroscientists who study resistance to influence among people with divergent moral perspectives, such as Tali Sharot (2017), also offer helpful insights and prescriptions for attempting to negotiate and mediate effectively across worldviews. They uniformly counsel against attempts to alter others' worldviews, recommending instead that we attempt to understand and persuade skilfully in ways that work within or align with them.

Mediate Within *Stakeholder Groups*

In our most protracted conflicts, in which worldviews and the (religious and/or secular) sacred values that accompany them often are implicated, there may be an extremely narrow margin for conflict resolution, if one exists presently at all (see, for example, Hassner, 2009: 91–110; Ramsbotham, 2017). When we 'stack the maps' in these conflicts, we may, at least on some issues, find no ground on which all parties can stand together while continuing to inhabit their own worldviews, and no realistic possibility of bridging gaps presently. When this is the case, progress transforming the conflict *among* groups often will require progress transforming the conflict *within* one or more of the groups.

This requires patient, skilful intra-party work (see Kelman, 1993; Rothman, 2012; Rothman and Alberstein, 2013; Ramsbotham, 2017). Peace mediators must find ways to support what can feel like riskier and more uncomfortable reflection, dialogue and action among all members of the community, including its non-combatants. Where contradictions exist between an espoused commitment to pro-peace values and a group's embrace of other values that tend to undermine efforts to resolve the conflict, these contradictions must be surfaced, teased apart and addressed. There is much useful research and practice know-how about how to go about this work.[12] Needless to say, this sort of work inside a community can create cognitive and emotional dissonance that can feel risky and unsettling; this is necessary to some degree and, in a sense, it is the point of such work. In order for work of this nature to be accepted, be effective and ultimately contribute to inter-party peacemaking, however, it cannot only expose and begin to upset contradictions among competing attachments and value commitments. It also must help people find ways to revise, or find new ways to honour, each of their legitimate value commitments, including a commitment to one's group and its heritage, security and well-being. To borrow a line from Rilke, those supporting others in this

[12] One important approach for dealing with individual and group immunity to change due to tensions among competing value commitments comes from the work of Robert Kegan and Lisa Laskow Lahey, adult development psychologists who are among the leading contemporary researchers on the topic (Kegan and Lahey, 2001; Kegan and Lahey, 2009). I discuss application of Kegan and Lahey's research to mediation practice in Seul (1999).

work must help them 'span the chasm between two contradictions' (Rilke, n.d.): they must help build conceptual, emotional and relational bridges that are secure on both sides of the chasm between two contradictions, as adult developmental psychologist Robert Kegan puts it (Kegan, 1994: 37).

Scale the Process

Among the challenges that have long vexed the conflict resolution field are the problems of knowledge sharing and building sufficient consensus among stakeholders, from official actors, to politically influential elites, to change agents operating at a grassroots level. This general category of problems has gone by different names at different times, including 'transfer' (see, for example, Chataway, 2002) between Track I and Track II processes and, more recently, 'inclusion' (see Nilsson, 2012; Paffenholz, 2014) with respect to grassroots, or Track III, peacemaking initiatives designed to engage civil society actors and others who traditionally have been marginalized from Track I and Track II processes. Today, it is fair to say there is widespread recognition that many of our most persistent and stubborn conflicts are so complex and multifaceted, and involve such a diverse range of local and international actors, that there is little hope of resolving them without the progressive construction of very broad-scale, inclusive, well-coordinated, locally led and internationally supported peace processes – processes that strain our prior conceptions and models of peace mediation practice. One recent manifestation of this realization is the emergence of the national dialogue paradigm (see Berghof Foundation, 2017). In-depth discussion of these challenges and approaches for meeting them in the context of worldview conflicts is beyond the scope of this chapter. Many efforts to transform such conflicts can, and likely should, start small (for example, as a conventional Track II process). These efforts are unlikely to succeed in the long term, however, without a carefully crafted plan for scaling the process to include large numbers of official and unofficial actors, recruiting and supporting inside mediators, coordinating multiple tracks of necessary activity, and directing those activities towards an outcome that is widely viewed as legitimate within all major worldview perspectives implicated in the conflict.

Conclusion

Divergent worldviews, and the difficulty of negotiating across them, may be the primary driver of our most persistent conflicts. The approaches we most typically use to try to resolve them are firmly grounded in one of these worldviews, and this frequently impedes our efforts to mediate the resolution of worldview conflicts. We need new perspectives and methods to mediate across worldviews – including the liberal worldview – more effectively. The ideas and tentative prescriptions offered in this chapter are intended to invite discussion about approaches for advancing peace mediation practice, both with respect to today's most challenging conflicts and in our future efforts to avert or more quickly resolve conflicts that emerge wherever worldviews collide.

As we rethink peace mediation, I hope these ideas and suggested approaches will be tested and further developed. Big questions about the future of peace mediation theory and practice must be confronted in the process. There will be tactical questions: how, for example, could and should a worldview lens influence how we prepare for and engage in high-level Track I processes, which have tended to be interest based and highly transactional? And there will be much deeper questions with which we undoubtedly must wrestle for years to come: how are worldviews entwined with power structures within the international system, and how might the system need to change if we were to take more seriously other worldviews that have had relatively less influence in international affairs up until now?

References

Atran, S. (2003) 'Genesis of Suicide Terrorism', *Science*, 299(5612), 1534–9.

Atran, S. (2010) *Talking to the Enemy: Violent Extremism, Sacred Values, and What It Means to be Human*, London, UK: Penguin.

Atran, S. and Axelrod, R. (2008) 'Reframing Sacred Values', *Negotiation Journal*, 24(3), 221–46.

Atran, S., Axelrod, R. and Davis, R. (2007) 'Sacred Barriers to Conflict Resolution', *Science*, 317(5841), 1039–40.

Bazerman, M. and Shonk, K. (2005) 'The Decision Perspective to Negotiation' in Moffitt, M. and Bordone, R. (eds.) *The Handbook of Dispute Resolution*, San Francisco, CA: Jossey-Bass.

Berghof Foundation (2017) *National Dialogue Handbook: A Guide for Practitioners*, Berlin [Online] May, available from: https://www.berghof-foundation.org/fileadmin/redaktion/Publications/Other_Resources/NationalDialogue/BF-NationalDialogue-Handbook.pdf (accessed 23 September 2019).

Chataway, C.J. (2002) 'The Problem of Transfer from Confidential Interactive Problem-Solving: What Is the Role of the Facilitator?', *Political Psychology*, 23(1), 165–89.

Desch, M.C. (n.d.) 'The Coming Reformation of Religion in International Affairs? The Demise of the Secularization Thesis and the Rise of New Thinking About Religion' in *Religion and International Relations: A Primer for Research (The Report of the Working Group on International Relations and Religion of the Mellon Initiative on Religion Across the Disciplines, University of Notre Dame)* [Online], available from: https://rmellon.nd.edu/assets/101872/religion_and_international_relations_report.pdf (accessed 11 September 2019).

Docherty, J.S. (2001) *Learning Lessons from Waco: When the Parties Bring Their Gods to the Negotiating Table*, Syracuse, NY: Syracuse University Press.

Du Sautoy, M. (2017) *The Great Unknown: Seven Journeys to the Frontiers of Science*, New York, NY: Viking.

Fisher, R., Ury, W. and Patton, B. (1981) *Getting to Yes: Negotiating Agreement Without Giving In*, New York, NY: Penguin.

Fiske, A.P. and Rai, T.S. (2015) *Virtuous Violence*, Cambridge, UK: Cambridge University Press.

Ginges, J. and Atran, S. (2009) 'What Motivates Participation in Violent Political Action: Selective Incentives or Parochial Altruism?', *Annals of the New York Academy of Sciences*, 1167, 115–23.

Ginges, J., Atran, S., Medin, D. and Shikaki, K. (2007) 'Sacred Bounds on Rational Resolution of Violent Political Conflict', *Proceedings of the National Academy of Sciences*, 104(18), 7357–60.

Greene, J. (2013) *Moral Tribes: Emotion, Reason, and the Gap Between Us and Them*, New York, NY: Penguin.

Haidt, J. (2012) *The Righteous Mind: Why Good People Are Divided by Politics and Religion*, New York, NY: Penguin.

Hassner, R.E. (2009) *War on Sacred Grounds* (Ithaca, NY: Cornell University Press).

Hoffman, A.J., Gillespie, J.J., Moore, D.A., Wade-Benzoni, K.A., Thompson, L.L. and Bazerman, M.H. (1999) 'A Mixed-Motive Perspective on the Economics Versus Environment Debate', *American Behavioral Scientist*, 42(8), 1254–76.

Hunter, S. (1989) 'The Roots of Environmental Conflict in the Tahoe Basin' in Kriesberg, L., Northrup, T.A. and Thorson, S.J. (eds.) *Intractable Conflicts and Their Transformation*, Syracuse, NY: Syracuse University Press, pp 25–40.

Kegan, R. (1982) *The Evolving Self: Problem and Process in Human Development*, US: Harvard University Press.

Kegan, R. (1994) *In Over Our Heads: The Mental Demands of Modern Life*, Cambridge, MA: Harvard University Press.

Kegan, R. and Lahey, L.L. (2001) *How the Way We Talk Can Change the Way We Work: Seven Languages for Transformation*, San Francisco, CA: Jossey-Bass.

Kegan, R. and Lahey, L.L. (2009) *Immunity to Change: How to Overcome It and Unlock the Potential in Yourself and Your Organization*, Boston, MA: Harvard Business School Press.

Kelman, H.C. (1993) 'Coalitions Across Conflict Lines: The Interplay of Conflicts Within and Between the Israel and Palestinian Communities' in Worchel, S. and Simpson, J.A. (eds.) *Conflict Between People and Groups: Causes, Processes, and Resolutions*, Chicago, IL: Nelson-Hall, pp 236–58.

Kelman, H.C. (1997) 'Nationalism, Patriotism, and National Identity: Social-psychological Dimensions' in Bar-Tal, D. and Staub, E. (eds.) *Patriotism in the Life of Individuals and Nations*, Chicago, IL: Nelson-Hall, pp 165–89.

Kumu (n.d.) 'Kumu' [Online], available from: https://kumu.io (accessed 1 September 2019).

Mavelli, L. and Petito, F. (2012) 'The Postsecular in International Relations: An Overview', *Review of International Studies*, 38(5), 931–42.

Moral Foundations (n.d.) 'Moral Foundations.org' [Online], available from: https://moralfoundations.org (accessed 1 September 2019).

Naugle, D.K. (2002) *Worldview: The History of a Concept*, Grand Rapids, MI, Cambridge, UK: Wm. B. Eerdmans Publishing Co.

Nilsson, D. (2012) 'Anchoring the Peace: Civil Society Actors in Peace Accords and Durable Peace', *International Interactions*, 38(2), 243–66.

Paffenholz, T. (2014) 'Civil Society and Peace Negotiations: Beyond the Inclusion-Exclusion Dichotomy', *Negotiation Journal*, 30(1), 69–91.

Palacio, A. (2019) 'The Twilight of the Global Order' [online] 2 September, *Project Syndicate*, available from: https://www.project-syndicate.org/commentary/g7-summit-biarritz-erosion-of-global-order-by-ana-palacio-2019-08 (accessed 9 September 2019).

Pew Research Center (2015) 'The Future of World Religions: Population Growth Projections, 2010–2050' [Online] 2 April, available from: https://www.pewforum.org/2015/04/02/religious-projections-2010-2050/ (accessed 23 September 2019).

Ramsbotham, O. (2017) *When Conflict Resolution Fails*, Cambridge, UK: Polity.

Rilke, R.M. (n.d.) 'As Once the Winged Energy of Delight' [online], available from: https://www.poetry.net/poem/29640/as-once-the-winged-energy-of-delight (accessed 23 September 2019).

Rothman, J. (2012) 'From Intragroup Pre-negotiation to Intergroup Peace', paper submitted for *Transforming Identities: Methods and Processes for Conflict Transformation panel* at International Political Science Association 22nd World Congress, Madrid, Spain, July 2012 (paper on file with author).

Rothman, J. and Alberstein, M. (2013) 'Individuals, Groups and Intergroups: Theorizing About the Role of Identity in Conflict and Its Creative Engagement', *Ohio State Journal on Dispute Resolution*, 28(3), 631–58.

Rothschild, Z.K., Abdollahi, A. and Pyszczynski, T. (2009) 'Does Peace Have a Prayer? The Effects of Morality Salience, Compassionate Values, and Religious Fundamentalism on Hostility Toward Out-groups', *Journal of Experimental Social Psychology*, 45(4), 816–27.

Routledge, C. (2018) *Supernatural: Death, Meaning, and the Power of the Invisible World*, New York, NY: Oxford University Press.

Sandel, M.J. (2018) 'Populism, Liberalism, and Democracy', *Philosophy and Social Criticism*, 44(4), 353–9.

Schirch, L. (2013) *Conflict Assessment and Peacebuilding Planning: A Strategic Participatory Systems-Based Handbook on Human Security*, Boulder, CO: Lynne Rienner Publishers.

Seul, J.R. (1999) 'How Transformative Is Transformative Mediation? A Constructive-Developments Assessment', *Ohio State Journal on Dispute Resolution*, 15(1), 135–72.

Seul, J.R. (2004) 'Settling Significant Cases', *Washington Law Review*, 79, 881.

Shapiro, D. (2016) *Negotiating the Nonnegotiable: How to Resolve Your Most Emotionally Charged Conflicts*, New York: Penguin.

Sharot, T. (2017) *The Influential Mind: What the Brain Reveals About Our Power to Change Others*, London: Little, Brown Book Group.

Tay, L. and Diener, E. (2011) 'Needs and Subjective Well-being Around the World', *Journal of Personality and Social Psychology*, 101(2), 354–65.

Taylor, A. (2019) 'The Free World Is Leaderless' [Online] 7 March 2019, *The Washington Post*, available from: https://www.washingtonpost.com/world/2019/03/07/free-world-is-leaderless/?noredirect=on (accessed 9 September 2019).

Tenbrunsel, A.E., Wade-Benzoni, K.A., Tost, L.P., Medvec, V.H., Thompson, L.L. and Bazerman, M.H. (2009) 'The Reality and Myth of Sacred Issues in Negotiations', *Negotiations and Conflict Management Research*, 2(3), 263–84.

Tetlock, P.E. (2003) 'Thinking the Unthinkable: Sacred Values and Taboo Cognitions', *Trends in Cognitive Sciences*, 7(7), 320–4.

Ugarriza, J.E. (2009) 'Ideologies and Conflict in the Post-Cold War', *International Journal of Conflict Management*, 20(1), 82–104.

UN (n.d.) 'United Nations and the Nobel Peace Prize' [Online], available from: https://www.un.org/en/sections/nobel-peace-prize/united-nations-and-nobel-peace prize/ (accessed 9 September 2019).

World Values Survey (n.d.) 'World Values Survey Online Data Analysis' [Online], available from: http://www.worldvaluessurvey.org/WVSOnline.jsp (accessed 1 September 2019).

Zalzberg, O. (2019) 'Beyond Liberal Peacemaking: Lessons from Israeli-Palestinian Diplomatic Peacemaking', *Review of Middle East Studies*, 53(1), 46–53.

PART III

Strategies of Engagement

12

Mediating Multilateral Proxy Conflicts

Francis Ward

Introduction

To achieve a mediated settlement, the challenge for any mediator is to ensure a minimal level of consent between the warring factions. To build this consent, the mediator needs to understand the aims and drivers of the parties, and how those drivers can be appealed to (using a combination of carrots and sticks) to craft a mutually acceptable settlement. In a conflict in which the primary actors are backed, guided or even controlled by an external third party, gaining this consent becomes even more challenging and can quickly turn a mediation process from a two-sided game of draughts into a multi-dimensional game of chess without clearly defined rules.

To date, classical mediation processes have struggled to effectively engage with and influence the behaviour of external supporters to a given conflict in the pursuit of a settlement. This is not helped by the fact that the subject of proxy wars is 'historically ubiquitous yet chronically under analysed' in contemporary security studies (Mumford, 2013a; 2013b), while analysis of mediation and proxy conflict has been all but ignored to date. Studies that have focused on this phenomenon have produced disagreement about what constitutes a proxy war and its key elements. There have been some notable efforts to analyse 'proxy warfare', 'limited warfare', or the 'indirect approach' (Liddell-Hart, 1967; Bar-Siman-

Tov, 1984; Byman and Kreps, 2010; Freedman, 2015; Byman, 2018; Carson, 2018) from state-centric perspectives (Bar-Siman-Tov, 1984; Hughes, 2014) to more flexible and holistic models which account for the increasing role of transnational non-state groups, private military providers and other non-state entities with sponsor–proxy relations (Loveman, 2002; Mumford, 2013a; Rondeaux and Sterman, 2019).

If there is one major point of agreement in the existing literature, it is that proxy warfare is characterized by a distinctive relationship between a principal-sponsor who delegates some authority over the pursuit of strategic war aims to a proxy-agent (Rondeaux and Sterman, 2019). For the sake of the present analysis, and bearing in mind operational objectives attached to mediation, this chapter takes a flexible and holistic view of proxy conflicts similar to that of Andrew Mumford, who defines proxy warfare as

> the indirect engagement in a conflict by third parties wishing to influence its strategic outcome. They are constitutive of a relationship between a benefactor, who is a state or non-state actor external to the dynamic of an existing conflict, and their chosen proxies who are the conduit for weapons, training and funding from the benefactor. (Mumford, 2013a)

The engagement of third parties in conflict by proxy has once again become a critical and defining element of contemporary conflicts and geopolitics. While there is some agreement on what proxy conflict is, there has been little attempt to analyse how to respond to it. As a result, the tools available to address these complicated conflicts are increasingly inadequate. Given the growing relevance of proxy sponsors in civil conflicts, and the evident gap in the literature, this chapter aims to assess the impact of modern proxy wars on attempts to mediate a resolution to conflicts, and offer possible suggestions for ways in which mediators can overcome the inherent challenge of proxy conflict.

The chapter will first consider proxy wars from a historical perspective to provide context on the evolution of modern proxy wars. Next the chapter will assess the typology of proxy conflict by looking at why actors engage in proxy war, who engages in proxy war, and briefly how proxy wars are fought. The chapter will then consider how proxy engagement in conflicts has greatly complicated the work of mediation in finding a viable resolution to contemporary conflicts. Finally, the chapter will analyse how mediators can confront these challenges and engage more effectively in conflicts which have proxy elements. The analysis demonstrates that many of the current tools available to help resolve or mitigate the negative impact of proxy wars are not working – either because they are outdated and based on inaccurate analysis of how modern proxy wars manifest, or because they have been structurally undermined by contemporary geopolitical dynamics. As a result, mediators and mediation processes need to be creative, dynamic and resourceful in today's conflict landscape in order to develop an effective hybrid response to the hybrid challenges faced.

From Bipolar to Multipolar to Polyarchic

The notion of the enemy of my enemy is my friend is not new. Sun Tzu outlined the indirect approach in *The Art of War* through the dictums 'the skillful leader subdues the enemy's troops without any fighting' (1910: 23), and 'avoid what is strong … strike at what is weak' (1910: 9). After witnessing the costly and bloody attrition of the First World War, Liddell-Hart set to create a doctrine for warfare which would limit tactical and strategic risk, while achieving set objectives. Liddell-Hart's *indirect approach*, first articulated in 1954, argued for an approach which avoided massive frontline battles, instead conserving strength while applying the means of war where the enemy is weakest and least prepared (Liddell-Hart, 1954; 1967). Modern war by proxy can be seen as the contemporary iteration of the indirect approach (Freedman, 2015: 138). There is evidence of actors utilizing specific localized events or conflicts to further an agenda (whether political or ideological) throughout history, be it during the Thirty Years War, where Protestant France and Catholic Spain covertly engaged to support their respective sides within the Holy Roman Empire, or during the Prussian War of 1870–1, where Britain influenced events by arming the French military to undermine the Prussians (Mumford, 2013a). The Industrial Revolution, which led to the production of more deadly and efficient weapons on a mass scale, enabled industrialized nations to further advance strategic influence over certain local dynamics through the provision of mass-produced weaponry (Towle, 1981: 21; Holsti, 1996: xi).

During the 20th century war by proxy became more common, predominantly visible during the Cold War, where the prospect of Mutually Assured Destruction (MAD) meant proxy war became the norm, with the direct engagement of a super power, such as the United States (US) engagement in Vietnam 1964–72 and Soviet engagement in Afghanistan 1979–89, the exception (Velina, 2019). De Soysa (2017) further demonstrated a direct correlation between the rise of great power rivalry during the Cold War and the increased onset and duration of localized civil wars. While the Cold War is often cited as a defining period of proxy warfare, Rondeaux and Sterman (2019) have suggested that 'an understanding of proxy war based on Cold War models fails to capture the strategic innovations since the Soviet collapse that have dramatically altered the character of armed conflict and the nature of proxy warfare' (2019: 51). Where Moscow and Washington once defined the rules, there is now a growing multiplicity of state and non-state sponsors of proxy forces.

Since the US invasion of Iraq in 2001 and the proclaimed 'war on terror', the scale of proxy engagement in conflict is arguably at a historical high. As Mumford has outlined, a heightened perception of risk, greater restrictions on military expenditure since the 2007 financial crisis, and minimal public appetite for direct engagement in foreign wars in the wake of Afghanistan and Iraq, has required the pursuit of 'national security' (and other) goals through indirect strategies (Mumford, 2013a: 8). Conflicts that arose in the wake of the Arab Spring further magnified this shift to the pursuit of states' interests, geopolitical rivalries and inter-state wars being played out through proxy conflict. This has led to what Mumford (2017) describes as the 'era of indirect war by proxy'.

Importantly, unlike during the Cold War, where confrontation was bipolar in nature, multipolarity has given way to a 'polyarchic' world order in which the monopoly on the use of force by nation states is often highly atomized, and occasionally non-existent (Pfaff, 2017a: 312). During this period the world has witnessed a dramatic rise in the geo-politicization of local and national conflicts and a forceful return of geopolitics (Mead, 2014; Oslo Forum, 2017; Harland, 2018). For example, in the Middle East and North Africa (MENA), strong regional actors such as Iran, Saudi Arabia, the United Arab Emirates (UAE), Qatar, Turkey, Egypt and to an extent Israel, as well as a number of non-state armed actors, are all engaging in a limited war strategy to undermine their rivals and ensure their own interests are met. Conflicts playing out today in places such as Syria, Yemen, Libya, Iraq, Somalia, Sudan and elsewhere are characterized by engagement by multiple sponsors and proxies, leading to what could be termed multi-party or multilateral proxy conflicts.

Regional and international actors see such conflicts and fragmented countries as an arena of competition. Engagement and intervention in these fragmented countries is perceived as an opportunity to further national security goals and financial interests, and is therefore of high strategic value. This trend is set to continue and increase as the price and risk of direct military engagement by large states remains too high, leading to a strategy of leveraging alliances to ensure interests are met. US policy in the Middle East since former President Barack Obama took office until now is a prime example (Krieg, 2016; Pfaff, 2017b). While the international system appears to be moving back towards great power rivalries, a strategy of containment by proxy warfare will remain a central approach (Yesley, 2011; Rondeaux and Sterman, 2019: 46).

As Rondeaux and Sterman (2019: 3) point out, 'a complex mesh of partnerships among states, corporations, mercenaries and militias is changing the way wars are fought'. This atomization and the polyarchic nature of conflict has been driven by a number of factors, including but not limited to, the spread of advanced weapons and communications. For example, the proliferation of missile technology and use of drones across the MENA region has changed the dynamics, allowing actors like Iran to more effectively empower and arm local proxies such as Hezbollah, and the al-Ḥashd ash-Shaʿbī (PMF) forces in Iraq, or arguably Ansar Allah (the Houthis) in Yemen (International Crisis Group, 2018). Israeli concerns about ballistic missile proliferation to Iranian proxies in Syria has led to direct strikes on Syrian territory and in turn has led to tension with both Damascus and Moscow. Libya today is sometimes described as a 'testing ground' for drone technology by the UAE and Turkey (Herbert, 2019; Interview with Libya Expert, 2019). In December 2019 US commanders blamed Russian special forces supporting Khalifa Haftar for shooting down a US predator drone in Libya (Stewart and Lewis, 2019). The advancement of cyberwar capabilities is also adding to this trend towards indirect conflict and proxy conflict. Today cyber is often seen as the weapon of first resort – cheap and limited in nature, but potentially highly effective. The US cyber strike on Iran following the attacks on the Saudi Aramco facilities in September 2019 is a strong case in point – a cyber response to a kinetic attack on behalf of a regional ally (Ali and Stewart, 2019). As technology develops further, and the likes of advanced ballistic missiles systems, remote targeting, unmanned and autonomous weapons systems, artificial intelligence, and cyberwar capabilities proliferate even for weaker states and non-state actors, this trend of atomized proxy war escalation and 'hybrid warfare' will continue (Collier, 2017; Rondeaux and Sterman, 2019: 52–53).

Furthermore, the role of globalized financial systems and simple access to multiple offshore banks has enabled quick and easy transfer of funds to 'conflict entrepreneurs' (Rondeaux and Sterman, 2019). For example, associates around the Syrian president Bashar al-Assad stored millions of dollars in offshore tax havens, which they used to help fund Syria's pro-government militias (Lake, 2012). Cryptocurrency further enables conflict actors to operate large flows of financial assets undetected to fund various groups and individuals to further their strategic aims from a distance. For example, the military wing of the Palestinian Islamic Resistance Movement (Hamas) has designed a sophisticated campaign to raise money using bitcoin (Popper, 2019). Conversely, the imposition of international sanctions is another form of indirect war, often used by the US and the European Union (EU). Under the Clinton administration in the US the idea of 'smart sanctions' was introduced, which aimed to target specific individuals or entities, rather than entire populations, through travel bans, asset freezes, arms embargoes, capital restraints, foreign aid reductions and trade restrictions. After 9/11 former US President George W. Bush took the use of sanctions to a new level, using the prevalence of US dollars in the global financial system to shut out 'rogue banks', while the Obama administration used targeted sanctions notably against Russia (Dyer, 2014). The 'maximum pressure' campaign imposed on Iran by the Trump administration in the US is an evident example of such indirect war, driven by forces inside the US, as well as by US allies in the region, notably Saudi Arabia and Israel (Indyk, 2019).

In addition, the 'democratization of communication' and proliferating use of social media has allowed multiple actors not only to influence, but also to control narratives surrounding conflicts. This was seen during the Arab Spring, where social media may not have been a causal mechanism in the uprisings, but evidently played a major role in influencing, controlling and communicating the narrative (Aday et al, 2012).

With the end of bipolarity and the changes described in modern warfare, the role and nature of non-state actors in particular has shifted dramatically. There is an evident and expanding spectrum of non-state actors who are directly engaged in conflict – whether classic organizations, 'hybrid actors', business people, 'conflict entrepreneurs' or networks (Moghadam, 2017; Slaughter, 2017; Cambanis et al, 2019; Rondeaux and Sterman, 2019). Once viewed only as proxy actors who implemented the desires of their state sponsors, in contemporary proxy warfare these non-state actors are both able to be sponsors and proxies, often developing their own sources of revenue, such as trans-border trafficking of arms, drugs or people. Hezbollah is an example of a non-state armed group that plays the role of proxy and sponsor. Hezbollah both directly implements strategies on the ground in support of Iran and provides training and logistics/weapons support to other groups, for example Ansar Allah in Yemen or pro-regime forces in Syria (Byman and Kreps, 2010; Corbeil and Amarasinggam, 2016; Hubbard, 2017). Other non-state actors have developed their own network of proxies, for example, al-Qaeda, unlike the Islamic State (ISIS) (at least until now), has often worked through front groups and coalitions rather than engaging in direct efforts to seize territory and exercise governance itself – a strategy which has been referred to as 'proxy terrorism' (Gartenstein-Ross et al, 2015; Rondeaux and Sterman, 2019: 51).

Importantly, all of the elements outlined have combined to develop multiple and often complex connections between conflicts, leading to many more transnational conflicts (Salehyan and Gleditsch, 2006; Salehyan, 2011; Malet, 2013; Sterman and Rosenblatt, 2018). As Harland (2018) outlines, while the number of inter-state and internal conflicts has remained roughly steady, the number of 'internationalised internal conflicts' has surged over the past decade, representing a major shift.

This shift to a 'polyarchic' order and the use of hybrid forms of conflict has had a dramatic impact on the way that conflict is conducted, which in turn has changed the face of conflict mediation. It is critical to understand this shift when analysing conflicts today, and specifically when engaging in mediation in order to develop a viable process. National and international peace agreements are becoming something of a rarity. The 2018 Oslo Forum asked the question, have we seen the 'end of the big peace?', and assessed whether comprehensive peace and power-sharing agreements of the 1990s are a thing of the past (Oslo Forum, 2018). Indeed, during the last decade, the number of national, regional or international peace agreements are few (Whitfield, 2015; Harland, 2018).[1] While there have been some other agreements in name, such as the 2015 Libyan Political Agreement, these have often fallen apart shortly after conclusion. At the same time there has been a surge in local-level agreements – whether peace agreements, ceasefires or humanitarian access agreements – within various conflicts, for example in Syria and Libya.[2] Within this new conflict landscape the mediator must adjust rapidly.

Typology of Proxy War

In order to consolidate this analysis, building on previous work by Mumford (2013a), it is useful to briefly outline the broad typology of a proxy war – why sponsors engage via proxy, who engages, and how?

---

[1] 2011 Doha Document for Peace in Darfur (DDPD); 2011 Ceasefire of Euskadi Ta Askatasuna (ETA); 2011/2012 GCC Initiative in Yemen; 2014 Comprehensive Agreement on the Bangsamoro in the Philippines; 2014 Minsk Protocol and Minsk II in Ukraine; 2015 Republican Pact in Central African Republic (CAR); 2015 Nationwide Ceasefire Agreement in Myanmar; 2015 Accord d'Algier in Mali; 2016 Acuerdo Final Para la Terminación del Conflicto y la Construcción de Una Paz Estable y Duradera in Colombia; 2019 Mupato Accord in Mozambique; 2019 peace accord in CAR.

[2] For example: in Syria, in December 2016 Turkish intelligence and the Russian military negotiated an agreement to allow civilians and moderate rebels to flee from Eastern Aleppo to Idlib (Shaheen, 2016); in Libya in April 2013 a peace agreement was signed in Sabha between the main tribal groups putting a halt to heavy fighting in the south-west.

These variables are key to understanding the nature of the conflict, and as a result, how a mediator can engage most effectively.

Actors engage in proxy wars for multiple reasons. One common feature is for state or non-state actors to seek to further their strategic goals while simultaneously limiting their risk, exposure to and cost of war. As Mumford states: 'In short, proxy wars are the logical replacement for states seeking to further their own strategic goals yet at the same time avoid engaging in direct, costly bloody war-fare' (Mumford, 2013a: 111). This chapter identifies four key reasons for engaging in proxy war – ensuring limited war, creating strategic depth, reducing costs while maintaining outputs, and reshaping norms – though there are evidently more.

As outlined by Lawrence Freedman (2014), the logic of proxy war is bound in the concept of 'limited war' – that being mutual acceptance of external constraints imposed by the prospect of mutual annihilation. Therefore, while rivals may want to compete with one another, they also wish to avoid direct military confrontation and escalation. War via proxy allows for this. For example, Russia's use of mercenary forces in Ukraine, Syria and Libya has provided some level of plausible deniability of direct ground engagement, enabling Russia to stay under the perceived threshold for direct retaliation from the US or NATO (Sukhankin, 2018). This plausible deniability, and secrecy, is key to limiting direct escalation, while still pursuing direct strategic goals. Limited war strategy is also evident between the countries of the Middle East, notably Iran and Saudi Arabia, both of whom continue to compete with one another, but neither of whom desires direct military confrontation (McManus, 2016).

Pakistan's Inter-Services Intelligence has long used investment in proxies, including relations with the Taliban and Laskar-e-Taiba, as a key way to create strategic depth in the face of threats from India (Coll, 2018). Iran also perceives its investment in proxies across the Middle East, such as Hezbollah in Lebanon, or the al-Ḥashd ash-Shaʿbī in Iraq, as a way of building strategic depth. This strategic depth comes with significant military tactical benefits of partnering with local forces, who can both shorten lines of communication and provide valuable local intelligence, enabling actors to project power beyond their existing capacity (Rondeaux and Sterman, 2019: 23).

The next benefit is that proxy warfare allows actors to conduct war 'on a shoestring', enabling battlefield gains at a fraction of the cost of using conventional forces, and avoiding the steep costs of occupying territory. As Mumford (2013a: 8) outlines, the 'inevitable cost' of the 'war on terror' – both financial and political – is that 'the US will revert to engagement in proxy warfare', as also happened following the Vietnam war. Indeed, part of 'Obama's doctrine' of relying on local proxy forces instead of authorizing US military deployments was clearly evident in both Libya and Syria, while in Yemen and Somalia the administration made prolific use of unmanned aerial drones against al-Qaeda and affiliated Al Shabab targets (Wherey, 2018). This modus operandi continued under Trump, who was set on further disengagement of direct military forces, notably in the Middle East (Gordon, 2018).

In addition to the financial and political efficacy, war via proxy allows the benefactor to engage in conflict without the public scrutiny and accountability that direct engagement would entail. The use of irregular forces hence allows the benefactor to bypass and often break established norms, and in turn increase the possibility of strategic surprise upon their adversary, while maintaining plausible deniability (Rondeaux and Sterman, 2019: 25). Actors engaging in proxy wars can range from state and non-state to commercial and criminal. There are examples where states use other states, such as Russia's support to Cuba and US support to former Zaire and South Africa during the war in Angola in the 1970s, Russia's support to Assad's regime in Syria after 2012 (in addition to direct engagement), and US support to Kenyan's regional counter-terror operations against Al Shabab. Alternatively, there is evidence of state support to non-state actors such as US support to the Angolan opposition groups the National Liberation Front of Angola (FNLA) and the National Union for the Total Independence of Angola (UNITA) from the 1970s until 2002; Iran's support to Hezbollah; Saudi Arabia, Turkey, and Qatar's support to opposition groups in Syria after 2011; or Pakistan's support to the Taliban in Afghanistan. Other examples show non-state actors using other non-state actors, for example Hezbollah's support, mainly through training, to Ansar Allah in the north of Yemen, or al-Qaeda Central's support to its network of affiliate groups. There is also evident involvement of private sector actors such as oil companies, which often use non-state militias to guard oil installations, as we have seen in Libya (Sylvers, 2015), as well as the increasing role of Private Military Companies (PMCs) or mercenaries fighting on behalf of certain states or non-state actors, such as Wagner Group, which has conducted operations on behalf of Russia in both Syria and Libya. The conflict in Libya was described by *The New York Times* in May 2020 as a 'mercenary on mercenary war' (Walsh, 2020).

There are various proxy war strategies that can be observed – the *type* and *level* of support are two critical variables. They can include manpower (such as Russian and Iranian support to Assad's regime in Syria after 2011); weapons and technical capacity (such as Iranian and Hezbollah support to Ansar Allah in Yemen, US arming of Mujahidin fighters in Afghanistan 1979–89, and US support to the Contra paramilitary groups against the Sandinista government in Nicaragua 1979–90); money (the Soviet Union's financial support to smaller proxies was estimated at 51 billion USD between 1955 and 1980); soft power and ideology (for example creating and supporting certain political groups, such as the US support to selected political parties in Chile during the 1964 and 1970 elections in order to discredit Marxist-leaning political leaders, or current alleged Russian support for far-right political parties in Europe); and intelligence/information (such as the provision of NATO intelligence to Libyan rebels during the 2011 uprising) (CIA, 2000; Kornbluh, 2003; Mumford, 2013a: 61–75; Klasa et al, 2019).

The Implications of Multilateral Proxy War on Mediation

The shift to a 'polyarchic' conflict landscape and the nature of proxy conflicts leads to a number of challenges for a mediator, which can seriously complicate any attempts at reaching a resolution in a number of ways. Unless there is unparalleled political support to a process, such as the process that led to the Dayton Accords in Bosnia (Holbrook, 1998), mediators often have few carrots and even fewer sticks to utilize within any given process to counter these challenges and drive through a solution to the conflict. Progress more often relies on some or all of: (a) understanding the dynamics – causes, aims of the parties, relations; (b) knowing the actors/points of influence; (c) using creative means to gain access/influence; (d) finding ways to build consent towards a settlement. All of these critical elements are dramatically complicated within conflicts with proxy elements. Before exploring possible ways and methods for mediators to overcome these challenges and operate more effectively within proxy wars, it is necessary to identify the particularities of the challenges faced.

Conflict Escalation

Despite the analysis that proxy war is supposed to reduce the chances of direct big power conflict, with the rise of non-state actors with access to state-level resources, the diffusion of remote targeting and high-powered weaponry, and proliferation of interconnected conflicts, the risk of proxy warfare expanding in scale and intensity as well as geographic scope is evident (Rondeaux and Sterman, 2019; 17).

The engagement of external sponsors in an internal conflict can dramatically change the nature of the conflict in terms of size and intensity.

This is multiplied by the fact that more often than not when one warring side receives external support other parties to the conflict will also receive concomitant support from their own benefactors, increasing the stakes and costs of the conflict (Pfaff and Granfield, 2019). From the perspective of the benefactor, proxy engagement in conflict gives the sponsor greater incentive to escalate rather than to resolve, enabling them to 'forgo risks around the negotiating table and pursue them in the battlefield' (Pfaff and Granfield, 2019). The often-massive change in capability and strategy that comes with proxy support can shift the dynamics and escalate the conflict, making it difficult for the mediator to assess and engage effectively. This was evident in Syria when Russia decided to provide direct air support to Assad in September 2015, dramatically shifting and escalating the direction of the conflict. The influx of weaponry to tribal elements in Yemen changed the dynamics on the ground, notably from 2015, increasing the intensity and lethality of the fighting, as was evident in clashes between the Hajoour tribe and the Ansar Allah in the north in November 2019 (al Ashwal, 2019).

In addition, with a lack of well-defined command and control there may be incentives or opportunities for local actors to take greater risks on the battlefield, raising the chances of escalation. Such lack of direct command and control, as well as sometimes contradicting war aims, can also lead to an inability to constrain local proxy forces from committing abuses on the ground, while local forces will often hide the strategic risks attached to a certain approach from their sponsor (Ladwig, 2017). Furthermore, the academic literature has revealed that external sponsorship of internal groups has often led to an increase in acts of (often state-sponsored) terrorism and atrocities being conducted (Byman, 2005; 2018; Byman and Kreps, 2010; Salehyan, 2010; Weinstein, 2012; Salehyan et al, 2014).

This potential for conflict escalation can have an adverse impact at the local level between forces on the ground, or at the remote level between sponsors. In an environment of proliferation of high-powered weaponry, such escalation on the ground can cause a devastating loss of life, often outside internal strategic calculations of the parties (Gaub, 2017). As conflict escalates and lives are lost, it becomes exponentially harder for a mediator to carve out any resolution to the conflict, especially if atrocities have been committed in the absence of any realistic prospect of justice or accountability.

Indeterminate Responsibility, Misaligned Strategies, and Opaque Command and Control

In addition to the risk of conflict escalation, understanding who is in control – the 'proxyness' of a conflict – and therefore who needs to be engaged in a mediation process and provide consent to a solution is a major challenge for the mediator in proxy conflicts. First, the support provided by a sponsor to a surrogate is often clandestine or deniable in nature, while supporters and financiers of conflicting parties are traditionally difficult to engage. Considering that one of the main appeals of proxy wars is to be able to influence the situation while reducing risks, the very appeal and strategic utility of irregular forces are that they tend to sit outside formal state structures and as such are deniable assets for the sponsor who can remain in the shadows. This allows sponsors to pursue strategic goals deniably. For example, in the early phases of the Russian involvement in Crimea the use of 'little green men' provided deniability of direct engagement (Freedman, 2014: 15–23). Such a strategy only thickens the Clausewitzian 'fog of war', making it hard for mediators to identify the correct entry point and decision makers to build the necessary consent. In a polyarchic environment, with the proliferation of high-powered weaponry, the covert nature of sponsor–proxy ties also raises the risk of strategic miscalculation and possible escalation.

The opaque nature of proxy conflicts can lead to misaligned proxy-sponsor war aims, sometimes intentionally (Rondeaux and Sterman, 2019: 24). Intentional misalignment can be on the part of the sponsor, who can use proxies to pursue strategic aims, for example, the support provided by the US to the Kurdish Democratic Union Party (PYD) forces in Syria to combat ISIS, which was not aligned to PYD ambitions of gaining a semi-autonomous state. This misalignment was revealed with the decision of the Trump administration to withdraw US troops from north-east Syria in late 2019, to the detriment of the PYD forces.

Misalignment can also be on behalf of the proxy who can use their local knowledge to redirect resources and strategic direction. For example, Field Marshall Khalifa Haftar, commander of the Libyan National Army (LNA) based in the East of Libya, launched his attack on Tripoli, Libya, in April 2019, allegedly without being pushed to do so by his supporters in Egypt, the UAE and France. France and the UAE even signed joint statements calling for the conflict to end (Irish, 2019). Haftar's attack created a 'with me or against me' dichotomy, which forced these backers into doubling down on their investment (Interview with Libya Expert, September 2019).

Yemen is a particularly good example of shifting war aims. While the UAE and Saudi Arabia are formally part of the same military coalition designed to combat Ansar Allah, the two countries have also been pursuing different strategic aims on the ground. This culminated in UAE-backed Southern Transitional Council (STC) forces temporarily taking parts of Aden from the Saudi-backed government of Mansour al-Hadi in August 2019, and in turn led to a clear rupture within the coalition (Ghantous, 2019). These differences were partially resolved through the Riyadh Agreement of November 2019. However, in April 2020, the UAE-backed STC declared autonomous rule in southern Yemen, once again undermining the Saudi-backed Yemeni government. This additional dynamic has further complicated the job of the UN in forging a viable political process in Yemen.

Such a misalignment of aims is routinely obvious where proxies provide specific counter-terror functions. For example, France uses several non-state armed groups, including Mouvement pour le Salut de l'Azawad (MSA) and Le Groupe Autodéfense Touareg Imghad et Alliés (GATIA), as proxy forces to combat the Islamic State for the Greater Sahara (ISGS) in the Mali–Niger border region. However, France has also played a key role in Mali's peace process since the 2015 Bamako agreement; MSA is not a signatory to this agreement, and they as well as GATIA regularly undermine the process through inter-communal violence with Felani communities (Katz, 2019). Indeed, understanding the differing war aims and navigating the misalignment of the sponsor's and proxy's war aims is one of the biggest challenges for a mediator.

It is also important to note that the 'proxyness' of a conflict can change over time. The Liberation Tigers of Tamil Elam (LTTE) were initially trained and armed in part by and in India in the early 1980s. However, with a change of leadership and approach in India, by 1987 the LTTE declared war on the Indian Peacekeeping Force in Sri-Lanka (IPKF). In 1991 an LTTE member assassinated the sitting Prime Minister Rajiv Gandhi and the group were banned from India (Mishra, 2011). The loose alliance of Syrian opposition that has made up the Free Syrian Army (FSA) since 2011 is an excellent example of the complex and changing nature of 'proxyness'. The FSA is a decentralized opposition coalition, which has consisted of over 80 armed groups during its lifespan, as well as foreign fighters, representing different agendas, and supported at one time or another by a multitude of sponsors, including the US, Turkey, UK, Jordan, Saudi Arabia and others (Barnard, 2013; Lister, 2016). This example is an important illustration of how careful a mediator must be when assessing from whom and to what degree consent towards peace must be gained.

This also leads to a more fundamental problem of understanding the command and control between principle sponsors and proxies. It is often assumed that proxies are merely implementing the orders of their paymasters in external capitals. While this is sometimes the case, this simplified chain of command and analysis of interests is often incorrect. In actual fact, within military strategy, command and control of local forces is seen as one of the greatest challenges and risks of war by proxy (Brown, 2016). Take again the example of the relationship between Khalifa Haftar in Libya and one of his principal sponsors, Egypt. Egyptian officials were dismayed when, in early 2019, Haftar refused to agree to the outputs of the Cairo military dialogue, a year-long process the Egyptians had led to reunify Libya's armed forces by bringing together military officials from all parts of the country. Yet, lacking a clear alternative, Egypt was compelled to continue its support to Haftar (Interview with Libya Expert, 2019). This challenge of command and control is magnified in instances where forces have more than one sponsor and/or are part of a loose alliance, as seen with the FSA.

This imprecise analysis is not an unimportant point. As Ollivant and Gaston (2019) have highlighted, 'the narrative of proxy warfare can misdiagnose the nature of the threat and help escalate a geopolitical standoff based on what are in reality local actors' strategic positioning and machinations'. Due to various dynamics since 2007, full proxy manipulation in Iraq is harder to attain – 'external influence is present, but in most situations it is overshadowed by internal, domestic political considerations' (Ollivant and Gaston, 2019). The research suggests that rather than proxy manipulation, the idea of 'convergence of interests' better captures the relationship between external powers and local actors in Iraq.

This is a critical point: seeing things purely through a proxy war lens can skew the analysis and can even escalate geopolitical tensions. This can also be seen playing out in Yemen, where Ansar Allah attacks on Saudi positions are sometimes interpreted as the work of Iran, when in actual fact Ansar Allah are principally pursuing a domestic agenda. However, this interpretation in turn heightens geopolitical tensions between Saudi Arabia and its allies, and Iran. The example of Hezbollah in Lebanon is also prescient. While Hezbollah undeniably gains political, financial and military support from Iran, and conversely implements strategy on behalf of Iran, it also has its own domestic constituency from which it gains legitimacy and support (Interview with Middle East Expert, 2019). As Ollivant and Gaston (2019) conclude, 'to de-escalate both the local and geopolitical tensions, it is important to differentiate the source and nature of the threat'. This is the critical point for the mediator.

Conflict Protraction

The provision of external support to one or more conflicting parties can lead to the prolongation and often stalemate of a conflict (Mumford, 2013a; De Soysa, 2017). The resolution of a conflict is often preceded by a mutually hurting stalemate between the parties, caused by the duration, loss of life, or cost (economic and political) of the conflict (Zartman, 2001). Because external sponsors do not feel the direct pain of the conflict, and bearing in mind most proxy engagement is economically and politically cheap, this mutually hurting stalemate often never arrives. While the local forces on the ground bear the cost and may wish to sue for peace, the level of agency they have to end the conflict can be limited, and even if they could concede, the cost may be total (and sometimes bloody) loss. For example, in Cambodia the conflict raged from 1979 to 1993, during which time the People's Republic of Kampuchea was supported by Vietnam and the Soviet Union, while the Coalition Government of Democratic Kampuchea was backed by China, the US and some members of the Association of Southeast Asian Nations (ASEAN). These external actors greatly hampered any substantive peace from being achieved due to Cold War competition. A viable settlement was only reached when an internal 'win-win' policy was devised, which included amnesty and integration of some former Khmer Rouge members (Sokkhoeurn, 2010).

Additionally, when local conflict parties are promised or expect external support, the leadership may sometimes hold out and hope for this support or intervention to arrive, even if major losses are being felt on the ground. This can lead to an unnatural (and often brutal) prolongation of the conflict. Kuperman demonstrates this perverse dynamic when analysing the negative side effects of humanitarian interventionism under the Responsibility to Protect (R2P) doctrine in Bosnia and Kosovo. Although R2P does not (necessary) represent a proxy–sponsor relationship, the effect can be the same: vulnerable groups hold out, and even actively incite a violent retaliation in order to solicit external support, which may come too late, or not at all (Kuperman, 2008). Indeed, it is possible that until external actors remove themselves from conflicts in Libya, Yemen, Somalia or Afghanistan, for example, the hope for a substantive resolution to the conflict remains slim-to-none, while the chances of further conflict escalation are high.

While a mutually hurting stalemate is often required to push the parties to peace, the development of an incentive structure is necessary to pull the parties into an agreement. While this is complicated to develop with local conflict actors, it becomes almost impossible when the demands and considerations of multiple external sponsors are considered. This can cause a scenario where no arrangement will satisfy the basic demands of all critical actors, and a violent stalemate can prevail. This has arguably been the case in Syria since 2011. This challenge is multiplied when one factors in the inherent difficulties in trying to influence the strategic calculations of state actors who are often benefactors to proxy wars and who see their engagement as part of a national security framework. Take, for example,

Russian support to Bashar al-Assad in Syria; this support is based on a complicated mix of Russian pursuit of strategic and security interests in the Middle East, provision of support to a long-term ally, and Putin's domestic agenda to project Russian strength. Considering the domestic security policies of state actors when trying to build consent towards an agreement greatly complicates the work of a mediator within a proxy conflict.

In addition, recent conflicts which have evident proxy engagement have led to large numbers of internally displaced people and refugees (UNHCR, 2018). This level of displacement threatens to greatly complicate and extend the duration of the war, especially for those most adversely affected. Mediation efforts can often break down when there is little to no hope of a safe and just return of displaced populations. Take, for example, the Israel–Palestine conflict, where the issue of the return of Palestinian refugees remains a serious stumbling block to a final settlement, even if a viable process could be established.

The Breakdown of Multilateral Institutions

The return of geopolitics and the end of the US unipolar structure has further complicated the work of a mediator in several ways. This dynamic has arguably led to a breakdown of the authority of multilateral institutions and international bodies, notably the United Nations Security Council (UNSC). This is an additional challenge for peace mediation actors – where powerful countries are willing to cooperate to resolve conflict through bodies such as the UN, much can be done. Where they see such conflicts as arenas for further internal agendas, established tools of peacebuilding breakdown (Harland, 2018: 6). The UNSC has often been divided between the superpowers. However, one of the main fall-outs from the Libya conflict was to initiate an even more decisive break between Russia and the US. While Russia abstained from a UNSC vote to establish a no-fly zone in Libya in 2011, NATO members used the turmoil to pursue geopolitical aims both directly and through NATO-backed Libyan proxy forces on the ground. From a Russian perspective, this approach and the subsequent breakdown in order was unacceptable in Libya, which had previously been a long-time client state of Moscow and a key node in Russia's energy trading chain (Steward, 2011). This breakdown over Libya was one of the formative events which led to Russian blocking of draft resolutions in Syria after 2011, and direct (and indirect) Russian intervention thereafter (Nichols, 2019).

The UNSC has in a sense become another forum of war by proxy. Importantly, the now dysfunctional nature of the Security Council is creating major challenges for UN political missions who are often mandated to mediate an end to certain conflicts. Without Security Council consensus and unanimous political backing for a resolution to the conflict, it is hard or even impossible to deploy the necessary resources to build consent from the warring factions towards a peaceful resolution. This is one example of the breakdown of multilateral institutions that we are currently experiencing, as has been evident during the Syrian conflict (Oweis, 2015), or even in the inability of the Security Council to initially support the UN Secretary-General's call for a global ceasefire to counter COVID-19. Resolution 2532 was eventually adopted 111 days after the pandemic was announced by WHO, calling for an immediate cessation of hostilities for 90 days. However, this belated resolution had little to no effect on the ground and failed to seize the initial momentum developed by the Secretary-General in late March/early April 2020 (Reliefweb, 2020a; Reliefweb, 2020b; United Nations, 2020). A further complication arising from the breakdown of the authority of multilateral institutions is the inability to address transnational issues and demands of diverse parties in interlinked conflicts. Rather than viewing specific conflicts as discrete problems to be solved, a transnational approach is required. The ability to address such interlinkages depends on a functioning multilateral system.

Overcoming the Challenges of Mediating Wars with Proxy Elements

Gone are the classical conflicts and resultant peace processes of old. Colombia was perhaps one of the last examples – a strong government and military pitted against a largely homogeneous revolutionary armed group, the Revolutionary Armed Forces of Colombia (FARC), who, after 50 years, had fought each other to a mutually hurting stalemate, with high degrees of independence and autonomy, and within a regional and international environment which was rather constructive towards a settlement (Jaramillo, 2017).

The challenges of proxy conflict – an evident shift to a polyarchic framework of conflict, the increasing relevance of proxy sponsors in civil conflicts, and the difficulties this imposes upon mediating a conflict – require mediators to rethink how they can counter these challenges effectively and gain the necessary consent to help move towards agreement within conflicts that have proxy elements.

Methods deployed to understand how best to mediate proxy conflicts are no different from those used for any conflict, just more complicated. This requires a detailed mapping of (a) who to engage and when to engage (key actors, relationships between them, how to gain and maintain access to these actors); (b) what to engage these key actors on (the key substantive issues, main drivers of the conflict/core interests, and how to influence these factors); and (c) and ultimately, how to build a process that can gain and maintain the necessary consent from the necessary actors for a settlement. Importantly, strategies deployed must aim to overcome the previous challenges outlined to the best extent possible.

Understanding 'Proxyness' of Conflict

Understanding the nature of the conflict, and notably the nature of the relationships in the conflict, is key to understanding how, as a mediator, one can engage the relevant actors most effectively. *Who* are the key actors, and how can they be engaged? The level of control of a sponsor or autonomy of a proxy (or the 'proxyness' of the relation(s)) is a critical variable when assessing how to engage actors, gain the necessary consent at the right point, and construct a successful mediation process. Where there are high levels of control, consent of the sponsor (as well as the local actor) to any settlement will be critical to develop a viable/lasting agreement. Where the necessary consent is not gained, the likelihood of any agreement being undermined by the sponsor is greater. Where control of a proxy by a sponsor is weaker the proxy/local actor may have more ability to strike a deal without the permission/consent of the sponsor. In such an instance the mediator can afford to spend less time and effort engaging with the sponsor and more engaging with the local actor(s). However, this understanding of control or autonomy is often highly unclear. If the mediator gets this calculation incorrect, it can undermine months or even years of work. Moreover, the degree of 'proxyness' is often not only unclear, but unknown, even to the parties on the ground. The limits of the relations often go untested until a critical moment and can change rapidly depending on internal and external dynamics. Within this web of uncertain relations, the mediator must find a way to develop a viable process.

Understanding the Minimal Demands and Building Incentive Structures

Understanding the parties' demands within the conflict is crucial to developing a viable settlement by consensus. *What* is it that the parties want? This requires a strong analysis of the dynamics, and trusted relations with the conflict actors. Linked to the question of from whom the mediator must gain consent, the mediator must also understand the minimum demands of these parties that must be met for a settlement to be viable. This is particularly the case in highly atomized conflicts where multiple parties often hold multiple maximalist positions. Finding a settlement which will satisfy all maximal demands is impossible, while finding a settlement that satisfies minimal demands is plausible. Failure to meet these minimal demands can jeopardize any process as parties to the conflict become spoilers to any agreement if they do not see that their interests are met and protected. Therefore, the minimal coalition for a settlement must be developed. The mediator should also work to understand the difference in demands of the proxies on the ground and the sponsor. Where differences exist, the mediator can exploit these to give prominence to positions which are more amenable to a resolution of the conflict.

In addition to creating a structural win-win for the parties and giving prominence to constructive positions, the mediator can also develop a strong set of both positive and negative incentive structures for the parties which promise to reward acquiescence to an agreement and punish refusal/actions which undermine an agreement. This is often easier for 'strong' mediators, who have greater resources, including, sometimes, military resources, and recourse to sanctions or financial incentives. 'Weak' mediators need to find creative ways to build such incentive structures, for example by enabling humanitarian access to domestic constituents, or facilitating (discrete) diplomatic contact for the parties.

Taking a Hybrid Approach

The next question is *how* can a mediator conduct the complicated task of building necessary consent from the necessary actors in the complex environment of modern proxy warfare? To help overcome the challenges posed by proxy wars and more broadly modern conflict, the mediator must be able to operate at multiple levels geographically – local, national, regional, international – and on multiple tracks. In a world of hybrid conflict the mediator requires a hybrid response, using state and non-state actors, resources and networks to craft the minimum consensus required from all relevant parties.

From a process design perspective, this requires a much more rigorous and comprehensive approach than dealing with two-party 'classical' conflicts. As Whitfield (2019: 9) outlines, 'we need more, and better, process design for the kind of multi-layered mediation efforts required by multi-layered conflict'. This is particularly important if the mediator is to be able to engage at all relevant levels. In today's conflicts a mediation process that ignores or neglects any one of the individual 'tracks' can be undermined rapidly, leading to the end of sometimes years of careful work by the mediator. For example, in Yemen the UN and (previously) the Gulf Cooperation Council (GCC) efforts often focused as much on the regional dynamics as the local dynamics, utilizing various channels and actors to build the necessary consent on all sides.

The Conductor

This multi-level, comprehensive approach requires that the mediator uses all resources at their disposal, including working closely with other third-party actors to increase their capacity and reach. As Feltman (2019: 4) outlines, 'UN mediators and facilitators today need to view themselves less as the star soloists ... and more as conductors of a coherent, coordinated orchestra of mediation actors who can reach more of the people who can influence the direction of a conflict and who are affected by the conflict'.

In an interview reflecting on his time as Special Representative to the Secretary General for Libya, Ghassan Salamé outlined the need for a multi-pronged approach to dealing with vested interests and external interference in the conflict (Centre for Human Dialogue, nd). During his tenure, Salamé 'conducted' other third parties effectively as a force multiplier, utilizing non-governmental actors such as the Centre for Humanitarian Dialogue (HD), Dialogue Advisory Group, the European Council on Foreign Relations and others who have been able to engage actors and run processes that the UN were not, broadening the reach and capacity of the UN-led mediation.[3] This also afforded Salamé and his team more time and space to engage with the national and regional actors to the conflict in order to generate consent at that level towards an approach, though unfortunately not a lasting settlement.

Multilateral Institutions

Multilateral institutions have often been used to gain leverage and influence on external actors in order to build a coordinated regional and international approach to dealing with a particular conflict. Examples include the role of the Economic Community of West African States (ECOWAS) in

[3] For example, the National Conference Process (NCP) run by HD, report delivered to the UN Security Council on 08 November 2018. See full report here: https://www.hdcentre.org/wp-content/uploads/2018/11/NCP-Report_English.pdf.

West Africa, the African Union (AU) or Intergovernmental Authority on Development (IGAD) in the case of Somalia, or the GCC in Yemen. However, as mentioned, one of the trends that has been witnessed in recent years is a breakdown and reduction in effectiveness of some of these multilateral bodies. This deprives the mediator of a key tool to help manage regional and international actors' involvement in a given conflict, even when the context requires multi-level negotiations (Whitfield, 2019: 9).

When such bodies are not readily available or useful to the mediator they must be creative in developing a support architecture that can help. The formation of a regional contact group/dialogue process, including state sponsors of proxies, can be an effective approach. For example, during the peace process between the government of the Philippines and the rebel group the Moro-Islamic Liberation Front (MILF), an International Contact Group (ICG) was set up to support the process after 2009. The ICG was a hybrid body composed of both states and international non-governmental organizations (INGOs), including Turkey, Saudi Arabia, the United Kingdom, Japan, the Asia Foundation, HD, Muhammadiyah, Conciliation Resources, and Sant'Egidio. This innovative approach led to the signing of the Comprehensive Agreement on the Bangsamoro in 2014.[4] The peace process in Colombia benefited greatly from a strong, purpose-built international support structure. This included: the guarantor countries Cuba and Norway, who facilitated the process with a wide mandate; accompanying countries Chile and Venezuela, who provided strong regional buy-in; special envoys from the US, EU and elsewhere, who ensured international support and assistance to the process; the UN, which supported the monitoring of the implementation of crucial parts of the agreement; as well as other international organizations, NGOs, experts and former conflict parties, to help key elements of the process and talks (Nylander et al, 2018). Other processes have benefited from 'groups of friends', 'regional platforms' or 'networks', which can create the necessary support and conducive environment at the regional and international level for a successful process.

Moreover, such a multilateral approach can provide space for regional and international actors who utilize local and national conflicts to further their agenda to resolve issues between themselves, or at least to reduce tensions and build confidence. If the Kuwaiti-led initiative which took place in 2016 had led to an agreement between the GCC (notably Saudi Arabia)

[4] See: Framework Agreement for the formation of the international contact group for the GRP-MILF process: https://www.hdcentre.org/wp-content/uploads/2016/06/Framework-Agreement-on-the-Formation-of-the-International-Contact-Group-for-hte-GRP-MILF-Peace-process-2009.pdf.

and Iran, it could have helped to dramatically defuse regional tensions, and reduce regional interference in some current conflicts. Unfortunately, the initiative failed, with negative consequences for the MENA region and beyond. Constructing a multilateral approach can be a complicated undertaking for a mediator, however it can serve to reduce regional and international proxy sponsors to the conflict, reduce possible spoilers, and increase support to a process and possible agreement, in order to enable the necessary consent towards a settlement and secure a successful process.

Non-official and Deniable

Sponsors of proxy wars are often major state actors, who are traditionally difficult for non-state third-party mediators to engage. For this reason, the mediation of international and proxy conflicts has traditionally been the realm of strong mediators, like the UN or the US. However, high-level public diplomacy and classical mediation processes have increasingly struggled to engage sponsors of proxies in conflict. Because these processes are often public or semi-public (more so today with the role of social media), the stakes are too high for actors who take a zero-sum game approach to explore alternative, non-violent options to de-escalate or resolve conflicts. Instead these processes are often considered as another forum of battle in which opposing parties can combat one another. However, non-state mediators or facilitators, such as private diplomacy organizations, well-connected non-official figures, or business people, offer possible alternative approaches. Being agile, low profile, confidential, apolitical, non-threatening and deniable, such actors can appeal to sponsors to a given conflict because they can test mechanisms to avoid unintended escalation, or explore alternative options to resolve specific conflicts, while reducing the exposure, risk and potential political costs. In addition, such non-state mediators/facilitators have the flexibility to simultaneously engage both state actors and hard-to-reach non-state actors, some of whom official or state mediators cannot access or engage. This hybrid approach is increasingly necessary in conflicts where state and non-state actors can be equally as influential and in turn can help to build consent on multiple levels. Such an approach can also be reinforced through coordination and cooperation with strong/state mediators, who can quietly facilitate access, as well as provide additional resources to help to influence the parties in a positive direction.

Technical and Humanitarian

In such multi-layered and complex conflicts, and with parties who take a zero-sum game approach, engaging the parties on specific technical or humanitarian issues of mutual concern can be highly effective in helping to de-escalate tensions and stabilize conditions on the ground, build confidence between the parties, and perhaps open the way for progress on political issues. Topics such as humanitarian access, cyber security, maritime security, military deconfliction and crisis management, or environmental concerns, while each important in and of themselves, can also serve to achieve this. Such an approach may sometimes be less direct, but also less threatening, and often more tangible. For example, in Ukraine HD have convened an ecological track focusing on the impacts of the conflict on the environment in Donbas, with the aim to promote cooperation on an area of mutual concern (Centre for Humanitarian Dialogue, nd). With the rapid spread of COVID-19 across the world in 2020, the Secretary-General (SG) to the United Nations called for a global ceasefire to counter the pandemic. A number of state and non-state groups responded by calling for a ceasefire or de-escalation. For example in Iraq, following the December 2019 attack on a US military base in Kirkuk and the killing of a US contractor, and the assassination of Iranian General Qassem Soleimani in January 2020, the US and Iranian-backed paramilitary groups have been engaged in a dangerous tit-for-tat escalation. Following the call of the SG, and with the support of non-state mediators, both parties called for a temporary de-escalation of the conflict in order to counter COVID-19, in turn opening the potential for longer-term de-escalation under a newly formed Iraqi government.

The measures discussed represent just some examples of possible approaches the mediator could take to overcome the multifaceted challenges caused by proxy wars within the framework of modern polyarchic conflicts. However, much also depends on the prevailing political dynamics, timing, personal relations, and other external and uncontrollable factors. With an appropriate approach, combined with conducive political dynamics, and a large slice of luck, a mediator could harness the necessary consent towards an agreement – whether a humanitarian or military ceasefire, peace agreement or other violence-reduction initiatives.

Conclusion: Rethinking the Framework of Mediation

While those who fight wars continue to restructure the framework for war, mediators must restructure the framework for mediation. As this chapter has demonstrated, since the US invasion of Iraq and the 'war on terror', the scale of proxy engagement has reached a historical high. This trend has been magnified by the 2011 Arab Spring and the events that have followed. Unlike the Cold War, conflicts today are highly atomized and 'polyarchic' in nature, and with the forceful return of geopolitics, we see a rise in 'multilateral' proxy conflicts involving a complex web of partnerships between states, militias, corporations and mercenaries. As a result, the simple linear conception of sponsor–proxy relation is inaccurate; both states and non-state actors can be both sponsor and proxy, with mutual path dependencies and complex power dynamics. This atomization has been driven by a number of factors, including the spread of advanced, high-powered and automated weaponry, advances in communications technology, the rise of powerful non-state actors, the globalized financial system and trans-border trafficking, and internationalized internal conflicts. This shift in the nature of conflict has had a dramatic impact on conflict mediation, reducing the occurrence of comprehensive peace agreements, instead requiring the brokering of more local-level agreements.

This rise in multilateral proxy conflicts within a polyarchic conflict framework has numerous negative implications for mediating conflicts, including the increased risk of conflict escalation, blurred lines of responsibility, opaque command and control structures, and misaligned conflict strategies. All of these risks increase the chances of conflict protraction. Furthermore, the gradual erosion of the authority of multilateral bodies has potentially significant implications for the ability of mediators to develop international or regional consensus on how to respond to and resolve specific conflicts, or to tackle transnational and interlinked conflicts. These challenges combined make it extremely difficult for a mediator to navigate the conflict and develop the necessary consent towards a resolution.

In order to help overcome these challenges, the chapter proposed several strategies which the mediator can adopt. First is to understand *who* needs to be engaged – essentially the 'proxyness' of the conflict. Secondly, to analyse and address *what* the minimal demands of the key conflict actors are as a step towards developing a minimal coalition for settlement, as well as to build both positive and negative incentive structures to encourage the parties to align with a resolution. Thirdly, to address *how* the mediator can conduct the complicated task of building the necessary consent, through adopting a hybrid and multi-layered approach – utilizing third-party actors where helpful, and developing multilateral architectures.

Those conducting warfare remain many steps ahead. The structures that exist to manage, mitigate and resolve conflicts are regularly undermined, outdated and inadequate to deal with the complexities of modern war. Those who wish to reduce the human suffering of war must respond rapidly to establish effective frameworks to counter this negative trend. In the meantime, there are things the mediator can do to respond creatively and to develop the necessary consent towards a resolution. If the international system is returning to bipolar or multipolar great power conflicts between the US, Russia and China, a strategy of containment by proxy will almost certainly remain a central approach, as risk management remains central to policy (Yesley, 2011; Rondeaux and Sterman, 2019: 46). Meanwhile, the escalatory pressures are only likely to increase as technical development accelerates. Areas such as remote targeting, cyberwarfare and artificial intelligence, and cryptocurrency enable multiple state and non-state actors to engage in proxy war to advance their strategic aims. As the costs and risks of conflict decrease and potential strategic benefits increase, the trend of increasing war by proxy is set to continue, and the populations caught in the middle of these conflict arenas will continue to suffer the direct consequences.

References

Aday, S., Farrell, H., Lynch, M., Sides, J. and Freelon, D. (2012) *New Media and Conflict after the Arab Spring*, Washington, DC: United States Institute for Peace.

al Ashwal, A. (2019) 'Hajoour Tribes, Houthis Locked in Key Battle in Northern Yemen', *al -Monitor* (14 March). Available at https://www.al-monitor.com/pulse/originals/2019/03/yemen-houthis-hajour-tribes-battle-war-saudi-arabia-strike.html (accessed 24 November 2019).

Ali, I. and Stewart, P. (2019) 'Exclusive: U.S. Carried Out Secret Cyber Strike on Iran in Wake of Saudi Oil Attack: Officials', *Reuters*, 16 October. Available at https://www.reuters.com/article/us-usa-iran-military-cyber-exclusive/exclusive-u-s-carried-out-secret-cyber-strike-on-iran-in-wake-of-saudi-oil-attack-officials-idUSKBN1WV0EK (accessed 24 November 2019).

Bar-Siman-Tov, Y. (1984) 'The Strategy of War by Proxy', *Cooperation and Conflict*, 19(4): 263–73.

Barnard, A. (2013) 'Syrian Rebels Say That Saudi Arabia Is Stepping Up Weapons Deliveries', *New York Times* (12 September). Available at: https://www.nytimes.com/2013/09/13/world/middleeast/syrian-rebels-say-saudi-arabia-is-stepping-up-weapons-deliveries.html (accessed 23 November 2019)

Brown, S. (2016) 'Purpose and Pitfalls of War by Proxy: A Systemic Analysis', *Small Wars and Insurgencies*, 27(2): 243–57.

Byman, D. (2005) *Deadly Connections: States That Sponsor Terrorism*, Cambridge: Cambridge University Press.

Byman, D. (2018) 'Why Engage in Proxy War? A State's Perspective', Brookings Institution (blog). Available at https://www.brookings.edu/blog/order-from-chaos/2018/05/21/why-engage-in-proxy-war-a-states-perspective/ (accessed 24 November 2019).

Byman, D. and Kreps, S.E. (2010) 'Agents of Destruction? Applying Principal-Agent Analysis to State-Sponsored Terrorism', *International Studies Perspectives*, 11(1): 1–18.

Cambanis, T., Esfandiary, D., Ghaddar, S., Wahid Hanna, M., Lund, A. and Mansour, R. (2019) *Hybrid Actors: Armed Groups and State Fragmentation in the Middle East*, New York, NY: The Century Foundation Press.

Carson, A. (2018) *Secret Wars: Covert Conflict in International Politics*, Princeton, NJ: Princeton University Press.

Centre for Humanitarian Dialogue (nd), 'Background on Activities in Ukraine'. Available at https://www.hdcentre.org/activities/ukraine/ (accessed 24 November 2019).

CIA (2000), 'CIA Activities in Chile'. Available at https://www.cia.gov/library/reports/general-reports-1/chile/ (accessed 21 May 2020).

Coll, S. (2018) *Directorate S: The C.I.A. and America's Secret Wars in Afghanistan and Pakistan*, New York: Penguin Press.

Collier, J. (2017) 'Proxy Actors in the Cyber Domain: Implications for State Strategy', *St Anthony's International Review*, 13(1): 25–47.

Corbeil, A. and Amarasinggam, A. (2016) 'The Houthi Hezbollah: Iran's Train-and-Equip Program in Sanaa', *Foreign Affairs*, 31 March.

De Soysa, I. (2017) 'Proxy Wars: Implications of Great-Power Rivalry for the Onset and Duration of Civil War', Norwegian University for Science and Technology (NTNU).

Dyer, G. (2014) 'Sanctions: War by Other Means', *Financial Times* (30 March). Available at https://www.ft.com/content/b18d2c74-b59e-11e3-81cb-00144feabdc0 (accessed 24 November 2019).

Feltman, J. (2019) *UN Envoys as Conductors, Not Soloists* Centre for Humanitarian Dialogue. Available at https://www.hdcentre.org/publications/un-envoys-as-conductors-not-soloists/ (accessed 24 November 2019).

Freedman, L. (2014) 'Ukraine and the Art of Limited War', *Survival*, 56(6): 7–38.

Freedman, L. (2015) *Strategy: A History*, Oxford: Oxford University Press.

Gartenstein-Ross, D., Fritz, J., Moreng, B. and Barr, N. (2015) *Islamic State vs. Al Qaeda: Strategic Dimensions of a Patricidal Conflict*, New America. Available at https://www.newamerica.org/international-security/policy-papers/islamic-state-vs-al-qaeda/ (accessed November 2019).

Gaub, F. (2017) *Arab Wars: Calculating the Costs*, European Union Institute for Security Studies. Available at https://www.iss.europa.eu/sites/default/files/EUISSFiles/Brief%2025%20Arab%20wars.pdf (accessed 24 November 2019).

Ghantous, G. (2019) 'Yemeni Government, Separatists Close to Deal on Ending Aden Stand-off', *Reuters*, October. Available at https://www.reuters.com/article/us-yemen-security/yemeni-government-separatists-close-to-deal-on-ending-aden-stand-off-sources-idUSKBN1WM0XF (accessed 24 November 2019).

Gordon, M. (2018) 'U.S. Seeks Arab Force and Funding for Syria', *The Wall Street Journal*, 16 April. Available at https://www.wsj.com/articles/u-s-seeks-arab-force-and-funding-for-syria-1523927888 (accessed 24 November 2019).

Harland, D. (2018) *The Lost Art of Peacemaking*, Centre for Humanitarian Dialogue. Available at https://www.hdcentre.org/publications/the-lost-art-of-peacemaking/ (accessed 24 November 2019).

Herbert, M. (2019) 'Libya's War becomes a Tech Battleground', Institute for Security Studies, Africa. Available at https://issafrica.org/iss-today/libyas-war-becomes-a-tech-battleground (accessed 24 November 2019).

Holbrook, R. (1998) *To End a War*, New York, NY: Random House.

Holsti, K.J. (1996) *The State, War and the State of War*, Cambridge: Cambridge University Press.

Hubbard, B. (2017) 'Iran Out to Remake Mideast With Arab Enforcer: Hezbollah', *The New York Times*, 27 August. Available at https://www.nytimes.com/2017/08/27/world/middleeast/hezbollah-iran-syria-israel-lebanon.html (accessed 24 November 2019).

Hughes, G. (2014) *My Enemy's Enemy: Proxy Warfare in International Politics*, Brighton; Portland, OR: Sussex Academic Press.

Indyk, M. (2019) 'Disaster in the Desert: Why Trump's Middle East Policy Can't Work', *Foreign Affairs*, November/December.

International Crisis Group (2018) *Iran's Priorities in a Turbulent Middle East, Middle East* Report No. 184. Available at https://www.crisisgroup.org/middle-east-north-africa/gulf-and-arabian-peninsula/iran/184-irans-priorities-turbulent-middle-east (accessed 24 November 2019).

Interview with Middle East expert, August 2019.

Interview with Libya expert, September 2019.

Irish, J. (2019), 'France, Britain, Egypt, UAE, U.S., Italy Call for Immediate End of Libya Violence', *Reuters*, 16 July. Available at https://www.reuters.com/article/us-libya-security/france-britain-egypt-uae-u-s-italy-call-for-immediate-end-of-libya-violence-idUSKCN1UB249 (accessed 20 January 2020).

Jaramillo, S. (2017) 'The Possibility of Peace', Lecture delivered at the Pearson Institute for the Study and Resolution of Global Conflicts, Chicago, IL, 24 March. Available at https://thepearsoninstitute.org/sites/default/files/2018-09/THE%20POSSIBILITY%20OF%20PEACE%20.pdf (accessed 24 November 2019).

Katz, B. (2019), *Imperfect Proxies: The Pros and Perils of Partnering with Non-State Actors for CT*, Centre for Strategic and International Studies (CSIS), 29 January. Available at https://www.csis.org/analysis/imperfect-proxies-pros-and-perils-partnering-non-state-actors-ct (accessed 20 January 2020).

Klasa A. et al (2019) 'Russia's Long Arm Reaches to the Right in Europe', *Financial Times*, 23 May. Available at https://www.ft.com/content/48c4bfa6-7ca2-11e9-81d2-f785092ab560 (accessed 24 November 2019).

Kornbluh, P. (2003) *The Pinochet File*, New York, NY: The New Press.

Krieg, A. (2016) 'Externalizing the Burden of War: The Obama Doctrine and US Foreign Policy in the Middle East', *International Affairs*, 92(1): 97–113.

Kuperman, A.J. (2008) 'The Moral Hazard of Humanitarian Intervention; Lessons from the Balkans', *International Studies Quarterly*, 52: 49–80.

Ladwig, W.C. (2017) *The Forgotten Front: Patron-Client Relationships in Counterinsurgency*, Cambridge: Cambridge University Press.

Lake, E. (2012) 'Inside the Hunt for Assad's Billions', *Daily Beast*. Available at https://www.thedailybeast.com/inside-the-hunt-for-assads-billions (accessed 24 November 2019).

Liddell-Hart, B. (1954) *Strategy: The Indirect Approach*, New York, NY: Praeger.

Liddell-Hart, B. (1967) *Strategy: The Indirect Approach*, London: Faber & Faber.

Lister, C. (2016) *The Free Syrian Army: A Decentralized Insurgent Brand*, The Brookings Project on US Relations with the Islamic World, No. 26, November. Available at https://www.brookings.edu/wp-content/uploads/2016/11/iwr_20161123_free_syrian_army.pdf (accessed 20 January 2020).

Loveman, C. (2002) 'Assessing the Phenomenon of Proxy Intervention', *Conflict, Security and Development*, 2(3): 29–48.

Malet, D. (2013) *Foreign Fighters: Transnational Identity in Civil Conflicts*, Oxford: Oxford University Press.

McManus, B. (2016) 'We Asked an Expert What Would Happen If Saudi Arabia and Iran Went to War', *Vice*, 14 January. Available at https://www.vice.com/en_us/article/av3qja/what-happens-if-saudia-arabia-and-iran-go-to-war (accessed 24 November 2019).

Mead, W. (2014) 'The Return of Geopolitics: The Revenge of the Revisionist Powers', *Foreign Affairs*, May/June.

Mishra, A. (2011) 'Indira Gandhi Helped Train Tamil Rebels, and Reaped Whirlwind', *First Post*. Available at https://www.firstpost.com/world/indira-gandhi-helped-train-tamil-rebels-and-reaped-whirlwind-13913.html (accessed 20 January 2020).

Moghadam, A. (2017) *Nexus of Global Jihad: Understanding Cooperation among Terrorist Actors*, Columbia Studies in Terrorism and Irregular Warfare, New York, NY: Columbia University Press.

Mumford, A. (2013a) *Proxy Warfare: War and Conflict in the Modern World*, Cambridge: Polity.

Mumford, A. (2013b) 'Proxy Warfare and the Future of Conflict', *The RUSI Journal*, 158(2): 40–46.

Mumford, A. (2017) 'The New Era of the Proliferated Proxy War', Real Clear Defence. Available at https://www.realcleardefense.com/articles/2017/11/16/the_new_era_of_the_proliferated_proxy_war_112648.html (accessed 24 November 2019).

Nichols, M. (2019) 'Russia Casts 13th Veto of UN Security Council Action During Syrian civil War', *Reuters*, 19 September. Available at https://uk.reuters.com/article/uk-syria-security-un/russia-casts-13th-veto-of-u-n-security-council-action-during-syrian-war-idUKKBN1W42CH (accessed 24 November 2019).

Nylander, D., Sandberd, R. and Tvedt, T. (2018) *Designing Peace; the Colombian Peace Process*, Norwegian Centre for Conflict Resolution (NOREF). Available at https://noref.no/Publications/Regions/Colombia/Designing-peace-the-Colombian-peace-process (accessed 15 November 2019).

Ollivant, D.A. and Gaston, E. (2019) 'The Problem with the Narrative of "Proxy War" in Iraq', War on the Rocks. Available at https://warontherocks.com/2019/05/the-problem-with-the-narrative-of-proxy-war-in-iraq/ (accessed 24 November 2019).

Oslo Forum (2017) *Peacemaking in a New Era of Geopolitics*, Centre for Humanitarian Dialogue. Available at https://www.hdcentre.org/wp-content/uploads/2017/11/OF-Report-2017.pdf (accessed 24 November 2019).

Oslo Forum (2018) *The End of the Big Peace? Opportunities for Mediation*, Centre for Humanitarian Dialogue. Available at https://www.hdcentre.org/wp-content/uploads/2018/12/Oslo-Forum-2018-Meeting-Report.pdf (accessed 24 November 2019).

Oweis, K.Y. (2015) *Sieges and Ceasefires in Syria's Civil War: Lessons Learned as Regional Players Undermine New Approach by UN Mediator*, German Institute for International and Security Affairs [Stiftung Wissenschaft und Politik].

Pfaff, C.A. (2017a) 'Proxy War Ethics', *Journal of National Security Law and Policy*, 9(2): 305–53.

Pfaff, C.A. (2017b) 'Strategic Insights: Proxy War Norms', Strategic Studies Institute (blog). Available at https://publications.armywarcollege.edu/pubs/3518.pdf (accessed 24 November 2019).

Pfaff, C.A. and Granfield, P. (2019) 'The Moral Peril of Proxy Wars', *Foreign Policy*. Available at https://foreignpolicy.com/2019/04/05/proxy-wars-are-never-moral/ (accessed November 2019).

Popper, N. (2019) 'Terrorists Turn to Bitcoin for Funding, and They're Learning Fast', *The New York Times*, 18 August. Available at https://www.nytimes.com/2019/08/18/technology/terrorists-bitcoin.html (accessed 24 November 2019).

Reliefweb (2020a) 'UN Security Council Fails to Support Global Ceasefire, Shows No Response to COVID-19'. Available at: https://reliefweb.int/report/world/un-security-council-fails-support-global-ceasefire-shows-no-response-covid-19 (accessed 6 June 2020).

Reliefweb (2020b) 'Salvaging the Security Council's coronavirus response'. Available at: https://reliefweb.int/report/world/salvaging-security-council-s-coronavirus-response (accessed 7 August 2020).

Rondeaux, C. and Sterman, D. (2019) *Twenty-First Century Proxy Warfare; Confronting Strategic Innovation in a Multipolar World Since the 2011 NATO Intervention*, New America. Available at https://www.newamerica.org/international-security/reports/twenty-first-century-proxy-warfare-confronting-strategic-innovation-multipolar-world/ (accessed 24 November 2019).

Salehyan, I. (2010) 'The Delegation of War to Rebel Organizations', *Journal of Conflict Resolution*, 54(3): 493–515.

Salehyan, I. (2011) *Rebels without Borders: Transnational Insurgencies in World Politics* Ithaca, NY: Cornell University Press.

Salehyan, I. and Gleditsch, K.S. (2006) 'Refugees and the Spread of Civil War', *International Organization*, 60(2): 335–66.

Salehyan, I., Siroky, D. and Wood, R.M. (2014) 'External Rebel Sponsorship and Civilian Abuse: A Principal-Agent Analysis of Wartime Atrocities', *International Organization* 68(3): 633–661.

Shaheen, K. (2016) 'Russia-Turkey Ceasefire Deal Offers Hope of Survival for Residents', *The Guardian* (14 December). Available at https://www.theguardian.com/world/2016/dec/13/deal-reached-to-evacuate-rebels-and-civilians-from-aleppo (accessed 24 November 2019).

Slaughter, A.M. (2017) *The Chessboard and the Web: Strategies of Connection in a Networked World*, New Haven, CT: Yale University Press.

Sokkhoeurn, A. (2010) 'Conflict Resolution in Cambodia', CICP Working Paper No 5: Cambodian Institute for Cooperation and Peace.

Sterman, D. and Rosenblatt, N. (2018) *All Jihad Is Local: Volume II: ISIS in North Africa and the Arabian Peninsula*, New America. Available at https://www.newamerica.org/international-security/policy-papers/all-jihad-local-volume-ii/ (accessed 24 November 2019).

Steward, C. (2011) 'Russia Accuses NATO of "Expanding" UN Libya Resolution', *The Independent*, 5 July. Available at https://www.independent.co.uk/news/world/africa/russia-accuses-nato-of-expanding-un-libya-resolution-2306996.html (accessed 24 November 2019).

Stewart, P. and Lewis, A. (2019) 'Exclusive: U.S. Says Drone Shot Down by Russian Air Defenses Near Libyan Capital', *Reuters*, 7 December. Available at https://www.reuters.com/article/us-usa-libya-russia-drone-exclusive/exclusive-u-s-says-drone-shot-down-by-russian-air-defenses-near-libyan-capital-idUSKBN1YB04W (accessed 20 January 2020).

Sukhankin, S. (2018) *'Continuing War by Other Means': The Case of Wagner, Russia's Premier Private Military Company in the Middle East*, Jamestown Foundation. Available at https://jamestown.org/program/continuing-war-by-other-means-the-case-of-wagner-russias-premier-private-military-company-in-the-middle-east/ (accessed 24 November 2019).

Sylvers, E. (2015) 'Libya's War Rages, but Eni Keeps Pumping Oil', *Wall Street Journal*, 7 April. Available at https://www.wsj.com/articles/libyas-war-rages-but-eni-keeps-pumping-oil-1428428079 (accessed 24 November 2019).

Towle, P. (1981) 'The Strategy of War by Proxy', *RUSI Journal*, 126/1.

Tzu, S. (1910) *The Art of War* (L Giles trans.), Leicester: Allande Online Publishing (2000 edn).

UNHCR (2018) *Global Trends, Forced Displacement in 2018*. Available at https://www.unhcr.org/globaltrends2018/ (accessed 24 November 2019).

United Nations (2020) Security Council Resolution 2532. Available at: https://undocs.org/en/S/RES/2532(2020) (accessed 7 August 2020).

Velina, J. (2019) 'Afghanistan: The Forgotten Proxy War', GlobalResearch, Centre for Research on Globalization.

Walsh, D. (2020) 'By Air and Sea, Mercenaries Landed in Libya. Then the Plan Went South', *New York Times*, 25 May. Available at https://www.nytimes.com/2020/05/25/world/middleeast/libya-mercenaries-arms-embargo.html (accessed 25 May 2020).

Weinstein, J. (2012) *Inside Rebellion; The Politics of Insurgent Violence*, Cambridge: Cambridge University Press.

Wherey, F. (2018) *Burning Shores: Inside the Battle for the New Libya*, New York, NY: Farrar, Straus, Girour.

Whitfield, T. (2015) *The Basque Conflict and ETA, The Difficulties of an Ending*, Special Report 384, Washington, DC: United States Institute of Peace.

Whitfield, T. (2019) *Mediating in a Complex World*, Centre for Humanitarian Dialogue. Available at https://www.hdcentre.org/publications/mediating-in-a-complex-world/ (accessed 24 November 2019).

Yesley, M.O. (2011) 'Bipolarity, Proxy Wars, and the Rise of China', *Strategic Studies Quarterly*, 5(4): 75–91.

Zartman, I.W. (2001) 'The Timing of Peace Initiatives: Hurting Stalemates and Ripeness', *Global Review of Ethnopolitics*, 1(1): 8–18.

13

Towards a More Integrated Approach? Cooperation Among the UN, AU and IGAD in Mediation Support

Jamie Pring

Introduction

While the number of guidance notes on peace mediation (UN, 2012) and types of mediation support actors (Mason and Sguaitamatti, 2011) has grown in the past, the institutional capacity of the UN and other regional organizations to provide 'effective support' has been relatively limited (Whitfield, 2015). The establishment of mediation support mechanisms gained momentum only in the past 15 years, most notably with the establishment of the UN Mediation Support Unit (MSU) in 2006. The UN MSU's establishment 'led to the rapid understanding of the utility of a standing support structure for good offices, conflict prevention and mediation efforts of an envoy' (Whitfield, 2015) and inspired other international organizations to create or revitalize their own mediation structures, including the European Union (EU) Mediation Support Team, the Organization for Security and Co-operation in Europe (OSCE) Conflict Prevention Centre, the various mediation support structures of African sub-regional organizations, and the African Union (AU) Peace and Security Council, among other examples.

Among the many challenges for developing effective mediation and mediation support, three are relevant for this chapter. The first challenge is that the multiple mediation support efforts by international organizations, states and international NGOs have resulted in a 'crowded field' characterized by overlaps, uncoordinated action and competition (Lanz and Gasser, 2013). In addition to the UN, continental and regional organizations have emerged as dominant mediating actors. To address this particular challenge, mediation structures of these actors have strengthened cooperation in knowledge management, training, and networking in mediation (following the categorization of mediation support of Lehmann-Larsen, 2014).

The second challenge is that despite the growth of these institutionalized mediation structures and principles of coordination among them, the fundamental decision of whether and when to mediate in an actual conflict remains a political decision by the organization's member states and outside the purview of the secretariat and technical experts that build up mediation support institutional capacities. Partnership efforts to streamline and integrate efforts of MSUs are centred on the coordination of technical assets once a mediation mission has been mandated, but not coordination in deciding on such mandates. As Nathan observes, 'partnerships are being built between the organization's secretariats and not at the vastly more important level of the member states' decisionmaking bodies' (Nathan, 2017: 160). Mediation practitioners have long noted the importance of a political decision before launching their initiatives and have focused on technical expertise. These efforts remain deliberately separate from the political decision making, and the link between the technical and the political remains under-examined in inter-organizational coordination in mediation support.

Lastly, the third challenge is the lack of order among standards and norms that aim to guide effective coordination among mediation actors. Mediation actors have developed various guidelines outlining principles of cooperation and coordination in mediation support. However, different norms also can conflict with one another and propose diverging prescriptions. For example, subsidiarity and primacy appear as two seemingly conflicting norms, where the former is the basis for the leadership of regional organizations, while the latter provides grounds for the leadership of the UN in the integrated mediation effort. The confusion as to who should lead in a mediation effort has been a product of the push and pull between these norms (Nathan, 2016).

This chapter aims to examine the link between technical cooperation, political decision making, and norms in understanding coordination and cooperation among mediating international organizations. It attempts to bridge the gap between the technical and the political through an eclectic understanding of the function of norms. In a two-level analysis, it first builds from a realist understanding of international organizations and norms, where member states' interests and strategic calculations guide the decisions of international organizations, in this case, on the mandate to mediate in a particular conflict and which norms to uphold. The first argument is that member states' strategic calculations guide the decision of an organization to lead in a mediation process and uphold the ordering principle.

On the second level, the normative claim backing up the political decision influences which technical assets, regardless of whether they are unique pre-existing, or need to be built from scratch, are deployed in support of the mediation process. In this second level of analysis, norms are a necessary intermediate factor between political decisions and the division of technical functions and assets. Norms arguably serve as a necessary link given that while other mediating states and organizations can contest the lead organization based on power and efficiency grounds, they can be compelled not to do so to avoid violating the invoked ordering principle.

In particular, this chapter examines the case of the Inter-Governmental Authority on Development (IGAD) and its mediation in South Sudan from 2013 to 2015. It analyses the strategic calculations of IGAD member states in the decision-making processes leading to the launch of the mediation in South Sudan in 2013 and in coordinating among the different mediation efforts of IGAD, the UN and the AU in this mediation process. It argues that the decision for IGAD to lead and uphold the principle of subsidiarity, particularly IGAD regional ownership,[1] was guided by the strategic calculations of IGAD's Big Four – Ethiopia, Uganda, Sudan and Kenya – which are South Sudan's immediate neighbours. Consequently, the principle of subsidiarity guided other actors such as the AU and the UN in specializing in support roles, maximizing existing assets that can support the IGAD-led mediation, and even shrinking already existing ones that overlap with the new IGAD mandate and functions.

This chapter is divided into three sections. The first section further discusses the gap between realpolitik decision making and functional integration and introduces a conceptual framework that links functional, power-based and normative factors in operational mediation support. The second section illustrates these linkages in the IGAD-led mediation process

[1] Subsidiarity can be invoked by both the AU and its RECs. The specific form of subsidiarity under study is IGAD's regional ownership.

in South Sudan from 2013 to 2015. The last section concludes with a summary of the main arguments as applied in IGAD and the findings' possible contribution in studying decision making and coordination in mediation processes at the general level.

Bridging the Perceived Gap Between the Technical and the Realpolitik: a Framework for the Role of Norms

In order to address the challenges of multiple mediation actors operating in one conflict context, technical experts and staff of the different mediation structures of states and international organizations work together to institutionalize cooperation with one another. These forms of cooperation come in the form of cultivating networks of mediation actors, establishing regular channels of communication and knowledge sharing, and engaging in joint training, among others. This form of cooperation aims to pool resources, maximize each mediation actor's comparative advantage and minimize collective action problems, such as redundancies, discoordination and even conflict, in the process of combining these mediation structures' resources.

For example, the UN MSU has played a central role in supporting mediation networks such as the Group of Friends of Mediation, a network of 51 member states, the United Nations, and seven regional organizations and other international organizations promoting a culture of mediation in their national and international policies, and fostering dialogue and cooperation among key mediation support actors through convening senior experts' meetings and facilitating knowledge exchange between regional organizations. The UN MSU also works closely with the Mediation Support Network (MSN), a global network of primarily non-governmental organizations that support mediation in peace negotiations (UN Department of Political Affairs, n.d.). The MSN meetings and similar gatherings promote regular interaction among mediation practitioners and facilitate the exchange of research findings and reflections on mediation processes around the world, and by doing so, foster collaboration among them (Mediation Support Network, n.d.). From an inter-organizational perspective, in 2015 the UN and the IGAD agreed to further cooperation in 'conducting joint analysis, sharing information and expertise on mediation processes as well as exploring further opportunities for capacity development' (IGAD and UN, 2015). The two organizations, together with the AU, also signed a Memorandum of Understanding underlining areas of cooperation (IGAD, 2010).

Minding the Gap: Functional Cooperation Among Mediation Structures vs Realpolitik Decision Making Among Member States

The common premise behind these forms of inter-organizational cooperation is its functional approach to addressing the integration of mediation efforts. The functionalist approach assumes that states can work towards a peaceful world society through gradual and pragmatic cooperation in technical and economic activities. The functionalist approach captures the prominent problem-solving discourse in envisioning cooperation among mediation support actors. This approach acknowledges that organizations indeed share a common concern and mandate to promote peace and security within their areas. As there is a general agreement to deal with common issues, in this case to promote peace, cooperation and integration of efforts are treated as technical and even apolitical endeavours (Biermann, 2008; Koops, 2012; Klabbers, 2014). The functional approach also points to the advantages of the adaptability of existing institutional assets (Wallander, 2000) in order to minimize inefficiencies from 'reinventing the wheel'.

Functionalism's focus on technical capabilities and efficiency resonates well with the calls by mediation actors to clarify roles and division of labour, to 'maximise the value and comparative advantage of the external actors' (ACCORD and AU, 2014: 59) and observe 'coherence, coordination, and complementarity in mediation efforts' (UN, 2012: 18). Given the UN's comparative advantage in terms of robust institutional capabilities, the functionalist approach can explain how the UN leads in assisting other international organizations such as the AU and its regional economic communities (RECs) in institutionalizing mediation support. The UN has provided assistance and technical support to the AU, including on formulating the AU's mediation strategy and operationalizing the AU Panel of the Wise (UN Office to the AU, n.d.).

However, when it comes to actual mediation processes, the UN, despite its comparative advantage in terms of institutional assets, need not lead an integrated mediation effort, and regional organizations have often led despite having relatively less capacity. In the Horn of Africa, IGAD has relatively minimal institutional capacities in mediation support but has often taken the lead when providing operational support to mediation processes in the region. For most of its history, IGAD offered operational support to mediation processes through ad hoc bodies that only later developed as specialized offices in the home country of the lead IGAD mediating country. For example, the Secretariat for the IGAD Peace Process on the Sudan and the Office of the Facilitator for Somalia Peace and National Reconciliation have their head offices in Nairobi, with satellite offices in Sudan and Somalia, respectively. Meanwhile the Office of the Special Envoy for South Sudan is based in Ethiopia.

In terms of support to actual mediation processes, functional considerations such as existing assets and comparative advantage are not sufficient to explain a decision to mediate. Instead, secretariat and technical experts point to the importance of the choice of the member states based on their strategic calculations of the specific conflict at hand (Confidential sources, 2019). In this regard, understanding the decision on whether or not to launch or lead a mediation process in a particular context falls outside of functional concerns. Instead, such lands in the realm of realist theorizing (such as Krasner, 1976; Gilpin, 1983; Mearsheimer, 1994/95). In contrast to the functional approach, the realist approach submits that the decision of whether, when and how to mediate in a particular conflict is based on the member states' assessment that mediation is the most effective way to protect or further state power, whether this power means resources or status in the international system, and that the international organization in question can deliver (Nathan, 2010). Hence, cooperation in actual mediation support, unlike the order of cooperation in training, knowledge management, and networking, among others, is not sufficiently explained by efficiency concerns, but more as a decision based on member states' power calculations. Away from the secretariat, these decisions put member states of international organizations as the decision makers, and this decision-making process is less streamlined.

There are thus two contrasting observations in the development and integration of mediation capacity. On the one hand, there is the dynamic institution building of mediation support through the establishment of mediation structures and technical cooperation among them, where integration efforts are concentrated. On the other hand, one aspect is stagnant, where member states in one international organization are 'muddling along' the decision to engage and provide mediation support depending on the context (Nathan, 2017: 159).

Bridging the Gap? An Eclectic Understanding of Norms to Bridge Functional Cooperation and Realist Decision Making

To bridge these two parallel trends, different norms for establishing order and integration have been examined, such as subsidiarity and primacy. Subsidiarity or regional ownership implies that the primary responsibility for peace and security in the region lies with regional organizations (O'Brien, 2000; Sibanda, 2007; Nathan, 2016). Meanwhile, primacy upholds the status of the UN as the final decision-making authority in matters of peace and security (UN, 1945; Nathan, 2017).

In constructivist theorizing, norms are 'collective expectations about proper behavior for a given identity' (Katzenstein, 1996: 15) and have been studied to have prescriptive, regulative and constitutive functions. Norms are prescriptive in that they describe behaviour that is imperative, *ought* to be performed, or appropriate for a given identity. Norms are regulative in that they incentivize the performance of certain behaviour and/or constrain other actions, therefore guiding how actors pursue their interests. Lastly, norms can have a constitutive function in that they can define the interests in the first place (Finnemore and Sikkink, 1998).

Through these functions, norms can enable functional cooperation. For example, the principles of coherence, complementarity and comparative advantage can have a 'constitutive effect' on functional concerns in that they help define what organizational assets can be considered advantageous and what can be liabilities in a mediation process. These constitutive norms support the approach that mediation support assets unique and/or most optimal in one organization should work together with another's in order to jointly address the conflict context in a manner that minimizes redundancies and conflicting efforts (Ancas, 2011; UN, 2012).

However, norms and functional considerations do not go always go hand in hand. Norms may also have a conflicting relationship with function when actors, acting in accordance with norms, act on reasons other than arriving at the most optimal solution in terms of efficiency, and comparative advantage, or other such functional concerns. Rather, actors may act based on the prescriptive function of the norm, prioritizing the appropriateness of such actions despite inefficiencies. For example, an organization might observe the norm of subsidiarity even where it means that another organization with less technical capacity leads the mediation effort. Here, compliance with norms may also generate sub-optimal processes such as redistribution of assets or shrinking of existing assets to make way for one built from scratch.

While adherence to norms can explain why existing cooperation and deployed assets are sub-optimal, looking at the constructivist theorizing of norms alone is unreliable in explaining political decision making in operational mediation support. Norms have been inconsistently observed (Nathan, 2013), are unclear or can oppose one another. In terms of clarity, the principle of subsidiarity can be invoked by a continental organization such as the AU or one of the AU's RECs. In terms of conflicting relationships, the principles of subsidiarity and primacy can show a tug-of-war between the UN and the regional organizations.

Instead of studying states' strategic calculations, functional cooperation, and norms, separately or in pairs, this chapter brings back the realist conceptualization of norms, where norms are treated as resulting from states' strategic calculations, to link these three dimensions. The resulting conceptual framework develops a two-stage analysis with norms as an intermediate factor bridging strategic decision making and technical cooperation in operational mediation support (see Figure 13.1).

In the first level of analysis, member states' strategic calculations play a crucial role in determining which organizations will take the lead and, relatedly, which norms will be upheld. This is consistent with the analysis that member states need to be convinced that the organization would best promote or protect their interest as well as an agreement on the principles of how such actions are carried out (Nathan, 2010). In the second level of analysis, the principles emanating from the political decision guide technical cooperation, by guiding the definition of advantageous assets (constitutive), providing boundaries within which organizations act and interact (regulative), and creating standards to evaluate organizations' actions and interactions (prescriptive).

Figure 13.1: Conceptualizing the relationship among strategic calculations, norms and technical cooperation in operational mediation support cooperation among international organizations

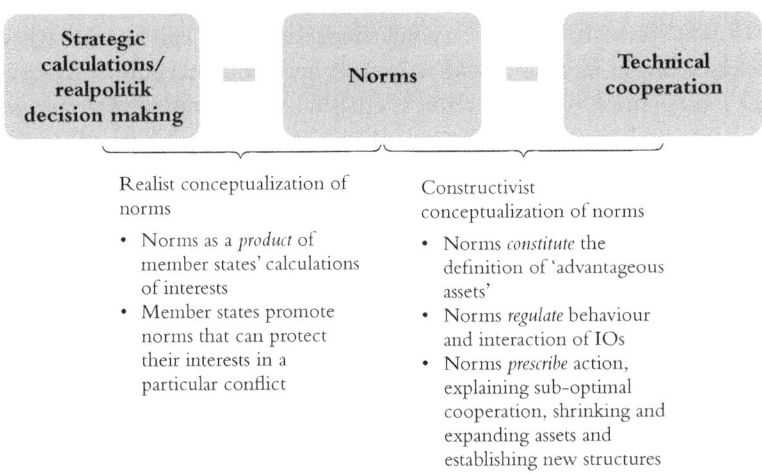

Examining Cooperation Among the UN, AU and IGAD in Mediation in the Horn of Africa: the Mediation Process in South Sudan

The dynamics among interests, norms and functional coordination are observable in the IGAD-led mediation in South Sudan (2013–15). IGAD initially prided itself as a competent peacemaker in its region after having brokered the 2005 Comprehensive Peace Agreement (CPA) between the government of Sudan and the Sudan People's Liberation Army (SPLM), which led to the independence of South Sudan. However, on 15 December 2013 violence once again erupted in South Sudan's capital, Juba, because of tensions between the President, Salva Kiir, and then former Vice President, Riek Machar Teny, both members of the ruling party, the SPLM. The CPA's long-term success and the credibility of a regionally owned peace process hung in the balance. IGAD, the AU and the UN have a long-standing presence in South Sudan and conducted their own political missions to prevent the escalation of the conflict prior to December 2013. These three organizations were all capable of assuming a mediating role.

Member States' Strategic Calculations: Identifying the Lead Mediating Actor and Upholding the IGAD Regional Ownership Norm

IGAD Member States have varied geopolitical interests in the South Sudan conflict (Apuuli, 2015). In launching the mediation process in South Sudan, observers noted a desire from the IGAD member states to have peace in the country, but the vision of how such peace would look varied among member states. Each of the 'Big 4' member states in IGAD – Ethiopia, Kenya, Sudan and Uganda – have particular national interests in the country, which, in turn, shape their desired outcome of the talks.

Ethiopia is driven both by national political interest as well as prestige. As a land-locked country, Ethiopia relies on its neighbours, all the IGAD member states except Uganda, for its economic activities (port access in Djibouti and Mombasa in Kenya, oil in the Sudans, and access to the large Kenyan market). Hence, keeping good neighbourly relations is paramount. Gambella, the Ethiopian region bordering South Sudan, has been home to Nuer communities, Riek Machar's tribe, and, before the 2013 war, the second-largest tribe in Gambella. With the influx of mostly Nuer refugees, many of whom have been granted Ethiopian passports, the Nuer has now grown to challenge the Agnuak, which previously dominated the politics in Gambella (Feyissa, 2014). Apart from these geopolitical interests, Ethiopia is the current chair of IGAD, and its national strategy documents have articulated its desire to play a regional role. Given such a multifaceted stake in South Sudan, key considerations are addressing Nuer grievances, keeping good neighbourly relations and showing a prominent Ethiopian peacemaking role in the region (Confidential source, 2016b; Confidential source, 2017a; Confidential source, 2017b).

Kenya has been home to many South Sudanese diaspora communities and was home to the SPLM when the Ethiopian government stopped its support around the 1990s. Its interest is mainly economic in that the new state of South Sudan was seen as a new market, and Kenyan investments quickly poured into the country before and after its independence, including establishing its national banks in Juba. South Sudan was the fourth-largest market for Kenya among the Common Market for East and Southern Africa (COMESA) members (Odhiambo and Muluvi, 2014). Many of these Kenyan businesses and banks were looted and destroyed during the conflict.

South Sudan's ties are closest and most extensive with Sudan, the country from which it seceded. Seeing South Sudan's independence in 2011 as a set-back, the Khartoum government aims to keep South Sudan under its sphere of influence in all its engagements. Ninety-eight per cent of South Sudan's economy lies in oil, which is refined and transported in processing plants and pipelines in Sudan (de Waal, 2014). Keeping South Sudan in its sphere of influence entails empowering the opposition and keeping the government of South Sudan in check.

South Sudan has also been an extension of the conflict between Sudan and Uganda. Uganda sees South Sudan as a buffer between its territory and the Lord's Resistance Army (LRA), which Sudan supported through funds, armaments and other equipment (Apuuli, 2014). Uganda has supported the SPLM from the very beginning of its fight against Sudan, and Presidents Museveni of Uganda and Kiir of South Sudan have developed strong personal ties. Riek Machar's role as a mediator in the Juba Peace Talks for the LRA did not win him favour with the Ugandan government, which accused Machar of using the talks to negotiate for the escape of LRA members. Uganda has strongly articulated its support for the government of President Kiir and does not favour any solution with Riek Machar reinstalled as Vice President (Taylor, 2016).

Hence, South Sudan was not only a battlefield for the government of South Sudan and the SPLM-IO but also for the 'Big 4' IGAD member states, whose national interests ride on either of the two. During the 23rd Extraordinary Meeting of the IGAD Heads of States and Government, IGAD Heads of States, despite having their own differences, agreed that IGAD would take the lead in the mediation process and uphold the principle of subsidiarity, particularly IGAD regional ownership. The deliberations show open concern about the importance of the regional impact of the conflict on these IGAD neighbours, in addition to IGAD being the broker of the previous agreement between Sudan and now South Sudan (IGAD, 2016).

Promoting its own version of the principle of subsidiarity, IGAD particularly chose to uphold IGAD regional ownership given the geopolitical constellation. As a security complex (Zeru, 2015), the high interdependence among States in the Horn of Africa on matters of security makes IGAD and, in particular, the Heads of States' meetings, a viable venue at which these member states pursue their interests. South Sudan and several IGAD member states are members of other regional organizations such as the East African Community (EAC) or the ICGLR, except for Ethiopia, which, as mentioned, has vital stakes in the peace on the shared border. In the absence of a regional hegemon, the consensus-building approach in most of the IGAD Heads of States' deliberations ensures that each of their positions is considered in the process of crafting the resolutions (Confidential source, 2016a), minimizing contestation against decisions that result through such a process. While they may need to accommodate their immediate neighbours' interests, regional ownership nonetheless allows these member states to keep their collective authority as the final decision maker in matters of peace and security, away from other bodies such as the UN and the AU, which host a wider (and more influential) set of actors (Francis, 2005; Healy, 2009).

The decision was published in the IGAD Communiqué of 27 December 2013 that mandated the mediation and in which it was stated that the summit 'commends the UN Security Council Resolution 2132 of 2013 which it notes as a prudent and timely move to *complement* on-going political efforts in alleviating the deteriorating security situation in the country'. The summit also made the decision that the UN, the AU, and the 'International Community' should '*support the IGAD process*' (IGAD, 2013: 3–4, author's emphasis). The Communiqué also established a mediation team that operated separately from the IGAD MSU and reported directly to the Heads of States. It also reiterated its call for the international community to support the 'IGAD-led' process, the term being repeated in several issuances (such as IGAD, 2014a, 2014b). Similar statements were reiterated in the IGAD Special Envoys' meetings with international organizations and state supporters such as the UN, the EU and the Troika countries (Norway, the United Kingdom (UK) and the United States (US)).

In deciding which organization to lead, the realist take on international organizations and norms as instruments of forwarding strategic calculations holds. The next section will illustrate how the role of subsidiarity, and particularly IGAD regional ownership, once politically decided, guided cooperation among organizations.

Regional Ownership: Defining Assets, Regulating Interactions, and Shrinking Already Robust Institutions to Make Way for New Initiatives

International observers and peace process supporters were aware of the salience of the strategic calculations of IGAD member states in the South Sudan conflict. They nonetheless supported the launch of the IGAD-led process, citing the benefit of regional ownership, which is that regional ownership would increase the buy-in of regional neighbours that can help sustain the peace (Confidential source, 2017a; Confidential source, 2017b). However, doubts about such benefits grew the longer the IGAD-led talks stagnated. The challenges of the mediation emanated not only from the conflict parties, but from the differences within the IGAD Heads of States as well, given their divergent national stakes and optimal outcomes on the issue (African Arguments, 2014; Apuuli, 2015).

To revive the talks and partly to minimize the effects of IGAD Summit disagreements, separate initiatives were launched, including those by influential states and organizations with more leverage. One of these other initiatives has been viewed as conflicting: specifically, the intra-SPLM talks, which focused on the SPLM and undermined the participation of other stakeholders, such as civil society, participating in the IGAD-led mediation. This process was eventually led by non-IGAD AU members such as Tanzania and South Africa and was called the Arusha Process. Mediation supporters also explored ideas alternative to the IGAD-led process, such as elevating the mediation to the AU, and transferring the talks to Washington DC as a process that upholds regional *co*-ownership, instead of regional ownership, allowing a more direct role for the US (Aromi, 2018; Vertin, 2019). Even in direct support of the IGAD-led talks, furthermore, there were separate attempts by the international community to meet with the warring parties and stakeholders that often conflicted with the gains in the IGAD-led mediation. One informant mentioned that after the IGAD-led talks during the day, "in the evening, they [the international community] would meet with one of the parties over drinks and tell them so many things. Then they [the negotiating parties] come back the day after saying they have changed their minds about certain agreements they made the day before" (Confidential source, 2017b).

Invoking IGAD regional ownership, IGAD consolidated the actors under the IGAD-Plus. Proposed by the lead mediator, Ambassador Mesfin of Ethiopia, and approved by the IGAD Heads of State, the IGAD-Plus format invited the Troika (the US, the UK and Norway), the AU, the UN and the EU to attend and participate in the talks. By having the 'Plus' countries participate directly in working-level meetings and deliberations, it centralized the efforts of the 'Plus' countries, with their political and economic leverage, to work not only in getting the warring parties' acquiescence, but also to make sure that IGAD member states followed up on their collective decisions.

Nonetheless, the 'process remained an IGAD-led peace process, providing an African solution to the crisis but with partners playing their own role to support the peace process' (Government of Ethiopia, 2015). The IGAD-Plus was also a response to the international community's growing criticism of the regionally owned process over several missed deadlines, deadlocks and recession of the talks. As one informant mentioned, "IGAD-Plus was a way … so we can say, 'if we fail, we fail together'" (Confidential source, 2017a).

In IGAD's continued call for upholding regional ownership under the IGAD-Plus, the efforts of the UN and AU became more integrated with the process. However, instead of expanding already existing robust UN and AU operational assets in South Sudan, such as the comprehensive UN Mission in South Sudan (UNMISS) or the AU Office in Juba, these organizations adjusted to support IGAD's ownership in a way that downsized these pre-existing institutional assets.

After successfully brokering the CPA's signing in 2005, IGAD transferred the responsibility for implementing the CPA to the AU. The AU then developed institutional assets and resources such as the AU Office in Juba, which, in terms of technical capabilities, such as a standing facility in the context and pool of experts in-house, could be used to address the 2013 conflict in the South as part of the overall mandate of successfully seeing the CPA through. However, IGAD aimed to secure its leadership in the peace process through swift actions, most especially by immediately mandating a new mediation mission and calling for other members of the international community to 'complement' IGAD's efforts (IGAD, 2013). These efforts provided a clear and early indication of who would lead in the Southern conflict. Instead of bolstering the AU Office in Juba, the IGAD Communiqué of December 2013 established the IGAD Office of the Special Envoys for South Sudan, composed of high-profile mediators that led in IGAD's previous peacemaking endeavours, including the CPA. Brokering the previous CPA peace process may have risked the impartiality of the mediator (one of the fundamental norms in mediation according to the UN) given that the desire to prove the previous mediation's success may lead to perceptions of bias towards the ruling government established under the CPA over the opposition. Conversely, in line with regional ownership, IGAD considered its previous experience and sharing a stake in the South Sudan peace process a beneficial element in fully grasping the regional implications of unresolved conflict in the new state and coming up with sustainable solutions (Confidential source, 2017b).

Nonetheless, while parallel processes emerged and were initiated by non-IGAD AU members, IGAD kept institutional cooperation with the AU through the High-Level ad hoc Committee (Sudan Tribune, 2015) and the AU Commission of Inquiry on South Sudan (AUCISS). The AUCISS was mandated to 'investigate the human rights violations and other abuses committed during the armed conflict in South Sudan and make recommendations on the best ways and means to ensure accountability, reconciliation and healing among all South Sudanese communities' (Deng, 2015), which complements IGAD in its statement that people responsible for atrocities will not be permitted to serve in the transitional government (Chonghaile, 2015). At the time when the report was to be presented to the AU Political-Security Community, the Ethiopian Prime Minister, Hailemariam Desalegn, raised a motion to defer the discussion and publication of the report to avoid the then ongoing IGAD-led peace process. While this attests to the benefits of IGAD member states' dual membership both in IGAD and the AU, President Jacob Zuma of South Africa (a non-IGAD member) also seconded this motion along with President Yoweri Museveni (Deng, 2015). Although there are criticisms of postponing the consideration and release of the AUCISS report, this nonetheless demonstrates the two organizations' similar priority of protecting the regional peace process.

Meanwhile, the UN has also maintained a strong and long-term presence in South Sudan through the UN Mission in the Sudan (UNMIS) in 2005 to help implement the CPA as well as through the UNMISS in 2011 to assist the new state of South Sudan after its independence. While most of the mission consists of military personnel, UNMISS has been under civilian leadership to the level of the Special Representative of the Secretary General. Its mandate went beyond military-related concerns such as civil protection and humanitarian intervention to foster 'longer-term state building and economic development … support the Government in exercising its responsibility for conflict prevention, mitigation, and resolution … and help the authorities in developing capacity to provide security, establishing the rule of law and strengthening the security and justice sectors …' (UN Security Council, 1996, 2011). Similar to the existing AU office, and given this broad mandate, the mission could also take on a peacemaking function. However, after the fighting in 2013, UNMISS's mandate was extended in 2014 but was also limited to monitoring, humanitarian relief, civilian protection and providing logistical and personnel support to the IGAD-brokered ceasefire (UN Mission in South Sudan, n.d.; UN Security Council, 2014).

In terms of dealing with other assets and parallel initiatives by other actors, invoking regional ownership enabled the outcomes of the Arusha Process to be subsumed under the agreement made in the IGAD-led process in Addis Ababa. While the conflict parties agreed to the reunification of the SPLM in Arusha, which could arguably be adequate to silence the guns among the armed factions (Awolich, 2015; Mabor, 2015), the IGAD-Plus provided continued pressure for the conflict parties to go to Addis Ababa and negotiate on the broader institutional reforms beyond the party. Invoking regional ownership also helped hinder the realization of transferring the process to Washington DC. When initially consulting members of the international community on the viability of such transfer to the US capital, Vertin notes that while there was enthusiasm on the potential greater leverage provided by a closer US role, members of the international community were not openly supporting it, citing the norm of regional ownership (Vertin, 2019). In this scenario, despite a viable peace from intra-party reunification or prospects for greater access to leverage from a global power, the international community still gravitated towards working with the IGAD-led process in the name of regional ownership.

Notwithstanding criticisms of the peace process, the organization's ability to rally the international community, including the UN and the AU, especially under the regionally owned IGAD-Plus mechanism, suggests the importance of IGAD's effective signalling of intent to uphold its ownership of the peace process from the beginning. While there are already existing AU and UN institutional assets on the ground, these two organizations launched ad hoc initiatives, limited these assets' mandates and, as in the AUCISS report, acquiesced in the timing of information, to complement rather than usurp the IGAD-led peace process. This illustrates that once invoked, the norm of regional ownership guided how existing institutional assets are implemented and modified, often in ways that do not maximize existing comparatively advantageous resources and institutional assets.

What can also be observed is that other actors, such as the US and several non-IGAD AU countries, were willing to contest IGAD leadership, given the obstacles posed by IGAD member states' strategic calculations. However, these parallel efforts were tempered and subsumed under IGAD by invoking the norm of regional ownership. This suggests that while strategic calculations drove the decision on who would lead the mediation, maintaining such leadership in terms of coordinating with other actors required invoking the principle of subsidiarity, particularly IGAD regional ownership.

Conclusions: Towards an Integrated Approach? Addressing the Gap Between Current and Envisioned Cooperation

In this chapter, the analysis of mediation support capabilities development and decision making drew attention to the applicability of both functional and realist approaches as well as their limitations if used in isolation. While the development of norms, such as subsidiarity and primacy, seeks to address coordination issues in mediation support, the constructivist view of norms is not self-sufficient and needs to be supplemented by a realist understanding of norms as invoked due to states' strategic calculations. The analysis in this chapter argues that there is not one approach or factor that can fully explain cooperation in mediation support, but rather an eclectic approach that can take into consideration functional concerns, strategic calculations, and norms all together.

The case presented illustrates that, in line with an instrumental perspective of norms consistent with realist theorizing, member states' strategic calculations guide the decision of a sub-regional organization to lead and to uphold norms such as the principle of subsidiarity. However, while member states' strategic calculations are necessary for deciding who leads, these calculations are not sufficient to maintain leadership, especially when such state calculations impede efficiency and any progress in the talks. In inter-organizational cooperation, member states' strategic calculations can be promoted to the extent that they can invoke internationally recognized principles, such as subsidiarity, to support the organization's leadership.

Moreover, once the principle is articulated, implemented and defended, it can have regulative, constitutive and prescriptive effects that facilitate streamlined coordination among actors, consistent with constructivist conceptualization of norms. Cooperation among the secretariats and technical mediation support structures work effectively when the question of who should mediate has been decided. In this case, advanced organizational assets for mediation support do not translate into consistent leadership in a peace mediation process or dependence on existing assets for operational support. The decision for this still lies at the member states' level, but instead of treating the technical and the political as two parallel fields, an eclectic understanding of norms may help link these worlds and guide in understanding order among the efforts of varied mediation actors.

In the case of South Sudan, the decision for IGAD to lead and the strong assertion of IGAD regional ownership, under the principles of subsidiarity and 'African solutions to African problems', were based on

IGAD member states' decision that IGAD would be the venue that would most optimally protect their vital national interests and away from other actors that may compete in their influence in South Sudan. Consequently, regional ownership animated institutional coordination among various mediation actors, including maintaining IGAD leadership amid powerful interested states such as the US and influential interested regional powers such as Tanzania and South Africa in the Arusha Process. In line with IGAD regional ownership, the existing assets and efforts of other mediating actors, including the UN and the AU, adapted to fit within the IGAD-Plus framework. Moreover, IGAD's firm assertion of regional ownership also helped shape actors' interpretation of advantageous and disadvantageous institutional assets. Emphasizing IGAD regional ownership, the proximity of member states in the conflict was promoted as an asset, rather than a hindrance, in mediating effectively.

The chapter has focused on a uni-directional relationship among the three factors: the flow from strategic calculations, to the selection of norms, to the organization of technical cooperation among mediation actors. Such a uni-directional relationship proved useful in analysing the temporal sequence of events in operational mediation support. Future studies may explore the applicability of the conceptualized relationships to other mediation contexts, as well as examine another direction of the relationships, such as feedback loops from experiences in technical cooperation to further norm building and member states' strategic calculations.

In the popular discourse on operational support to mediation, the aspired trajectory is an integrated approach within frameworks of coordination based on functional comparative advantage and clear division of labour. However, it is doubtful whether this will be achieved if integration of mediation efforts among organizations is focused only on technical networking, knowledge management, and institution building and training, which is the trend. Coupled with dissimilar interests as well as unclear and competing norms, the employment of similar technical capacities in ongoing mediation processes may be more conflicting or overlapping, rather than cooperative or integrated. The suggestion is for a holistic approach to studying coordination and cooperation in mediation support. For research to help connect silos of political officers and mediation practitioners, scholars studying mediation support to actual operations would benefit from bridging the gaps among functional, realist and constructivist schools of thought.

References

ACCORD and AU (2014) *African Union Mediation Support Handbook*, South Africa: ACCORD [online], 13 October, available from: https://www.accord.org.za/publication/african-union-mediation-support-handbook/ (accessed 25 July 2019).

African Arguments (2014) 'Addis Dispatches (Part Two): IGAD's Credibility Seriously Damaged by South Sudan Summit Fiasco' [online], 3 September, available from: https://africanarguments.org/2014/09/03/addis-dispatches-part-two-igads-credibility-seriously-damaged-by-south-sudan-summit-fiasco/ (accessed 11 October 2017).

Ancas, S. (2011) 'The Effectiveness of Regional Peacemaking in Southern Africa: Problematising the United Nations-African Union-Southern African Development Community Relationship', *African Journal on Conflict Resolution*, 11(1), 129–52.

Aromi, O. (2018) 'IGAD Mediation Model Is Flawed: It's Time for African Union (AU) or AU/UN Hybrid Mediation to Take Over South Sudan Peace Process' [online], 25 March, available from: http://www.southsudannation.com/igad-mediation-model-is-flawed-its-time-for-african-union-au-or-auun-hybrid-mediation-to-take-over-south-sudan-peace-process/ (accessed 12 October 2018).

Apuuli, P.K. (2014) 'Explaining the (Il)legality of Uganda's Intervention in the Current South Sudan Conflict', *African Security Review*, 23(4), 352–69.

Apuuli, P.K. (2015) 'IGAD's Mediation in the Current South Sudan Conflict: Prospects and Challenge', *African Security*, 8(2), 120–45.

Awolich, A. (2015) 'The Mediation Pendulum and the Challenges that Underlie the Peace Implementation in South Sudan. Policy Brief' [online], 02 December, available from: http://suddinstitute.org/publications/show/the-mediation-pendulum-and-the-challenges-that-underlie-peace-implementation-in-south-sudan/ (accessed 10 December 2015).

Biermann, R. (2008) 'Towards a Theory of Inter-organizational Networking', *The Review of International Organizations*, 3(2), 151–77.

Chonghaile, C.N. (2015) 'African Union Must Release South Sudan Report, Rights Groups Say', *The Guardian* [online], 4 February, available from: https://www.theguardian.com/global-development/2015/feb/04/african-union-report-south-sudan-delayed (accessed 25 July 2019).

Confidential source (2016a) interviewed by Jamie Pring, June.

Confidential source (2016b) interviewed by Jamie Pring, June.

Confidential source (2017a) interviewed by Jamie Pring, April.

Confidential source (2017b) interviewed by Jamie Pring, May.

Confidential sources (2019) feedback from reviewers, November.

de Waal, A. (2014) 'Visualising South Sudan: The Oil Shutdown' [online], 20 March, available from: https://sites.tufts.edu/wpf/visualizing-south-sudan-the-oil-shutdown/ (accessed: 15 November 2018).

Deng, D. (2015) 'No Peace, No Justice: How the African Union is Failing South Sudan', *African Arguments* [online], 2 February, available from: https://africanarguments.org/2015/02/02/no-peace-no-justice-how-the-african-union-is-failing-south-sudan-by-david-k-deng/ (accessed 25 July 2019).

Feyissa, D.D. (2014) 'The Spillover Effect of South Sudan in Gambella', *Horn of Africa Bulletin*, September–October 2014 issue [online], 18 November, available from: https://hornaffairs.com/2014/11/18/the-spillover-effect-of-south-sudan-in-gambella-ethiopia/ (accessed 02 March 2016).

Finnemore, M. and Sikkink, K. (1998) 'International Norm Dynamics and Political Change', *International Organization*, 52(4), 887–917.

Francis, D. (2005) *Uniting Africa: Building Regional Peace and Security Systems*, Aldershot: Ashgate Publishing Limited.Gebrekidan, G.Z. (2015) 'Tackling the South Sudan Conflict Within a Complicated Regional Security Complex', *The Southern Voices Network Research Paper* [online], September, available from: https://www.wilsoncenter.org/sites/default/files/getachew_research_paper_final.pdf (accessed 25 July 2019).

Gilpin, R. (1983) *War and Change in World Politics*, Cambridge: Cambridge University Press.

Government of Ethiopia (2015) 'Prime Minister Hailemariam launches the IGAD-Plus mediation on South Sudan' [online], 15 June, available from: https://reliefweb.int/report/south-sudan/prime-minister-hailemariam-launches-igad-plus-mediation-south-sudan (accessed 19 April 2019).

Healy, S. (2009) 'Peacemaking in the Midst of War: An Assessment of IGAD's Contribution to Regional Security in the Horn of Africa', *Crisis States Research Centre, London School of Economics Working Papers Series*, 2(59) [online], November, available from: http://eprints.lse.ac.uk/28482/1/WP59.2.pdf (accessed 25 July 2019).

IGAD (Intergovernmental Authority on Development) (2010) 'Memorandum of Understanding Among African Union Mission in Somalia (AMISOM), IGAD Office of the Facilitator for Somalia Peace and National Reconciliation and United Nations Political Office for Somalia'. Nairobi, Kenya [online], available from: https://unpos.unmissions.org/sites/default/files/old_dnn/100428%20MOU%20AMISOM-IGAD-UNPOS.pdf (accessed 6 October 2020).

IGAD (2013) 'Communiqué of the 23rd Extraordinary session of the IGAD Assembly of Heads of State and Government on the Situation in South Sudan' [online], available from: http://igad.int/attachments/725_Communique%20of%20the%2023rd%20IGAD%20Extraordinary%20Summit.pdf (accessed 25 July 2019).

IGAD (2014a) 'Communiqué of the 25th Extraordinary Session of the IGAD Assembly of Heads of State and Government on the Situation in South Sudan' [online], available from: https://igad.int/communique/781-communique-of-the-25th-extra-ordinary-session-of-the-igad-assembly-of-heads-of-state-and-government-on-the-situation-in-south-sudan (accessed 25 November 2015).

IGAD (2014b) 'IGAD-led Peace Talks on South Sudan Continue in Bahir Dar', *IGAD Press Release* [online], 22 September, available from: https://southsudan.igad.int/attachments/article/265/09_22_2014_Press_Release_on_Official_Opening_of_the_Sixth_Session_of_South_Sudan_Peace_Talks.pdf (accessed 9 August 2019).

IGAD (2016) *Report of the Special Envoys on the Conclusion of the IGAD-led Mediation to Resolve the Conflict in the Republic of South Sudan (2013–2015).*

IGAD and UN (2015) 'IGAD-UN High Level Dialogue on Peace and Security: Joint Communiqué' [online], available from: https://igad.int/attachments/1242_IGAD-UN%20Joint%20Communique.pdf (accessed 25 July 2019).

Katzenstein, P. (1996) *The Culture of National Security: Norms and Identity in World Politics*, New York, NY: Columbia University Press.

Klabbers, J. (2014) 'The Emergence of Functionalism in International Institutional Law: Colonial Inspirations', *European Journal of International Law*, 25(3), 645–75.

Koops, J.A. (2012) 'Assessing the European Union as an Inter-organizational Actor: From Policy-oriented Analysis to Theory-guided Research', prepared for GREEN Scientific Workshop, Institute for European Studies, 'The EU in International Organizations Across Time: Structure, Commitment and Consistency'.

Krasner, S.D. (1976) 'State Power and the Structure of International Trade', *World Politics* 28(3), 317–47.

Lanz, D. and Gasser, R. (2013) 'A Crowded Field: Competition and Coordination in International Peace Mediation', *Mediation Arguments* (2) [online], February, available from: https://repository.up.ac.za/bitstream/handle/2263/21679/Lanz_Crowded%282013%29.pdf?sequence=1&isAllowed=y (accessed 25 July 2019).

Lehmann-Larsen, S. (2014) 'Effectively Supporting Mediation: Developments, Challenges and Requirements', *Oslo Forum Papers* 3 [online], June, available from: https://www.hdcentre.org/wp-content/uploads/2016/07/Oslo_Forum_paper_n__3_-_Effectively_supporting_mediation_-_WEB-June-2014.pdf (accessed 25 July 2019).

Mabor, B. (2015) 'Understanding Arusha Agreement and the IGAD Process for South Sudan', *Sudan Tribune* [online] 21 February, available from: https://www.sudantribune.com/spip.php?article54068 (accessed 17 April 2018).

Mason, S. and Sguaitamatti, D. (2011) 'Mapping Mediators: A Comparison of Third Parties and Implications for Switzerland', *Center for Security Studies* [online], available from: https://ethz.ch/content/dam/ethz/special-interest/gess/cis/center-for-securities-studies/pdfs/Mapping-Mediators.pdf (accessed 25 July 2019).

Mearsheimer, J. (1994/95) 'The False Promise of International Institutions', *International Security*, 19(3), 5–49.

Mediation Support Network (n.d.) 'About Us' [online], available from: https://mediationsupportnet.ethz.ch (accessed 25 July 2019).

Nathan, L. (2010) 'The Peacemaking Effectiveness of Regional Organizations', *Crisis States Research Centre, London School of Economics Working Papers Series*, 2(81) [online], October, available from: http://www.lse.ac.uk/international-development/Assets/Documents/PDFs/csrc-working-papers-phase-two/wp81.2-peacemaking-effectiveness-of-regional-organisations.pdf (accessed 25 July 2019).

Nathan, L. (2013) *Community of Insecurity. SADC's Struggle for Peace and Security in Southern Africa*, Aldershot: Ashgate Publishing Ltd.

Nathan, L. (2016) 'Will the Lowest Be First? Subsidiarity in Peacemaking in Africa', prepared for International Studies Association 2016 Annual Convention [online], available from: https://www.up.ac.za/media/shared/237/PDFs/Publications/competition-and-subsidiarity-in-peacemaking-in-africa.zp84164.pdf (accessed 25 July 2019).

Nathan, L. (2017) 'How to Manage Interorganizational Disputes over Mediation in Africa', *Global Governance*, 23(2), 151–62.

O'Brien, D. (2000) 'The Search for Subsidiarity: The UN, African Regional Organizations and Humanitarian Action', *International Peacekeeping*, 7(3), 57–83.

Odhiambo, P. and Muluvi, A. (2014) 'Impact of Prolonged South Sudan Crisis on Kenya's Economic and Security Interests' [online], 12 March, available from: https://www.brookings.edu/blog/africa-in-focus/2014/03/12/impact-of-prolonged-south-sudan-crisis-on-kenyas-economic-and-security-interests/ (accessed 17 April 2016).

Sibanda, S. (2007) 'Beneath It All Lies the Principle of Subsidiarity: The Principle of Subsidiarity in the African and European Regional Human Rights Systems', *Comparative and International Law Journal of Southern Africa*, 40(3), 425–48.

Sudan Tribune (2015) 'African Union Appoints High Representative for South Sudan', *Sudan Tribune* [online], 2 June, available from: http://www.sudantribune.com/spip.php?article55202 (accessed 25 July 2019).

Taylor, M. (2016) 'From Conflict to Cooperation? Sudan, South Sudan and Uganda', *International Crisis Group* [online], 20 June, available from: https://www.crisisgroup.org/africa/horn-africa/south-sudan/conflict-cooperation-sudan-south-sudan-and-uganda (accessed 15 August 2019).

UN (1945) 'Charter of the United Nations' [online], available from: https://www.un.org/en/charter-united-nations/ (accessed 25 July 2019).

UN (2012) 'Guidance for Effective Mediation' [online], available from: https://peacemaker.un.org/sites/peacemaker.un.org/files/GuidanceEffectiveMediation_UNDPA2012%28english%29_0.pdf (accessed 25 July 2019).

UN Department of Political Affairs (n.d.) 'Group of Friends of Mediation' [online], available from: https://peacemaker.un.org/friendsofmediation (accessed 15 July 2019).

UN Mission in South Sudan (n.d.) 'Background' [online] available from: https://unmiss.unmissions.org/background (accessed 9 August 2019).

UN Office to the AU (n.d.) 'UNOAU: United Nations Office to the African Union' [online], available from: https://dppa.un.org/en/mission/unoau (accessed 25 July 2019).

UN Security Council (1996, 2011) 'Security Council Resolution 1996 (2011)', *Reports of the Secretary-General on the Sudan*, 8 July 2011, S/RES/1996 [online] available from: https://www.refworld.org/docid/4f1d3b322.html (accessed 8 August 2019).

UN Security Council (2014) 'Security Council Resolution 2155 (2014)', *on extension of the mandate of the UN Mission in South Sudan (UNMISS) until 30 November 2014*, 27 May, S/RES/2155 (2014) [online], available from: https://www.refworld.org/docid/538f17a64.html (accessed 8 August 2019).

Vertin, Z. (2019) *A Rope from the Sky: The Making and Unmaking of the World's Newest State*, Stroud: Amberley Publishing.

Wallander, C.A. (2000) 'Institutional Assets and Adaptability: NATO After the Cold War', *International Organization*, 54(4), 705–35.

Whitfield, T. (2015) 'Support Mechanisms: Multilateral, Multi-level and Mushrooming', *Global Peace Operations Review* [online], 17 December, available from: https://peaceoperationsreview.org/thematic-essays/support-mechanisms-multilateral-multi-level-and-mushrooming/ (accessed 25 July 2019).

Zeru, G. (2015) 'Tackling the South Sudan Conflict within a Complicated Regional Security Complex. The Southern Voices Network Research Paper', September 2015 [online], available from: https://www.wilsoncenter.org/publication/tackling-the-south-sudan-conflict-within-complicated-regional-security-complex (accessed 16 July 2016).

14

Women's Mediator Networks: Reflections on an Emerging Global Trend

Irene Fellin and Catherine Turner

Introduction

It is a well-acknowledged fact that women are underrepresented in the ranks of high-level peace mediators. One recent study, conducted by the Council on Foreign Relations (2019), found that women accounted for only 2 per cent of all mediators appointed between 1992 and 2017. Further research by Aggestam and Svensson (2018) has also sought to map the presence of women mediators in Track I negotiations. According to their research, which adopted a slightly broader definition of mediator, only 8 per cent of these positions were filled by women.

The persistent underrepresentation of women in Track I mediation has recently prompted a response from a number of states. Seeking to address the apparent invisibility of women in the field of mediation, several new Networks have been created with the aim of increasing the representation of women in high-level mediation and the visibility of women mediators at all levels.[1] The creation of these Networks globally is rooted in United Nations Security Council Resolution 1325(2000) (UNSCR 1325),

[1] In this context Networks are a mechanism for enhancing the visibility of women in mediation, and creating opportunities for women to engage in mediation.

which made normative commitments to increase women's participation in peace and security. Since UNSCR 1325 was adopted in October 2000, successive resolutions on Women, Peace and Security (WPS) have called for an increase in the number of women in high-level mediation roles (Turner, 2018). This commitment was reinforced in 2017 by the United Nations (UN) Secretary-General Antonio Guterres, who pledged to expand the pool of UN Envoys and senior mediators, with a particular focus on women (UN, 2017). Whereas policy in relation to women in mediation originates primarily in the field of WPS, this particular commitment from the Secretary-General was made in the context of a report on strengthening the UN mediation support capacity and, as such, originates in the field of mediation, rather than WPS, creating a potential bridge between the two professional spheres, which have traditionally remained separate. The international environment therefore appears supportive of the emergence of initiatives such as Networks.

Given the relative infancy of the Networks, and the absence of much scholarly scrutiny of their creation, this chapter does three things. First, it provides an introduction to the Networks, focusing on the legal basis for their creation and locating them within the broader foreign policy context. Second, it distils the core aims and objectives of the different Networks, paying particular attention to the relationship between women mediators and gender advocacy. Finally, it offers an initial critique of some of the conceptual and practical difficulties facing the Networks as they set about achieving their aims. In particular, it considers the origin of the Networks in the field of WPS and what this means for their ability to impact meaningfully in the field of mediation. In presenting these arguments the chapter advances two core aims. The first is to provide a contemporaneous and insider account of the creation of the Networks. The chapter brings together disparate sources of information on the Networks and presents nuanced insight into the negotiations that led to their creation. In this way it aims to create a resource for understanding the Networks, their origins and the historical global context in which they emerged. The second aim is to provide some food for thought for the Networks and those interested in their study as they develop into established mechanisms of foreign policy and engage in the peace mediation field.

The Networks

Since the announcement of the creation of a new Network of Nordic Women Mediators at the Nordic African Foreign Ministers' meeting in

Oslo in April 2015[2] there has been a rapid increase in the number of official Networks created. In only four years, four additional Networks were established,[3] and an increasing number of countries and multilateral organizations are expressing interest in setting up or supporting similar initiatives.[4] The Networks aim to more closely connect the work of women in the fields of mediation and peacebuilding with governmental-level policy and practice. They are therefore not simply grassroots Networks of women practitioners,[5] but have a common political genesis and have been created in support of a specific (foreign) policy agenda.

With the exception of FemWise-Africa, which is an organ of the African Union (AU), the other Networks are created at the state level, funded by Ministries of Foreign Affairs, with the operational responsibility devolved to national partners, mainly from civil society.[6] Yet, despite being unified by a seemingly common goal, there are substantive differences between the nature and the approaches of the Networks. Perhaps unsurprisingly, their composition and approach reflect existing national or regional experiences of conflict and mediation. The following section provides an overview of the creation of each of the Networks, locating them within the existing foreign policy priorities of the states and regions in which they have been created, and the history of engagement with conflict and mediation in those regions. Understanding these dynamics helps to better understand the aims of states in creating the Networks, and as such can help assess their relative impact going forward.

Nordic Women Mediators

The first regional Network to be created was the Nordic Women Mediators (NWM). The NWM was launched in Oslo in November 2015, taking its inspiration from a South African initiative that brought together women with mediation experience from Southern Africa for

---

[2] https://gps.prio.org/Events/Event/?x=11 (accessed 7 October 2020).

[3] For more information about the Networks, visit the Global Alliance page: https://globalwomenmediators.org/ (accessed 7 October 2020).

[4] For example, work is ongoing to create an Arab Network of Women Mediators. An ASEAN Women for Peace Registry is also being created.

[5] In this regard, they can be distinguished from, for example, the Network of women mediators in Colombia. See United States Institute of Peace (2016).

[6] The case is different for FemWise-Africa, whose secretariat is part of the African Union structure, and for the Nordic Women Mediators Sweden, whose operational partner is the Folke Bernadotte Academy, the Swedish government agency for peace, security and development.

skills development and exchange of experience (Norwegian Ministries, 2019: 16).

The mission of the NWM is to enable its members to advance the inclusion and meaningful participation of women in all phases of peace processes in order to contribute to achieving and sustaining peace. The creation of the NWM builds on the extensive experience of Nordic countries in peace mediation, and their associated reputation as peace brokers. For instance, Norway has played a key role in peace processes since the 1990s, when it helped facilitate peace agreements in countries such as Guatemala, Mali and Sudan. In the most recent period, the country has been involved in a number of peace initiatives in different parts of the world, including formal peace processes, such as in Colombia and the Philippines, in addition to dialogue initiatives with one or more parties to a conflict where the goal is to bring the parties to the negotiating table (Norwegian Ministries, 2019: 14). In these engagements Norway pays particular attention to the inclusive dimension of the process. The Norwegian facilitative style of mediation is known for being based on an 'ownership' approach to peace efforts, meaning that only the conflicting parties and their constituencies can ultimately resolve conflict (Norad, 2018). Building on its well-established efforts to support the implementation of peace agreements, in its Fourth National Action Plan (NAP) on WPS (2019–22), Norway declared its intention to have a more systematic focus on WPS and on strengthening the gender perspective in international operations and missions.[7] The creation of the NWM flows from this commitment.

If Norway can be defined as a pioneer of new peace diplomacy, Sweden, Denmark and Finland have all, in one form or another, adopted peacemaking and conflict resolution as a key dimension of their foreign policy agendas (Lehti and Saarinen, 2014: 13). In the case of Sweden it has become a core element of the 'Feminist Foreign Policy' adopted and promoted by the country. This high-level expertise in mediation is reflected in the membership of the Network.[8] For example, each of the women recruited to the national Networks has professional expertise in a related field, such as multilateral organizations, diplomacy or civil society,

[7] The Norwegian Government's Action Plan, Women, Peace and Security (2019–22) 14–19, https://www.peacewomen.org/sites/default/files/actionplan_wps2019.pdf (accessed 7 October 2020).

[8] https://fba.se/en/areas-of-expertise/dialogue-mediation/swedish-womens-mediation-network/members-of-the-swedish-womens-mediation-network/ (accessed 7 October 2020). As of September 2019, the respective national Networks have the following numbers of members: Denmark has 18; Finland has 7; Iceland has 10; Norway has 50; and Sweden has 15 members.

and on a variety of issues relevant to all phases of peace processes, including mediation, ceasefire agreements, constitutional reforms, communication and inclusive strategies.

Finnish efforts to develop a distinct profile and capacity in the sphere of peace mediation are of relatively recent origin although the promotion of mediation as an integral part of the country's foreign policy leans on previous experiences (Joenniemi, 2014: 110). Finland has accumulated a vast experience and expertise engaging Finnish peace mediators in various peace processes, including, inter alia, Northern Ireland, the Western Balkans, Aceh, the Horn of Africa and the South Caucasus. Internationally renowned for its commitment in promoting the use of mediation as a tool for addressing the entire peace cycle, starting from conflict prevention to its control and resolution, in 2010 Finland established in partnership with Turkey the Group of Friends of Mediation active within the framework of the UN, succeeding in its objective to strengthen mediation in practice. Since its establishment the Group has drafted and negotiated four mediation resolutions (Ministry for Foreign Affairs of Finland, n.d.).

The NWM is therefore a collaborative forum that builds on national women mediators' Networks and associated expertise in all five Nordic states. The Network itself operates at the inter-state level, with a governmental-level contact group comprised of representatives of each of the respective Ministries of Foreign Affairs providing strategic-level oversight and coordination for the regional Network. Operationally the Network is supported by a number of in-country partner organizations who are responsible for the implementation of the Network's activities. The NWM meets once a year, with some ten representatives participating from each country.

Mediterranean Women Mediators Network (MWMN)

Acknowledging the need to foster women's participation in a key region for global peace and stability, Italy decided to establish the Mediterranean Women Mediators Network (MWMN). Launched in October 2017 during the Italian mandate as non-permanent member of the United Nations Security Council (UNSC), the MWMN is an initiative inspired by the NWM. It has its basis in the Third Italian NAP in accordance with UNSCR 1325, falling under the first strategic goal of 'strengthening the role of women in peace processes and in all decision-making processes', which underpins the support for the creation of a Network of women mediators (Ministero Degli Affari Esteri E Della Cooperazione

Internazionale, 2016: 16). The MWMN initiative was developed and launched by the Ministry of Foreign Affairs and International Cooperation (MAECI) in conjunction with the Rome-based Istituto Affari Internazionali (IAI) and Women in International Security (WIIS) Italy and it is funded under the umbrella of the national WPS funding.

Like the Nordic Network, the MWMN aims to increase the number of women involved in peacemaking efforts and to facilitate the appointment of women mediators at the local and global level. This initiative combines Italy's top priorities within the UNSC and its role in a strategic area such as the Mediterranean: it keeps the focus on the stability of the region, it supports preventive diplomacy and the peaceful resolution of conflicts, and it commits to bolstering the role of women, especially in conflict prevention and resolution processes, with a focus on high-level political positions (Track I mediation). The MWMN includes members across all 25 countries from both shores of the Mediterranean represented in the initiative. Members of the Network have been identified through a mixed procedure that included the support of the Permanent Representations to the UN of the various countries involved, as well as through civil society organizations, to ensure the involvement of a diverse group of women. The number of members, 44 at its foundation, is increasing due to the consolidation of the Network locally.

The MWMN also strives to become a catalyst for peace mediation efforts in ongoing and potential crises and post-conflict stabilization processes. To achieve that, the Network works as a community of practice and provides opportunities for women mediators to strengthen their existing capacities through peer-to-peer learning, mentoring and targeted training. Further, the scope of the Network's activities is consolidated locally through the establishment of 'Antennae' in the various Mediterranean countries. In 2019 the first Antennae were launched in Cyprus and in Turkey (MWMN, 2019). Through the structure of these local satellites, the Network aims not only to increase the numbers of members, but also to foster synergies, build opportunities and coordinate with existing initiatives, connecting practice on the ground and supporting local initiatives.

The Network is designed specifically to connect local actors with the global reality of peace mediation. Specifically, it aims to address the disconnection between the work that women do at the local level and the world of international mediation processes to which women do not enjoy access. At the policy level it works in close cooperation with the UN, the Organization for Security and Cooperation in Europe (OSCE) and more recently the EU to support their mediation activities. It also liaises with initiatives developed and promoted at the local level, for example in Libya and Cyprus, where its effectiveness is bolstered through close cooperation with civil society.

The African Network of Women in Conflict Prevention and Peace Mediation (FemWise-Africa)

Officially launched in July 2017, FemWise-Africa was created as a subsidiary body of the five-member Panel of the Wise and the expanded Pan-African Network of the Wise,[9] placing it in a strategic location for influencing policy formulation on women's inclusion and advocating for narrowing the gap between the commitments for women's inclusion and their implementation. The Network itself builds on a stronger tradition of grassroots and local Networks of women mediators in Africa. Established pursuant to an initiative of the AU and endorsed by the UNSC, FemWise-Africa aims to strengthen the role of women in conflict prevention and mediation efforts in the context of the African Peace and Security Architecture (APSA).[10]

The Network provides a platform for strategic advocacy, capacity building, and networking aimed at enhancing the implementation of the commitments for the inclusion of women in peacemaking in Africa (Limo, 2018). FemWise-Africa has a clear governance strategy that allocates responsibility for strategic direction and operational implementation of the initiative. A Steering Committee, a high-level panel, gives guidance to the Network and approves matters of membership and accreditation. The membership of this Committee includes the members of the Panel of the Wise as well as notable African women who have proven mediation skills.

[9] The Panel of the Wise is one of the critical pillars of the Peace and Security Architecture of the African Union (APSA). Article 11 of the Protocol establishing the Peace and Security Council (PSC), sets up a five-person panel of 'highly respected African personalities from various segments of society who have made outstanding contributions to the cause of peace, security and development on the continent' with a task 'to support the efforts of the PSC and those of the Chairperson of the Commission, particularly in the area of conflict prevention' (African Union, 2018a). See 'Strengthening African Women's Participation in Conflict Prevention, Mediation Processes and Peace Stabilisation Efforts Operationalisation of "FemWise-Africa"', http://www.peaceau.org/uploads/final-concept-note-femwise-sept-15-short-version-clean-4-flyer.pdf, p 1 (accessed 7 October 2020).

[10] FemWise-Africa was officially established through a decision of the AU Assembly of Heads of State (AU Summit) on 4 July 2017 (Assembly/AU/Draft/Dec.21(XXIX)). See http://www.peaceau.org/uploads/final-concept-note-femwise-sept-15-short-version-clean-4-flyer.pdf (accessed 7 October 2020).

In addition to the high-level members, the Committee also includes, on a non-voting basis, representatives of the relevant departments of the Commission, of international organizations, and thematic experts who can provide expert guidance to support the work of the Network (Secretariat of the Panel of the Wise, n.d.). The operational work is supported by a dedicated Secretariat that is responsible for the coordination, monitoring and reporting of Network activities. It also manages relations with external bodies, such as other Networks. Finally, the Assembly of FemWise-Africa comprises all the members of the Network. Membership is open to both institutions and individual women and girls, with either a proven track record in mediation or who aspire to serve in mediation initiatives, including in the field of election observation missions across Africa.

Women Mediators Across the Commonwealth (WMC)

In 2018 the UK government announced funding to support the work of women peacebuilders, including mediators.[11] This commitment arose from the UK's NAP on WPS for the period 2018–22, which includes the following strategic outcome: '[t]o increase women's meaningful and representative participation in decision making processes, including conflict prevention and peacebuilding at community and national levels' (UK Government, 2018: 6). This strategic outcome in the NAP underpins funding and support for the creation of a looser Network called Women Mediators Across the Commonwealth (WMC). The geographical scope of the Network – being Commonwealth-wide – reflects the UK's position as Chair in Office of the Commonwealth (during the two-year mandate 2018–19), with the funding being announced at the Commonwealth Heads of Government Meeting hosted in London in 2018. As with the other Networks, the operational running of WMC has been devolved to a civil society partner, in this case the UK-based peacebuilding organization Conciliation Resources.[12]

As WMC remains in its infancy it does not yet have a separate governance structure. Conciliation Resources has overseen the initial recruitment of members and continues to act as the Secretariat for the Network. After an initial round of recruitment in 2018, which increased the initial number of five founding members to 37, as of October 2020 the WMC has 50 members (Conciliation Resources, n.d.), recruited

[11] https://globalwomenmediators.org/wmc/ (accessed 7 October 2020).

[12] https://www.c-r.org/programme/women-mediators-across-commonwealth (accessed 7 October 2020).

from among activists and peacebuilding practitioners who engage in mediation and dialogue from the community level to official processes. WMC aims to provide a platform for peer-to-peer learning across the different areas of mediation activity and across the diversity of the Commonwealth (Conciliation Resources, 2020), which is reflected in its recruitment procedures.

The Global Alliance of Regional Women Mediator Networks

The mushrooming of Regional Women Mediator Networks across the globe is a clear reflection of the need to find effective mechanisms for ensuring that women's common aspirations to participate in and lead peace processes is fulfilled. It reflects a belief that women are equal stakeholders in society and, therefore, they should have a place at every table where peace is being discussed, negotiated or brokered, including as mediators. In the past few years, Networks have emerged as key actors in the quest for fair and meaningful representation of women across the whole peace cycle. Following several months of informal collaboration, the Networks identified a need to embody a collective voice to amplify their common goals while maintaining their respective independence and characteristics.

As a result, since March 2018 the Networks have worked together towards the launch of a Global Alliance of Regional Women Mediator Networks (Global Alliance). The specific aims of the Global Alliance are to provide visibility to women mediators, to organize networking and capacity building opportunities and, most notably, to facilitate the deployment of its members in the field. The Global Alliance was launched in the Seventy Fourth Session of the UN General Assembly in September 2019. As part of the launch, a list of deployable women mediators was handed to the UN Deputy Secretary-General Amina Mohammed, in a direct challenge to the persistent myth that there are simply not enough qualified women mediators.

The initial idea of formalizing an already existing collaboration was developed within the framework of the NWM, and in close dialogue with the UN, back in early 2018, when Norway invited representatives of all the established Networks to an initial meeting. The meeting, which was held in Oslo in March of the same year, demonstrated the benefits of getting together, sharing experiences and learning from each other (Norwegian Ministries, 2019: 18). The event gathered together more than 80 women and men, including representatives from the UN Secretary-General's High-Level Advisory Board on Mediation as well as representatives of UN entities (including the Executive Office of the Secretary-General, the Department of Political Affairs and UN Women). Other multilateral actors also attended the meeting: the AU, the EU, the OSCE and the Association of Southeast Asian Nations (ASEAN), as well as delegates from several countries and representatives of civil society and academia.

Considering that all the Networks were in the very initial stages of their activities (and that, at that time, the WMC had not yet been launched), the Networks agreed to postpone the establishment of a Global Alliance and take some more time to strengthen their respective individual capacities before engaging with a broader initiative at the global level. The Oslo meeting was then followed by a second event in New York at the margins of the General Assembly Open Debate on UNSCR 1325 in October 2018. The open event, organized in collaboration with UN Women and Permanent Mission of the Arab Republic of Egypt to the United Nations, was followed by an internal meeting of Network members aimed at sharing experiences between their members on mediation issues and as an opportunity for further strategizing the development of a Global Alliance. As an output of the event, an advocacy letter was sent to the UN Secretary-General Antonio Guterres on behalf of the four regional Networks, stressing the importance of recognizing the work done at many levels by women mediators and the urgency of appointing women mediators to the highest positions.[13]

The Global Alliance is a collective of voices demanding that policy and decision makers alike hasten the implementation of UNSCR 1325 and consciously create spaces for more women to participate in and lead peace processes. During the launch, discussions went beyond the achievements and barriers to access, focusing more on opportunities and possible modalities through which women's participation can be facilitated and enhanced and what kind of support Networks can provide to their members for engaging with key policy makers in the mediation field.

The Global Alliance has four main objectives for its activities. First, it aims to create awareness of the respective Networks, showcasing the work being done by them and by their members to promote and enhance women's participation in peace processes in pursuit of the broader WPS agenda. Second, it aims to engage with key policy makers to leverage support from the UN, the AU, the EU, the OSCE and UN Member States, to build partnerships to advance the roles and participation of women in mediation processes at the global, regional and national levels. Third, it aims to identify opportunities for collaboration with, among and

[13] On file with lead author.

between the respective Networks represented within the Global Alliance and other stakeholders. And last, but not least, it aims to expand and reinforce the connections among the members and key stakeholders, including policy makers, identifying networking and relationship-building opportunities.

Aims and Objectives of the Networks

The new Regional Women Mediator Networks have an explicit goal to address the underrepresentation of women in mediation. But their intellectual genesis in the field of WPS means that they are not exclusively focused on the individual role of mediator. Rather, they take a broader approach to the capacity of women mediators to amplify the voices of women peacebuilders across the spectrum of the WPS agenda and to address the relative invisibility of women's peace work at institutional level. The emphasis placed on each activity varies according to the individual Network and the geographical and political context in which it was created. Nevertheless, there are core common objectives that can be distilled across all initiatives.

The first objective is increasing the visibility of women mediators. The low numbers of women achieving high-level mediation positions internationally is symptomatic of a broader trend whereby women's contribution to the field of peace and security is not recognized. It is common to hear, by way of justification of the failure to appoint more women, that there are simply not enough qualified women. Women's contribution to sub-national and local mediation initiatives go largely unrecognized and are weakly supported (African Union, 2018b; Turner, 2018). This problem arises for both conceptual and practical reasons. Conceptually, the way in which women's skills, experiences and career trajectories are assessed does not easily match with the traditional 'career' path in international mediation. The lower representation of women at high level in the peace mediation field is symptomatic of the way in which the requirements of the job have evolved over time. In particular, Envoys and Special Representatives are traditionally drawn from the ranks of former heads of state, ambassadors or UN officials. These professions themselves are male dominated, meaning that the numbers of women coming through are relatively low (Aggestam and Svensson, 2018; Heyworth and Turner, 2019). What the Networks seek to do is to fill this gap created by the exclusion of women from the traditional spaces of peace and security. They create new networking opportunities to bring qualified women together and to enhance their visibility and facilitate access to key decision-making spaces and actors. For example, the NWM aims to 'facilitat[e] access and provid[e] Networking opportunities with mediating and peacebuilding actors globally' (PRIO, 2015). Similarly, the MWMN is clear that it aims to facilitate the appointment of high-level women,[14] and WMC cites profile raising as one of its key activities, including enhancing the visibility of women qualified for high-level appointment (Conciliation Resources, n.d.). Networks can directly counter the claim that there are no qualified women by maintaining rosters of such qualified women, matching women with opportunities as they arise. Promoting the visibility of women who have achieved high-level positions is also important as it helps to build a leadership brand for women mediators and can create mentoring opportunities for younger women – a stated goal of FemWise in particular (African Union, 2018b). This frames the development of a new positive narrative around women mediators, one that highlights the achievements and successes of women actively involved in mediation efforts at different levels all around the world.

The second common objective is the development of skills and capacity of women in mediation. With this objective there is a slight difference in approach between the Networks. All of them build in a peer-to-peer learning and support function, including drawing on the expertise of members through knowledge exchange. FemWise-Africa is the most clearly focused on skills development, with a core objective of professionalizing the role of women in mediation across all tracks. One of the expected outcomes of the Network is the 'enhanced capacity of African women engaged in conflict prevention and mediation ...' (African Union, 2018b). This derives from the premise that to contribute more effectively to mediation and negotiation in Africa, women's capacity in mediation and negotiation skills needs to be improved and extended to all areas of work (African Union, 2018b). The other Networks take a slightly less direct approach to skills development. Rather than focusing specifically on training and capacity building, their narrative centres the importance of peer-to-peer learning and support whereby women's existing expertise can be more effectively shared. The very purpose of a Network is to enable the wealth of expertise to be more efficiently disseminated.

The third common objective is using the Networks to make more effective connections between both global actors and local initiatives to enhance women's visibility in mediation. There are two aspects to this. The first speaks to the 'networking' function in that more effective connections need to be made with international organizations and global actors to ensure women's expertise in mediation is made visible.

[14] https://womenmediators.net/ (accessed 7 October 2020).

One of the roles of the Networks is therefore to facilitate access and networking opportunities with global actors. The other side of this is to make connections not only 'up' to the global actors but also 'down' to local organizations, including civil society organizations. The role of the Networks in this regard is to create clear links between the different Tracks of mediation practice and to provide channels of communication between local actors and global processes. FemWise-Africa, for example, names as an explicit priority '[b]ridging the gap between Tracks 1, 2 and 3 mediation …' (African Union, 2018b). Similarly, the MWMN aims to foster synergies and coordination with other actors, including globally, with institutions such as the UN Department of Political and Peacebuilding Affairs (UN-DPPA) and locally with civil society. WMC builds this function into its design, with the membership of the Network including grassroots women mediators and peacebuilders, as well as women with national and international experience, as a way of fostering peer learning.

Finally, the Networks aim to contribute to the broader goal of strengthening inclusive mediation and promoting the sustainability of peace agreements. Through their work, all of the Networks seek to contribute to the sustainability of mediation and peace agreements. For some, such as the MWMN and FemWise-Africa, there is a specific regional connection and an aim to contribute to sustainable peace in their own region. For the NWM, a region less afflicted by violent political conflict than others, the ambition relates to international peace and security. One of the key ways in which the Networks seek to pursue this goal is through advocacy on the importance of women's participation in peace processes. This can be achieved through direct support for local grassroots women's organizations, through providing access to local women's organizations to national and international actors, or through amplifying both the voices and the message of women's civil society in international processes. All of these activities form part of a broader goal of advocacy in favour of inclusive processes that seek to enhance women's access to and participation in mediation.

What is clear from these objectives is that the Networks are not narrowly focused on increasing the representation of a small number of women in high-level international processes, but rather on increasing the visibility of all women's voices in mediation, from grassroots peacebuilding organizations focused on women's participation right up to UN Special Envoys. They sit clearly within the much bigger normative frame of WPS and adopt a holistic approach to mediation and to women's roles in mediation that enables a multi-level approach to both mediation and leadership. They seek to amplify women's voices in peace processes not only through their own work, but also by actively bringing the experiences of grassroots women's organizations to the attention of mediation support organizations and making connections between the local and the global.

These are clearly important objectives which are coherent within the broader context of WPS. It is too early to evaluate, in a technical sense, the success of the Networks. Most have only recently been established and have not had time to embed their work. Moreover, with the exception of FemWise-Africa, the Networks have not developed comprehensive governance structures or performance indicators that would enable technical evaluation outside the parameters of the NAPs under which they are created. Much will depend on the directions the Networks take in their early years and how they set their own priorities. Nevertheless, it is worth highlighting some conceptual and practical challenges faced by the Networks as mediation support actors.

Conceptual Questions That Remain

Exploring the role of Networks through the lens of mediation support offers some insight into the first conceptual difficulty faced. From a mediation perspective, the mediation support function of the Networks lies in three potential areas: first, the identification of more female mediators to be included in the selection pool, thus redressing the gender balance of mediation and mediation support activities; second, the promotion of inclusive models of mediation, with a particular focus on the inclusion of women in all roles in the mediation process, including as negotiators and advisors; and finally, the provision of technical expertise in gender-sensitive mediation and support to women and women's groups who are invited to participate in mediation, which is a key function of mediation support. Yet there remains a gap between mediation actors and the Networks that suggests that more will need to be done to bridge it.

In relation to the identification of women mediators, the Networks face the challenge of identifying appropriate women for the role. The questions of *which* women should be included in peace processes, including in the role of conflict mediators, is a key one for WPS scholars and practitioners. Whether women should be included simply on the basis of representation, or whether their participation is a means to the end of gender sensitivity is a recurrent theme in the literature (Charlesworth, 2008). This is particularly salient when it comes to mediation, where there is an underlying tension between gender and mediation (Palmiano Federer, 2016; Turner, 2020). It can be argued that the fundamental 'logics' of WPS and mediation do not sit easily together. WPS scholars identified mediation early on as a site of exclusion for women and one where advocacy for greater inclusion was needed. There has been a strong push in WPS circles to develop normative commitments relating to the participation of women in mediation. Norms have been deployed as a means of putting pressure on mediators to include women and to adopt a gender sensitive approach to conflict analysis and process design. For many WPS advocates these norms are non-negotiable. However this normative approach is not one which has been fully embraced within the mediation field, and indeed there are potentially conflicting understandings of norms at play. Where WPS has focused on substantive norms related to the substance of negotiations, mediation has tended to look more closely at process-related norms and how they shape the activity of the mediator (Hellmüller, 2019). Mediation as a form of conflict resolution is a voluntary activity which relies on the consent of the parties (UN, 2012). It is not unusual for mediation to occur in contexts where social and political norms exclude women from public life. These social norms then also exclude women from having a role in political negotiations. In these circumstances the participation of women may conflict with religious or social norms of the parties to the mediation, making it less likely that they will consent to women's participation. When this occurs, mediators face the choice of pushing a normative agenda that challenges the parties and risks alienating them, on the one hand, or marginalizing women and gender on the other. Palmiano Federer (2016) highlights how 'gender' has not been accepted as a core norm of mediation, but rather exists as a non-core norm that can be displaced in favour of other (core) considerations, such as consent. There is therefore a fundamental absence of agreement between the WPS and mediation communities of practice related to the purpose of women's participation and the extent to which mediation is an appropriate vehicle for advancing gender equality during and after conflict (Standfield, 2020). This creates a particular difficulty for women mediators, who find themselves caught between the professional logics of mediation on the one hand, and pressure to advance gender sensitivity on the other (Turner, 2020).

This tension is one which must be navigated by the Networks if they are to be effective. In particular, as a starting point, recognizing that women play a range of different roles in processes and that each role needs to be appropriately developed is key. There is a risk with a gender-focused approach that the Networks will replicate existing structures which equate 'women' with 'gender' and sideline women into 'soft' or gendered portfolios. It also risks overlooking women who are experienced mediators but who do not have any gender expertise, who remain less visible in the WPS sphere (Turner, 2020). This is a core question that the

Networks will need to address – are they promoting mediators, or WPS experts? And how can the Networks help to reduce the gap between the two by integrating WPS into mediation thinking? There are differences of approach between the Networks in this regard. The NWM draws from a relatively large pool of women with direct experience in mediation, who are also supportive of inclusive mediation. The MWMN, on the other hand, has prioritized the recruitment of women with high-level political experience or experience related to gender but not necessarily to mediation. While it is clear that the Networks have attempted to address this very divide, recruiting both mediators and thematic experts to advise on the work of the Network, a lack of crossover between Networks and the mediation support community of practice remains.[15]

As outlined in the first section of this chapter, the Networks have, with the exception of FemWise-Africa, been adopted nationally as commitments on WPS included in NAPs on Resolution 1325. This means that nationally the Networks exist primarily as gender-focused policy commitments. Policy and financial support for the Networks comes nationally, but also internationally, from departments with responsibility for gender equality, including WPS, and not those with the broader mandate of political affairs or peace and security, including mediation support. This gap has potential implications for effective collaboration between the different bodies. The Networks risk falling into a chasm that already exists at the UN level between mediation and gender (Turner, 2018), and despite the desire for coordination and being a possible solution to the problem, they have not yet succeeded in bridging this gap. Establishing effective working relationships with mediation support actors and governments will be key to finding entry points for women mediators. Yet the differences in approach create a conceptual question surrounding the understanding of mediation and mediators being advanced by the Networks and how this will either enable or hinder effective relationships within the broader professional field of mediation support.

While it is still too early to fully assess the impact the Networks can have in the broader field of mediation and mediation support, it is nevertheless worth asking where the influence of the Networks should be felt the most. Where, and to whom, should their activities be directed? At the global level, the Networks have gained an impressive popularity among international and regional organizations that provide them with regular support. Yet, none of the Networks has succeeded thus far in having one of its members appointed as a UN Special Envoy or to any other high-

[15] https://themediateur.eu/wp-content/uploads/2019/07/EEAS-CoP-mediation-Report.pdf (accessed 7 October 2020).

level position in an international or regional organization, nor to the mediation support teams of the non-governmental providers.

Another way for the Networks to have a more innovative approach could be by supporting local buy-in to mediation processes. The UN is no longer the only, nor indeed even the principal, actor in the mediation field. While it may take the lead in coordinating activities, it is simply one of an increasing constellation of mediation actors. With their stated objectives of forging more effective connections between global mediation actors and mediation and peacebuilding work that takes place locally, the Networks could be well placed to collaborate more deeply with mediation support actors in pursuit of this particular aim, enhancing the capacity of mediation support actors to engage more meaningfully with women and with gender in their work.

More time is required to evaluate whether Networks present the right tools for increasing the representation, and indeed the recognition, of women in peace and security. Early indications show that the Networks, widely acclaimed as innovative initiatives, still align themselves with the current mainstream model of conflict mediation (Track I, II, III) – a model which itself creates gendered hierarchies that tend to marginalize and exclude women. With their focus on skills development and capacity building, it seems that the Networks are inviting women to make additional efforts to adapt to a system that is putting them at the periphery of the debate. Is there a role for the Networks to disrupt current understandings of mediation, and to advocate a fundamentally different way of listening? Why not challenge the system with a different and innovative approach to inclusive peace mediation?

Practical Difficulties

During the first years of activity of the Networks a number of obstacles emerged which need to be addressed to maximize the benefits of their activities.

One of the most critical issues is the medium- to long-term sustainability of the initiatives, in terms of both economic resources and political commitments. The Networks require core and regular funding to be sustainable. As noted, a number of the Networks are funded within the frameworks of NAPs concerning UN Resolution 1325, and their commitments can vary from one period to another, depending, on the one hand, on the political will of the sponsoring state, and, on the other, on the number of competing projects demanding funding through the same mechanism. Experience shows that Networks require efficient Secretariats in support of their work and enough funding for organizing the initiatives. If the Networks are to be sustainable, and to make a discernible difference to women's participation in peace processes, there needs to be a secure commitment to funding that allows not only response to immediate needs or requests, but also longer-term strategic planning that extends beyond the temporal scope of the relevant NAP. One way to address this would be to establish a dedicated financial mechanism, enabling the Networks to bring their activities forward independently of political choices.

A second, related, aspect is the chronic undervaluing of women's peace work. It is often cited that women carry out mediation roles as part of their function within families or communities (El-Bushra, 2007). This translates into a problematic assumption that the women involved in the Networks are available and willing to work for free. To make a meaningful difference to women's capacity to participate in these initiatives, funding needs to be not only sustainable, but also set at a level that recognizes the professional nature of the work the women are undertaking, as well as the financial burden incurred in doing it, whether through direct expense or the loss of other employment opportunities. This is particularly true where women from civil society are being asked to dedicate substantial amounts of time to the Network.

Finally, the rapid growth of the number of Networks, and the positioning of these initiatives in relation to current foreign policy priorities, create a risk that the Networks will not develop independently of government priorities. If Networks remain tools for the projection of soft power, for example, will this distract from the core work of delivering meaningful change in mediation processes? Will the funding and support be directed where they are most needed? The nature of the relationship between the sponsoring governments and the operational activities of the Networks is one which will shape the success of the Networks for better or for worse.

Conclusion

Although the Networks remain in their infancy, the rate at which they have become established suggests that they are tapping into a clear perceived need to make more effective connections between gender and mediation. Some concluding observations can be offered for the Networks. First, they need to be clear regarding their aims and objectives, and where they want their impact to be felt most. The majority include a dual function of helping to promote women as mediators as well as amplifying the voice of women in mediation processes. These are complementary goals but not necessarily the same thing, and Networks need to be clear how these aims work together rather than conflating the two. Second, Networks can help to bridge the gap between the professional fields of mediation and WPS. They can help to define the skills necessary to be a good mediator and maintain rosters of suitably qualified women from different professional backgrounds, enhancing the diversity of the pool of candidates from which mediators are drawn.

Third, Networks are uniquely placed to begin to bridge the divide between women's mediation work at the local and civic society levels with that of intergovernmental bodies. Access to government is crucial to bridge the problematic divide between local and global work that has characterized efforts to increase the role of women in mediation to date. The role of Networks is therefore to reach out and forge connections – connections between the local and the global, but also between the WPS community of practice and the mediation support community of practice, and between civil society and governments. These connections are at the heart of attempts to increase women's meaningful participation in mediation at all levels.

Ultimately, establishing mechanisms for in-depth and effective coordination between Networks, states and international organizations will be key to their long-term success.

References

African Union (2018a) 'Panel of the Wise (PoW)' [Online] 24 April 2018, available from: http://www.peaceau.org/en/page/29-panel-of-the-wise-pow (accessed 28 September 2019).

African Union (2018b) 'Strengthening African Women's Participation in Conflict Prevention, Mediation Processes and Peace Stabilisation Efforts: Operationalisation of "FemWise-Africa' September 2018, available from: http://www.peaceau.org/uploads/final-concept-note-femwise-sept-15-short-version-clean-4-flyer.pdf.

Aggestam, K. and Svensson, I. (2018) 'Where Are the Women in Peace Mediation?' in Aggestam, K. and Towns, A.E. (eds.) *Gendering Diplomacy and International Negotiation*, Cham: Palgrave Macmillan, pp 149–68.

Charlesworth, H. (2008) 'Are Women Peaceful? Reflections on the Role of Women in Peacebuilding' *Feminist Legal Studies*, 16, 347–61.

Conciliation Resources (n.d.) 'WMC Members' [Online], available from: https://www.c-r.org/programme/women-mediators-across-commonwealth/wmc-members (accessed 28 September 2019).

Conciliation Resources (2020) *Women Mediators: Bridging the Peace Gap* [Online], available from: https://www.c-r.org/learning-hub/women-mediators-bridging-peace-gap (accessed 2 November 2020).

Council on Foreign Relations (2019) 'Women's Participation in Peace Processes' [Online], 30 January, available from: https://www.cfr.org/interactive/womens-participation-in-peace-processes (accessed 28 September 2019).

El-Bushra, J. (2007) 'Feminism, Gender and Women's Peace Activism' *Development and Change*, 38(1), 131–47.

Hellmüller, S. (2019) 'Beyond Buzzwords: Civil Society Inclusion in Mediation' in Ho-Won Jeong (ed.) *Conflict Intervention and Transformation: Theory and Practice*, Lanham, MD: Rowman and Littlefield.

Heyworth, F. and Turner, C. (2019) 'Advancing Inclusive Mediation Through the Lens of Leadership', *Geneva Centre for Security Policy* [Online], 1 March, available from: https://www.gcsp.ch/publications/advancing-inclusive-mediation-through-lens-leadership (accessed 28 September 2019).

Joenniemi, P. (2014) 'Peace Mediation and Conflict Resolution: The Policies Pursued by Four Nordic Countries' in Lehti, M. (ed.) *Nordic Approaches to Peace Mediation: Research, Practices and Policies*, Tampere Peace Research Institute, TAPRI Studies in Peace and Conflict Research No. 101 [Online], available from: https://trepo.tuni.fi/bitstream/handle/10024/94740/nordic_approaches_to_2014.pdf (accessed 28 September 2019).

Lehti, M. and Saarinen, J. (2014) 'Mediating Asymmetric Conflicts: A Survey on Nordic Studies on Peacemaking' in Lehti, M. (ed.) *Nordic Approaches to Peace Mediation: Research, Practices and Policies*, Tampere Peace Research Institute, TAPRI Studies in Peace and Conflict Research No. 101 [Online], available from: https://trepo.tuni.fi/bitstream/handle/10024/94740/nordic_approaches_to_2014.pdf (accessed 28 September 2019).

Limo, I. (2018) 'What Do Networks of Women Mediators Mean for Mediation Support in Africa?', *Accord* [Online], 31 May, available from: https://www.accord.org.za/conflict-trends/what-do-Networks-of-women-mediators-mean-for-mediation-support-in-africa/ (accessed 28 September 2019).

Ministero Degli Affari Esteri E Della Cooperazione Internazionale (2016) 'Italy's Third National Action Plan, In Accordance with UN Security Resolution 1325(2000), 2016–2019' [Online], available from: https://www.peacewomen.org/sites/default/files/49123_f_PlanofAction132520162019%20(1).pdf (accessed 28 September 2019).

Ministry for Foreign Affairs of Finland (n.d.) 'Mediation' [Online], available from: https://um.fi/mediation (accessed 28 September 2019).

MWMN (2019) 'Launch of the Cyprus Antenna of the MWMN' [Online] May, available from: https://womenmediators.net/launch-of-the-cyprus-antenna-of-the-mwmn/ (accessed 28 September 2019).

Norad (2018) 'The Norwegian Peace Engagement: New Challenges in a New World Order' [Online], 20 August, available from: https://norad.no/en/front/evaluation/news/2018/evaluation-views-the-norwegian-peace-engagement---new-challenges-in-a-new-world-order/ (accessed 28 September 2019).

Norwegian Ministries (2019) 'The Norwegian Government's Action Plan: Women, Peace and Security (2019–2022)' [Online], available from: https://www.regjeringen.no/globalassets/departementene/ud/dokumenter/planer/actionplan_wps2019.pdf (accessed 28 September 2019).

Palmiano Federer, J. (2016) 'On Gender: The Role of Norms in International Peace Mediation', swisspeace.

PRIO (2015) Nordic Women Mediators (NWM), [Online], November, available from: https://www.prio.org/Projects/Project/?x=1725 (accessed 7 October 2020).

Secretariat of the Panel of the Wise (n.d.) 'Strengthening African Women's Participation in Conflict Prevention, Mediation Processes and Peace Stabilisation Efforts: Operationalisation of "FemWise-Africa"' [Online], available from: http://www.peaceau.org/uploads/final-concept-note-femwise-sept-15-short-version-clean-4-flyer.pdf (accessed 28 September 2019).

Standfield, C. (2020) 'Caught Between Art and Science: The Women Peace and Security agenda in United Nations Mediation Narratives', *International Feminist Journal of Politics*, DOI: 10.1080/14616742/2020.1716632.

Turner, C. (2018) 'Absent or Invisible? Women Mediators and the United Nations' *Global Policy*, 9(2), 244–53.

Turner, C. (2020) 'Soft Ways of Doing Hard Things: Women Mediators and the Question of Gender in Peacebuilding', *Peacebuilding*, DOI:10.1080/21647259.2019.1664369

UK Government (2018) 'UK National Action Plan on Women, Peace and Security 2018–2022' [Online] January, available from: https://assets.publishing.service.gov.uk/government/uploads/system/uploads/attachment_data/file/677586/FCO1215-NAP-Women-Peace-Security-ONLINE_V2.pdf (accessed 28 September 2019).

UN (United Nations) (2012) 'Guidance for Effective Mediation' [Online], available from: https://peacemaker.un.org/sites/peacemaker.un.org/files/GuidanceEffectiveMediation_UNDPA2012%28english%29_0.pdf (accessed 25 July 2019).

UN (2017) 'United Nations Activities in Support of Mediation: Report of the Secretary-General', UN Document, 27 June 2017, A/72/115.

United States Institute of Peace (2016) 'Colombian Women Mediators Prepare to Support Peace' [Online] 11 August, available from: https://www.usip.org/blog/2016/08/colombian-women-mediators-prepare-support-peace (accessed 28 September 2019).

15

Technology and Peace Mediation: A Shift in the Mediator's Profession?

Miguel Varela

Motivation

This chapter examines the challenges and opportunities of the online space for peace mediation process design. While peace mediation as a core competence may remain largely unchanged, the design of interventions, from preparation to addressing questions of inclusivity or confidentiality or facilitating the implementation of an agreement, must now account for an additional layer of complexity that technology provides.

The chapter begins with an analysis of the functions that technology may serve in mediation. Fusing Brendan McAllister's functions of mediation and Anne Kahl and Helena Puig Larrauri's exploration of technology in broader peacemaking, it outlines four specific functions for technology in mediation: improving understanding, expanding and securing the mediation table, supporting creativity, and facilitating agreement. The broader fields of peace and social studies have been historically intertwined with the development of communication technologies, a dynamic that is explored later in the chapter and into which peace mediators have been thrown by the rise of social media and the COVID-19 pandemic.

Four changes are anticipated for peace mediation in adapting to technology: first, it is expected that mediation teams add profiles specialized in technology, following skills-based recruitment, and build linkages with the private sector. Second, the mediation table will continue to expand thanks to the use of video-tele-conferencing (VTC) systems in preparation for and around mediation sessions, also enhancing opportunities for training. Third, digital technologies will be key for communities of practice and coordination of efforts, an area that continues to be a key hurdle for peace workers. Lastly, mediators may look to technology to enhance the inclusivity of the process.

These changes will likely only come about once mediators understand technology not just as a tool, but as a transversal component in the societies where they operate.

Introduction

Communication is at the heart of mediation. Be it in the formulation of a common understanding of conflict issues or to aid in the unearthing of deep-rooted needs and interests, words represent one of the main tools at the disposal of mediators. Yet the field is still coming to grips with one of the main ingredients in modern communications: the digital sphere.

Technology provides channels that have accelerated and diversified our communications. Social media and instant messaging have created space where billions of messages are shared every day around the world. Through posts, 'tweets', comments, video calls, live broadcasts and texts, mobile phones and laptops serve today as personal media platforms. Every minute, users of websites like Twitter, Facebook or Instagram produce hundreds of millions of new posts and images (Martin, 2019). Online applications handle over 50 billion messages every day. Search engines claim they receive over 4 million queries in only 60 seconds, while online encyclopaedias collect hundreds of new edits and new articles per minute. Meanwhile, news sites and blogs produce millions of news pieces every day as the hunger for information grows with no end in sight (Al-Heeti, 2018).

Not only have social media become the centre of attention for people of all ages with access to the internet, but they have become a key medium for political campaigning and social activism. With social media, conflict actors have gained new ways to express needs, reinforce positions and state demands. There are many and well-known examples of the role of these channels in social developments. Movements like the Arab Spring across North Africa and the Middle East, the Revolution of Dignity in Ukraine, or the protests in Hong Kong in 2014 and the summer of 2019 made intensive use of the internet to spread their message, gain visibility and build their image.[1] Meanwhile, campaigns of counter-information and misinformation accompanied the rallies and spread quickly in social media and blogs, offering an alternative view for better or worse and reinforcing the position of those who did not support the protests. Group chats continue to be used by violent groups to recruit members, while democratically elected presidents take to the internet to attack their rivals and spread their political messages.

But if there is an event that has materialized the impact of digital technologies for peace mediators and dialogue actors, that is the COVID-19 pandemic. As the UN Secretary-General (UNSG) called for a global ceasefire, online communications played a key role in sustaining existing processes and supporting new initiatives. In Yemen, an eight-day round of virtual Track II consultations was hosted by the Office of the Special Envoy of the Secretary-General to Yemen (OSESGY) and the European Union Delegation to prepare for a potential resumption of negotiations. Digital technologies enabled a depth of discussion that would have been impeded by global lockdowns and travel blockades.

In parallel to social media, artificial intelligence (AI) has garnered the attention of peace practitioners for some time now. Data scientists and social researchers have developed groups of mathematical equations to label comments and attempt narrative analysis and used big data to analyse the impact of social reforms,[2] while fake social media profiles continue to spread information like wildfire. The role of AI in social dynamics has

[1] In the 2014 Umbrella Revolution in Hong Kong, photo-manipulations circulated online played an important role in the redefinition of legitimacy and governance, and were 'produced neither by the centre nor by the privileged few [but] by the netizen through mass participation and public reinvention' (Wing-Ki, 2019: 41). Similarly, the use of imagery along with the #Euromaidan hashtag online helped create a visual identity for the protests in Ukraine, made possible by the democratization of photography via mobile phones and social media (Domb Sadof, 2017). Meanwhile, the role of social media in the Arab Spring has been debated at length, with authors claiming that '[t]he first noteworthy success of new media in the Middle East and North Africa (MENA) region was creating, building and strengthening civil society' (Khan, 2013: 68).

[2] The use of AI to automatically label content online is one of the current frontiers for social studies, faced with challenges of interpretation and scale. Two examples come to mind from personal experience: in Ukraine, social media was used to measure the impact of different areas of reform as expressed by social media discussions. In Bosnia, AI was developed to detect comments in news sites and different forums that may reveal radicalization dynamics.

been highlighted by electoral processes or the migration crisis in Europe, demonstrating just how fragile social stability can be.[3]

In 2020, technology is barely *just a tool*. Instead, it is now a fundamental part of how we relate to each other and how sentiment is built, deeply embedded into our communications.[4] As such, mediators can find opportunities in approaching it as a transversal competence.

Mediation in an Ocean of Information

There is an easy exercise that mediators can do to place themselves in the bigger, online picture. Google Trends is an online resource provided by the search engine giant. It gives an overview of how the number of searches for a term or topic varies over time, from its highest point to its lowest point, since 2004.

Typing 'peace mediation' into Trends reveals the visibility of the practice online (Figure 15.1). The term peaks in 2004, sparks back into discussion in 2009 (perhaps with the development of the European Commission's concept on mediation) and has deflated ever since. The same dynamic can be observed when searching for 'peacebuilding' and 'conflict transformation' (Figure 15.2). Online attention to peace practice comes and goes, but it would seem it is relatively present – until compared with conflict terms.

When 'shootings', 'Syria' or 'terrorism' are introduced, the visibility of peace practice is nearly null (Figure 15.3), and the event-driven nature of online attention becomes even more noticeable.

Should mediators worry that their practice is not a trending topic online? In workshops and communities of practice, mediators have shown resistance to this idea, and understandably. Rightly, they note that mediation is a professional undertaking that relies on confidentiality, not a public relations stunt. Yet the practice of peace, generally, is situated within a social context that is increasingly fragmented, where attention has become a key currency for business, social and political actors alike. Mediators are not strangers to that dynamic: whether they work at the highest track or deep within community dialogue, information leaks and new social dynamics pose a constant risk to their processes.

[3] The EU's adoption in December 2018 of an Action Plan and Rapid Alert System on disinformation, which includes heavy investment in digital tools capable of detecting misinformation online, is a clear sign of the relevance of AI and the online space in governance. For an exploration of AI in global governance, see Pielemeier (2019).

[4] The UN Secretary-General's High-Level Panel on Digital Cooperation refers to this as 'the age of digital interdependence'.

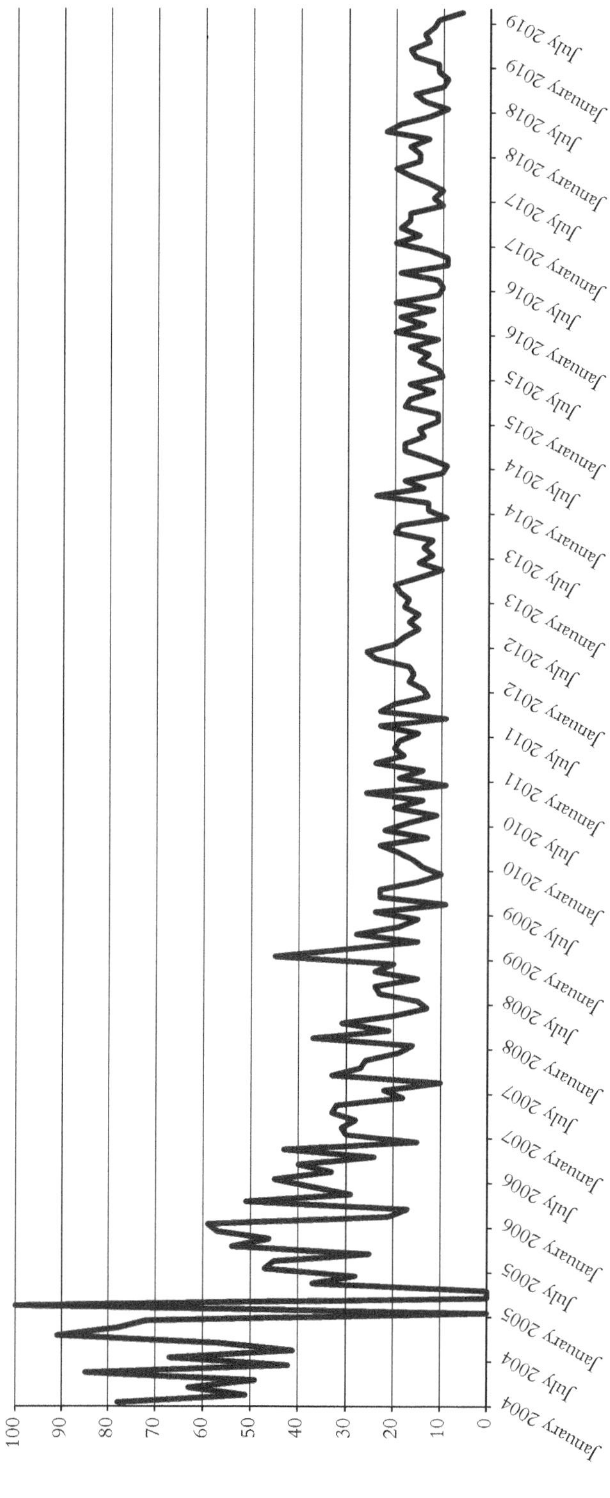

Figure 15.1: Standardized distribution of the searches on Google Trends for 'Peace Mediation' from 2004 to 2019

Source: Google Trends, 2019

Figure 15.2: Standardized distribution of the searches on Google Trends for 'Peace mediation', 'Peacebuilding' and 'Conflict transformation' from 2004 to 2019

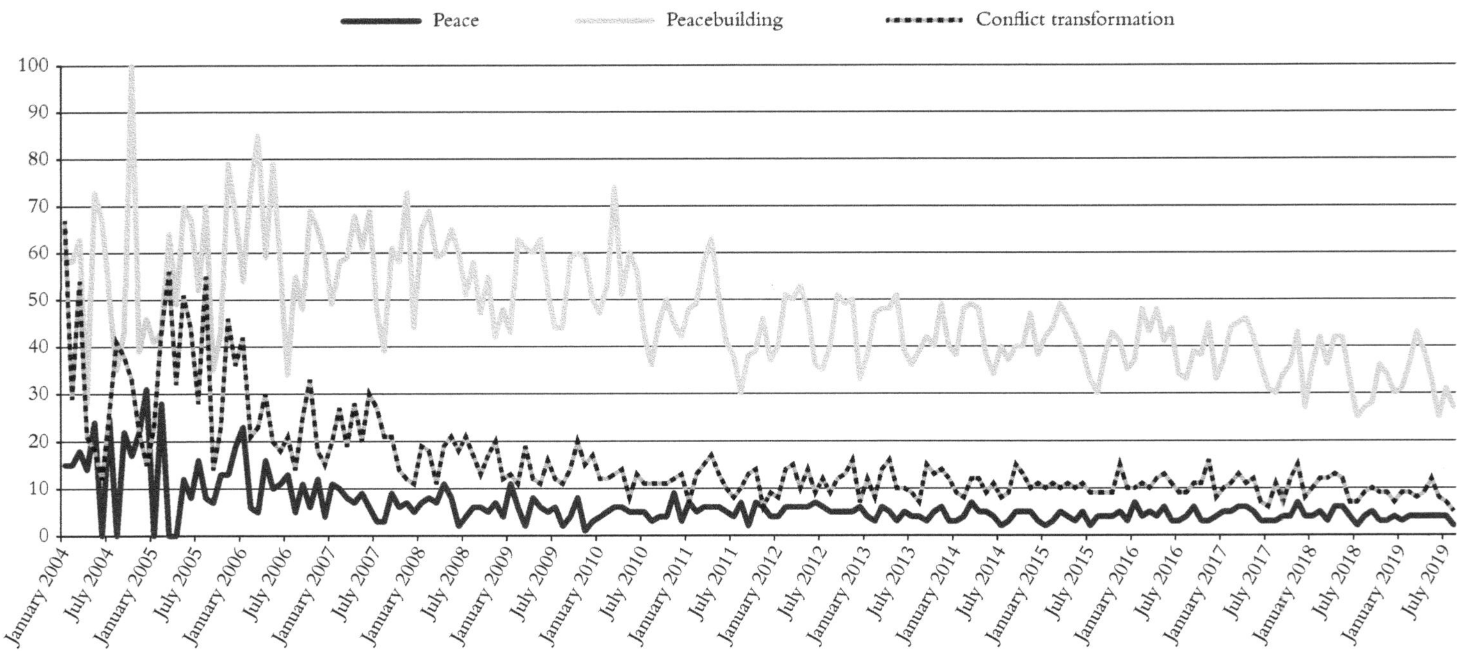

Source: Google Trends, 2019

Figure 15.3: Standardized distribution of the searches on Google Trends for 'Terrorism, 'Shooting', 'Syria', 'Peace' and 'Peacebuilding' from 2004 to 2019

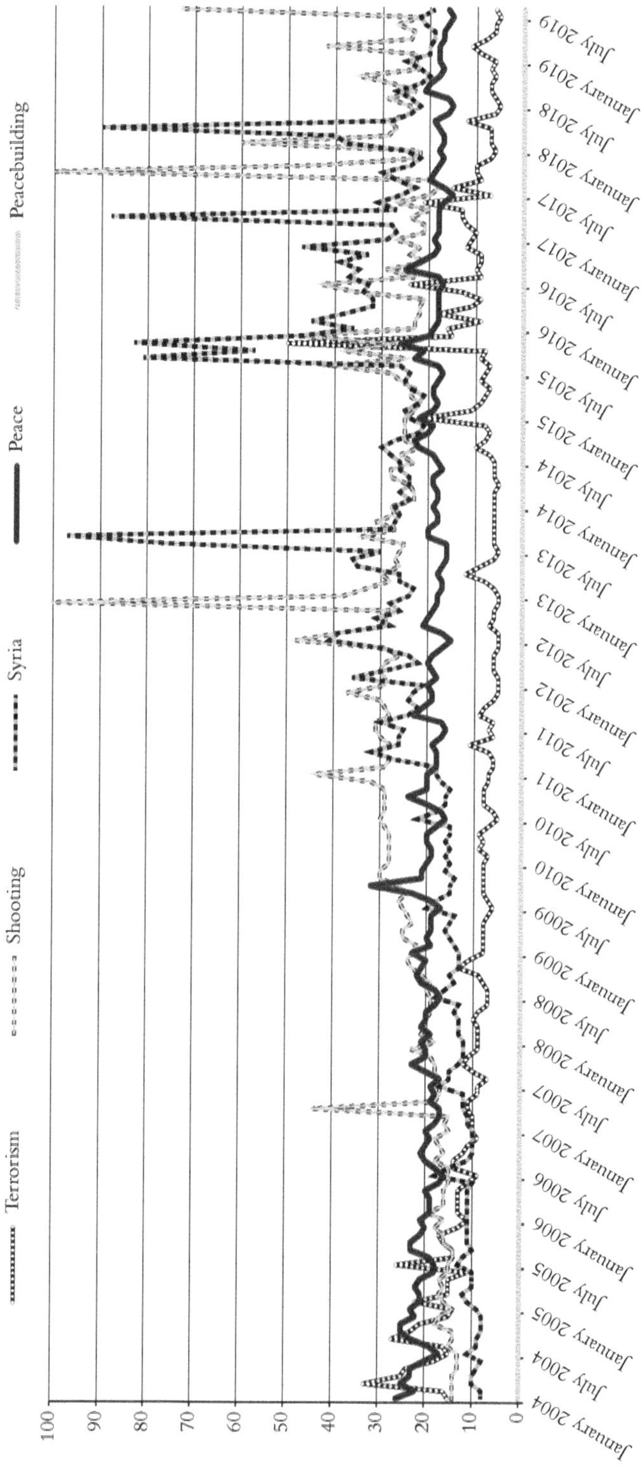

Note: A peak indicates a high volume of searches for the given term on a given date.

Source: Google Trends, 2019

Figure 15.4: Standardized distribution of the searches on Google Trends for 'Terrorism, 'Shooting', 'Syria', 'Peace' and 'Lady Gaga' from 2004 to 2019

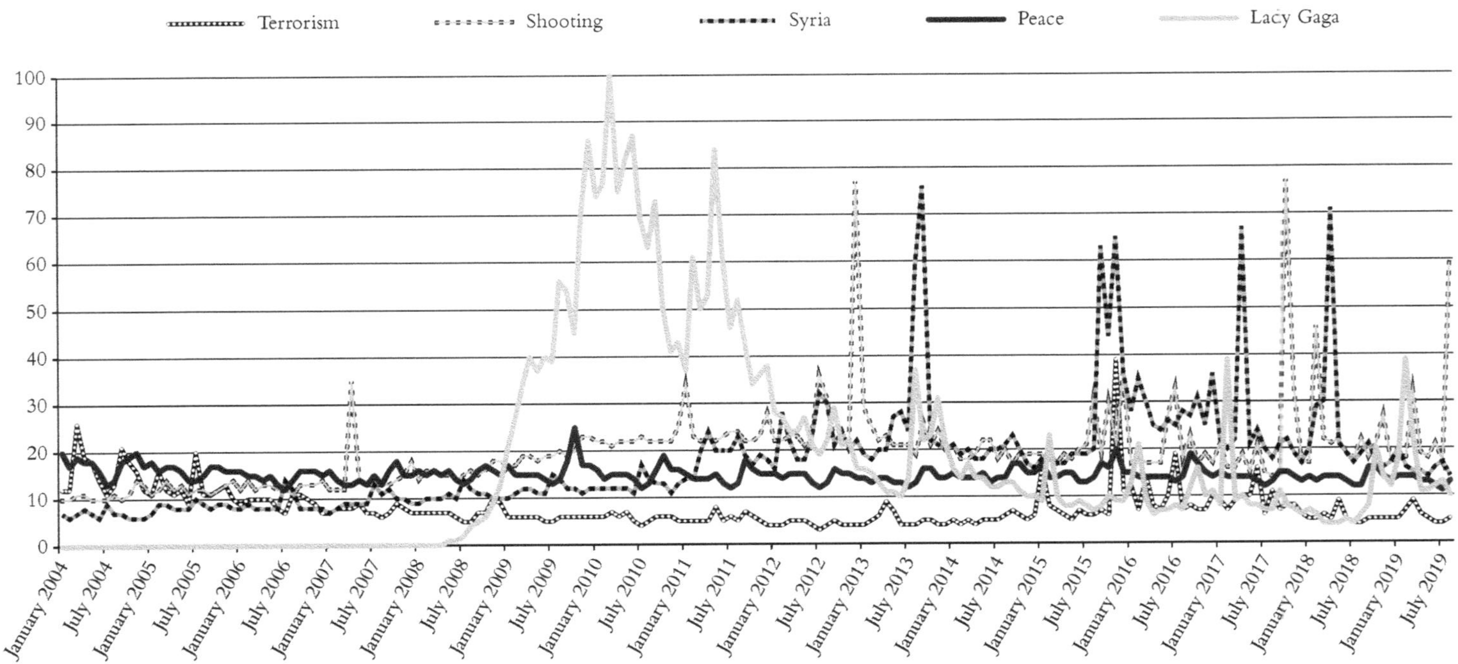

Source: Google Trends, 2019

Incorporating online tools and capacities, monitoring the online space, and analysing the role of technology in each context are steps for mediators and the broader mediation team to design processes that respond to said contexts.

An Evolution in the Peace Mediator's Profession

The digital world comes with challenges to the profession, which mediators acknowledge: 'It is evident that while mediation is and will remain a predominantly human endeavour requiring human skills and sensitivity, the mediation environment is increasingly impacted and influenced by digital technology' (UN DPPA and HD Centre, 2019: 32).

An important question relates to attention: how to maintain the interest of interlocutors throughout the process while accepting the fact that technology will inevitably appear as a disruptive element.[5] Mediators deal in language, words, feelings and stories; how can they compete with flashing images on a mobile phone or catchy 'tweets' that constantly reinforce the position of their interlocutors? And importantly, how are peace mediators to capture the attention of those who are already outside their process, most likely uninterested in what they can contribute to them and instead finding comfort in the reassuring warmth of internet arguments?

Brendan McAllister, a former member of the United Nations (UN) Standby Team for Mediation Experts, often speaks about the 'quality of [the] attention' of mediators and conflict parties. Discussing peace in Northern Ireland, he reflects:

> The quality of our attention to the legacy of conflict and the wounds of division is now deficient and a once-in-a-generation opportunity to attend to deeper truth, with compassion, is fading with each passing year since the Good Friday Agreement of 1998. Perhaps at the heart of such a failing

[5] A simple exercise to understand the extent to which the constant flow of information affects attention is the one proposed by Jeffrey Colkin in his *Dialogue Mapping* book, an excellent resource for mediators (Colkin, 2006). Colkin proposes a three-minute game of noughts and crosses, with a twist: playing the game on a 4×4 grid without using pen or paper. Most players struggle to complete even one game before the three-minutes mark. As they manage more information than their brain is prepared to process, players stress out and fail to keep their attention on the game. The same logic can be applied to this landscape of information: handling such vast volumes of data can be a daunting task.

> is a widespread inability between the two main traditions of Northern society for mutual recognition of each other. (McAllister, 2015)

It is worth questioning what the online 'ocean' of information does to our capacity for mutual recognition. The online space can affect the attention of both mediators and stakeholders, not only during the mediation session, but also around it. While professional capacity from the mediator to avoid participants falling into their social media *at* a mediation session should be expected, it is increasingly difficult to control the safe space created by the mediation in the long-term process. As much as mediators can assist communication at the mediation table, does the inevitable disruption threatened by the online space mean that mediators and their teams should constantly engage in online discussions too?

Digital technologies can distract parties from the mediation process, or even derail it entirely through misinformation or online mobilization, but they also provide a space to continue the conversations and act as a bridge. The case of Yemen is illustrative. As the country rolled into another year of war and the momentum of the Riyadh agreement was yet to be translated into local measures, the COVID-19 pandemic 'joined the chat'. As international travel bans were implemented and dialogue actors became trapped in their homes, international and local organizations sought to continue supporting efforts at all levels. With the UNSG's call for a global ceasefire, the opportunity was there for a potential resumption of negotiations. Hosted by the OSESGY and the European Union Delegation, peace practitioners used VTC to formalize a series of working groups to address key topics in such a scenario, advancing the work of OSESGY and enhancing coordination.

Using social media to connect mediation teams and the public has also helped enhance their legitimacy. In 2016 the Office of the United Nations Special Coordinator for Lebanon (UNSCOL) organized a live Q&A session with the then Special Coordinator in the country, helping connect the mission with the public and enhance transparency (UNSCOL, 2016). Conversely, social media can underpin the disconnect between mediation teams and their target audiences. In 2018 the UN Special Representative to Afghanistan faced heavy criticism online after he was perceived to not be meeting the expectations placed on him; it was only once the Envoy set up an account on Twitter that he could respond to online reports on him and build an image of approachability.[6]

[6] The UN and HD Centre's Digital Toolkit collects this and other cases in its 'Case Studies' section (UN DPPA and HD Centre, nd).

Increasingly, as social media expands the negotiation table, the frontier between peace practice and mediation is blurring, and the time is nigh for a review of the function of mediation in conjunction with technology. The five core functions of mediation outlined by McAllister are a good starting point (McAllister, 2015):

- assisting communication
- improving understandings
- supporting creative thinking
- exploring accommodations
- facilitating agreement

McAllister's approach is one of peace mediators as 'sensitive outsiders', capable of engaging with and understanding the content of the conflict without it impacting their clarity of assessment. His work can be merged with that of Kahl and Puig Larrauri, who outline four ways in which technology can contribute to broader peacebuilding (Kahl and Puig Larrauri, 2013). Fusing both, it is possible to draw four areas where technology may become vital to mediators.

First, Kahl and Puig Larrauri refer to technology for *data processing*. This includes the use of social media to 'listen' into online discussions, or the use of geographical mapping systems to pinpoint areas of need. Generally, digital technologies that serve this function are seen as an opportunity to obtain information about a given conflict and prepare for it. Mediators can thus look at social media to draw a general picture of drivers and dynamics (see also Lanz and Eleiba, 2018). But, beyond the challenges of echo-chambers and the digital divide, handling such data poses both technical and intellectual difficulties, as noted in a DFID practice note: 'only when the volume, velocity and variety of these data can be handled, and the veracity and virtue established, can researchers begin to extract meaningful information' (Williams et al, 2016: 5). And so, increasingly, donors are turning their attention towards complex technologies that strengthen and *accelerate* this work, moving from analyst-driven observation to computational research.

Symptomatic of this move into data processing for broader peace process design is the publishing of the 'E-Analytics Guide' (Wählisch and Masood, 2019) at the Department of Political and Peacebuilding Affairs of the UN (UN DPPA) in January 2019. It covers a variety of tools and approaches to conducting digital analysis for peace work. One such approach is the use of big data, an area that has received increasing attention in recent years. Collecting and processing large amounts of information, researchers can extract a list of the main topics being discussed online in each context quickly. Further, they can use AI[7] and 'sentiment analysis'[8] to report on whether social media users perceive each of those topics positively or negatively. Researchers have also used social media to draw social networks of key actors and the connections between them, helping them understand the linkages between different groups of interest. With digital technologies, they can keep those networks updated as they evolve and use the information to communicate strategically (Williams et al, 2016: 19). Similarly, speech analysis has been used to attempt to detect extremist content online and feed Countering Violent Extremism programmes or to quickly react to potential spoilers (Williams et al, 2016: 22).[9] Ultimately, this first function of technology in mediation can be labelled as *improving understanding*, borrowing from McAllister's terminology, if not between the conflict parties then at least within the mediation team. Using appropriates technologies in conjunction with local knowledge and empathy can help build a picture of the situation mediators must help address.

Second in Kahl's and Larrauri's exploration is the function of technology in *assisting communication* of a peace process where it is sensible to do so, demonstrating progress and keeping stakeholders updated. This

---

[7] Masood and Wählisch explore the ways in which machine learning and AI can support a peace process by tracking the perception of local issues in different regions (Masood and Wählisch, 2019). Simply put, these are combinations of mathematical models capable of adapting their own design through trial and error. By repeatedly presenting the model with data previously labelled by an analyst, programmers can 'teach' it to replicate the labelling process in a previously unseen set of data. Naturally, the process takes a significant amount of time and effort from both programmers and analysts, but once set up, some models have been observed to reach accuracy levels much higher than that of analysts, especially when it comes to avoiding false positives. This type of work has received increasingly more attention by both international organizations and government agencies when it comes to detecting hate speech online, for instance.

[8] In simple terms, sentiment analysis assigns positive and negative meanings to certain words and their combinations within a sentence. Thus, when a social media post contains words such as 'good' or 'great', they may be labelled as positive, whereas words such as 'bad' or 'disaster' may be labelled as negative. Meanwhile, keyword or topic identification is used to find the most-mentioned concepts and the words that relate to them. While it is not a foolproof method (sentiment analysis is particularly difficult when sarcasm is used, for instance) nor available for all languages, it gives analysts the possibility of extracting a list of key issues almost immediately.

[9] The use of AI in this field has been debated intensively given the limitations of AI in placing online content within a social context. For an exposition of how machine learning AI works when it comes to text analysis and extremism, see González Fraile and Barton-Henry (2019).

component is directly translated into McAllister's function of mediation with the same name. With digital technologies, mediators have a set of tools to increase their reach, but they are also forced to be on the lookout for potential disturbances, perhaps more so than in their absence. In the words of Teresa Whitfield, Director of the Policy and Mediation Division at the United Nations Department of Political and Peacebuilding Affairs: 'common features of peace processes today include data breaches; leaked information; monitoring and surveillance; intense scrutiny on social media; misinformation and disinformation; and competition, disruption or control of crucial internet resources' (Whitfield, 2019: 9). These dynamics leave mediators susceptible to a set of new threats from both within and outside the mediation circle. Conflict actors can use social media to question the legitimacy of the process; to show defiance; to mobilize their circumscription; to react to developments in the mediation process; or simply to exert pressure on mediators to meet their demands. Admittedly, mediators can apply similar techniques, strategically leaking information or pushing for parties to meet.[10] In these cases, online technologies appear not just as a channel, but as an accelerator of group dynamics that can block processes or derail them. Thus, digital technologies may serve a second function of *expanding and securing the mediation table*.

The third element in Kahl and Puig Larrauri's analysis of peace technology is that of *gaming*, or the use of games to expose individuals to new ideas and motivate their participation in a peace initiative. In a peace mediation context, this type of work could be envisioned as a mechanism to build due regard, to explore accommodations, stimulate creative thinking and anticipate potentials blockages. Or, simply, *supporting creativity*.

Lastly, Kahl and Puig Larrauri outline how technology can assist with *engagement*, motivating stakeholders into action and offering them new ways to contribute to the process. A whole body of work is being developed by the Centre on Conflict, Development and Peacebuilding at the Geneva Graduate Institute that looks into the opportunities and challenges technology creates with regard to inclusion.[11] From a mediation lens, this last element may be useful in three ways: to request input from circumscriptions between mediation rounds; strengthening

[10] A relevant example is that of the G7 meeting in Biarritz in the summer of 2019. Twitter played a key role in pressuring US President Donald Trump to attempt a meeting between the President and the Foreign Minister of the Islamic Republic of Iran, Javad Zarif.

[11] The report is available online at https://digitalpeacemaking.com (accessed 15 September 2020).

linkages with underrepresented groups; and to motivate citizens during the implementation phase of an agreement. That is, *facilitating agreement*.

These four functions of technology in mediation (improving understanding, expanding and securing the mediation table, supporting creativity, and facilitating agreement) do not come without risks, as Kahl and Puig Larrauri admit. Among them, the digital divide (or the problematic assumption that everyone has access to the same technology), the risk of a confidentiality breach, ethical conundrums or the echo effect of technology are some of the most commonly mentioned. In their words, '[i]n exploring the application of technology to peacebuilding, it is important to keep in mind that technologies are *not* neutral. … technologies can also become *dividers* in a conflict context' (Kahl and Puig Larrauri, 2013: 2; original emphasis).

Similarly, the introduction of large-scale and automatic data analysis poses particularly difficult challenges for mediators. What is *public* in the public online sphere? And to what extent can analysts use the information collected? Can machines be trusted to give accurate interpretations to the content studied? And how much capacity do mediation teams have to engage with them while also attending to the process?[12] Online ethnographers have discussed questions of privacy in online research at large and are still looking for consensus, generally accepting that the principle should be to do no harm and to earn consent whenever possible.[13] So, if mediators are to approach technology while protecting the privacy of their interlocutors and the integrity of their profession, they need to carefully assess the function that they want technology to fulfil in their work, and not just the advantages or disadvantages of using it: in other words, understand technology as a transversal topic.

Ultimately, the eruption of digital technologies into the peace mediation sphere may lead to the reshaping of the mediation team. If peace mediators are to work with technology, does that mean they need

[12] This is a common challenge for people working in Countering Violent Extremism (CVE) programming, for instance. The type of algorithms that can mark content as extremist are known as 'machine learning' algorithms, which require very careful supervision by analysts to make sure the context is considered and that the algorithms are progressing correctly. While the algorithms will eventually 'learn' and interpret text on their own, the initial phases are very heavy work, especially for mediation teams that might be understaffed and want to focus on the process instead. Based on experience, in projects where the aim is for machine learning algorithms to correctly mark online posts as radical, hate speech or extremism, analysts should be ready to label up to 5,000 posts manually.

[13] The University of Aberdeen, for instance, provides a framework for social media ethics (Townsend and Wallace, 2016).

to become technology *experts*? The predictable answer is 'no'. Instead, mediators may want to ensure their professional needs are listened to and incorporated into the development of technologies that can assist them. Thus, the process of learning should be bidirectional, from technologists to mediators, and vice versa. While approaching some areas of technology – such as AI or the use of mapping systems – may require training, mediators are not expected to become software developers nor data analysts, but may benefit from becoming informed users. This is a common misconception when peacetech proponents and mediators come together, and one that the COVID-19 has put in the spotlight.[14]

Peace mediation teams might look at skills-based recruitment to acquire the technological expertise required *when* it is required. As underlined by Catherine Turner and Fleur Heyworth, 'the complexity underlying contemporary conflicts demands both new approaches, and new skills' (Turner and Heyworth, 2019: 9). In their defence of skills-based recruitment in mediation teams, Turner and Heyworth explore a series of skills underlying the mediators' practice, mainly interpersonal skills,[15] which, they continue, must come in agreement with the mediators' 'ability to work within the context of a conflict' (Turner and Heyworth, 2019: 10). It is precisely as part of that capacity to work the context that mediators may approach technology. Alternatively, it may be understood as a transversal competency, seeing as technology affects most of the interpersonal skills required of the mediator. Lanz and Eleiba recognize this shift that new technologies bring about for mediation teams and highlight that 'senior mediators will seek to include specialized expertise in their team' (Lanz and Eleiba, 2018: 4).

Lastly, obtaining information from social media has become increasingly difficult, and it may require the support of actors that peace mediators are not used to working with, such as research institutions or the private sector. In the wake of data breaches and privacy scandals, large social media providers have made it harder to access relevant information, making it available only to research groups and individual researchers affiliated with

[14] A useful example here is that of a project for dialogue in Ukraine that made use of mapping technologies to detect patterns in the content of dialogues across the country. The project team found it a challenge to connect with facilitators and mediators, who instead chose to stay focused on their processes and participants. Similarly, at a workshop in Brussels early in 2019, a community of practice of mediators expressed their concern that focusing on harnessing the advantages of technology would take their attention away from the process.

[15] The list is composed of effective communication and listening; team work; emotional intelligence; ability to build trust; empathy; resilience; self-awareness; and the ability to be inclusive (Turner and Heyworth, 2019: 10).

a university department.[16] In addition, while the peacetech community has made a great effort to promote open-source and non-profit models in technology for peace, most software development and data analysis organizations remain for-profit. Peace mediators who wish to explore the development of new technological solutions for their work may need to accommodate to this reality, which is often unfamiliar to them.[17]

How Do Peace Practitioners Look at Technology Today?

The interest in the role of technology in governance and social peace is not recent, but its shape has evolved over the second half of the 20th century. A look at the volume of academic papers since the beginning of the 20th century shows that scholarly interest in the nexus between technology and peace (or technology and war) began in the wake of the Second World War and accelerated greatly in the 1970s and 1980s.[18]

In a 1964 essay in the *Virginia Quarterly Review*, the historian Melvin Kranzberg reflected on the suspicion that technology raised in his time among humanists. He argued that technology was 'in the process of restoring human dignity by freeing man from the repetitious tasks which dull the human personality' (Kranzberg, 1964: 582), while theorists continued to frown upon it. He went on to elaborate a defence of technology that, 'far from destroying democracy, may have actually increased it' (Kranzberg, 1964: 584). He covers a breadth of social aspects, from governance to the arts or the division of labour – and peace, too. The current push for digital work in peace is partly inspired by this vision, with a dose of caution.

In parallel, the 1960s saw intensive scholarly debates on peace research, born of the perceived failure of traditional theories to adapt to the nuclear age (Burton, 1964: 283; Chaudhri, 1968: 365). Johan Galtung's work in this area is seminal and makes a direct link between the theory of peace, the theory of conflict and the theory of development (Galtung, 1969: 183). That is, peace research was concerned with both physical and non-

[16] A case in point is that of Facebook, which locked access to its data following the breaches detected early in 2018 related to the US election campaign of 2016.

[17] When it comes to media and social media work for peacebuilding and security, for-profit outfits have steadily gained more access to public funding, particularly in the UK and the US, an added challenge for traditionally non-profit mediation organizations.

[18] Search conducted on the Journal Storage (JSTOR) database, filtering results by decade. The search included the terms 'peace' and 'technology' within a maximum distance of ten words.

physical aspects, in which technology played a big role and would go on to play a much larger role as communications evolved.

At the heart of this new discipline was the need to respond to the changes that technology had brought about in society. At the time, technology in peace was mainly framed through the lens of potential nuclear warfare, looking at machinery, military technology and other infrastructure – in sum, looking at hardware. In Kranzberg's words, 'technology made warfare more complex and most costly, it helped increase the power of the state and the destructiveness of modern armed combat' (Kranzberg, 1964: 590).

This security paradigm would continue to dominate the study of technology in peace for decades. Researchers discussed the values that technologists should apply to their work, how humanists could influence the development of new technological tools, or how technology should be distributed to support economies and social groups in disadvantage. In the late 1980s, scholars and thinkers were still submitting letters to the editors of leading journals in peace research that outlined their concerns about technology and called for a careful approach to it (see Bardis, 1985; Hunt, 1989). Meanwhile, technology was steadily coming to a point where it would change human relationships entirely.

Fast-forward into the 2000s and, with them, the rise of social media and online exchange. As communications became larger, faster and more unpredictable, researchers turned their attention from the 'hard' side of technology (machinery, armament and infrastructure) to the 'soft' side, that which impacted perceptions and feelings. New dynamics in communications emerged and information became more readily available. In this context, the contribution of mediators, peace researchers and behavioural scientists becomes even more important to understand conflict dynamics. Kranzberg's closing remarks from 1964 are still relevant today:

> Technologists must perforce educate themselves in ... a more responsive attitude to human and social demands in their ultimate implications ... Some technologists are increasingly aware of the humanistic imperatives and are trying to do something about fulfilling them. Can the same be said of the humanists in understanding the demands of a technological society? (Kranzberg, 1964: 592)

The answer is 'yes', at least from a broad peacebuilding perspective. In recent years, peace practitioners have put increasingly more attention on technology. Efforts have predominantly looked at technologies accessible to non-technical users: information and communication technologies like mobile phones, web applications, messaging platforms and media software. These technologies can be encapsulated in four functions: enabling communications; collecting information about the world we live in; analysing said information; and presenting results clearly while keeping them updated. In doing so, peace workers hope to fulfil some of the core competencies of their trade: establishing facts, understanding dynamics and analysing their impact, and including as many perspectives as possible.

In 2018, the UN and the Centre for Humanitarian Dialogue (HD Centre) published their Digital Mediation Toolkit, a collection of online technologies meant to help mediators and peace practitioners do their jobs better. The toolkit is the culmination of a process of research, community engagement and practical development that organizations like Build Up, ICT4Peace or the United States Institute of Peace have been spearheading for years. Mediation outfits like the HD Centre, swisspeace or mediatEUr have done intensive work in this area as well.[19]

The HD Centre's 'Peacemaking and New Technologies' practice series is another example of a thorough review of the technological tools available to mediators, while encouraging mediators not to lose sight of the nature of their work: 'technological tools may provide benefits and risks in addition to this [the mediator's practice], but they do not change its essence' (Jenny et al, 2018: 46).

Generally, studies on digital technologies for peace blur the lines between mediation and broader peace work. As organizations that had traditionally conducted direct mediation and dialogue are increasingly putting their focus on supporting insider mediators, the focus on tools that can help analyse dynamics and build inclusive processes will become more important in the future.

This support role of technology is clear from the #CyberMediation initiative by the Diplo Foundation[20] and the work of David Lanz and Ahmed Eleiba. In their 2018 review of options for peace mediators to approach technology, Lanz and Eleiba call on mediation teams to

[19] See HD's work in the Libyan Peace Process (Centre for Humanitarian Dialogue, 2018); mediatEUr's work to support dialogue facilitators and mediators in Ukraine (mediatEUr, 2016); or swisspeace's exploration of the implications of information and communication technologies in peace processes (Widmer and Grossenbacher, 2019).

[20] The #CyberMediation Initiative is a project launched by the Diplo Foundation in 2018. It aims 'to explore how digital technology is impacting the role of mediation in the prevention and resolution of violent conflict, how digital tools can be used by peace mediators and what safeguards are needed to protect the integrity of the mediation process' (Diplo Foundation, 2018).

'incorporate social media in their communication strategy' and to 'take social media seriously' (Lanz and Eleiba, 2018: 4).

Specifically, in the field of mediation, efforts have moved mostly in the direction of conflict assessment, coordination and informal dialogue. In Ukraine and the Middle East, mediatEUr used a mapping methodology to connect different mediation and dialogue initiatives and inform the European Union (EU) and the UN Development Programme (UNDP) programming on local needs (mediatEUr, 2015; 2019). Also in Ukraine, Donbass Dialogues shines as an example of successful connections across the contact line in the East through videoconferences; their work also includes a crowdsourcing component when it comes to selecting the themes to address at the discussions. In Colombia, *La Conversación Más Grande del Mundo* ('the world's largest conversation') was a project supported by the International Organization for Migration (IOM) and the Swedish International Development Agency (SIDA) that launched questions about the development of the country and the negotiation process between the government and the Revolutionary Armed Forces of Colombia (FARC). Users could contribute to the discussion in a format that helped avoid toxic commentary and gave visibility to well-articulated arguments.

While not mediation efforts per se, the work done by organizations aiming to counter misinformation and extremism online is a key component of addressing competing perspectives too. Such is the work of Stop Fake, the EU vs Disinfo initiative, the *Observatorio Proxi* in Spain, or Factmata in the United Kingdom, among many others.

Conclusion: Beyond Discussing Technology

Examples of initiatives using digital technologies for peace abound, with no lack of challenges and lessons to be shared and discussed. Be it as an early-warning mechanism, as a tool to measure social cohesion, or as a thermometer on conflict, the use of technology for peace nowadays is mainly – and naturally – an information and communications effort. Research in this area has grown significantly in the last decade, and conferences like Build Peace[21] or projects like the #CyberMediation initiative or Digital Peacemaking help connect practitioners and

[21] Build Peace is an annual conference organized by Build Up. Its stated aim is to 'bring together practitioners, activists, academics, policy makers, artists and technologists from around the world to share experience and ideas on using technology, arts and other innovations for peacebuilding and conflict transformation' (Build Peace, nd).

design new approaches to digital technology in peace work. Yet mediators are largely a satellite to these discussions despite the few and positive exceptions.

In the information society, technology is intertwined with governance, power struggles, community relations and conflict. In higher-income countries, we witness the return to conflict dialectics of 'us against them' in the aftermath of the economic crisis and in the face of migration, largely fuelled via social media. In lower-income countries, communication technologies have created new social divisions and reinforced existing socials structures.[22] Humanitarian and development organization have been harnessing the power of technologies to connect social groups and accelerate assistance for years, with peace practitioners recently joining them in that effort.

Peace mediators must be part of the discussion. A key trait of the peace mediator is their ability to operate within the context of the peace process and to respond to its dynamics; whether it is complex or rudimentary, technology is a fundamental component of society, and so mediators should be ready to adapt it. Several developments may be expected in this regard:

First, incorporating digital tools will require changes in the composition of the mediation team, bringing in more analytical capacity as well as technological expertise, and with new and existing skills like data analysis or strategic communications gaining more importance. Mediation teams may look at skills-based recruitment to secure that expertise and build the capacity of current members to become informed users of technologies that can enhance their preparation and outreach. In some cases, this may also entail cooperating with the business sector.

Second, mediators may engage in online discussions through regular Q&A sessions, open or private groups, or crowd-sourced session design, particularly in preparation for and around mediation sessions.[23] Using video-teleconferencing systems, this may also be an opportunity for online training for local mediators, increasing the reach of the profession.

Third, as mediation outfits move into supporting local mediators and continue pushing for more coordination among organizations, digital tools should be an opportunity to strengthen communities of practice,

---

[22] Discussed by Kahl and Puig Larrauri as the 'bias of connectivity' (Kahl and Puig Larrauri, 2013: 2), the reflection on how access to technology replicates existing social structures is an important point to consider, and yet another manifestation of how technology has been incorporated into the social fabric.

[23] Crowd-sourced design has been practised in Ukraine for several years now, with the work of Donbass Dialogues pulling from the experience of a group of over 400 Facebook users who participate in a private group regularly.

connecting local and international practitioners for an exchange of experiences and, when sensible and safe to do so, information. This is an important step towards better coordination among Track II organizations, with local organizations and with donors.

Finally, digital technologies may impact the design of the mediation process and its levels of intervention, allowing for easier exchange across all demographic indicators and tracks. This might help create more inclusive and better-coordinated processes that have a measurable impact on decision making, provided that the challenges of online inclusion are observed.

Much of the discussion around technology and peace in general, and technology and peace mediation specifically, is framed around the advantages and disadvantages of using technology in a peace mediation context. This chapter would suggest that the time to decide *whether* technology should be a part of peace work has passed. Instead, mediators may need to approach the analysis of technology (particularly information and communication technologies) as a transversal element in each context of operation and prepare to respond to it with the right expertise.

The decision for peace mediators to use certain technological tools will necessarily respond to the needs of each process, including technical, ethical and sociological considerations.[24] Perhaps, in the spirit of the peace research scholars, mediators are at that stage where they 'need to start moving from a science of peace [or mediation] to a technology of peace [or mediation]' (Eckhardt, 1971: 68). Or, simply, it may be time to move from discussion to practice.

References

Al-Heeti, A. (2018) 'WhatsApp: 65B messages sent each day, and more than 2B minutes of calls', CNET, [online], available from: https://www.cnet.com/news/whatsapp-65-billion-messages-sent-each-day-and-more-than-2-billion-minutes-of-calls/ (accessed 21 August 2019).

Bardis, P.D. (1985) 'Technology and Peace', *International Journal on World Peace*, 2(4): 112–16, [online], available from: https://www.jstor.org/stable/20750972 (accessed 21 August 2019).

Build Peace (nd) *Build Peace 2019*, [online], available from: https://howtobuildpeace.org/ (accessed 27 August 2019).

[24] In earlier, wiser words: '[t]he technologist himself may judge a device on the basis of: will it work? Yet the practical decision to apply a technological innovation involves factors which are social, political, and ethical, as well as technical, in character' (Kranzberg, 1964: 591).

Burton, J.W. (1964) '"Peace Research" and "International Relations"', *The Journal of Conflict Resolution*, 8(3): 281–6, [online], available from: https://www.jstor.org/stable/172740 (accessed 18 August 2019).

Centre for Humanitarian Dialogue (2018) *The Libyan National Conference Process: Final Report*, [online], available from: https://www.hdcentre.org/wp-content/uploads/2018/11/Libyan-NCP-Report_English_web.pdf (accessed 27 August 2019).

Chaudhri, M.A. (1968) 'Peace Research and the Developing Countries', *Journal of Peace Research*, 5(4), 365–74, [online], 1 May, available from: https://www.jstor.org/stable/422470 (accessed 19 August 2019).

Colkin, J. (2006) *Dialogue Mapping: Building Shared Understanding of Wicked Problems*, Hoboken, NJ: Wiley.

Diplo Foundation (2018) '#CyberMediation Initiative Launched to Address Potential and Challenges of Digital Tools in Peace Mediation', *Diplo*, [online], 15 March, available from: https://www.diplomacy.edu/blog/launch-of-cybermediation-initiative (accessed 19 August 2019).

Domb Sadof, K. (2017) 'Finding a Visual Voice The #Euromaidan Impact on Ukrainian InstagramUsers', in U.U. Frömming, S. Köhn, S. Fox and M. Terry (eds), *Digital Environments: Ethnographic Perspectives Across Global Online and Offline Spaces*, Bielefeld: Transcript Verlag, pp 239–50, [online], available from: https://www.jstor.org/stable/j.ctv1xxrxw.19 (accessed 22 August 2019).

Eckhardt, W. (1971) 'Symbiosis between Peace Research and Peace Action', *Journal of Peace Research*, 8(1): 67–70, [online], available from: https://www.jstor.org/stable/422563 (accessed 21 August 2019).

Galtung, J. (1969) 'Violence, Peace, and Peace Research', *Journal of Peace Research*, 6(3), 167–91, [online], available from: http://www.jstor.org/stable/422690 (accessed 21 August 2019).

González Fraile, J. and Barton-Henry, K. (2019) 'Data Science in International Development', *Towards Data Science*, [online], 9 January, available from: https://towardsdatascience.com/data-science-in-international-development-part-i-working-with-text-44ebb6e0feef (accessed 21 August 2019).

Hunt, C.L. (1989) 'Peace Through Technology', *International Journal on World Peace*, 6(2): 4–7, [online], available from: https://www.jstor.org/stable/20751348 (accessed 21 August 2019).

Jenny, J., Greenberg, R., Lowney, V. and Banim, G. (2018) 'Peacemaking and New Technologies: Dilemmas and Options for Mediators', *Centre for Humanitarian Dialogue Practice Series*, [online], December, available from: https://www.hdcentre.org/wp-content/uploads/2018/12/MPS-8-Peacemaking-and-New-Technologies.pdf (accessed 4 August 2019).

Kahl, A. and Puig Larrauri, H. (2013) 'Technology for Peacebuilding', *Stability: International Journal of Security & Development*, 2(3): 1–15, [online], available from: https://www.stabilityjournal.org/articles/10.5334/sta.cv/ (accessed 21 August 2019).

Khan, M.A. (2013) 'Slow and Steady Wins the Race: New Media as Variable of Change in the Arab Spring', *Pakistan Horizon*, 66(1/2): 65–76, [online], January–April, available from: https://www.jstor.org/stable/24711492 (accessed 22 August 2019).

Kranzberg, M. (1964) 'Technology and Human Values', *Virginia Quarterly Review*, 40(4): 578–92, [online], Autumn, available from: https://www.jstor.org/stable/26444899 (accessed 19 August 2019).

Lanz, D. and Eleiba, A. (2018) 'The Good, the Bad and the Ugly: Social Media and Peace Mediation', *Swisspeace Policy Brief*, [online], available from: https://www.swisspeace.ch/assets/publications/downloads/Policy-Briefs/aa3fc8830f/Social-Media-and-Peace-Mediation-Policy-Brief-12-2018.pdf (accessed 4 August 2019).

Martin, N. (2019) 'How Much Data is Collected Every Minute of the Day', *Forbes*, [online], 7 August, available from: https://www.forbes.com/sites/nicolemartin1/2019/08/07/how-much-data-is-collected-every-minute-of-the-day/#1a8db9213d66 (accessed 21 August 2019).

Masood, D. and Wählisch, M. (2019) 'AI & Global Governance: Robots Will Not Wage Future Wars but also Future Peace', *United Nations University, Centre for Policy Research*, [online], available from: https://cpr.unu.edu/robots-will-not-only-wage-future-wars-but-also-future-peace.html (accessed 9 August 2019).

McAllister, B. (2015) 'The Quality of Our Attention', *Words of Peace – mediatEUr Blog*, [online], available from: http://themediateur.eu/the-quality-of-our-attention/ (accessed 15 May 2020).

mediatEUr (2015) *Building a Dialogue Support Platform in Ukraine*, [online], 29 July, available from: http://themediateur.eu/building-a-dialogue-support-platform-in-ukraine/ (accessed 27 August 2019).

mediatEUr (2016) *Dialogues in the Donbas: Fifth Report of the Dialogue Support Platform in Ukraine*, [online], available from: http://themediateur.eu/wp-content/uploads/2017/12/DSPU_Report_May_2016_WEB.pdf (accessed 27 August 2019).

mediatEUr (2019) *mediatEUr's team had a first mission to Jordan for its project The Future of Syria*, [online] 21 March, available from: http://themediateur.eu/mediateurs-team-had-a-first-mission-to-jordan-for-its-project-the-future-of-syria/ (accessed 27 August 2019).

Pielemeier, J. (2019) 'AI & Global Governance: The Advantages of Applying the International Human Rights Framework to Artificial Intelligence', *United Nations University, Centre for Policy Research*, [online], 26 February, available from: https://cpr.unu.edu/ai-global-governance-the-advantages-of-applying-the-international-human-rights-framework-to-artificial-intelligence.html (accessed 21 August 2019).

Townsend, L. and Wallace, C. (2016) *Social Media Research: A Guide to Ethics*, Aberdeen: University of Aberdeen, [online], available from: http://www2.port.ac.uk/research/ethics/CurrentDownloads/filetodownload,198032,en.pdf (accessed 2 May 2019).

Turner, C. and Heyworth, F. (2019) 'Advancing Inclusive Mediation Through the Lens of Leadership', *Strategic Security Analysis*, Geneva: Geneva Centre for Security Policy.

UN DPPA (United Nations Department of Political and Peacebuilding Affairs) and HD Centre (Centre for Humanitarian Dialogue) (2019) *Digital Technologies and Mediation in Armed Conflict*, [online], March, available from: https://peacemaker.un.org/sites/peacemaker.un.org/files/DigitalToolkitReport.pdf (accessed 4 August 2019).

UN DPPA and HD Centre (nd) 'Digital Technologies and Mediation', *United Nations Peacemakers*, [online] March, available from: https://peacemaker.un.org/digitaltoolkit (accessed 21 August 2019).

UNSCOL (Office of the United Nations Special Coordinator for Lebanon) (2016) 'Live #Twitter Q&A w/ UN Special Coordinator for #Lebanon @SigridKaag 2 Feb,14:00–15:00 (GMT+2), Send questions to #AskSigridKaag @LebAmUniv', *Twitter*, [online] March, available from: https://twitter.com/unscol/status/693003418072408066 (accessed 27 August 2019).

Wählisch, M. and Masood, D. (2019) *E-Analytics Guide: Using Data and New Technology for Peacemaking, Preventive Diplomacy and Peacebuilding*, New York: United Nations University Institute on Computing and Society, Department of Political and Peacebuilding Affairs and UN Global Pulse, [online], available from: https://reliefweb.int/sites/reliefweb.int/files/resources/E-analytics%20Guide.%20Using%20data%20and%20new%20technology%20for%20peacemaking%20and%20peacebuilding.pdf (accessed 27 August 2019).

Whitfield, T. (2019) 'Mediating in a Complex World', *Oslo Forum Background Paper*, Geneva: The Centre for Humanitarian Dialogue, [online], available from: https://www.hdcentre.org/wp-content/uploads/2019/07/Mediating-in-a-complex-world.pdf (accessed 27 August 2019).

Widmer, J.N. and Grossenbacher, A. (2019) 'Information and Communication Technologies in Peacebuilding', *Swisspeace*, [online], available from: https://www.swisspeace.ch/assets/publications/downloads/Essentials/87df4dac25/Information-and-Communication-Technologies-Essential-1-2019.pdf (accessed 27 August 2019).

Williams, M.L., Burnap, P., Sloan, D. and Jessop, C. (2016) 'DFID Practice Note: Using Social Media in International Development Research, Monitoring and Evaluation', *Department for International Development*, [online], available from: https://www.gov.uk/dfid-research-outputs/dfid-practice-note-using-social-media-data-in-international-development-research-monitoring-evaluation (accessed 27 August 2019).

Wing-Ki, L. (2019) 'Derivative Work and Hong Kong's Umbrella Movement: Three Perspectives', in P. Dibazar and J. Naeff (eds), *Visualizing the Street: New Practices of Documenting, Navigating and Imagining the City*, Amsterdam: Amsterdam University Press, pp 29–55, [online], available from: https://www.jstor.org/stable/j.ctv9hvqjh.5 (accessed 22 August 2019).

16

The Nexus of Peace Mediation and Constitution Making: The Case for Stronger Interaction and Collaboration

Mir Mubashir, Julian Klauke and Luxshi Vimalarajah*

Introduction

In many contexts of armed intra-state conflict or social unrest calling for democratic transition, the core issues are of deep constitutional relevance, such as distribution of power and resources, and participation in – or transformation of – the political system. To address the constitutional issues in such conflict contexts, peace or transition processes often involve

* The chapter is informed by a joint project of the Berghof Foundation and the United Nations Department of Political and Peacebuilding Affairs' Mediation Support Unit (MSU), supported by the German Federal Foreign Office, which has developed a Primer on constitutions and peace processes (Berghof Foundation and the United Nations Department of Political and Peacebuilding Affairs, 2020). See the project website www.berghof-foundation.org/pmcb for all related publications. At the time of writing this chapter, the Primer is in draft stage; the content of this chapter is heavily influenced by the deliberations of the project team members and their notes and

peace mediation[1] and constitution making. Consequently, in recent years, most peace agreements have included provisions on constitutional and/ or legislative reform, to be taken up by subsequent constitution-making processes (Nathan, 2019). In some other cases, constitution-making processes have been used directly to negotiate an end to hostilities.

Despite this clear connection, scholarship on the relationship between mediation and constitution making is largely absent. Handbooks, guides and references in both fields have hardly considered their relationship or mutual relevance (for example, see Moore, 2004; UNITAR and UNDPA, 2010; UNSG, 2012; Brandt et al, 2011; Gluck and Brandt, 2015; Georgakopoulos, 2017). Only recently, the connections between 'political settlements' and constitution making have been thoroughly investigated, such as on procedural issues of sequencing, inclusion, elections and so on (for example, see Bell and Zulueta-Fülscher, 2016; Bell et al, 2016; Sapiano et al, 2016), and the role of mediation in particular constitutional issues has been researched (for example, see Raffoul, 2019, regarding power sharing). The relationship between national dialogues and constitution making has also been deliberated upon (for example, see Berghof Foundation, 2017; Murray, 2017). The discourse on the peacemaking role of constitutions and constitution making has been limited to constitutional means of resolving conflict (negotiations, constitution writing/drafting), post-conflict reconstruction/statebuilding/peacebuilding/reconciliation, and 'justice after war' (for example, see Edrisinha, 1998; Grossman, 2002; Widner, 2005; Easterday, 2014; Turner and Houghton, 2015).

This chapter argues for rethinking and (re)assessing our understanding of how mediation is related conceptually and practically to constitution making,[2] and how a mutual relationship may be forged to better contribute to the transformation of conflict for sustaining peace. Mediation and

---

drafts. Attribution is due to the Berghof Foundation colleagues (apart from this chapter's authors) Sara Abbas, Charlotte Huch and Véronique Dudouet, and the MSU colleagues Rohan Edrisinha and Christina Murray. The project has interviewed a number of experienced mediators and mediation support actors, references to whom are made, whenever applicable, *anonymously* in footnotes as 'Project interview(s)'. References in footnotes marked as 'Project notes' imply notes from the project's conferences and internal discussions where practitioners from both the peacemaking and constitution making fields expressed their opinions and experiences on the nexus. Examples not referenced are from the authors' previous and ongoing work.

[1] Keeping in mind that it is referring to mediation in the pursuit of peace in socio-political conflict and not to other forms of mediation such as in family, civil or corporate cases.

[2] 'Constitution making, including the drafting of the constitution (the codified legal document), encompasses processes intended to lead to agreements that concern the

constitution making – as socio-political processes encompassing a broader scope in time and space than peace processes, political settlements and peace agreements – may intersect. Both have unique approaches and techniques that may be mutually resourceful. A comprehensive deliberation on every aspect of this relationship is, however, beyond the scope of this chapter, let alone examining the intricacies of the vast field of constitutions and constitution making. The modest aim here is to pique the curiosity of – and raise awareness among – practitioners and scholars.

Three phenomena illustrate the relationship between mediation and constitution making. First, constitutional deliberation may already be initiated in a mediation process and may have implications on any subsequent or concurrent constitution-making process. Second, constitution-making processes, in place of or in addition to mediation processes, may take on a mediative role. Third, constitution making may be a site of contention, given that it tries to navigate a pluralistic vision of a state, and therefore may warrant facilitated negotiation (mediation) during deadlocks and constitutional crises. These phenomena, their mutual relationship and its aspects, and their interface comprise what this chapter calls the 'nexus' between mediation and constitution making.

Generally speaking, mediation and constitution making have the same long-term goal of transforming conflict and sustaining peaceful socio-political relations. However, their short-term aims, approaches, the required environmental factors, and the norms and principles that guide them may appear to be in tension and potentially jeopardizing each other's work. Some scholars and practitioners have used this as a basis to argue for a clear separation of mediation and constitution-making processes (for example, see Benomar, 2003; Samuels, 2006b; Ludsin, 2011).[3] This implies that *mediators* would attempt to *resolve violent conflict* through *peace agreements*, and *thereafter* in constitution making, *constitution makers* would codify the agreements into a *constitution* that defines the rules and institutions of governance for sustaining peaceful socio-political relations that *prevent further violent conflict*.

---

exercise of public power. Constitutional issues include (but are not limited to): who exercises executive authority, how laws are made, autonomy for regions, governing arrangements for security services, judiciary, rights, public administration, [and so on]. While drafting of constitutions requires legal prudence and skills, the broader "making" process is ideally a democratic exercise that necessitates getting public opinion and buy-in on matters that affect their lives most in addition to getting elite buy-in' (from a 2019 working draft of the Primer on constitutions and peace processes mentioned in the note on p 333 (credit: Christina Murray)).

[3] Ludsin (2011) uses the term 'constitution-drafting' but it can be argued that she is in effect implying the broader 'constitution making'.

Such linear and simplistic views on actors, processes, sequence and roles do not reflect the reality of peace processes where the relationship between the different sub-processes is *non-linear, mutual* and *complex*. The actors and their expertise are varied and often convergent, and the roles the two processes play are not mutually exclusive. Both need to be seen as political processes (with technical aspects), which have shared goals, albeit different means, and their substance and processes are interlinked over time and space.[4] Apart from this theoretical argument, in conflicts with a strong connection to the constitution, it is often practically impossible to separate the two and exclude deliberations on constitutional issues from the mediation process as they lie at the heart of the conflict. Despite this, it has been observed that there is a lack of awareness about the nexus among mediation and constitution-making practitioners alike. This sometimes leaves them uninformed about each other's activities and the consequences of their own practices, and unaware of the need to interact and collaborate.

In this chapter, first the core of the nexus is elaborated through the three phenomena along with examples, so that the nexus might be better recognized. Second, not to romanticize the nexus, it is problematized by highlighting the key tensions, challenges and dilemmas between and within the fields in theory and practice. Third, the opportunities at the nexus are deliberated upon by putting forth considerations for reassessing and reframing the tensions, challenges and dilemmas, and for rethinking mediation in relation to constitution making.

The Core of the Nexus

Both mediation and constitution making are related to conflict in one way or the other and in most cases *conflicts are around socio-political issues that have deep constitutional relevance*. In current times, societies thus tend to seek constitutional means to resolve a multitude of issues around power, resources, territory, system of governance, identity, religion, language, exclusion, representation, autonomy, justice and so on (Brandt et al, 2011). In transition contexts, restructuring the political system often requires a new or significantly reformed constitution. The perception or experience that the current constitution suppresses democratic expression and exercise, prevents government accountability, favours a particular

[4] See n 3. While constitution drafting may be largely a legal affair confined to legal experts, constitution making is the broader field that encompasses the processes before and after drafting.

group and marginalizes others (for instance based on ethnicity or religion), or distributes wealth unfairly may also heighten the perceived need for constitutional reforms.[5] In a peace or transition process, constitutional issues are negotiated and codified into a new or reformed constitution, or they may be set out in formal, binding laws.

With this basic premise in mind, three important phenomena illustrating the nexus are highlighted and elaborated in the following section.

Phenomenon 1: Mediation Dealing with Constitutional Issues, Constitutions and Constitution Making

While formal constitution making is the pertinent process for negotiations around constitutional issues and for the codification/drafting of the constitution, in many peace or transition processes, mediation becomes confronted with these issues.[6] This may happen if a formal constitution-making process is not yet in place, if conflict actors are not willing to move to an agreement without progress on particular issues, or if the context is not ready for a constitution-making process. In many such cases, mediation processes have dealt with the constitutional issues arising, and produced peace agreements that 'expressly require constitutional reform' as 'a vital means of entrenching their settlement and consolidating and maintaining peace in the long-term' (Nathan, 2019: 4). Historically, peace agreements have (i) incorporated constitutional provisions that would be carved out in a subsequent (new or reformed) constitution ([North] Macedonia 2001, El Salvador 1991, Burundi 2000, Nepal 2015); (ii) incorporated an agreement that a constitutional reform process would follow (with or without specifying its scope) (Rwanda 1993); (iii) annexed a whole constitution (Bosnia and Herzegovina 1995); or (iv) been required to adhere to preceding constitutions (Mali 1992, Niger 1995) (Nathan, 2019: 4).[7]

[5] From a 2019 draft of the Primer mentioned in the note on p 333 (credit: Christina Murray).

[6] To this end, depending on the conflict context, national dialogue, elections and referenda may be used instead of or in addition to mediation.

[7] In analysing the relationship between comprehensive peace agreements (CPAs) and post-conflict constitutions (PCCs), Nathan (2019) examined 34 CPAs: 58.8 per cent of CPAs required PCCs, 8.8 per cent of CPAs were followed by PCCs, although not expressly required, and 11.8 per cent of CPAs required adherence to preceding PCCs (Nathan, 2019: Appendix 1). Easterday (2014) uses the term 'constitutional peace agreements' for constitutions arising out of peace agreements, pointing out that 34 per cent of peace agreements now contain some provision on constitutional

This is primarily because conflict actors want the constitutional deliberations and agreements to become *constitutionalized and legalized*. The legal status and enforceability of peace agreements is often questionable, whereas the constitution 'offers greater assurance ... that their opponent will adhere to the terms of the agreement', since the constitution 'has the status of supreme law and is therefore durable, justiciable and enforceable' and since 'many of the provisions typically contained in a [peace agreement] can only come into effect through constitutional or legislative enactment' (Nathan, 2019; see also Bell, 2006; Weiner, 2011).

In some cases, to circumvent the legal questions around peace agreements and their implementability, interim constitutions are drafted in peace processes (South Africa 1993, Iraq 2004, Libya 2011) (International IDEA, 2015). These are flexible and provisional, offering conflict actors and mediators creative ways to deal with the challenges in negotiations while deferring final constitutional decision making to a later stage. To this end, interim constitutions are seen to act 'as a safety valve to the pressure-cooker of transitions' (Rodrigues, 2017). During the Arusha peace talks in Burundi, for example, conflict actors agreed on interim arrangements and established processes and guidelines for a subsequent constitution-making process. In fact, the peace accord had addressed the constitutional demands of the rebels to lure them in and incentivize a ceasefire (Nindorera, 2019). Rwanda's (1993) and Sudan's (2005) peace agreements eventually became interim constitutions (International IDEA, 2015). Nepal included parts of its peace agreement as an annex to the interim constitution so that the peace agreement would continue to be enforced during the initial transition phase.

Phenomenon 2: Constitution Making Taking on a Mediative Role

In certain conflict contexts, the process of constitution making is intended to perform (or ends up performing) a mediative role in the midst of ongoing violence. Not necessarily resorting to a formal mediation process, such constitution-making processes comprise of constitutional deliberations that attempt to resolve differences among conflict actors. For example, interim constitutions can be described as 'mediating tools that serve to bridge transitions from one constitutional order to another' (International IDEA, 2015: 27). Particularly in deeply divided

---

reform. Turner and Houghton (2015: 126) note how peace agreements may have a constitutional form, that is, their constitutional provisions may achieve constitutional status at least until a longer constitutional process is complete.

societies, constitution making is sometimes seen as providing a forum for reconciling differences, negotiating issues of conflict, and addressing grievances (Hart, 2001; 2003). In Tunisia (2011–14), it was key to resolving conflict and securing the transition. In Afghanistan (2002–4), it 'provided an opportunity for dialogue between the people and the military and political elites' (Samuels, 2006a: 14). In Iraq (around 2006), it sought to resolve deep ethnic and confessional divisions and address the issue of the autonomy of the Kurds (Weiner, 2011).

Constitutions themselves sometimes become synonymous with peace agreements, and constitution making with a peacemaking process. Colombia's 1991 Constitution, for example, is often dubbed as the 'Peace Agreement Constitution'. The constitution-making process was one of the key drivers of the peace process since it set the ceasing of hostilities by insurgent groups as a precondition to their participation in the process. Its institutional design and processes provided for substantial public participation and guaranteed the representation of a wide range of political actors (Cepeda Espinosa, 2016).[8] Based on the new Article 22 'Right to Peace', the Constitutional Court has gradually evolved to become a trusted actor for strengthening the rights of the underprivileged and vulnerable (the displaced, women, minority groups, indigenous people) (Benomar, 2003; Merhof, 2015), and shielding subsequent peace processes from legal challenges.

Phenomenon 3: Constitution Making Warranting Mediation

Constitution-making processes essentially involve negotiations and sometimes warrant third-party negotiation support, especially when deadlocks or crises occur around contentious constitutional issues. Although this is usually not termed as mediation or seen as a mediation process in itself (Bland and Ross, 2008; Weiner, 2011),[9] it is an important aspect of the nexus. It underlines the distinction between having mediation as a specific process and using mediation as an approach and

---

[8] Cepeda Espinosa (2016) writes: 'The 1991 Constitution is seen as a peace treaty in several senses: it consolidated the end of violence by four guerrilla groups, it created institutions to include marginalised or challenging political actors in a sustainable way, it provided a commonly agreed navigation charter to channel disagreements and conflicts, it laid the foundation of peaceful coexistence within one polity'.

[9] These authors make an interesting point about constitution making being a process of negotiation, which helps conflict actors articulate *a vision of a mutually bearable shared political future*, without necessarily trying to embrace a *shared vision of the future*.

technique, and mediation skills as useful resources to deal with conflict within a constitution-making process.

The heavy reliance on the constitution-making process as the primary peacemaking tool in Tunisia's recent transition process paid limited attention to changing factors on the ground. The resulting constitutional crisis warranted ad hoc, albeit well-structured insider mediation. In its mediation approach, the Quartet recognized the crisis as a political issue rather than a technical one – that it was essentially a governance crisis with several components, which had to be tackled comprehensively. This approach helped shore up the constitution-making process and put it back on track. The mediation was also effective in reducing the risk of spoilers in the process by informally expanding participation of both political and civil society elites who were not formally part of the National Dialogue.[10]

On the other hand, Nepal's staggering nine years (2006–15) of protracted constitution-making process may be cast as an example that did not manage to take sufficient advantage of mediation (Raffoul, 2019: 19–24). The process was constantly deadlocked due to seemingly irreconcilable elite interests and it failed to sufficiently bring forth the grievances of ethnic minorities. The constitution that came about in 2015 deepened ethnic, social and political fractures, immediately plunging Nepal into a deadly constitutional crisis (International Crisis Group, 2016; Strasheim and Bogati, 2016; Cottle and Thapa, 2017). While informal and insider mediation had played an important role in the process leading to the 2006 comprehensive peace agreement, it decreased afterwards, giving way to direct bilateral negotiations. When bilateral negotiations were deadlocked, mediation had kicked in as required (Raffoul, 2019: 24).

Elaborating these three phenomena has been an attempt to draw a picture of mutuality and interconnectedness between mediation and constitution making. As a result, one might expect strong interaction and collaboration between the two fields. Surprisingly however, this is rarely the case. Some possible reasons for this are explored in the next section, along with further critical issues that strain the work at the nexus.

Tensions, Challenges and Dilemmas at the Nexus

Academic and practitioner reflections often either do not acknowledge the very existence of a nexus or theorize and suggest the need for clear(er)

[10] This paragraph is an adaptation of the analysis from a desk study on Tunisia by Sara Abbas as part of the project mentioned in the note on p 333.

separation of the fields. Furthermore, (potential) collaboration at the nexus is faced with practical challenges and dilemmas.

Perceived Incompatibility of Goals

Some scholars and practitioners have pointed out what they perceive as fundamental incompatibilities between the goals of peacemaking and constitution making (Benomar, 2003; Samuels, 2006b; Ludsin, 2011). They argue that, in an effort to secure elite consensus and to achieve a timely end of hostilities, peace agreements may include provisions primarily catering to the interests of the main conflict actors, which may be detrimental to long-term stability and a functioning political system. The suggestion is therefore to decide on constitutional issues 'through a transitional process that provides for wide-ranging elite discussions as well as public participation' (The Oslo Forum, 2015: 93). As a negative example, the Dayton peace agreement for Bosnia and Herzegovina is often cited, as an elite deal that '[q]uite unnecessarily … created enduring constitutional arrangements which were both unworkable and discriminatory' (Harland, 2017: 2). The efficacy of a complete merger of peacemaking and constitution making is therefore questioned (Ludsin, 2011).

Similarly, if constitution making is conducted in the midst of violent conflict, it is argued that this may challenge important procedural principles and potentially bias the negotiations. Constitutions' purpose is seen as 'less about war-ending and more about the broader, future-oriented work of peace-building' (Benomar, 2004: 82–3). Simultaneously creating peace and designing a stable foundation for the state, it is cautioned, may put too much pressure on constitution making and an unstable security situation may distort perceived needs for expansive rights for the security organs (Ludsin, 2011). Therefore, an end to armed violence (through peace/ceasefire agreements) and an (ensuing) sense of security and stability are seen as preconditions for participatory constitution making. If that proves difficult, an interim constitutional process is suggested as an alternative, which may allow parties to make the immediate constitutional change necessary for a ceasefire in a temporary constitution while giving society the room to meet constitutional needs when drafting a permanent constitution (Ludsin, 2011). However, interim constitutions may not be able to stabilize the situation (Central African Republic 2013–14). Additionally, while interim constitutions usually devise a process to create a final constitution, they may become quasi-permanent. In fact, nine interim constitutions adopted since 1990 in the midst of violent conflict are in force (reported in 2015) (International IDEA, 2015). This calls into question the ability of interim constitutions to end violent conflict, in contrast to peace agreements.

Professional Divide

In many conflict contexts, mediation and constitution-making processes are assisted by different sets of (international and local) actors, often strictly separated (simultaneously or sequentially). According to some practitioners from both fields, there is a lack of dialogue on the nexus, partly due to a lack of awareness of the core of the nexus, elaborated earlier, and partly due to professional ego and turf consciousness.[11] Constitution-making practitioners have noted that mediation practitioners and conflict actors often immerse themselves in constitutional deliberation without *early* and *adequate* engagement with them.[12] This can lead to ceasefire or peace agreement provisions that may neither be managed nor guaranteed at later stages, or which may become the source of further conflict. On the other hand, constitution-making practitioners are sometimes seen to be dismissive or sceptical of the mediation approach and its techniques of dealing with constitutional issues.[13] Moreover, some mediation practitioners feel they do not have the mandate or access to get involved in constitution making.[14] This may lead to missed opportunities in constitution making to take advantage of mediation expertise and approaches or at least to deal with the conflict issues through a mediation lens.

Guiding vs. Working Principles

Although a number of principles are shared by mediation and constitution making, there may be variations in how they are understood *between* and

[11] Project notes. Some scholars and practitioners from both fields had expressed the view that the exchange events of the project mentioned in the note on p 333, where they were present, were the first opportunity they had to be in dialogue with each other on topics of the nexus.

[12] Project notes.

[13] Project notes; Project interviews (Anonymous, 2018; Anonymous, 2019a; Anonymous, 2019c; Anonymous, 2019d).

[14] Project notes.

even *within* the fields, and how they are implemented in practice. The following exemplifies this on two critical principles.[15]

National Ownership and Expertise

The principle of local/national ownership is often at stake in internationally driven mediation and constitution-making processes. One aspect of this challenge is how much emphasis is placed on the particular expertise, skill set and experience that international experts bring. There is a general tendency to value (comparative) international over (context-specific) local knowledge, experience and expertise. Although constitution making is seen as a sovereign process where the choice lies with the people, in many cases drafting is often dominated by international experts (Turner and Houghton, 2015: 134–7).[16] Recycling and copy-pasting of ideas from 'successful' contexts is not uncommon (Carl, 2019), despite conflict actors' acute knowledge of (aspects of) their legal system and of ways to navigate it. On the other hand, depending on their background, conflict actors may in fact not possess the necessary knowledge or there may be an asymmetry in legal expertise between participants in constitution making, such as between the government and the public. In terms of drafting, 'in many processes, constitutional commissions and constituent assemblies take it upon themselves to produce the final words of the [constitution], even though they do not fully understand the words' legal meanings and implications' (Brandt et al, 2011: 354). Additionally, local support actors may also be strongly influenced by their own experiences, thinking in similar prisms as the conflict actors and thus not able to break out of the conflict dynamics.[17]

Mediation typically fares even worse with regard to dominating peace processes through international expertise and their 'toolboxes'. The general tendency to put a strong emphasis on Track 1 mediation to reach ceasefire and peace agreements often means missed opportunities to engage with insider mediation and to benefit from 'insider knowledge' about conflict

[15] The role of norms and principles in mediation and constitution making are fields of study on their own. See Easterday for the relationship between constitutional peace agreements and *jus post bellum* (justice after war), which posits a 'broad, holistic concept that includes a spectrum of rules, norms, and principles applied post-conflict with the goal of promoting sustainable peace' (2014: 379). See also Turner and Houghton (2015) for the role of international law in providing a normative framework for constitutional reform and the tension between international involvement and local ownership.

[16] See Turner and Houghton (2015, 134–7) for an elaboration on competing priorities in debates on local vs international ownership.

[17] Project interviews (Anonymous, 2019b).

dynamics and stakeholder interests and from ongoing efforts of intra- and inter-group mediation. This is exacerbated by the fact that sometimes diplomats or heads of state are deployed whose mediative skills and experience and/or their knowledge of the context can be questioned.[18]

Inclusion and Participation

Nature, scope and connotation of inclusion, participation and consultation vary between mediation and constitution making. Formal mediation in peace processes primarily deals with elites, power holders and a certain level of conflict actors at Track 1. Confidential arrangements are often needed to build trust within – and ensure buy-in of – these crucial conflict stakeholders, and to avoid the perceived danger of sceptics undermining the process. Non-formal and insider mediation generally tend to be broader within – and deeper across – tracks. Today, constitution making is defined as a democratic, highly inclusive process, thus already differentiating itself from many mediation processes. Additionally, different standards between the two fields about what constitutes an inclusive and participatory process can make it even more difficult for practitioners to engage with each other and collaborate. Generally, transparency is needed for broader societal buy-in and trust in the process, in order to (re)build a long-term stable political system. Striking the right balance between confidentiality and transparency can be challenging.

In contexts of intra-state armed conflicts, a majority of the population may be against certain necessary compromises with armed groups. For example, the public consultations in Colombia during the constitution-making process revealed that a majority of the people were against electoral participation of former guerrilla leaders due to atrocities and human rights violations committed during the armed conflict (Cepeda Espinosa, 2016). Nepal's case was different in this regard since the Maoists had the support of their huge constituency and a part of the population was sympathetic towards their cause or at least not opposed to their running for office.

In contexts of democratic transition from authoritarian regimes, where a new constitution usually needs to be adopted to establish a new political order, social groups who never had the chance to play a meaningful role in national political life may strive to advance their particular visions of society (Weiner, 2011).[19] This 'may sharpen political differences and

[18] Project interviews (Anonymous, 2019a; Anonymous, 2019c).

[19] 'In some cases, the end of authoritarian regimes has unearthed deep divisions over such issues as confessional/sectarian identity, tribal identity, regional identity, or the liberal versus religious character of the state' (Weiner, 2011: 8–9).

heighten the political salience of controversial issues or social cleavages' (Weiner, 2011: 8–9). Additionally, seeking a constitutional resolution of the most contested issues may discourage the development of a joint vision of the future in which there is an acceptable role for all parties. Finally, even a highly inclusive, participatory and consultative constitution-making process may not lead to a genuinely inclusive constitution, as Nepal illustrates (Castillejo, 2018). If there is a lack of consensus on constitutional principles, certain actors may also attempt to disrupt the effectiveness of the new constitution, as was the case in Brazil, Colombia and Nicaragua (Benomar, 2003). The constitution may commit to inclusive governance and institutions, but, in reality, the nature of power and access to resources may (continue to) be exclusionary, as in Afghanistan.

Opportunities at the Nexus: Considerations for Reassessing the Tensions, Challenges and Dilemmas

The tensions, challenges and dilemmas mentioned earlier certainly need to be acknowledged by practitioners and scholars working at the nexus. However, they do not represent a fully convincing argument for the total separation of mediation and constitution-making processes. Keeping mediation and constitution-making processes separate 'is an illusion. The interconnectedness remains even in formally separate processes. At the very minimum, one process element directly impacts the others' (Töpperwien, 2019: 12). Forced separation of issues and processes is not conducive to addressing conflict holistically. With constitutional issues at the core of many conflicts, it is unavoidable that they arise in the mediation process. The discourse, therefore, ought rather to be around how the tensions, challenges and dilemmas could be constructively dealt with, in order to discover opportunities for collaborative and coordinated efforts. The following are some considerations in this regard.

The perceived incompatibility of goals can be attributed to a narrow understanding of mediation and peace processes. The (often short) time-bracketed formal process with international third-party involvement can be seen as concerned with 'negative peace'. Longer-term pursuit of 'positive peace' involves societal forces and (largely informal) processes that are at play *before international intervention starts and after it ends*. Seeing the documents that mediation and constitution making produce – ceasefire agreements, peace agreements and constitutions – as the end of a peace process misses out on seeing the continuity of a multitude of efforts to address and transform conflict towards sustaining peace. These efforts would yield best results when high-level, formal, diplomatic Track 1 (power) mediation is connected to locally rooted and led insider mediation.[20] These efforts are part of 'whole of society peacebuilding' processes that seek to transform conflicts (Brunk, 2016; Martin et al, 2016: 65) through back channel diplomacy, bridge building, confidence building, dialogue facilitation and reconciliation on Tracks 1.5, 2 and 3.

Mediation and constitution-making theory and practice have undergone changes over the recent decades that increase the extent of their interdependence. Mediation, at least in theory, has become less about security and 'management' of conflict through ceasefire and peace agreements and more about attending to the underlying grievances and issues of conflict (many of which are constitutional in nature).[21] Similarly, in constitution making, concepts of 'new'/'participatory'/'democratic'/ 'transformative' constitutionalism regard a constitution not merely as a contract to be negotiated, signed and observed, but as 'a conversation, conducted by all concerned, open to new entrants and issues, seeking a workable formula that will be sustainable rather than assuredly stable' (Hart, 2003: 3; see also Hart, 2001; Langa, 2006; Baxi, 2008; Brandt et al, 2011; Gluck and Brandt, 2015). In this (sometimes difficult) conversation, mediation (and its practitioners) and more broadly mediation approach and techniques may be useful resources in a constitution-making process to facilitate agreement, loosen deadlock and crisis, and support previously crafted agreements. One example in this regard is (local and international) NGOs' mediation in Fiji during its constitutional review process.

In constitution-making processes, when local/national actors can freely select their experts and decide on support options, the net result is likely to be more sustainable and be perceived as legitimate, as was the case in constitution-making processes in Poland, Eritrea and Albania. The Ohrid process in [North] Macedonia, although based heavily on international experts, emphasized national ownership by trying not to undermine political structures. Ideally, international experts would limit their engagement to explaining options, helping local actors better understand legal consequences of particular provisions and 'expand imagination of the parties' where such support was necessary. To allow for more participation of the population, one contemporary approach

[20] In some contexts, insider mediation may be more effective than (or complementary to) international mediation (Wehr and Lederach, 1991; Elgström et al, 2003; Hislaire et al, 2011; Roepstorff and Bernhard, 2013; Svensson and Lindgren, 2013; Ropers, 2014; UNDP, 2015; Mir et al, 2016; Dziatkowiec, 2017).

[21] According to Papagianni (2010: 244), mediation can strengthen political processes by 'creat[ing] the political space within which long-term reconstruction, development, and reconciliation issues can be discussed [and by] encouraging dialogue'.

of retaining national ownership is for international actors to support the writing of constitutions in a universally accessible language and with a wider variety of issues that are relevant to ordinary people.[22]

Challenges around inclusion and participation may be overcome through 'incremental' models of inclusion, inclusion at specific points in the process, and clear delineations of process and outcome inclusivity (Berghof Foundation, 2015; Berghof Foundation, nd). Their exact design is, of course, context dependent. In [North] Macedonia, for example, although the rebels were not represented at the table, through a creative use of parallel security/political tracks, their views were represented in the negotiations and agreements (Stankovski, 2019). Also, although women were not included at all at the negotiation table, women's rights greatly improved in the constitution. Similarly, in Burundi, although women were only invited as observers in the Arusha process, they managed to get gender clauses into the agreement.[23] Generally, inclusion should not be an end in itself, but its design should answer the question '*who* should be included, *at what stage* and *to what end?*' (Berghof Foundation, 2015). In mediation, early inclusion (for instance during ceasefire negotiations) can have a strong impact on the outcome of the entire peace process. A way to overcome the different levels of inclusion is to include 'hooks' that offer the possibility of later inclusion in early agreements.

Concluding Reflections

Today, most conflicts are of intra-state nature and are becoming increasingly complex, due to changes in geopolitics, use of social media and extremism, among other factors (Buchhold et al, 2017; Howard and Stark, 2018; Whitfield, 2019). More conflict contexts will seek or warrant mediative approaches geared towards constitutional resolution of the conflict. Given the intricate relationship between mediation and constitution making and the challenges involved, a joint framework would need to be designed that is prudent in breaking down – and sequencing the steps to solve – the complex puzzle of contemporary conflict. This framework would have to hold together the different goals, approaches and principles to elicit complementary and collaborative engagement of mediation and constitution making. It should not try to eradicate differences between processes and merge them, but see mediation and constitution making as *intricately interconnected sub-processes* of a peace

[22] Project interviews (Anonymous, 2019b).

[23] Project notes.

process, each contributing in their own way to the broader goal of societal transformation, conflict transformation and sustainable peace, thus harvesting each field's unique strengths and opportunities.

This inevitably calls for a complex and adaptable design of peace processes and their constituent sub-processes in terms of: *what* needs to be sequenced (substance/issues: power, territory, identity, rights, justice, and so on), *how* (process/order), *by whom* (experts, support actors, insiders/outsiders), and *with/for whom* (inclusion, participation, consultation of conflict actors, elites, public). Nonetheless, working along this framework alone would certainly not alleviate the individual and shared challenges and dilemmas of mediation and constitution making. Taking them into consideration when designing the peace process may, however, help make informed decisions. Furthermore, to keep pace with the dynamic nature of conflict, the framework would essentially need to be flexible and utilize 'adaptive approaches' (for example, see Coleman et al, 2017; de Coning and Gray, 2018; de Coning, 2019).

Collaboration problems, especially across professional fields, are recurrent in peacebuilding. Even if practitioners may not want to give in to a joint, collaborative and adaptive process at the nexus, for the sake of seeing their own efforts sustained, they ought to, at least, be aware of each other's knowledge, strengths, experience and efforts, and sufficiently communicate, interact and seek advice. This requires humility of the actors about their own strengths and weaknesses, and a readiness to reach out to each other. For mediation practitioners this is about being open to benefit from constitutional expertise. For constitution-making practitioners it is about realizing that mediation as an approach and technique may be something they could integrate into their work. One incentive in this regard is the constant reminder that the ultimate goal of mediation and constitution making is the transformation of conflict for sustaining peace. Succeeding in signing an agreement or ratifying a constitution may only be a milestone in the journey towards that goal, not the finishing line. It is the responsibility of mediation and constitution-making experts to ensure that they have contributed to the creation of a trajectory towards this goal.

References

Anonymous (2018) interviewed via Skype by the authors, 14 December.
Anonymous (2019a) interviewed via Skype by the authors, 6 March.
Anonymous (2019b) interviewed via Skype by the authors, 7 March.
Anonymous (2019c) interviewed via Skype by the authors, 24 April.
Anonymous (2019d) interviewed via Skype by the authors, 26 April.

Baxi, U. (2008) *Preliminary Notes on Transformative Constitutionalism*, BISA Conference: Courting Justice, Delhi, [online] 27–29 April, available from: https://docplayer.net/37394149-Preliminary-notes-on-transformative-constitutionalism-upendra-baxi.html (accessed 30 July 2019).

Bell, C. (2006) 'Peace Agreements: Their Nature and Legal Status', *The American Journal of International Law*, 100(2): 373–412.

Bell, C., Rodrigues, C., Suteu, S., Daly, T.G. and Sapiano, J. (2016) 'Constitution-Making and Political Settlements in Times of Transition', *Edinburgh School of Law Research Paper No. 2016/23*.

Bell, C. and Zulueta-Fülscher, K. (2016) 'Sequencing Peace Agreements and Constitutions in the Political Settlement Process', *International IDEA*, Policy Paper No. 13.

Benomar, J. (2003) 'Constitution-Making and Peace Building: Lessons Learned from the Constitution-Making Processes of Post-Conflict Countries', *United Nations Development Programme (UNDP)*.

Benomar, J. (2004) 'Constitution-Making After Conflict: Lessons for Iraq', *Journal of Democracy*, 15(2): 81–95.

Berghof Foundation (2015) *Broadening and Deepening Participation in Peace Negotiations. A Strategic Framework*. Berlin: Berghof Foundation, [online] available from: https://www.berghof-foundation.org/fileadmin/redaktion/Publications/Other_Resources/Strategic_Frameworks/Framework_Inclusivity_final.pdf (accessed 30 July 2019).

Berghof Foundation (2017) *National Dialogue Handbook. A Guide for Practitioners*. Berlin: Berghof Foundation, [online] available from: https://www.berghof-foundation.org/fileadmin/redaktion/Publications/Other_Resources/NationalDialogue/BF-NationalDialogue-Handbook.pdf (accessed 30 July 2019).

Berghof Foundation and the United Nations Department of Political and Peacebuilding Affairs (2020) *Constitutions and Peace Processes: A Primer*.

Berghof Foundation (nd) *Incremental Inclusivity in Peace Process Design*, [online] available from: https://www.berghof-foundation.org/en/programmes/conflict-transformation-research/incremental-inclusivity-in-peace-process-design/ (accessed 30 July 2019).

Bland, B. and Ross, L. (2008) 'Relational Barriers: Reflections on Peacemaking', *Stanford Center on International Conflict and Negotiation (SCICN) Working Papers No. 210*, [online] 13 August, available from: https://law.stanford.edu/publications/relational-barriers-reflections-on-peacemaking/ (accessed 30 July 2019).

Brandt, M., Cottrell, J., Ghai, Y. and Regan, A. (2011) *Constitution-Making and Reform: Options for the Process*, Interpeace, [online] November, available from: https://www.interpeace.org/wp-content/uploads/2011/09/2011_11_Constitution-Making_Handbook_English.pdf (accessed 30 July 2019).

Brunk, D. (2016) '"Whole-of-Society" Peacebuilding: A New Approach for Forgotten Stakeholders', *International Journal: Canada's Journal of Global Policy Analysis*, 71(1): 62–87.

Buchhold, C., Harlander, J., Quamber, S. and Pitts, P. (2017) 'Peacemaking in a New Era of Geopolitics', *Oslo Forum 2017 – Meeting Report*, Oslo: The Centre for Humanitarian Dialogue and the Norwegian Ministry of Foreign Affairs, [online] 13–14 June, available from: https://www.africaportal.org/publications/oslo-forum-2017-peacemaking-new-era-geopolitics/ (accessed 30 July 2019).

Carl, A. (2019) *Constitution-Making in Contexts of Conflict: Paying Attention to Process*, Berlin: Berghof Foundation.

Castillejo, C. (2018) 'Inclusive Constitution Making in Fragile and Conflict-Affected States', *Norwegian Centre for Conflict Resolution (NOREF)*, [online] 15 May, available from: https://noref.no/content/download/169207/767799/version/8/Castillejo_Inclusive constitutions_FINAL_May2018.pdf (accessed 30 July 2019).

Cepeda Espinosa, M.J. (2016) 'The Peace Process and the Constitution: Constitution Making as Peace Making?', International Association of Constitutional Law (IACL)-Association Internationale de Droit Constitutionnel (AIDC) Blog, [Blog] 5 July, available from: https://blog-iacl-aidc.org/the-colombian-p/2018/6/1/iacl-roundtable-the-peace-process-and-the-constitution-constitution-making-as-peace-making-lzk6m (accessed 30 July 2019).

Coleman, P.T., Kugler, K.G. and Chatman, L. (2017) 'Adaptive Mediation: An Evidence-Based Contingency Approach to Mediating Conflict', *International Journal of Conflict Management*, 28(3): 383–406.

Cottle, D. and Thapa, S. (2017) 'The Role of Political Parties in Nepal's Peace Building Process', *PEOPLE: International Journal of Social Sciences*, 3(2): 1117–34.

de Coning, C. (2019) 'Complexity Thinking and Adaptive Peacebuilding', *Accord*, Issue 28, London: Conciliation Resources, pp 36–8.

de Coning, C. and Gray, S. (2018) 'Adaptive Mediation', *Conflict Trends*, No. 2 [online] 18 September, available from: https://www.accord.org.za/conflict-trends/adaptive-mediation/ (accessed 30 July 2019).

Dziatkowiec, P. (2017) 'The Inside Story. The Impact of Insider Mediators on Modern Peacemaking', Geneva: Centre for Humanitarian Dialogue (HD), [online] available from: https://www.hdcentre.org/wp-content/uploads/2017/06/The-Inside-Story-The-impact-of-insider-mediators-on-modern-peacemaking.pdf (accessed 30 July 2019).

Easterday, J.S. (2014) 'Peace Agreements as a Framework for Jus Post Bellum', in C. Stahn, J.S. Easterday and J. Iverson (eds) *Jus Post Bellum: Mapping the Normative Foundations*, New York, NY: Oxford University Press, pp 379–415.

Edrisinha, R. (1998) 'Trying Times: Constitutional Attempts to Resolve Armed Conflict in Sri Lanka', *Accord*, Issue 4, London: Conciliation Resources, pp 28–36 [online] available from: https://www.c-r.org/downloads/Accord%2004_4Trying%20times_1998_ENG.pdf (accessed 30 July 2019).

Elgström, O., Bercovitch, J. and Skau, C. (2003) 'Regional Organisations and International Mediation: The Effectiveness of Insider Mediators', *African Journal on Conflict Resolution*, 3(1): 11–27.

Georgakopoulos, A. (ed) (2017) *The Mediation Handbook: Research, Theory, and Practice*, New York, NY: Routledge.

Gluck, J. and Brandt, M. (2015) *Participatory and Inclusive Constitution Making: Giving Voice to the Demands of Citizens in the Wake of the Arab Spring*, Peaceworks, United States Institute of Peace (USIP), [online] available from: https://www.usip.org/sites/default/files/PW105-Participatory-and-Inclusive-Constitution-Making.pdf (accessed 30 July 2019).

Grossman, H.I. (2002) 'Constitution or Conflict?', *Conflict Management and Peace Science*, 21(1): 29–42.

Harland, D. (2017) 'Never Again: International Intervention in Bosnia and Herzegovina', Geneva: Centre for Humanitarian Dialogue, [online] available from: https://peacemaker.un.org/sites/peacemaker.un.org/files/BH_InternationalInterventionsBiH_2017.pdf (accessed 30 July 2019).

Hart, V. (2001) 'Constitution-Making and the Transformation of Conflict', *Peace & Change*, 26(2): 153–76.

Hart, V. (2003) 'Democratic Constitution Making', *United States Institute of Peace (USIP) Special Report 107*.

Hislaire, P., Smith, R. and Wachira, G. (2011) *Insider Mediators in Africa: Understanding and Enhancing the Contribution of Insider Mediators to the Peaceful Resolution of Conflicts in Africa*, Geneva: PeaceNexus Foundation.

Howard, L.M. and Stark, A. (2018) 'Why Civil Wars Are Lasting Longer', *Foreign Affairs*, [online] 27 February, available from: https://www.foreignaffairs.com/articles/syria/2018-02-27/why-civil-wars-are-lasting-longer (accessed 30 July 2019).

International Crisis Group (ICG) (2016) 'Nepal's Divisive New Constitution: An Existential Crisis', *Asia Report No 27* [online] 27 February, available from: https://d2071andvip0wj.cloudfront.net/276-nepal-s-divisive-new-constitution-an-existential-crisis.pdf (accessed 30 July 2019).

International IDEA (2015) *Interim Constitutions: Peacekeeping and Democracy-Building Tools*, [online] October, available from: https://www.idea.int/sites/default/files/publications/interim-constitutions-peacekeeping-and-democracy-building-tools.pdf (accessed 30 July 2019).

Langa, P. (2006) 'Transformative Constitutionalism', *Stellenbosch Law Review*, 3: 351–60.

Ludsin, H. (2011) 'Peacemaking and Constitution-Drafting: A Dysfunctional Marriage', *University of Pennsylvania Journal of International Law*, 33(1): 239–311.

Martin, M., Bojicic-Dzelilovic, V., van der Borgh, C. and Frerks, G. (2016) 'Theoretical and Methodological Framework', *Whole of Society Conflict Prevention and Peacebuilding (WOSCAP) Theoretical Framework Paper*, [online] 16 May, available from: https://www.google.com/url?sa=t&rct=j&q=&esrc=s&source=web&cd=1&ved=2ahUKEwj-4YKovN3jAhUJShUIHR9WCmQQFjAAegQIABAC&url=https%3A%2F%2Fdataverse.nl%2Fapi%2Faccess%2Fdatafile%2F4024&usg=AOvVaw1XrnrOkWAX_K48fWuI6dmi (accessed 30 July 2019).

Merhof, K. (2015) 'Building a Bridge between Reality and the Constitution: The Establishment and Development of the Colombian Constitutional Court', *International Journal of Constitutional Law*, 13(3): 714–32.

Mir, M., Morina, E. and Vimalarajah, L. (2016) *OSCE Support to Insider Mediation. Strengthening Mediation Capacities, Networking and Complementarity*, Organization for Security and Co-operation in Europe (OSCE), [online] 13 December, available from: https://www.osce.org/support-to-insider-mediation?download=true (accessed 30 July 2019).

Moore, C.W. (2004) *The Mediation Process: Practical Strategies for Resolving Conflict*, San Francisco, CA: Jossey-Bass Publishers.

Murray, C. (2017) 'National Dialogues and Constitution Making', *National Dialogue Handbook Background Paper No. 2*, Berlin: Berghof Foundation.

Nathan, L. (2019) *The Imperative of Constitutionalizing Peace Agreements*, Berlin: Berghof Foundation.

Nindorera, W.P. (2019) *Les Interactions entre le processus de paix et l'élaboration constitutionnelle au Burundi: Facteur de stabilité ou de crise?*, Berlin: Berghof Foundation.

Papagianni, K. (2010) 'Mediation, Political Engagement, and Peacebuilding', *Global Governance*, 16(2): 243–63.

Raffoul, A.W. (2019) 'Tackling the Power-Sharing Dilemma? The Role of Mediation', *swisspeace report*.

Rodrigues, C. (2017) 'Letting off Steam: Interim Constitutions as a Safety Valve to the Pressure-Cooker of Transitions in Conflict-Affected States?', *Global Constitutionalism*, 6(01): 33–62.

Roepstorff, K. and Bernhard, A. (2013) 'Insider Mediation in Peace Processes: An Untapped Resource?', *Sicherheit & Frieden*, 31(3): 163–9.

Ropers, N. (2014) 'Insider Mediation as a Tool of Collaborative Security: Trends, Discourses and Insights from Asia', *International Studies*, 49(3–4): 189–205.

Samuels, K. (2006a) *Constitution Building Processes and Democratization: A Discussion of Twelve Case Studies*, Stockholm: International IDEA and Democracy-building & Conflict Management (DCM).

Samuels, K. (2006b) 'Post-Conflict Peace-Building and Constitution-Making', *Chicago Journal of International Law*, 6(2): 663–82.

Sapiano, J., Bell, C., Zulueta-Fülscher, K., Bisarya, S. and Welikala, A. (eds) (2016) 'Constitution-Building in Political Settlement Processes: The Quest for Inclusion', *International IDEA, Political Settlement Reports*.

Stankovski, B. (2019) *Peacemaking and Constitutional Change: Negotiating Power-sharing Arrangements and Identity Issues. The Republic of (North) Macedonia and The Ohrid Framework Agreement*, Berlin: Berghof Foundation.

Strasheim, J. and Bogati, S. (2016) 'Nepal's Quest for Federalism: A Driver of New Violence', *GIGA Focus*, no. 1, [online] May, available from: https://www.giga-hamburg.de/en/system/files/publications/gf_asien_1601.pdf (accessed 30 July 2019).

Svensson, I. and Lindgren, M. (2013) 'Peace from the Inside: Exploring the Role of the Insider-Partial Mediator', *International Interactions*, 39(5): 698–722.

The Oslo Forum (2015) *On Peacemaking: A Decade of Reflections 2006–2015*, Oslo: The Centre for Humanitarian Dialogue and the Norwegian Ministry of Foreign Affairs, [online] May, available from: http://www.hdcentre.org/wp-content/uploads/2016/07/On_Peacemaking_-_A_Decade_of_Reflections_2006-2015-June-2016.pdf (accessed 30 July 2019).

Töpperwien, N. (2019) *From Armed Intra-State Conflict to a Functioning Constitutional Order. Reconciling Principles of Third-Party Support – A Reflection*, Berlin: Berghof Foundation.

Turner, C. and Houghton, R. (2015) 'Constitution Making and Post-conflict Reconstruction', in M. Saul and J. Sweeney (eds) *International Law and Post-Conflict Reconstruction Policy*, London: Routledge, pp 119–40.

United Nations Development Programme (UNDP) (2015) *Supporting Insider Mediation: Strengthening Resilience to Conflict and Turbulence* [online] available from: https://www.undp.org/content/dam/undp/library/crisis%20prevention/Supporting-Insider-Mediation---Strengthening-Resilience-to-Conflict-and-Turbulence--EU%20Guidance%20Note.pdf (accessed 30 July 2019).

United Nations Institute for Training and Research (UNITAR) and United Nations Department of Political Affairs (UNDPA) (2010) *A Manual for UN Mediators: Advice from UN Representatives and Envoys*, [online] available from: https://unitar.org/pmcp/sites/unitar.org.pmcp/files/uploads/manualunmediators_un2010.pdf (accessed 30 July 2019).

United Nations Secretary-General (UNSG) (2012) 'Guidance for Effective Mediation' in United Nations General Assembly, Resolution A/66/811 on Strengthening the role of mediation in the peaceful settlement of disputes, conflict prevention and resolution, [online] 25 June, available from: https://undocs.org/A/66/811 (accessed 24 July 2019).

Wehr, P. and Lederach, J.P. (1991) 'Mediating Conflict in Central America', *Journal of Peace Research*, 28(1): 85–98.

Weiner, A.S. (2011) 'Constitutions as Peace Treaties: A Cautionary Tale for the Arab Spring', *Stanford Law Review*, 64: 8–15.

Whitfield, T. (2019) 'Mediating in a Complex World', *Oslo Forum Background Paper*, Geneva: The Centre for Humanitarian Dialogue, [online] available from: https://www.hdcentre.org/wp-content/uploads/2019/07/Mediating-in-a-complex-world.pdf (accessed 30 July 2019).

Widner, J. (2005) 'Constitution Writing and Conflict Resolution', *The Round Table*, 94(381): 503–18.

17

Rethinking the Professionalization of Peace Mediation

Anne Holper and Lars Kirchhoff

Introduction

This chapter comments on the changes the field of peace mediation experienced under the impact of the last decade's professionalization and partial regulation. These processes, so closely intertwined, deeply affect the practice of peace mediation today: its styles and approaches, its conceptual understanding, the self-perception of and interaction between actors, and the resulting shape of roles, processes and agreements. However, it is still unclear whether and how professionalization and regulation affect the outcomes of mediated negotiations.

The chapter examines ways in which the major paradigm shift from mediation's traditional reliance on individualized, non-transferable skills to nuanced mediation expertise, clustered in support structures and distinct organizational profiles, has changed – or has not yet managed to change – the field of peace mediation. We argue that professionalization tested the peace mediation field and its ability to cooperatively improve its own professional basis in an unintended, fundamental way. Even if this litmus test is not yet finished, the chapter proposes a model to 'sort out' the status quo in this process and to help readjust mediation as a properly functioning instrument for addressing political conflict. The chapter uses the other contributions to this volume as a basis and as a quasi-representative mirror of a decade of underlying knowledge on professionalizing peace mediation.

A Defined Profession Lacking a Defined Reference Frame

While peace mediation is now widely recognized as a professionalized activity carried out by experts (see Kastner, in Chapter 2, this volume) within a defined normative arena, there is still no 'hard' empirical evidence demonstrating whether and how this professional expertise and the underlying normative system(s) lead to more satisfying outcomes and graspable changes towards peace. In other words, nobody knows whether recent adjustments actually have improved the quality of peace mediation work. For a long time, there seemed to be a tacit agreement in the community to either ignore this middle-sized elephant in the room or argue it away. Now that the field has become better acquainted with its own merits and flaws, the issue is becoming the focus of a new kind of self-reflective curiosity.

From a scientific perspective on professionalization, regulation and impact evaluation, the problem can be explained relatively easily. Any attempt at evaluating the impact of peace mediation so far (see, for example, Lanz et al, 2008) has lacked the necessary reference frame or coordinate system, which would require at least the following three elements: (a) clear standards relating to what a professional peace mediator is expected to do; (b) specific knowledge about concrete behaviour of peace mediators on the ground 'before' and 'after' becoming 'professionals' (and possible changes therein); and (c) precisely definable impact chains between the behaviour of mediators on the one hand and outcomes in conflict systems on the other. This lack of a defined reference frame still hinders solid commentaries on any topic of impact measurement in peace mediation. The basic hypothesis of this chapter is that because of this lack the concrete effects of professionalization efforts on mediation processes and mediated agreements cannot be measured, which thus hinders solid peace mediation work in general.

After a short assessment of the matter from the perspective of regulation theory, this chapter focuses on the various dimensions of professionalization to develop an analytical framework for exploring the interplay of impact factors in professionalizing peace mediation. Using this framework, the insights that other chapters of this volume offer in terms of regulating and professionalizing peace mediation are then filtered out and evaluated. The final section summarizes the main hypotheses that emerged from this exercise, which, it is assumed, will stimulate further investigations into practice and research.

Regulation: Peace Mediation as a Unique Arena for Regulation

Dimensions of Regulation

Some basic thoughts on regulatory approaches and systems prove worthwhile before delving into the professionalization of peace mediation. Departing from a wide definition as suggested by Lodge and Wegrich (2012: 16), the authors understand regulation as the intentional and, to a certain degree, institutionalized use of any form of authority that affects the behaviour of a different party (namely, in this context, peace mediation actors of whatever nature). According to Lodge and Wegrich (2012: 14), the core idea of regulation is the interconnected functioning of standard setting, behaviour modification, and information gathering:

> The three aspects are separate, but their functioning is interdependent: without a standard, we do not know what should be enforced or monitored, without any detection regarding activities on the ground, standards are meaningless and attempts at achieving compliance will be more or less random. Equally, without the ability to ensure compliance and modify behavior, no change in behavior is likely to occur, especially if this is not in the self-interest of the regulatee. (Lodge and Wegrich, 2012: 14)

A significant point of analysis of regulatory systems is the quality of standards. Standard setting, as the spine of regulatory processes, should aim to develop 'tough and comprehensive' norms (Lodge and Wegrich, 2012: 47). In other words, standards should be 'knowable and stable, acceptable and visible, consistent, verifiable and provide robust categories' (Lodge and Wegrich, 2012: 49). Another relevant dimension of regulation involves the question of who in fact regulates, and why. In addition, one must ask whether we observe voluntary self-regulation, enforced self-regulation or commanded regulation, each having distinct dynamics and possible flaws.

Application to Peace Mediation

The assessment in this chapter, in brief, is that the ongoing regulatory developments in the field of peace mediation carry unique traits that also account for some key dynamics in the more general professionalization of peace mediation. These traits are to be spelled out as follows.

In the last decade or so, the peace mediation field underwent a, predominantly voluntary, self- regulation. The process was initiated mainly by (western) peace mediation actors and promoted by the UN Mediation Support Unit (MSU) as their representing body – in technical terms, the regulatees – rather than by higher authorities. A typical risk of the self-regulatory approach, as pointed out most prominently by Convergne (2016) and Kastner (in Chapter 2, this volume), is that the driving actors promote the dominant value- and culture-based model of their particular group as universal or neutral, which is accepted as so 'normal' within this group that it is not even recognized anymore as a culture specific, potentially biased and therefore contestable prescription (see Kastner, Chapter 2, this volume). In the view of other actor groups that are not part of such a self-regulatory movement, the concrete dangers are the implicit exclusion of their institutional or cultural identities when setting and claiming adherence to standards; and the placement of the self-regulators' own policy objectives rather than true necessities of the field and clients/beneficiaries into the centre of attention.

Regarding the first constitutional element of regulation (standard setting as such), the diagnosis in this chapter is that the norms developed so far are 'comprehensive' yet not 'tough': by no means does the normative framework of peace mediation provide a robust category for shaping behaviour. With the exception of a small number of truly consolidated ('settled') norms (such as the 'right to life' and 'consent' as content- and process-related norms respectively (see Hellmüller et al, 2015: 5), it rather offers flexible, overlapping, sometimes contradictory reference frames (German Federal Foreign Office and Initiative Mediation Support Deutschland, 2019b; see also Hirblinger and Landau, Chapter 7, this volume).

When it comes to the second and third elements of regulation (behaviour modification and information gathering), the enormous relevance of confidentiality and restricted information flows becomes evident: modifications in the actual behaviour of peace mediation actors (NGOs or states) are not monitored or cannot be documented in the first place because the cases are politically too sensitive. Often enough, monitoring completely relies on the retrospective, partisan and possibly strategic self-descriptions of actors. When there is no access to independent monitoring data, the typical dangers (Lodge and Wegrich, 2012: 197) of selective interpretation, 'box ticking' (to ensure own formal compliance with standards) and *ex post* rationalizations (when acting against standards) prevail and actually do pose a risk to the professionalization of peace mediation practice. With regard to information gathering, in many other contexts 'light-handed' ideologies – assuming 'that regulatees would be interested in and capable of monitoring their own behavior' – proved to be entirely misplaced (Lodge and Wegrich, 2012: 28). Although there might be no overwhelming reason to believe this is fundamentally different for peace mediation (as compared to, say, the conduct of financial actors in the equally opaque international banking system), there might indeed be one striking difference: as the motivation for regulating peace mediation came from the peace mediation actors themselves, and was intrinsic to the drive to improve the practice, one might assume that there indeed is a tendency to observe standards of good practice. For many actors in the field of peace mediation, a key motivation for more professionalization and regulation was the desire to define more precisely the shared, yet rather abstract, notion of 'do no harm' as the overriding principle of activity. In other words, the very fact that the regulation was started from within the field – its genuinely voluntary character, combined with one essential altruistic 'guiding stick' ('do no harm') – might contribute to its broad and long-term efficacy and a compliance pull that by far exceeds the draw within other self-regulatory systems.

At the same time, the emerging picture clarifies the key danger of any regulatory system of peace mediation: an increasing discrepancy between the elaborated standards and an honest depiction of what actually works in peace mediation processes. While the first can be seen as the 'myth system', the latter can be viewed to be the 'operational code' of the field (Reisman, 1977). Myth system and operational code will never be the same but it must be the aim of any regulatory activity to narrow rather than widen the discrepancy between the mythical and the operational worlds. Given these basic thoughts on the special traits of regulating peace mediation, a 'bird's eye view' on professionalization seems to be even more useful.

Professionalization: Reference Factors for Measuring the Impact of Professionalizing Peace Mediation

Dimensions of Professionalization

The term 'profession' usually describes a distinct, formally associated and regulated occupation with a technical, expert knowledge base that claims to serve public and ethical goals (Silbey, 1993: 349; Evetts, 2018: 44). The key to a 'professional' status is the mastery of a special skill in conformity with certain technical and ethical standards (Hay et al, 1984: 228). The term 'professionalization' is normally understood as the process by which a typically newly emerging 'occupation organizes itself to ensure its practitioners perform their services well and thereby earn a larger share of societal respect and reward' (Pederson, 2005: 52), 'often by standardization of the education, training and qualification for practice' (Evetts, 2018: 44). A broader sociological perspective sees professionalization also as a 'process to pursue, develop and maintain the closure of the occupational group to maintain practitioners' own occupational self-interests in terms of their salary, status and power as well as the monopoly protection of the occupational jurisdiction' (Evetts, 2018: 44).

We can distinguish between three basic motivational patterns behind the development of a given activity into a profession that overlap with the traditional conceptual distinction made by the sociology of professions (Hoyle, 2001: 15472; Evetts, 2018: 44–6):

(a) professionalism: improving skills to enhance the quality of the work performed and results achieved;
(b) professionalization: improving status through a closure of the occupational group; and
(c) discourse of professionalism: constructing, regulating and legitimating an occupational identity through narratives and norms.

While professionalism and professionalization (re)organize the quality of work and its conditions in a technical, methodological and institutional sense, the discourse on professionalism governs the self-understanding of a professional group in a cognitive, normative and social sense. The narratives and norms in the centre of this discourse are collective self-descriptions and self-prescriptions of a self-referential group, with all the distortions this can entail. While professionalism/skills improvement and professionalization/status improvement shape the 'operational code' of work, the discourse on professionalism forms its 'myth system' (Reisman, 1977).

We further distinguish between 'internal' (within the occupational group) and 'external' (in the addressed social systems) demands for improving the quality of work and status of an occupation. Interestingly, most conceptions of professionalization are not explicitly concerned with the external needs of the social systems it addresses. This conceptual blind spot seems to mirror a perceptual failure resulting from the identity dynamics in a profession's pioneering phase: an emerging professional identity struggling to assert a still-contested expertise and status might tend to a more self-affirmative rather than client-oriented approach to needs assessment. Professionalization, a primarily self-referential endeavour (an 'occupation organizes itself to ...', see earlier), seems particularly at risk of forgetting its external *raison d'être*. Against the background of a mainly voluntary self-regulation, this risk becomes even more eminent.

Application to Peace Mediation

The authors consider this tendency towards self-referentiality to be partly responsible for today's lack of reliable empirical (experiential and scientific) data on the impacts of professionalizing peace mediation: if external needs (for example, those of conflict parties) regarding professionalizing peace mediation had been explicitly 'on the radar' (defined, investigated and monitored) from the outset, there would likely have been more data on the respective impacts, despite all legitimate notions of confidentiality. One additional, more general, reason for the lack of reliable impact data is the complexity of impact chains within, and the contextual diversity between, conflict systems. Together, these factors make it very difficult to identify clear generic cause–effect relationships (Snowden and Boone, 2007; Mason, 2016). Thus there is still no reliable methodological approach to assessing the tangible impact of mediation interventions on the outcomes of negotiations nor is there a dependable way to isolate and assess the impact of single factors, such as the regulation and professionalization of mediation.

From this background emerges a twofold agenda for this chapter: to develop a model for (a) a systematic mapping of assumed impact factors of professionalizing peace mediation and (b) an exploration of the interplay between these factors so as to reveal their potential cause–effect relationships and, if possible, identify their underlying impact chain. This includes, of course, the question as to which untested elements in the chain would have proven useful.

This chapter proposes including the following categories in this model as reference factors for investigating professionalization: *needs*; *skills*; *status and structures*; *narratives and norms*; *processes*; and *outcomes*.

In the following, these categories will be used to carry out an exemplary analysis of their (lack of) connectedness, their interplay and their impact on professionalizing peace mediation. Where suitable, the observations and assumptions stated elsewhere in this volume will be drawn on in an effort to identify or rule out cause–effect relationships and more general patterns of impact. As most of these observations and assumptions are not empirically validated, the analysis should generate hypotheses – hopefully thought provoking even if selective and incomplete – to be tested in further research and critically assessed in practice.

A look into the intertwined topics of regulation and professionalization of peace mediation reveals that the actual regulative elements are less complete and powerful than expected, while impact assessment seems to demand a differentiated, 'tailor-made' approach.

Mapping the Interplay of Impact Dynamics in Professionalizing Peace Mediation

In the following, the last decade's process of professionalizing peace mediation is recapitulated and five essential impact dynamics are considered. The latter are characterized by an inherent tension between desired effects, achieved or not; undesired drawbacks; and unintended impacts. Supposing that these dynamics follow certain ongoing incentives in the field, they might persist in the future.

Impact Dynamic One: Needs *in Conflict Systems Trigger* Skills *Adjustment, But ...*

Kastner identifies the increased complexity and new anatomy of contemporary conflicts as the initial and most essential shift that triggered an 'external' need for improving peace mediation skills (see Kastner, Chapter 2, this volume). He argues that the type of intra-state, often internationalized, armed conflict that has dominated peace mediation for about a decade requires different, more sophisticated, skills than the once dominant inter-state conflicts, which could be resolved by conventional high-level diplomatic interventions. Intra-state internationalized conflicts are marked by difficult asymmetric relationships, multiple issues requiring resolution, and a greater number of conflict actors and experts involved. The authors assume that peace mediators' discomfort with the lack of adequate skills given these new realities was due to their having deeply internalized the 'do no harm' principle. Thus emerged a new sophistication of conflict analysis, process design and much more elaborated 'skills toolboxes' (German Federal Foreign Office and Initiative Mediation Support Deutschland, 2019a).

However, Kastner also observes (in Chapter 2, this volume) that – given the still rather broad definitions of mediation and the strong commitment to diversity and flexibility in the field – no clear consensus has emerged as to the definition of competent mediation. The hypothesis in this chapter is that, without a basic methodological consensus, the field was unable to distil the core skills of peace mediation. Consequently, it was also impossible to assess the extent to which existing skills could meet the new realities of conflict, or whether adjusted or entirely new approaches were needed. This resulted in an uncoordinated, 'piecemeal' approach to skills improvement and intensive but inconsistent capacity building, not in a systematic needs-based adjustment and training. In those early years, there was a tendency to quickly formulate (methodical/ethical/legal) norms for peace mediation, such as the UN and other guidance (see Palmiano Federer, Chapter 5, this volume; UN, 2012), and to overlook the fact that the necessary methodical skill set still had to be consolidated and further developed.

Impact Dynamic Two: Skills *Adjustment Triggers Growth of* Status *and* Structures, *But ...*

The need for a skills upgrade and the resulting capacity-building offensive seem to have furthered the goal of peace mediation actors to distinguish themselves from such approaches as power diplomacy by underlining their expertise, competence and ambition. It also boosted institutionalized mediation structures. This development was accompanied and promoted by intensive exchange and production of mediation-related expertise among states, international organizations (IOs) and non-governmental organizations (NGOs); today there is an extensive corpus of policy directives, written guidelines, manuals, guidance notes, workshops and training (see Palmiano Federer, Chapter 5, this volume).[1] Whether intentionally or not, the replacement of traditional, individualistic, anecdotal accounts of mediation with inter-subjective expertise clarified the legitimacy of intermediaries. It placed them on a more solid, less subjective foundation, like that of judges or arbitrators, prior to and largely independent of the approval of negotiating parties (see Kastner, Chapter 2, this volume).

In a self-enforcing cycle, the increased legitimacy and improved status of peace mediation actors and interventions led to a growth in the relevant budget lines of donors. This led, in turn, to a differentiation of the types of actors, aspired-to mandates and proclaimed potential

[1] In addition to the UN 'Guide for Effective Mediation', examples include the Mediation Guidance of OSCE, Accord Series of Conciliation Resources and the Fact Sheet Series of the German Federal Foreign Office.

(see Palmiano Federer, Chapter 5, this volume). With every new peace mediation division, the scene became more crowded and competitive (Lanz and Gasser, 2013). But the field also was acknowledged as a distinct profession with general principles and specialized knowledge and skills.

However, as skills development and capacity building have been neither joint nor coordinated, today's institutional profiles seem to overlap or even conflict, rather than facilitate cooperative or integrated approaches (see Pring, Chapter 13, this volume). Attempts to map the comparative strengths of different actors (Sguaitamatti and Mason, 2011) and stimulate better cooperation have not resulted in the design of complementary competence profiles. The missing consensus on methodical standards for the profession translates into a heterogeneous landscape of actors, status and structures. While the multiplicity of approaches allows a flexible response in diverse contexts (see also the conclusion of this chapter), the absence of shared denominators, given the intense competition in the field between NGOs and between states, is dangerous: conflict parties today are confronted with a confusing variety of mediation services with no joint understanding of quality and no internal quality assurance mechanisms.

Impact Dynamic Three: Skills *Adjustment Triggers* Norm *Discussion, But …*

The rampant growth of status and structures prompted a call for further normative regulation of the emerging market and its services. On one hand, this desire for regulation grew out of competition between the growing number of peace mediation actors; on the other hand, the field saw a need for standards and principles (see Kastner, Chapter 2, this volume).

The UN MSU took up the role to formulate these joint principles in a participatory process involving a broad range of non-governmental and governmental mediation actors. After the UN launched its 'Guidance for Effective Mediation' in 2012, an intensive discussion about norms unfolded – which was surprising, since it was evident that these norms could not be enforced without regulative leverage. Ironically, the UN guidance may have unwittingly contributed to this (over)reaction: the fundamentals are formulated in a way that is too general to be ignored but also too general to be implemented (see Hirblinger and Landau's criticism in Chapter 7, this volume). Even if they are unsanctionable, the 'double bind' within the ambitious but unimplementable prescriptions creates an irritating normative pressure. At the same time, the hot emotional debates on 'flexibility' vs. 'principledness' reveal how this young profession used normative narratives to develop new sub-identity groups within the community ('*contra*' vs. '*pro*' norms).

Actually, from a legal point of view, large parts of this oft-cited, ever more normative approach do *not* constitute genuine normative (let alone regulatory) approaches to peace mediation. Instead, these are tendencies to *incorporate* regulatory and normative elements of the international system (including *ius cogens* norms from which no derogation is permitted by way of particular agreements, literally 'compelling law', as well as judicial and quasi-judicial systems and multilateral treaty systems) into the realm of peace mediation. While this will undoubtedly prove to be a decisive step towards professionalizing peace mediation, it must not be confused with normative or even regulatory approaches to peace mediation – the *how* of conducting peace mediation organized by methodical and ethical norms – which is still in its infancy.

The focus of attention on the 'normative turn' the UN 'Guidance for Effective Mediation' allegedly triggered tended to conceal its major real achievement: to finally provide a proper definition of peace mediation that is now widely accepted as the one shared terminological and conceptual reference frame for the whole field.

Impact Dynamic Four: Norms *Starting to Influence* Processes, *But ...*

Due to the (comparably) underwhelming adjustment of the field's skills and the (comparably) overwhelming discourse on norms, the norms started to actually influence processes of mediating peace, rather than (as desired) the skills.

On a pragmatic note, explicit reference to normative frameworks today is utilized to clarify and legitimate the specific contributions and roles of mediation actors. Given the multitude of actors now sharing the field, a normative framework could articulate what a particular organization represents and hence what the negotiating parties can expect from a mediator. This, in turn, can fulfil considerable expressive functions and increase the mediator's legitimacy, at least symbolically (see Kastner, Chapter 2, this volume). Palmiano Federer observes that NGO mediators demonstrate agency in reinterpreting the concept of normative mandates as entry points that allow manoeuvring and political flexibility (see Chapter 5, this volume).

On the one hand, external legal norms concerning the *what* of negotiations (while mediation principles concern the *how* of mediation, see Hellmüller et al, 2015) seem to provide some certainty for navigating (in most other respects) uncertain territory. First, law can provide certainty by delineating the legal from the illegal bargaining zone, thereby bestowing legitimacy on the process (see Kastner, Chapter 2, this volume), while the constitutional order, political and military power structures, control over wealth sources, and even political identities are subject to negotiation (see Ozcelik, Chapter 6, this volume). Secondly, international law starts to serve as a common language in which mediators, negotiating parties and other affected actors can frame their issues and positions ranging from ceasefires to elections and political parties (see Ozcelik, Chapter 6, this volume). It also increases agreement among states on the 'rules of the game' and the standards of evaluation by which state values and interests play out (see Pring, Chapter 13, this volume).

On the other hand, higher expectations for the inclusion of external legal parameters at the peace table and in resulting peace agreements (see Palmiano Federer, Chapter 5, this volume) are perceived as a significant limitation on the flexibility of mediators and on the space for pragmatic bargaining (see Ozcelik, Chapter 6, this volume). The metaphor of peace mediation suffocating under the impact of norms has become a commonplace narrative in the '*contra* norms' sub-group in the peace mediation community:

> [T]he international community should tread much more carefully than it is doing nowadays with the mushrooming normative framework to which it claims to subject peacemaking. However attractive it may be to fuse peacemaking requirements with all the other values the international community currently stands for, this temptation must be resisted, not embraced. (Arnauld, 2014: 25)

This perception is seen as a result of the overly ambitious but vague language of normative calls to incorporate international law into peace mediation combined with a lack of knowledge of the relevant legal norms and the resulting expectations regarding the concrete behaviour of mediation actors. As well, primarily ethical norms such as inclusivity might be formulated or seen as too absolute, overstating the pragmatic need for inclusion in a given process as well as the actual influence that mediators exercise at the negotiation table (see Hirblinger and Landau, Chapter 7, this volume). This had an even more confusing impact since methodical guidance on implementation of these norms is only developing step by step (for example, see German Federal Foreign Office and Initiative Mediation Support Deutschland, 2019a).

Impact Dynamic Five: Increasing Expectation on Processes *to Impact* Outcomes, *But...*

The expectation is growing that ten years of professionalizing peace mediation in response to the need in conflict systems would also impact the outcomes of mediated peace processes. Both mediation actors and donors are refining their impact assessment and monitoring tools. But we still have a long way to go before we fully understand the interplay of impact dynamics that would allow for the reconstruction of a full cause–effect chain between the application of defined skills and norms during peace processes and their short-term outcomes and long-term impacts.

As yet there is no clear answer to the key question of how all this finally translates into outcomes. What is clear, however, is that efforts to professionalize peace mediation did not automatically lead to better outcomes: '[T]he increase in the quantity and diversity of actors involved in peace mediation as well as their greater expertise and preparedness do, unfortunately, not mean that more conflicts are actually being resolved through mediation nowadays. In fact, there have been fewer "success stories" in recent years' (Kastner, Chapter 2, this volume, quoting Lehti and Lepomäki, 2017: 103). Kastner even dares to pose the question as to whether the increasingly explicit articulation of a normative framework might be responsible for a diminished effectiveness of roughly concurrent peace mediation activities: '[w]hile there is no clear evidence supporting this, a correlation cannot entirely be ruled out and would merit further investigation' (Kastner, Chapter 2, this volume).

Conclusion: Reading the Traces of the Impact Snail

Summarizing the observations and insights from this journey through the fields of regulating and professionalizing peace mediation brings out the following hypotheses:

The need for professionalizing peace mediation seems to have been triggered by an 'external' factor, among others: the new anatomy of contemporary conflict. First of all, this presents a truly trustworthy picture of the field as it suggests that the initial trigger for professionalization was not a primarily status-driven dynamic among peace mediators, a dynamic that the sociology of professions considers one of the three basic motivational patterns behind the development of a given activity into a profession; rather, the key driving force was the increasing complexity of conflicts and of the international arena within which peace mediation takes place. Many developments can be traced back to the search for adequate answers to the new challenges that exceeded the capacity of states, organizations and individuals in providing 'good offices': in such difficult environments, as is widely acknowledged now, conflict analysis, communication, process design, thematic issues, legal norms, coordination and complementarity necessitate highly specialized expertise.

However, the ensuing process lacked a clear overall reference frame: robust standards of what a professional peace mediator is expected to do; knowledge of concrete behaviour of peace mediators before and after professionalization; and measurability of impact chains between the behaviour of mediators and outcomes in conflict systems. Without such a coordinate system, professionalization activities seem to have had difficulties in directly responding to the specific challenges on the ground, and, maybe also for this reason the professionalization process developed a strange indirectness and self-referentiality.

Accordingly, the impact chain reconstructed in this chapter looks rather like an 'impact snail' meandering from *needs* to *skills* via *norms* and *structures* to *processes* and – possibly – *outcomes*. Seeking the concrete, tangible results at the end of this chain, the relation between needs and responses appears to be rather slow, blurred, incomplete and random. Particularly the most relevant last steps of the chain – where high-minded efforts of professionalizing skills, status, structures and norms had to be translated into concrete peace mediation processes and mediated outcomes – are blurry, first because of confidentiality and, secondly, because of uncertainties in causality: *does* it finally make a difference given the outcomes of mediated processes if a 'professional' mediator is in charge or not, and if yes, what exactly is the difference? In short, the hypotheses resulting from the analysis in this chapter produce a critical but thought-provoking picture: there seems to have been an honourable, reality-driven impetus for adjustment of skills, but then – most likely due to the lack of a coordinate system for professionalization – no sufficiently targeted response in skills improvement, no sufficiently targeted implementation in processes, and finally no mechanism to assess the actual impact of professionalization efforts on mediation outcomes.

Norms play an interesting yet ambivalent role in this picture. It comes as no surprise that so many of the contributions to this volume (for instance Kastner, Palmiano Federer, and Hirblinger and Landau) deal with this topic: the comparably weak self-regulatory approach to professionalizing peace mediation helped formulate and define the ethical and methodical principles of peace mediation in a first step but did not translate them into a common understanding of the *how* of peace mediation practice (the current debate on inclusivity is an example). However, the overrated normative discourse paved the way for better integration of international law – which concerns some parts of the *what* – into peace processes. Yet, for the time being, in the authors' eyes, there is no significant danger of over-regulating peace mediation. In terms of legal norms, it was actually inevitable that the norms and values of the international community (and the multitude of debates triggered by this very question) finally found their way into the long-isolated and opaque field of peace mediation just as the field aspired to a professional status. The timing was right and leaves mediators with enough room to manoeuvre.

Two issues seem to require better self-regulation. The first concerns an imbalance in the recognition of international and contextual/local approaches to peace mediation: the lack of more positive outcomes might result from the fact that professionalization has not taken contextual and local knowledge and experience of conflict contexts sufficiently into account (Palmiano Federer, Chapter 5, this volume; Hellmüller et al, 2015). Particularly in those intra-state, internationalized conflicts that highlighted the need for professionalizing in the first place, local expertise is an indispensable complement to (if not the basis for) the decontextualized standardized skill set and experience of international experts (Kastner, Chapter 2, this volume; Mubashir et al, Chapter 16, this volume). This has an essential ethical dimension. We need both a culture of honest, non-patronizing cooperation, and a redistribution of status and market shares: are international experts, who accumulated the most market power within the peace mediation system, ready to accept a facilitating yet reliable role in long-term conflict transformation processes while allowing local experts to make these processes truly nationally owned and driven (Mubashir et al, Chapter 16, this volume)?

The second issue involves designing avenues for dealing professionally with the functional differentiation and specialization of mediation actors. One way to accomplish this would be to establish consistent terms for capacity profiles that stress the complementary value of various approaches transparently, rather than trigger implicit competition due to blurred terminology. In other words: differences in normative convictions and methodical competences (for example, facilitative mediation vs. high-power diplomacy) can be seen as comparative strengths in clear role divisions that improve collaboration in conflicts, in the interest of mediators but, first and foremost, in the interest of conflict parties and affected groups.

The process of professionalizing peace mediation finds itself in an advanced yet highly volatile stage. In the absence of effective regulative approaches, or even a basic consensus on the methodological heart of the profession, the necessary future gravity will only be generated by a much closer investigation of the complex, context-dependent and non-linear impact chains during actual peace mediation processes: do the skills applied, structures established and norm systems suggested lead to real-world consequences in processes and outcomes? Only after this question has been elucidated in a scientifically sound fashion can safe assumptions be made as to whether or not the steps towards professionalization fit with the anatomies of contemporary conflicts in a highly challenged international arena. Reliable answers to this central question would also reduce the wide discrepancy between the myth system of professional peace mediation and its operational reality on the ground. Looking at the bigger picture, convincing research on the impact question would finally help mitigate one of the most dangerous risks of the field: that professional peace mediation be perceived as an empty promise because there are too many unclear and inflated expectations but still no reliable evidence of its very specific and conditional but hard added value compared to high-powered diplomacy.

References

Arnauld, J. (2014) 'Legitimacy and Peace Processes: International Norms and Local Realities' in Ramsbotham, A. and Wennmann, A. (eds.) *Legitimacy and Peace Processes: From Coercion to Consent*, London: Conciliation Resources.

Convergne, E. (2016) 'Learning to Mediate? The Mediation Support Unit and the Production of Expertise by the UN', *Journal of Intervention and Statebuilding*, 10(2), 181–99.

Evetts, J. (2018) 'Professions in Turbulent Times: Changes, Challenges and Opportunities', *Sociologia, Problemas e Práticas*, 88, 43–59.

German Federal Foreign Office and Initiative Mediation Support Deutschland (2019a) 'Methodology and Communication Tools in Peace Mediation', *Fact Sheet Series: Peace Mediation and Mediation Support*, [online], May, available from: http://www.peacemediation.de/uploads/7/3/9/1/73911539/methodology_and_communication_tools_in_peace_mediation.pdf (accessed 27 July 2019).

German Federal Foreign Office and Initiative Mediation Support Deutschland (2019b) 'The Normative Framework and the International Legal Basis of Peace Mediation', *Fact Sheet Series: Peace Mediation and Mediation* Support, [online], June, available from: http://www.peacemediation.de/uploads/7/3/9/1/73911539/the_normative_framework_and_the_international_legal_basis_of_peace_mediation.pdf (accessed 27 July 2019).

Hay, L.I., Carnevale, C.M. and Sinicropi, A.V. (1984) 'Professionalization: Selected Ethical Issues in Dispute Resolution', *The Justice System Journal*, 9(2), 228–44.

Hellmüller, S., Palmiano Federer, J. and Zeller, M. (2015) 'The Role of Norms in International Peace Mediation', *swisspeace and NOREF* [online], April, available from: https://www.swisspeace.ch/fileadmin/user_upload/Media/Publications/The_Role_of_Norms_in_International_Peace_Mediation.pdf (accessed 25 July 2019).

Hoyle, E. (2001) 'Teaching as a Profession' in Smelser, N.J. and Baltes, P.B. (eds.) *International Encyclopedia of the Social & Behavioral Sciences*, Amsterdam: Elsevier Ltd., pp 15472–6.

Lanz, D. and Gasser, R. (2013) 'A Crowded Field: Competition and Coordination in International Peace Mediation', *Mediation Arguments* (2) [online], February, available from: https://repository.up.ac.za/bitstream/handle/2263/21679/Lanz_Crowded%282013%29.pdf?sequence=1&isAllowed=y (accessed 25 July 2019).

Lanz, D., Wählisch, M., Kirchhoff, L. and Siegfried, M. (2008) 'Evaluating Peace Mediation', *swisspeace, Center for Peace Mediation and Crisis Management Initiative* [online], available from: https://www.oecd.org/derec/ec/Swiss%20Peace%20-%20evaluating%20peace%20negotiations.pdf (Accessed 27 July 2019).

Lehti, M. and Lepomäki, M. (2017) 'The Era of Private Peacemakers: A New Dialogic Approach to Mediation: A Case Study of Three Finnish Private Organizations, *Tampere Peace Research Institute* [online], April, available from: https://um.fi/documents/35732/48132/the_era_of_private_peacemakers__a_new_dialogic_approach_to/66830ecc-b175-ee3f-a252-b9a2e052156d?t=1525645981371 (Accessed: 27 July 2019).

Lodge, M. and Wegrich, K. (2012) *Managing Regulation: Regulatory Analysis, Politics and Policy*, Basingstoke: Palgrave Macmillan.

Mason, S. (2016) 'Combining Best, Good, and Emergent Practice', *Nadel Newsletter*, 1, pp 3–4.

Pederson, A. (2005) 'Professing Archives – A Very Human Enterprise' in McKemmish, S. Piggott, M., Reed, B. and Upward, F. (eds.) *Archives. Recordkeeping in Society*, Wagga Wagga: Centre for Information Studies, Charles Sturt University, pp 51–74.

Reisman, M. (1977) 'Myth System and Operational Code', *Yale Journal of International Law*, 3(2), 229–49.

Sguaitamatti, D. and Mason, S. (2011) 'Vermittler im Vergleich', *Zürcher Beiträge zur Sicherheitspolitik*, 83, 69–109.

Silbey, S.S. (1993) 'Mediation Mythology', *Negotiation Journal*, 9(4), 349–53.

Snowden, D.J. and Boone, M.E. (2007) 'A Leader's Framework for Decision Making' *Harvard Business Review*, 85(11), 68–76.

UN (2012) 'Guidance for Effective Mediation', [online] available from: https://peacemaker.un.org/sites/peacemaker.un.org/files/GuidanceEffectiveMediation_UNDPA2012%28english%29_0.pdf (accessed 25 July 2019).

Index

Note: Page numbers for figures appear in italics.
Page numbers followed by 'n' refer to notes.

Printed and bound by CPI Group (UK) Ltd, Croydon, CR0 4YY

15/09/2026

14962384-0008